THE DIVINE DAUGHTER

A NAMING CEREMONY

ANDREW GILCHRIST

Suite 300 - 990 Fort St
Victoria, BC, V8V 3K2
Canada

www.friesenpress.com

Copyright © 2019 by Andrew Gilchrist
First Edition — 2019

All rights reserved.

Aduri photograph used with permission from The Amarok Society and the Munro Family

Author photograph by Tammy Tischbein

No part of this publication may be reproduced in any form, or by any means, electronic or mechanical, including photocopying, recording, or any information browsing, storage, or retrieval system, without permission in writing from FriesenPress.

ISBN
978-1-5255-3905-3 (Hardcover)
978-1-5255-3906-0 (Paperback)
978-1-5255-3907-7 (eBook)

1. SOCIAL SCIENCE, FOLKLORE & MYTHOLOGY

Distributed to the trade by The Ingram Book Company

TABLE OF CONTENTS

vii	Foreword	
1	Introduction	Signs, Spirits, and the Symbolic
3		*Agamemnon and Jephthah*
4		*From Actions to Observations*
6		*Beginning, and Beginning Again*
8		*Icons and Idols, Signals and Symbols*
11		*Novelty and Nausea*
13		*Voices in Song*
17		*Apollo and Dionysus*
20		*Starting New Songs, Taking Her Hand*
23	Verse 1	Family Stock and Character Sketches
25		*Shriners and the Supernatural*
28		*Magic, Mask, and Metaphor*
29		*The Figure and Ground of Definitions*
32		*Namastes, Plural*
35		*Mother—Empowering and Devouring*
39		*Father—Tyrannizing and Encouraging*
44		*Son—Innovating and Retreating*
50		*Daughter—Observed and Unrecognized*
59		*A Divine Debut*
66		*Jyoti—Allatonce in the Family*
69		*The Aporia (Puzzle) of Apostles and Advocates*
71		*Reflection*
77	Verse 2	Settings and Structures
79		*Children of the Sun*
81		*Concerns, Cultures, Monuments, and Meditations*
84		*The Pyramid—Derrida and Competition*
94		*The Panopticon—Foucault and Anticipation*
99		*The Theatre—Levinas, Lonergan, and Responsibility*
108		*The Agora (Marketplace)—Nietzsche and Trade*
117		*Malala—I'm Fine with My Crooked Smile*
120		*Reflection*

123	Verse 3	Story Arcs and Social Circles
125		*Narcissus and the Self-Correcting Process of Inquiry*
128		*A Kiss That Was Just a Kiss*
131		*Peterson and the Line in the Sand*
137		*Plato's Disillusionment*
140		*Joseph Campbell's 10,000 Hours*
143		*Northrop Frye Made Waves*
148		*Circles and Lines, Emergence and Responsibility*
150		*Thresholds, Decisions, Observations, Actions*
155		*Birth, Death, and a Doctor's Love of Inquiry*
159		*Ayaan—When Your Daughter Becomes Her Own Woman*
162		*Reflection*
165	Verse 4	Speaking in Tongues: Sales and Services, Sacrifices and Solutions
167		*Canadian Poetics*
170		*The Critical and the Kerygmatic*
176		*Instrumental*
181		*Descriptive*
188		*Prescriptive*
197		*Imaginative*
204		*Aduri*
209		*Reflection*
215	Coda	Standing on New Shores
217		*Pushing, Proving, and Improving*
220		*One-Eyed Giants and Generational Debts*
222		*Standing on One Foot*
225		*Looking into the Maelstrom*
227		*Rituals, Celebrations, and Dances*
228		*Something Old, Something New, Something Borrowed, Something Blue*
231	Acknowledgements	
233	Resources, Retrievals	
249	Endnotes, Extensions	

An Appendix with
Summary Charts of Associations
Made in Each Chapter
is available at the book's website,
http://thedivinedaughter.org.

This book is dedicated to
Fern
—a sister, a daughter, lost but still teaching.

FOREWORD

What do you do if you find yourself in a maelstrom in the middle of the sea?

Imagine the current of a social media account. Imagine the flow of a television nightly news report. Stories crowd into the spaces, breaking against the constant movement of the news ticker. Advertising pop-ups compete with the anchor's steady presence and the babble of talking heads, all taking your attention. The swirl of text, image, and sound creates a feeling of total immersion in the information. Did the lead story just touch the surface or dive toward a story's undertow? How far down will the information take us?

What you see from a screen of new information is not always the same as what you hear from that same information. As a result, the normal attitude toward writing—distant, watchful, analytical—may fail to find a remedy for the nausea of novelty. The point of this book is not to get you to follow the logic of the writer. Instead, prepare for *exploration* and *association*.

Ride before breaking. Survive while surfing.

When the time comes, when the rhythm and the sounds of the text draw upon your senses, position your board to see where your ride takes you.

The scope of topics covered in this book is deliberately wide, deep, and tall. I wanted to look at literature, art, religion, and psychology and ended up with an arrangement of ideas. A song can call your attention back to what's important.

I have no intention of making metaphysical claims. I have no intention of making theological claims. I found these heuristics scattered on the shore like leaves under a great tree. They might come in handy riding out the next squall.

Unfortunately, surfers don't get to ride every wave. I apologize for not saying everything.

INTRODUCTION

Signs, Spirits, and the Symbolic

Alas, where is the guide, that fond virgin, Ariadne, to supply the simple clue that will give us courage to face the Minotaur, and the means then to find our way to freedom when the monster has been met and slain?

—Joseph Campbell
The Hero with a Thousand Faces

*The power of a god
was the power to know
when to change your mind.*

Agamemnon and Jephthah

I invited two men to join you as you read this book. Imagine them standing or walking beside you, one on your left and one on your right. Some readers may consider them not real, while others may take them to be historical or even authoritative figures. They come as symbolic reminders, invoked spirits from the dawn of what I will refer to as the West. A phrase like the West can appear vague, but I want to use it as a quick abstraction, an explanatory fiction, to start this conversation with you.

By one shoulder is Agamemnon Atreides, a king of ancient Greece. He was bold and confident, a clever leader. His ambitions led him to sacrifice his daughter Iphigenia. His warriors had enraged the goddess Artemis. Agamemnon calculated the sacrifice would win him favourable sea winds so that he could sail to conquer the prized city of Troy. He drove his Achaeans to victory over the walled city of King Priam and then claimed the king's daughter Cassandra as a prize of war.

When he returned home, mighty Agamemnon died at the hands of his wife, Clytemnestra, and her lover. His own son and daughter, Orestes and Electra, then killed his two murderers. An entire family fell into war against itself because of Agamemnon's choices. Afterwards, the children of this king among men stood before a court of gods, humans, and forces of nature in judgment for what they had done and what had become of the family.[1]

By your other shoulder is Jephthah. He was the bastard son of Gilead, hated by other sons in the family. Jephthah became a fearless leader of men, known for his strength and pride. Before one battle, Jephthah made an oath. He would make a sacrifice if he achieved victory. He said he would give to God whatsoever first came out of his home to greet him after he claimed victory.

Jephthah won the battle and returned home. His daughter ran out to meet him, making Jephthah weep in realization—was this the price of his vow to God? He ripped his clothes and pulled his hair, but his only child gave herself to God with the consent of a willing sacrifice. Jephthah could have searched for help outside the authority of his own thoughts, but instead he remained faithful to his pride and his word.

The experience changed the man, according to the story. He measured his oaths differently, knowing the true costs involved. Jephthah left a legacy as a mighty judge of Israel, but by the end of his story he became a broken man. Pieces of his body were scattered and buried, left behind in the cities of Gilead. Daughters of Israel spent four days each year lamenting the daughter of Jephthah, and remembering her father's attempt to exercise control over a divine power.[2]

The sacrifices of these two men are hard to understand today. What hubris would drive people to think they must destroy the lives of their daughters and plummet generations of their families into chaos? What ambitions could be so compelling as to trade a daughter for fair weather, or a child for a single victory on a battlefield? What is the value of such a prize if it comes at such a price?

The stories of Agamemnon and Jephthah sound so distant and alien to many of us now. Yet in our globally connected world, the West has sent soldiers of war and representatives of peace over practically every sea to fight for whatever the West is supposed to stand for. Soldiers have followed orders from officers much like these two men and faced other individuals just as strong-willed and ambitious. There are people in this world who will deliberately use a daughter as a shield in battle. There are leaders in this world who will forcefully train ten-year-old boys to fire rifles and charge at an enemy.

It can seem too horrible to imagine people acting this way, too hard to believe such acts could be *real*. Today we quickly discriminate between fiction and fact, mythology and history, religion and science, as easily as we identify the differences between colours like yellow, red, and blue. But when it comes to the things that move us, the things that guide our own actions, we shift between event and story, assumption and imagination, as the sailors who followed Agamemnon, gazing into what the writer Homer might have called a *wine-dark sea*.[3]

While you read this book, you can imagine that you hold your own daughter. The two figures of authority standing beside you act as cautionary symbols of just what is at stake, what motivated people are willing to do to reach their goals.

From Actions to Observations

On December 16, 2012, a bus driver, five men and one teenage boy raped a woman in Munirka, a neighbourhood of New Delhi. Jyoti Singh was a physiotherapy student enjoying a night out with her male friend. They were returning home after seeing the movie, *Life of Pi*. He was beaten unconscious. She died in a hospital bed days later. India's courts found the driver and passengers guilty of rape and murder. India's courts sentenced the men to death and the minor to three years in a reform facility.

Police records suggest stories like this can be quite common. A rape is reported on average every eighteen hours in some neighbourhoods of New Delhi. But something made this one event different, almost novel. Of over 700 rape cases reported in New Delhi in 2012, one became global news.[4]

What made this bit of news different? People paid attention to this story, horrified by the graphic violence, and felt compelled to do more than just let the case go. Citizens of India gathered in protest and outrage. It wasn't enough to let old ways continue. More than a billion people worldwide heard about the news story. Courts tried the accused and enforced sentences. Some people continued to work for further changes in the Indian culture and legal system. The attention of the global public moved on to other stories.

What compelled these men to behave like this? What possessed them? And what compelled so many people to react and do something about this single violent event? Did all the attention put an end to the acts of rape or the culture of shame in New Delhi, in Asia, or in any part of our world?

When I first heard of Jyoti's story, I wondered what motivations could be behind such violent acts. Blame could be placed on the alcohol the men were drinking that night. But blaming a drink is about as satisfying today as claims of supernatural possession. Did Dionysus *really* make them do it? Blaming a hormone like testosterone can amount to hand-waving as well. Even if we say the whisperings of some demon caused such behaviour, that explanation will no longer work with today's audience. Words may label things and ideas, but they don't resolve the motivations behind our actions. In Jyoti, we had a real and living daughter sacrificed to the motivations of others.

The West came to know of Jyoti through the network of world media. Readers know of the daughters of Agamemnon and Jephthah from ancient texts. A story about two other men illustrate another moment of change in the development of the modern world. A Catholic priest in the late 1700s by the name of Johann Joseph Gassner earned a reputation as a formidable exorcist in the last part of his career. For much of his life he suffered from despair, but at one point he experienced a kind of revelation, a personal apocalypse. As he worked on himself and his demons, he devised a method he could use with others as well.

Gassner did not use the authoritative, official exorcism rituals from the Catholic Church at the time. Instead, he would walk quietly into a room and invite a troubled soul to sit with him. He interviewed the person with a few questions. When he had a sense of the problem, he would begin the exorcism by asking, in the name of Jesus Christ, for the demon causing the problem to show itself in a display of symptoms. He often repeated this step several times. If no symptoms showed, Gassner reasoned the problem wasn't demonic. He would suggest the person see the local doctor for medical attention instead. If a symptom did appear, Gassner would take that as evidence the problem was demonic. He would then order the demon to be gone, in the name of Jesus Christ. This was repeated until the symptoms were under control.

After the initial session, Gassner trained his patient to call the demon and expel it using a similar process. Patients would use the same techniques and same script as the priest. According to Gassner, if the patients truly believed in Jesus Christ and truly believed in the power of words, they could calm themselves, manage their symptoms, and exorcise their demons. They could possess some method of control rather than be possessed.[5]

Gassner's methods did not go unchallenged. A doctor by the name of Franz Mesmer studied the work of the priest and declared that, although Gassner was sincere in his beliefs and his intentions, his cures were better attributed to something other than religious power or supernatural superstition. Officially, Mesmer reported that Gassner's cures came from the priest's high degree of *animal magnetism*.

Mesmer and Gassner stand as two very different authoritative fathers of a more modern era—one from a religious tradition and the other from a scientific tradition. Mesmer was a doctor and a student of magnetic forces. He applied magnetism to many medical treatments. He coined the term *animal magnetism* and theorized that magnetism influenced people's personalities and medical conditions. At one point, Mesmer even attempted to treat a young woman's blindness with magnetism. Though unsuccessful, he stuck to his theories and expanded his treatments. His name became a word used to describe the treatments—people would be *mesmerized* by the physician's presence.

Mesmer's secular theorizing marked the end of Gassner's religious coaching with troubled individuals. It also marked a cultural shift in authority in the West. These two men stood at the emergence of psychology as both a subject of academic study and as an authoritative practice for helping people manage and regulate behaviours and motivations.

Gassner, a Catholic priest, retired despite the documented effectiveness of the treatment and the humble restrictions he placed on the use of his methods. Mesmer, a doctor, believed his own innovative ideas had rather unlimited applications to health and wellness. He and his magnetic treatments became quite popular for a short while, though Mesmer's theories expired with the man. After his death, Mesmer's students looked at the data and abandoned the doctor's procedures. A new term, *hypnosis*, described the technique eventually drawn out of the work of Mesmer and his students.

War and conquest and family make up the context for the stories we have of Agamemnon and Jephthah. They were men of action. The context for Gassner and Mesmer can be described as theory and practice and social relationships. They were individuals of observation. In Agamemnon and Jephthah, we have two figures willing to sacrifice their daughters to reach their goals. In comparison, Gassner and Mesmer pursued treatments for clients such as young women who were hoping to make sense of their lives and their worlds.

Mesmer is an example of how novelty, not fully understood or authoritative but appearing to be fresh and creative, can captivate us and hold us in awe. Time has judged Mesmer's methods to be not worthy of worship or practice, despite the attention and influence he once received. Mesmer had taken a bite from the proverbial fruit of knowledge and found a flavour that captivated his thinking. But those who came after abandoned his knowledge, his theories, and his methods.

Beginning, and Beginning Again

In the popular account of the creation story of Genesis, Adam and Eve ate an apple from the tree of the knowledge of good and evil. It was a moment of curiosity and novelty. This was an act, consuming something for digestion, experiencing tastes and textures. Adam and Eve had two children, Cain and Abel. In a moment of rage and resentment, one son killed the other. This was another action, portraying what human beings can do because of their motivations.[6]

A different kind of genesis took place with Isaac Newton in the 1600s. According to some stories, Newton sat under an apple tree in contemplation and was witness to the fall of a fruit from above. He did not take an action in this story. He did not eat in that moment, for example. He observed. From his observation he found a new way of looking at the world, a new beginning.[7]

The puzzle of gravity intrigued Newton. He desired to understand how objects could attract one another, and he focused his attention on the relationships between objects as much as the objects themselves. He published his *Mathematical Principles of Natural Philosophy*, explaining the mechanical nature of the universe and preserving his Christian God.

Not only did Newton's ideas from his observations explain *why*; they predicted *how*. Accurately. Powerfully. The universe became a clockwork machine in the eyes of humanity in the West, set to the order of Newton's God. Newton delivered very few lectures in his academic career and rarely dealt with students. Unlike Agamemnon and Jephthah, Newton did not sacrifice his daughter. He had no children other than his work and his studies. Maybe this was why he could believe in such an orderly universe. His figurative walled garden and academic world had little in common with the characters, setting, or plot from the Adam and Eve story. Newton had a mystical side, though. He studied alchemy, hoping to obtain insights into what was considered the magical processes of transformation, creation, and combination. Newton may have participated in bringing about the scientific way of observing the world, but he was still drawn to the authority of mystery.[8]

In his second major publication, Newton investigated optics. A glass prism released a spectrum of colours hidden within simple white light. In time, not only could colours be defined with more and more discrimination, but they could be quantified and measured. Today, the Pantone Matching System lists over 430 different kinds of blue—zephyr, vapour, royal, turquoise, twilight, ultramarine, and more (but notably, not one of them has the name wine-dark sea).[9] The colour blue has almost become a language of its own. Printers, designers, marketers, and businesses use the Pantone system daily as an absolute authority. This precision brings consistency and predictability for logos and brands and advertising.

Beginnings can come from either actions or observations. In the stories of Agamemnon and Jephthah, one simple observation could have changed the fates of their families. They could have looked upon their daughters as divine, for example, or listened for the voices of their daughters. Could they still have been men of action, driven only by their motivations, after such an insight?

Unfortunately, observations can be imperfect or incomplete. Decades after Mesmer's rise and fall, Sigmund Freud used observation to separate the psyche into the id, the ego, and the superego. In some respects, Newton, Gassner, Mesmer, and Freud all took part in naming some elements of the explanatory architecture of the human experience. Through a progression of data to pattern to concept to practice—attending, understanding, reasoning, and participating—newly named things helped us understand what swayed our motivations and behaviours, and how to manage changes of mind. Each time, it gave us a chance to begin again. The scientific revolution gave birth to a new relationship between observer and observed. Where will it lead us?

As Freud explored his "talking cure" of psychoanalysis, which put an emphasis on verbal expression and language, Carl Jung peered further into the images and sounds of dreams, the archetypal symbols embedded in mythology. These two men raised psychology out of the animal magnetism of Mesmer and into the realm of academic study. Erich Neumann, a student of Jung and Freud, wrote the book *The Great Mother*, which was an analysis of an archetype and a kind of bridge between old and new. An archetype is a recurring symbol in mythology, literature, art, or experience. An archetype is a kind of abstraction from the information of experience, or a projection onto some part of an experience. Part example, part mystery, an archetype is a concentration of different ideas or associations. A single word like "mother" can mean many things—an authority, a person who gave birth, a role, or an identity. Neumann linked mythological and religious developments of spiritual transformation to psychological developments of consciousness and the unconscious. Neumann also recognized a change in the cultural headwinds of the modern world:

> Today a new shift of values is beginning, and with the gradual decay of the patriarchal canon we can discern a new emergence of the matriarchal world in the consciousness of Western man....
>
> How can the individual, how can our culture, integrate Christianity and antiquity, China and India, the primitive and the modern, the prophet and the atomic physicist, into one humanity? Yet that is just what the individual and our culture must do. Though wars rage and peoples exterminate one another in our atavistic world, the reality living within us tends, whether we know it or not, whether we wish to admit it or not, toward a universal humanism.[10]

Neumann believed this ancient symbol did not correspond or link directly to one material being, a magical entity, or even to one specific cultural concept. Neumann was also careful to suggest that the Great Mother archetype has a plural nature and can point to more than one idea at a time. It could be both benevolent and terrifying, inspiring optimism and drawing attention to danger.

To the modern mind in the West, it can seem strange that a symbol would point to more than one thing. And yet our entire evolution has prepared us for living in such an environment. The rustle of leaves can be associated with a welcoming warm lift of wind or the advancing steps of a predator, *all at the same time*. Water can refresh us, or it can drown us. A young boy can be terrified and exuberant and seemingly unchanged, all at once, when a young girl enters a room. Hope and anxiety can both be felt at the same time while we process, name, or respond to a call from our environment.

To approach the modern problem expressed by Neumann, to see the faces of today's challenges, I have fixed my sights in this book on how we tell stories. The elements of a story work together to leave an impression on an audience. Characters, settings, plot progressions, and resolutions of themes expressed are all important for how a story affects us. The first chapter of this book examines character. Jyoti came to be known as "India's daughter," the nation's child. Her story changed India. Her story acts as a reflection on the light and shadow sides of four types of characters.

ICONS AND IDOLS, SIGNALS AND SYMBOLS

The *Vierge Ouvrante*, or *Opening Virgin*, is a religious image, an icon of worship from medieval Europe. The contents of the image are older than the Christian representation and certainly not exclusive to Western traditions. Neumann, and others, demonstrated that carvings, illustrations, and references to images of the mother and child appeared in Egypt and Africa, India and Asia, and throughout a great number of the world's cultures before the spread of Christianity. This image is often considered a spiritual icon, expressing something meaningful in terms of beliefs. However, it can also be considered a biological symbol. The health of the relationship between mother and child—in humans, apes, and mammals especially—can mean the difference between survival and death, between a life of wellness or illness.

In the *Vierge Ouvrante* example of the symbol, however, there is more than just mother and child. Within, a bearded figure holds a cross. The sacrificial figure of Christ hangs upon the cross. The mother, father, and the individual are all authoritative symbols worthy of our attention, according to the figures in the icon and Western Christian traditions.

If we are to take an icon like this as a representation of what is important to a culture or an individual, then each figure bears some significance to motivation, to what could, potentially at least, compel our actions. To people not initiated in the religious tradition, it may appear as antiquated superstition or opaque artistry. Looking at a piece of art like this can be associated with staring into another wine-dark sea.

Each of these archetypes—mother, father, individual—represents not only something that compels identities, roles, and relationships, but also demonstrates the limits of our language. Each archetype points to something about different aspects of life beyond the physical icon, something not fully encapsulated by mere words or figures. Like the artist, we attempt to express our identities as fully as we can and transcend the frustration of limitation.

When I learned about Jyoti's story, and then thought about Iphigenia and Jephthah's unnamed daughter, I came back to this image of the *Vierge Ouvrante*. It held a surprise for me because, as if for the first time, I noticed there were others in the icon. On each side, a group of witnesses or onlookers stand present while the drama of mother, father, and individual plays itself out in the centre. If each part of the icon conveys something significant, how are we to understand the presence of this group of others? And do we have the words to recognize the role of the audience, the observed, the other, in the artwork of our lives?

We do not master the wine-dark sea by subduing it when we learn to sail. We do not become wise by naming more colours. We study an art, or craft, with wonder and respect, following the goals and trials of achievement. We do it because that discipline helps create what some might call *divine moments*, peak moments in our consciousness and being, opportunities for insights to emerge. Even the addicted soul can experience "a moment of clarity."[11] Art helps us approach those first clarifying questions, bringing us to both the *meaning* and *use* of images, ideas, symbols, and words. Art helps us put our desires in order and reveals what we find important. A naming ceremony is important to more than the one born. The family, community, and the very elements of the world all participate in attendance.

My parents have been long-standing and active members of the United Church of Canada. The United Church comes from the Protestant tradition, combining elements from Presbyterian, Methodist, Congregationalist, and Union churches. As a result, the United Church does not have a deep love, history, or trust of Catholic or Orthodox iconography. Instead, the church placed its trust and hope in the simple and sturdy pioneer attitude of a frontier country. Symbology, in the ritual and language of this liberal-minded Western church, was tempered with a great deal of textual analysis, scores of committee meetings, and plodding conversations about how to serve the community. All that, and putting papers in filing cabinets. The United Church of Canada is far from the evangelical revival of charismatic, fire-branding preachers and hand-waving choirs. If anything, the United Church I grew up in seemed completely comfortable with being *subdued* and *pewed*. There's thinking to do, and food drives to organize, and meetings to attend.

Like many children brought up in the religious households of the modern world, after my confirmation I stopped going to church. It wasn't a conscious decision, but my behaviour did change gradually over the course of my early teen years. Participating in the church became less and less a part of my own identity. My friends didn't talk about Jesus as an ultimate example of how to live, for example. The religious kids in school were boring and traditional. Their behaviour and attitudes were predictable, not novel at all. All the teenage fun seemed to be with the newest productions of pop culture and the illicit adventures of weekend bush parties. "Jesus" was an exclamation to go with eye-rolls and disbelief rather than respect, wonder, and awe.

Novelty and Nausea

Kurt Cobain and the band Nirvana crashed into the music scene when I was in high school. In less than three years, Cobain was dead by suicide. The tragedy of his inner turmoil and self-destruction was all the more compelling to angst-fuelled teenagers of the '90s because it was so predictable. Some generations watched as their best minds were destroyed by madness. I watched one of the heroes of my generation fall as a figurative sacrifice to novelty, burning out to popular culture and drug use. The drama was a cliché instead of an archetype. To make things more tragic, he left behind a daughter hardly two years of age.

Agamemnon and Jephthah found it worth sacrificing daughters for the sake of their ambitions. For Cobain, the haunting demands of his career, lifestyle, and addiction held authority over him. Their possession of his thoughts became a priority over his responsibility to his own child. Witnessing these events unfold publicly left me with a sense of nausea and hopelessness. But I kept staring into the screen, into the icon-generating scene.

According to Mark Fisher, in the book *Capitalist Realism: Is There No Alternative?*, Cobain's story tells us something about contemporary culture:

> In his dreadful lassitude and objectless rage, Cobain seemed to give wearied voice to the despondency of the generation that had come after history, whose every move was anticipated, tracked, bought and sold before it had even happened. Cobain knew he was just another piece of spectacle, that nothing runs better on MTV than a protest against MTV; knew that his every move was a cliché scripted in advance, knew that even realizing it is a cliché. The impasse that paralyzed Cobain is precisely the one that [Fredric Jameson] described: like postmodern culture in general, Cobain found himself in "a world in which stylistic innovation is no longer possible, where all that is left is to imitate dead styles in the imaginary museum."[12]

The novelty of it, the story of his life and his family, amusing and stimulating for a mere moment in the media, confirmed a cynicism for me, a withdrawal. Why participate if it is all a puppet show? Though not conscious or deliberate, the test of what should win my attention was not a question like, "Is it so?" or "Does this serve life?" or even "Is there a better way?" Instead, the authoritative question had become something more like, "Is it new?" And it disgusted me. But I played along anyway. In the bumbling adolescent process of building my personal identity, the old and traditional played one part, but it was by no means authoritative or central. That was the past. I didn't want dead people holding my leash, as if I were a neutered pet for a sedentary family. What fun or meaning could be gained on the street, the stage, or the sports field with such an existence? But, unfortunately, even the fun that was flickering on the screen of pop culture had become little more than a museum tour of dead people's imaginations.

Added to that, I couldn't settle in myself how a *supernatural* supreme being established a particular old book as magically authoritative and unchanging. Even in my adolescence I had some vague understanding that the magic of a book didn't come from its historical alignment with actual events or its authoritative status. The magic of a book was the relationship it created with a reader, the identity it offered. My brother brought into our house J. R. R. Tolkien's *The Hobbit* and *The Lord of the Rings*. I found the adventures and burdens of Bilbo, Sam, and Frodo more compelling, more heroic, than any scriptures of Jesus and his disciples. Though set in a world with different continents and creatures, Middle-earth seemed closer to home than the Bible. If Isaac Newton was considered the last of the magicians, Tolkien could be thought of as the last of the medievalists. Something from the Middle Ages felt closer to the contemporary world than the Bronze Age, and more engaging than the soulless ticking of a mechanical clock.

Tolkien was a devout Catholic. When I grew out of adolescence and into adulthood I was able to recognize more of the mythological and religious patterns in his stories. Still, the enchantment that comes from reading a good book for the first time can be hard to shake. The fantastic vision of *The Lord of the Rings* left a significant impression on me. When Frodo returned to the Shire, spiritually hollowed out and unable to participate in the physical fight for his own home, I felt hollowed out as well. And scared. It took me years to realize that an answer to that experience was not to continue staring at and worrying about Frodo (or myself). Now, when I return to *The Lord of the Rings*, I shift my attention away from the main character and observe what all the supporting characters do for the sake of the adventure. The character of Samwise Gamgee provides a very different model for personal attitude and behaviour.

My adolescent interests shifted to the future and to science fiction. In the adventures of Luke Skywalker and Captain James T. Kirk I found something, to me at least, new and compelling. The future in science fiction felt so much closer to the contemporary world than the world of religious stories. Science fiction seemed much better equipped to face today's problems than any lessons from the dusty ages of religious thinking.

As the name of the genre suggests, science fiction knows its place in literature and culture—*fiction*. It is not nervous or preoccupied with justifying its contents as *real*, as in corresponding with actual events. If Gene Roddenberry was one of the last of the optimistic futurists, George Lucas may be one of the last of the mythologists. Where the authority of sacred texts tends to take the form of the written word, Roddenberry and Lucas found a different kind of authority and attention in creating multi-sensory experiences. The sounds and screen images that make up *Star Wars* and *Star Trek* are just as compelling to their audiences as holy foundational scriptures coming from the ancients.

Magic and the supernatural permeate science fiction storytelling, even if embellished and rationalized with scientific terms. However, the supernatural is not used as a source for authoritative explanation. The goal holds more kinship to coherence than correspondence. Science fiction brings the audience's attention to questions like, "Could it be so?" or "Is it possible?" and "What if...?" In the stories of science fiction, characters are constantly updating their tools, their skills, and their attitudes to face new and novel surprises. I didn't see that happening in my parents' church, or in religious practice at all. How do you update things specifically designed to ignore new information and endure novelty? What would win a young boy's attention—joining a team on a spaceship that flies across the galaxy, or joining a congregation comfortable with sitting quietly in pews? It seemed like the religious community would rather bring in sheep than prepare lions.

I grew up in the classrooms and movie theatres of Canada. A girl by the name of Malala grew up in the classrooms of her father's schools and the streets of the Swat Valley in Pakistan. The second chapter describes four symbolic settings found in our stories today. Malala Yousafzai's love of classrooms and love of her hometown drew my attention to what is at stake if we do not pay attention to the environments and places we build for our families.

Voices in Song

If ever there were a broad-tent church open to talking about things, it is the United Church. Though not as progressive as some would wish, the United Church was one of the front-runners for recognizing women as ministers. People of different sexual orientations have been accepted as full members and even clergy. Some members are even openly atheist. When a minister identified herself as an atheist, the church received some media attention. This came about, in part, because she believed the use of the authoritative word "God" was too closely associated today with magical and supernatural thinking.[13] In a figurative way, this is all part of a church coming to terms with its own identity in the modern world. It could also stand as a signal of capitulation to the shifting, modern—and now postmodern—popular mindset. The power of novelty pops, again and again and again.

Still, something kept me away. From adolescence and into adulthood, something about the religious tradition conflicted with my personal identity. My father began to play with wine-making kits. It eventually became something of a hobby we would share. That hobby captivated my interest more than going to church and putting on a smile for such nice, well-meaning people. Even the United Church, as open-minded as it tries to be, wasn't having the conversations I wanted to have. At one point, my mother gave me *A Song of Faith* to read as part of a progression of faint-hearted attempts to win me back to the fold. For my mom, the spiritual journey was not one made with ecstatic dance or emotional displays. It meant reading, and then thinking, and then doing something about it.

In 2006, the United Church of Canada produced a "timely and contextual statement of faith, with a view to circulation throughout the whole church for study and response while honouring the diversity of our church and acknowledging our place in a pluralistic world and in an ongoing and developing tradition of faith."[14] That's quite a mouthful. Quite a wordy explanation. And quite a challenge for today.

The result was the church's statement called *A Song of Faith*. The initiators of the document wanted to open a conversation on the nature of the church. I think they also wanted to pull together the church's identity. In the beginning there were words, and they made the church sing, and explain. For the United Church of Canada, that happened in document form.

A Song of Faith was not meant to be an official creed, but instead a poetic expression, an attempt to transcend and connect through text. I didn't find the spiritual journey my mother hoped I would find, but what I did find surprised me. In just the first few words, I could see a lingering, subdued version of the attitude that took possession of Agamemnon and Jephthah.

The Song begins:

God is Holy Mystery,
beyond complete knowledge,
above perfect description.

Yet,
in love,
the one eternal God seeks relationship.

So God creates the universe
and with it the possibility of being and relating.
God tends the universe,
mending the broken and reconciling the estranged.
God enlivens the universe,
guiding all things toward harmony with their Source.

Grateful for God's loving action,
We cannot keep from singing.

With the Church through the ages,
we speak of God as one and triune:
Father, Son, and Holy Spirit.
We also speak of God as
Creator, Redeemer, and Sustainer
God, Christ, and Spirit
Mother, Friend, and Comforter
Source of Life, Living Word, and Bond of Love,
and in other ways that speak faithfully of
the One on whom our hearts rely,
the fully shared life at the heart of the universe.

We witness to Holy Mystery that is Wholly Love.[15]

According to *A Song of Faith*, the United Church first associates God with mystery. But then it recognizes God as one, as three, and as a complex multiplicity or community. The words "Father, Son, and Holy Spirit" are mentioned, as could be expected from most Christian documents. Even the word "Mother" is used. But ultimately the church distills this God as the one on "whom our hearts rely, the fully shared life at the heart of the universe."

Although perhaps implied in the list, the family's "Daughter" is not present. That word is not mentioned in the entire *Song*. Not the text. Not the appendices. The word "God," especially capitalized, has other traditional Christian associations with it—masculinity, dominance, an ideal, authority, leadership, and traditional wisdom. Of course, we can add other words to that list uncomfortable to the modern ear—*magic* and *superstition*.

What is it about the symbolic idea of a *daughter* that seems so distant from the authoritative associations? Is it not possible, or is it unthinkable, for a heart to rely on a daughter in the tradition of the West? Perhaps this omission is just an oversight, perceptible only by someone brought up with the fixations of the postmodern consciousness. But what is it that comes dragging along with the word "God" that stops this association? Why would one of the more progressive, receptive, exploratory, and text-based churches of the West not associate the word "God" with the word "Daughter"? What would it look like to recognize and respect the role of daughters in a religious or divine language? Maybe there are reasons for not recognizing such a divinity or such an authority over our motivations. Maybe it is worth exploring.

If you have ever lived with a daughter, you may know how much authority even a little girl can carry in a household. The smallest of sounds from a baby girl, for example, can change a heart and compel action in the darkest hours of the night.

I believe *A Song of Faith* is a beautiful, lyrical, and inspired work that can help an open-minded church face the challenges of religious faith in a world of pluralities. But, this one document shed another light for me on the limitations of the West. It presented me with a challenge and a chance to explore what it might be like to bring a new divine symbol into recognition. What would her name be? What have others called her? And what would she be like if we figuratively looked upon her and saw her for the first time *as our own*? What if I belonged to her?

But I was already disillusioned with religious thinking as much as I was nauseated by pop culture. I knew of Lady Wisdom, Sophia, the Daughter of God as she is sometimes known in Western thought. The expression of that relationship is poetic, but the phrase Daughter *of* God is not the same as the equation Daughter *is* God or the comparison God *as* Daughter. I knew of wise Athena, daughter of Zeus. How is it that Athena supported, advised, criticized, and disobeyed, but never plotted to overthrow her father's rule of Olympus? I didn't see people worshipping wisdom, taking up hard challenges like knowing when to change their minds. Instead, people were playing with novelty but not really questioning their own routines, their own motivations.

In 1879, an amateur archaeologist named Marcelino Sanz de Sautuola explored a cave in Spain. A hunter and his dog came across the cave on Sautuola's property and told him about it. Sautuola surveyed the cave. He brought his young daughter, Maria, with him on a later trip. When in the cave, his daughter looked up and gave an exclamation of wonder and surprise. This exclamation got her father's attention and revealed something he did not see the first time. He may have never considered looking up when by himself. But it was something so very natural for a child with a parent. Sautuola and his daughter *looked up*.

Above their heads was one of the oldest treasures of human art that we have ever found. The place is now known as the Cave of Altamira and it holds depictions of bison, hunters, human hands, and families. Some researchers suggest the paintings may be more than 25,000 years old.

Susanne K. Langer also struggled with the problem of symbolism and meaning. She noticed two very different systems of thought emerge from the last century of the modern Western world. These two systems of thought harnessed the power of symbolization. The psychological analysis of dreams and religion, by people like Freud and Jung, brought about a study of symbols in terms of *meaning*. The mathematical analysis of science and logic brought about a study of symbols in terms of *use*. *Meaning* and *use* are not always the same. In art, content and form are used together in order to express ideas. In any act of communication, meaning and use play their parts. Archetype, function, relation, and identity all contribute to the language of symbolism. Langer further illustrated the difference in her book *Philosophy in a New Key*:

> One conception of symbolism leads to logic, and meets the new problems in theory of knowledge; and so it inspires an evolution of science and a quest for certainty. The other takes us in the opposite direction—to psychiatry, the study of emotions, religion, fantasy, and everything but knowledge. Yet in both we have a central theme: the human response, as a constructive, not a passive thing.
>
> Epistemologists and psychologists agree that symbolization is the key to that constructive process, though they may be ready to kill each other over the issue of what a symbol is and how it functions. One studies the structure of science, the other of dreams; each has his own assumptions— that is all they are—regarding the nature of symbolism itself. Assumptions, generative ideas, are what we fight for. Our conclusions we are usually content to demonstrate by peaceable means. Yet the assumptions are philosophically our most interesting stock-in-trade.
>
> In the fundamental notion of symbolization—mystical, practical, or mathematical, it makes no difference—we have the keynote of all humanistic problems. In it lies a new conception of "mentality," that may illumine questions of life and consciousness, instead of obscuring them as traditional "scientific methods" have done. If it is indeed a generative idea, it will beget tangible methods of its own, to free the deadlocked paradoxes of mind and body, reason and impulse, autonomy and law, and will overcome the checkmated arguments of an earlier age.[16]

In her work, Langer suggested each change in the history of thought can be understood metaphorically as a change of musical key. The pitch of the notes expressed have changed but the next contributors bring rhythms, harmonies, and counterpoint until that movement plays itself out in a resolution of the root chord. The use of a musical metaphor by Langer is significant because it suggests a shift from one sense to another. We often associate sight with thought, as in seeing where people are going with their ideas. But thought is not just a matter of optics and light. We can just as easily be swayed by following the melody of a tune or by the surprise of a noise, an entirely different band on the wave spectrum. As Langer suggests, the symbols of the material world or the dream world can captivate and motivate us. What we learn from both worlds, through observation and participation, can help us manage the regulation of both reason and impulse.

When Sautuola explored the Altamira cave by himself, he found nothing beyond the focus of his own perspective. The moment of change, however, came when he invited his daughter. She expressed amazement at what she saw, with a voice likely very different from his own, in a pitch much higher. It was that change, that sound, that brought his attention up to something remarkable. That sound, that moment of communication, changed the way we looked at ourselves, our art, our history, and the world in which we live.

If we let imagination direct our own attention up, this story symbolically points to something that could be understood as the *divine* nature of a daughter. But in order to understand it, we need to explore some of the most basic assumptions we have about things like authority, motivation, and compulsion—what makes us act, and the artistry around us we may not fully see or hear.

A father in Somalia probably did not know of Sautuola's discovery or the lesson that came from his daughter. The third chapter of this book outlines four potential maps of action within story. Stories give us many chances to change our perspective, to search out meaning, and to look up. The plot of a narrative follows events and decisions important to the characters. Plot also gives shape to the relationship we have with the call of mystery and personal curiosity. Ayaan Hirsi Ali is a daughter from Somalia. She abandoned the life her father wanted for her and found her own way. Her journey toward self-identity and independence became an important lesson for me. If we fall in love with inquiry, we can combine observation and action, and give ourselves opportunities to begin again.

Apollo and Dionysus

Camille Paglia wanted to know why art and literature went through such a dramatic change of direction in the twentieth century. She perceived a shift, not just in the methods of expression or the technology behind media, but in the message. She described a binary conflict at the heart of Western civilization in her book *Sexual Personae: Art and Decadence from Nefertiti to Emily Dickinson*. One tradition she labelled Apollonian, fixated on symmetry and the structured state of an ordered social world. The other she called Dionysian for the revolutionary spirit that celebrated the disordered, creative potential of the natural world. She, along with others, recognized a pattern in the rise and fall of civilizations and the signs that seem to come with each stage.

The late stages of many civilizations show a similar loss of confidence, doubting the beliefs or foundational ideas that first helped it to flourish. Some of the signs of this shift can be seen in the language, as literature might become more ironic and challenging instead of celebrating triumphs. The figures once worshipped as embodying the mind, heart, and soul of the collective culture are cast in doubt or outright disrespect. Differences between the sexes in the Apollonian stages tend to be clear and distinct. In the Dionysian stages, however, identities are questioned and topics like androgyny are explored more. Artists exchange, intertwine, mock, or simply play with the traditional roles in families and relationships. From the Dionysian perspective, it is a sin to be mundane, traditional, and unoriginal. It is somehow missing the mark in life to do the same things over and over, expecting the simple dignity of getting the same results each time.[17]

If an artist were to remake the *Vierge Ouvrante* today, that artist may be tempted to portray the onlookers in the scene as though gazing every which way. The audience would be attending to every distraction or interest except that old, traditional construction of the mother-father-child family that was once believed to be the centre of Western civilization.

Paglia is a student of the long chronologies of art history, as the subtitle of her book suggests. She made things clear to her readers that the last century in the West presented symptoms of a civilization drawing to a close. We have separated each of the archetypal figures into isolated institutions and motivating forces. We have sacrificed their relationships and functions to the surprise of spectacle, to the novel idea that happens to come along and mesmerize us. Perhaps now we sacrifice everything to the observed and to the other. Is this what it means to worship the *Daughter-as-God*? Is there a light side and shadow side to this divinity?

Each time a civilization declines into decadence and navel-gazing, according to Paglia, other civilizations wait on the borders and encroach on the frontiers. Those others are either too desperate for identity or too ambitious for power to waste their time doubting what they believe, what they worship, or what they want. Even the most benign or optimistic revolutionaries come to realize that the disintegration of any system of power and culture does not simply make way for a more fair or just ideology. Instead, all other motivated forces energize, from within and from without, to contend for the spoils.

Paglia gives a general, possibly dated, and deliberately provocative commentary in her book about what happens when a civilization worships just one thing without consideration of the other forces at work. "The last western society to worship female powers was Minoan Crete. And significantly, that fell and did not rise again."[18]

Paglia received attention, commendation, and criticism for her ideas. Her work does draw our attention to a compelling challenge—no matter how distant we think the apocalypse might be, we are on a course to do the same thing over again and get the same results. Things will collapse. Things fall apart.[19]

Jeremy Rifkin took a different approach to the phenomenon of how civilizations rise and collapse. Instead of examining art, he looked at technology, energy consumption, and modes of communication. He wrote a book titled *The Empathic Civilization*. Instead of the binary conflict between the Apollonian and the Dionysian perspectives, Rifkin used contemporary interests like empathy, entropy, technology, and the environment, and he stressed the relationship between these figurative forces. In the process, he accomplished something quite remarkable in his writing—he can somehow sound optimistic and cynical, simultaneously.

> At the very core of the human story is the paradoxical relationship between empathy and entropy. Throughout history new regimes have converged with new communication revolutions, creating ever more complex societies. More technologically advanced civilizations, in turn, have brought more diverse people

> together, heightened empathic sensitivity, and expanded human consciousness. But these increasingly more complicated milieus require more extensive energy use and speed us towards resource depletion.
>
> The irony is that our growing empathic awareness has been made possible by an ever-greater consumption of the Earth's energy and other resources, resulting in a dramatic deterioration of the health of the planet.[20]

Civilization is not a simple game between the individual and culture. Agamemnon and Jephthah threw their families into ruin because of their ambitions. Now we risk our families, the stability of the community, and the relationship to our physical world as we become more and more connected. Rifkin seems to suggest we need to pay better attention to the relationships between our ambitions.

> Our journey begins at the crossroads where the laws of energy that govern the universe come up against the human inclination to continually transcend our sense of isolation by seeking the companionship of others in ever more complex energy-consuming social arrangements. The underlying dialectic of human history is the continuous feedback loop between expanding empathy and increasing entropy.[21]

To drive this double-sided point even further:

> The recognition of another's finite existence is what connects empathic consciousness to entropic awareness. When we identify with another's plight, it's their will to live that we empathize with and seek to support. The laws of thermodynamics, and especially the entropy law, tells us that every living moment is unique, unrepeatable, and irreversible.... When we empathize with another being, there is an unconscious understanding that their very existence, like our own, is a fragile affair, which is made possible by the continuous flow of energy through their being. Only recently, however, we have become consciously aware that we each owe our well-being, in part, to the buildup of our own personal entropic debt in the surrounding environment....
>
> While our empathic gains are impressive, our entropic losses are equally foreboding.[22]

The stakes are high. But the risks and the rewards of our pursuits seem linked, according to Rifkin. Many of the civilizations he examined made their contributions only to fall away later. Although his title was probably smart for the book market, Rifkin could have just as easily called his book *The Entropic Civilization*. Paglia suggests that despite the decline, the end times of civilization can be incredibly creative, vibrant, evocative, and revealing. Instead of simply and tragically enjoying the descent, finding quibbles and beliefs and words to argue over, we can use our awareness to make better decisions. Agamemnon and Jephthah carved out their own fates with their ambitions and their daughters. However, with one change of mind, we can continue to enjoy the rewards of the high-stakes game of civilization without sacrificing our daughters and families and neighbourhoods and ecosystems.

What can we do, if anything, to transcend this cyclical up and down of civilization and the suffering it promises to future generations? How wise or courageous is it, really, to stand as passive witnesses, almost as if revelling in the end of days? What have we learned that could change the coming fearful apocalypse into a hopeful revelation, make peace between polarizing extremes, and build a dialogue in search of something to share?

Starting New Songs, Taking Her Hand

In the quotation that opened this introduction, Joseph Campbell asked his readers where Ariadne might be found.[23] Ariadne was the daughter of a Minoan king. She fell in love with the Greek hero Theseus. She gave him the tools and insights needed to triumph over the Minotaur and the labyrinth. But according to some versions of the story, Theseus left her on the shores waiting. He returned to his home without her. She was left behind to perish along with the Minoan culture.

We can look to different stories, though. Perseus, another Greek hero, rescued a foreign princess and became her husband. Such a marriage is sure to have its own family tensions and its own problems. Yet despite the different motivations bred into one family against another, we can also find another kind of nobility in a young couple taking up the significant challenge of marriage. Compared to a violent war based on oppression or power, a marriage based on mutual love is a more promising symbolic model for relationships.

A little girl in a slum in Bangladesh named Aduri may have found a response to the challenges we face in the West and in the East. It likely wasn't her intention. If anything, she was probably doing little more than following her own personal interest and acting on a chance to help make her corner of the world a little better. A Canadian family wanted to do something about the lack of education children received in the slums. That family looked to the mothers in the slums for a solution. Aduri watched as her mother received an education. Aduri's mother then educated her. And despite her young age, Aduri took up the role of educator and began teaching children younger than her. She took an idea from the West that was delivered to her mother. Then she adopted it as part of her identity. She took a compelling idea and made it her own. The fourth chapter in this book coordinates four uses of language and expression. To find resolutions to our problems we use these different modes of communication. Aduri models the use of language and expression that can help us pass the tests of entropy.

Four female figures from the contemporary world offer us new ways of seeing our relationships to the other—Jyoti, Malala, Ayaan, Aduri. In each case, the woman or girl was acting as the hero of her own life. If we stand as observers to these lives, then the lessons from the observations could give us the tools for new peaks in consciousness. If we pay attention to their stories and to their names, that may be enough to lift our heads up and find a new vision for the world. It may give us something to show Agamemnon and Jephthah as we walk with them, something that could either change their minds or prepare us for their ambitions.

A simple idea may be enough to help us keep afloat in a storm. It may even provide us with a course of action to prevent much of the damage that comes from a deluge. But first comes preparation. After all, absolutes can breed more disillusionment. Quick certainties can create dangerous motivations. The challenge before me wasn't to place a daughter above the rest of the family, but to recognize her archetypal role in the family of motivations that compel our actions. For that reason, I can only invite you to carry a little girl with you, a daughter and her name, on this journey with Agamemnon and Jephthah.

The way we conduct our relations with the observed other, the stranger and our own reflection, can bring consequences great and terrible. Each new relationship is a chance to share new words, sing new songs, greet one another and awake to new ideas. And in each relationship, there may be an antidote to the nausea of novelty and the ambitions that accelerate entropy and war.

Unaware, complicit, or defiant, children often must face the sins and successes of their parents. We have a choice about the lessons we take from stories. We don't need to complete the stories of the past the way Jephthah's unnamed daughter and Iphigenia did, simply for the ambitions or expectations of parents. The ancients may not have had the same words we do, but they addressed the problems of fear and motivation with an inkling of what we might call today the test of entropy. Agamemnon drove his family into chaos and ruination because of his actions and motivations. He failed the test of entropy. Jephthah wept at the realization that his desires, and his interpretation of their authority over him, meant he stared at his own family's open grave. He too failed the test of entropy. These two characters stand as examples of a problem, raising a critical question. The test of entropy is your relationship with the observed. What actions and motivations potentially minimize entropy? This can be understood on the individual level, risking chaos in our regular lives, and on a more global scale, risking the cultures and environments that surround us.

Though she has always been a part of us, the Divine Daughter is proving to be just as important in compelling our behaviour as our paternal gods, matronly goddesses, and adventuring sons. She slips in and out of our consciousness. But we ignore her quiet, still voice at our own peril. She is as real to our existence as the natural world in which we live, the cultures we create, and the heroes we worship. What in the Western tradition tells us how to have a relationship with the observed, the other that may be just as divine as our own motivations? This book is about expanding our conception of the symbolically divine to recognize a place of authority for a daughter in our spiritual family. She need not rule in an absolute sense, just as each and every other divinity contends for our attention. She need not be tethered to any limiting issues of gender. This is about finding her place, finding a room for each divinity in the chambers of our hearts and minds.

Each of the following chapters explores four ideas. With the shift of perspective in each chapter, the four ideas take on different shapes, different pitches. And to do that, I turn and turn again to the repeated elements of story—character, setting, plot, the workings of a problem, and communicating a solution. Like the refrain of a pop song, the same thing might be expressed again and again, but differences stand out and impressions move, leading to a resolution of the theme.

Quiet moments of distraction and doubt may whisper in the ear or flicker in the eye's periphery. What is another book, another child, in a world freeing itself from all moorings of religious practices and enlightened traditions? What is our relationship to novelty and to wisdom? Examination of the elements of narrative can uplift us, toughen us, and prepare us for the demands of a hyperconnected world. By paying attention, we can make ourselves more aware of how information, in whatever form, works us over completely.

I want to start a different conversation about authority and literacy—about our relationship to the information in our observable environments and the actions that make up our experiences. The Divine Daughter appears in the stories of Agamemnon and Jephthah. She walks in the streets of Munirka and the slums of Bangladesh. She lives in places like the Swat Valley and Mogadishu. She also makes her way about our country lanes, quiet home towns and busy urban cores in the West. And she asks us how to manage our fears and how best to direct our motivations.

My own motivations in starting this journey are not academic or religious, but personal—as old and as common as time itself. An entire world can remain quiet and hidden, waiting for that first time a lover perceives a beloved.

This is a song to a girl.

§

Take her hand.
Not leading her
to the altar.
She may show
us another way.

1

Family Stock and Character Sketches

And where we had thought to find an abomination, we shall find a god; where we had thought to slay another, we shall slay ourselves; where we had thought to travel outward, we shall come to the center of our own existence; where we had thought to be alone, we shall be with all the world.

—Joseph Campbell
The Hero with a Thousand Faces

> *The character of a god*
> *was the expression*
> *of your sacrifice.*

Shriners and the Supernatural

In August 2015, more than 2,000 Shriners gathered with city officials and families to attend the ribbon-cutting ceremony of a new Montreal Hospital for Children. This hospital replaced an older building. Like all the hospitals under the care of the Shriners, this one was built to serve the needs of children, particularly those with musculoskeletal illnesses.

The new hospital cost $127 million. The funds to pay for the construction and medical equipment were raised through private donations from international members of the Shriners clubs. The decisions, organization, and construction took the better part of a decade.[1]

A Haitian girl by the name of Waina had a bone infection that destroyed her left tibia. In Haiti, treatment would have meant amputation. A journalist sponsored Waina's visit to Montreal and raised funds for accommodations. Shriners paid for the expenses involved with the surgery. Waina received a series of treatments so that she could walk independently again.[2]

Waina is one example of the many lives changed by the Shriners. The Shriners began as a fraternal community-service group through members of the Masonic Lodge. In 1870, two Masons, William Florence and Walter Fleming, wanted to create a group based on fun and fellowship. Florence was invited to an elaborate party held by an Arabian diplomat that involved a comedy stage show. Florence told his friend Fleming about the experience. Fleming took the ideas from the show and developed an entire theme for the new group. They called it the Ancient Arabic Order of the Nobles of the Mystic Shrine. They initiated others into the group by use of elaborate ceremonies loosely based on what Florence and Fleming knew of the Middle East. Meeting places for the group were called "temples."[3]

Despite the theme and name, the group has little to do with Arabic or Islamic culture. The only religious element of membership comes from Freemasonry. To be a Shriner, a person first needs to become a Mason. To be a Mason, a person must profess a belief in a Supreme Being. The fine details of what is meant by Supreme Being are up to the person professing the belief. The name of the group has changed officially to Shriners International, and many meeting places are no longer called temples.

People brought up with identity politics, politically correct etiquette, and trigger warnings may find the history of the Shriners offensive. Before passing judgment on the Shriners, it is worth considering their relationship to children like Waina. Imagine the effort and dedication needed to raise over $100 million. Imagine the logistics managed and obstacles overcome in a ten-year project. Imagine the staffing, purchasing, and custodial costs involved in running a hospital. Multiply that by twenty-two—the number of Shriners Hospitals in the world. All to give about 25,000 children each year a place to recover from surgery or treatment. Approximately ten times that number receive care each year on an outpatient basis.

If one were to look at the Shriners with one eye closed, one might only see an insensitivity toward cultural issues. The red hats, extravagant titles, and grand halls are not essential to achieving the level of support and philanthropy the Shriners give to children. But something in that network of fellowship and fun helped to inspire the level of persistent resolve needed to accomplish so much for so many kids.

Membership numbers in Shriners clubs are in decline. People in the West no longer turn to service and community groups for fellowship and fun in the same numbers as people did in the past. This comes at a time when the tasks of parenting have changed too. Today people expect children to be busy with sports leagues, dance classes, music lessons, and other highly organized activities. Children are more likely to be dedicated members of community clubs than their parents.

The merry pomp and circumstance of the noble Shriners can hardly be taken as mystical or spiritual or magical, but even a quick glimpse at the history and work of the group does reveal a change in attitude in the West. The Shriners may have built twenty-two hospitals and helped a lot of children, but how will that good work continue if fewer and fewer people become Shriners? The Masons and the Shriners explain the work of their clubs simply as "making good men better." For these clubs, part of that work involves a belief in a Supreme Being. That requirement is necessary for membership, although many clubs may not probe much further into it. The rituals and secrets of the clubs might have an air of the mystical about them, but again, that hardly seems like a necessary feature for the task of making a good man better.

Gretta Vosper grew up in the United Church of Canada and became a minister. She loved the work of the church. She believed it gave her the chance to make her community, and the world, better. But she came to realize that her own beliefs and her own readings of the sacred texts had very little to do with the rituals of a Sunday morning service. Her understanding of a Supreme Being didn't seem to correspond with anything she was saying in the call to worship, the hymns, or the prayers. She wondered if the two could be reconciled in any way, when her use of a word like "God" was not reflected in the rituals of her church or congregation. In 2008, she published *With Or Without God*. She was convinced the way we live is more important than what we believe. With support from her church community, she began eliminating the supernatural language of her services. The songs and prayers were rewritten to lead people toward living well with others rather than promoting conviction in supernatural powers. She wanted people to address the issue of what these difficult words really mean and how we use them. This has meant bringing attention to questions, again and again, about the words and rituals used in spiritual practice.[4]

Words can mean one thing to one audience but something else to another. To the busy person of today the word "supernatural" might mean magic. To the theologian, "supernatural" may be part of a specialized jargon, closer to something like "superordinate." In simple terms, the material world of nature might be understood as real, as in "what is." But something might be more important or authoritative. For example, people often do not want to be limited to "what is" and instead leap quickly to "what should be" or "what could be" or "how will I use this?"

The membership of Rev. Vosper's church went through a dramatic shift. Many left. Others, curious, came and went. Some returned and stayed. The bureaucratic parts of the larger national organization, United Church of Canada (UCC), have chosen not to act swiftly or impulsively. In 2013, Rev. Vosper identified herself as an atheist because of this problem with words. The UCC reviewed her standing as a minister and allowed her to continue as a leader in her spiritual community. In 2015, after the Charlie Hebdo massacre in France, she wrote an open letter to the church's leaders. She used the incident as an example of how belief in God can motivate people to perform atrocities.[5] The statement of belief in a Supreme Being is not sufficient to make a person good, or a good person better. The church eventually released a statement in 2016 saying she was deemed unsuitable for a ministry position.[6] In 2017, they planned to re-evaluate her position as a church minister.[7]

The church first appeared both complacent and experimental in spirit. Instead of reaching for the sinister brush and immediately painting a label on her, or throwing in the righteous towel, the administrative body of the church decided to watch and wait. It is worth noting just how peaceful this process was. Careers, communities, and people's confidences were at risk, but not lives. Each step involved books, letters, and meetings to explore and talk about the issue. If this is what burning heretics at the stake has become, evidently some progress has been made in the executive power of religious authority.

In the 1950s, long before my time, the UCC hit a high point in membership. It made a good attempt to rival the Catholic Church in Canada, not that Canada is known for heated religious rivalries (hockey being an exception). Since the 1980s, attendance numbers have dropped by an average of 2.5 percent each year. It took about twenty years to fall to half of its highest mark. And according to projections, it won't take that long to diminish by half again.[8]

This persistent issue isn't a problem only for the Shriners or the United Church. Active membership in religious and service communities in the West is in serious decline. The West hasn't fully sorted out what to do about the place of magic in a rational, materialist, and scientific world. The use of words and the meaning of words can be important. Despite our attempts to govern our lives intelligently, we haven't conclusively found non-mystical foundations for authority. Even legal rights and responsibilities—sometimes justified as "self-evident"— don't stop the conversation with foundational answers to *why* the law or institution *should* be binding or *ought* to compel behaviour. Instead, legal documents explain how something became binding and what punishments will be carried out on those who break the restrictions as articulated in documents. For some, maybe that's enough. Others, however, seek something more compelling than reward and punishment.

The reason both the Shriners Hospital and Rev. Vosper appear as illustrations of differences in religious beliefs is to raise questions about what is *necessary* and what is *sufficient*. Any useful definition addresses necessary and sufficient conditions. Sufficient means *enough*. It'll do. Necessary means required or essential. It must have a particular condition to meet the definition. Rev. Vosper seems to be saying that a belief in the supernatural is neither sufficient nor necessary, even in religious or spiritual pursuits. The traditions of the Shriners seem to suggest that it is both sufficient and necessary for group membership. According to statistics in Canada, roughly one in two people are involved in community volunteer work of some kind.⁹ So, what is happening to religious beliefs and the change in motivations around community membership? Perhaps the project of modernity can be thought of as the search, not for a Supreme Being, but for a *Supreme Way of Being*.

Magic, Mask, and Metaphor

In the introduction, I mentioned a news story about a daughter from India by the name of Jyoti. After the 2012 murder of Jyoti, protesters came out in massive numbers. The rallies in Munirka needed no magical justification or institutional organization for their motivation. But they needed a beginning, an impetus, and a goal. People took up action to move toward change. The people involved somehow identified with Jyoti, and they were willing to go to the streets for her.

The problem might be our relationship with what is authoritative as much as our relationship with the supernatural. Authority requires some rationalization or story, but must it rely on mystical beginnings as well? Is there no other way to know ourselves, to come to terms with the push and pull of what compels us besides appealing to magic? Sometimes, we must act before we can put into words a satisfying explanation of our actions. After all, almost any motivation or want can seem authoritative to us depending on circumstances. In the contemporary world, "We don't know" will not sufficiently answer our desire for explanation. The closest we dare come to the mystery is possibly, "We don't know, but..." And unfortunately, as many people know, anything before "but" ends up not counting anyway.

I stopped going to church when I realized just how many different definitions people used for the word "God." It wasn't merely some pointer toward a Supreme Way of Being for other people. It may as well have been a brand or graphic on a shirt. I realized that some of my schoolmates came from different Christian denominations. Some didn't go to church at all. By the time I learned about other world religions, I was questioning my own beliefs. My family's version of God started to sound like just another story. I can remember having a short conversation with my dad about the afterlife and belief. He was a minister at the time. I watched as he strutted and fretted behind the pulpit on Sunday mornings. He wrestled with two near-impossible goals: make an ancient text relevant to a modern world, and inspire his congregation to do more than just sit and listen to stories.

I realize now what was behind that struggling, hesitant, conflicted authority figure on Sunday mornings. He was in the process of working things out himself. He probably also realized his influence on me was changing. My participation was changing. And he probably also realized that my life, filled at the time with high school basketball, electric guitar, video games, and nachos, was going to take place in a world far different from the one he understood.

I asked him if belief— belief in God—was really necessary to get to heaven. I wasn't so sure about heaven or hell at the time either, but who can handle more than one big question at a time?

A direct connection between the afterlife and belief, never a real concern of my parents that I can remember, made little sense to me. I don't remember my father's exact response, but I remember it was honest. No pretense or subversion. No trickery or magic words. Belief in God wasn't what was important. What matters is what your beliefs made you do.

My trust in our family's version of "I don't know, but..." grew fainter in the years that followed. I started collecting definitions from others for the word "God." Nobody's explanation satisfied. Nothing in their words seemed necessary or sufficient. This wasn't a quest for truth. It was a passive distraction. Over time, I came to realize the word itself no longer compelled me. It no longer had any magic, any authority. I listened to the beliefs of others and forgot them as soon as another distraction came along. But then, years later, I came across a story from Joseph Campbell.

Campbell, a world-renowned teacher of mythology, loved to recount a coming-of-age ritual from New Guinea. The story, so distant from the Christian world, awoke in me something fresh and new. It was an intriguing illustration of how children and grown-ups use gods and words and masks.

> The boys are brought up to be in fear of the masks the men wear in their rituals. These are the gods. These are the personifications, the powers, that structure the society. When the boy gets to be more than his mother can handle, the men come in with their masks, or whatever their costume is, and they grab the kid. He thinks he's being taken by the gods. Taken out to the men's new ground, and he's beaten up and everything else.
>
> But in New Guinea, there is a wonderful event where the poor kid has to stand up and fight a man with a mask. He's fighting the god. The man lets the kid win, takes the mask off, and puts it on the kid.
>
> Now the mask is not there defeated. They don't simply say, "This is just myth." The mask represents the power that is shaping the society and has shaped you, and now you are a representative of that power.[10]

There is a way to understand the word "God" and writings about the character of "God" that can preserve some of the historical significance, re-establish some of the respect lost through time, bring attention to the mysterious elements of life, and still remove the superstitions that once seemed so necessary. The journey from magic to mask to metaphor can be incredibly difficult. But we can make the journey worth it. And perhaps we can go further, if we find good questions to ask.

The Figure and Ground of Definitions

Campbell's story reawakened my interest in definitions for the word "God." I had something to compare other ideas *against*. I went to another authority to test Campbell's story. I went to Google. According to Google, we use the word "god" (not capitalized) to mean

- a supernatural being,
- immortal, supreme, or superhuman creator of the universe,

- a power that has control over nature or human fortunes, a personification of fate,
- the subject of traditional stories and object of worship or prayer, or
- the source of moral authority.

My earlier quotation from *A Song of Faith* associated "God" with mystery. Campbell associated gods with masks and metaphors. These explanations did not even register for first-page consideration with Google. (I have omitted from the list above some of the more informal and non-religious definitions, such as "an adored, admired, or influential person" or "the gallery in a theatre.") Google may not be an authority in a traditional sense, but the list reveals current popular attitudes. Writer Wendy Piersell said it well: "Google only loves you if everyone else loves you first."[11]

Although each of these definitions has won its own measure of attention, none of them conclusively stands up well against the tests of necessity or sufficiency. They do not seem to be required and they just won't do for people taking up the challenge of asking better questions. If anything, these attempts at definitions inspire argument and quibbling. What does it say about our understanding of information if the words "mystery" and "metaphor" do not appear in the quickest of answers we assemble? Pop goes the popular accounts of things again, inviting us to look a little deeper.

Michael Dowd was born and raised Roman Catholic. He studied religion and philosophy and became an evangelical minister. He once called himself a young-earth creationist, but a series of friendships opened him up to the idea of evolution on an intellectual level. Then evolution took hold of him on a spiritual level. He wrote a book titled *Thank God for Evolution!* He suggests, as have others, that our ancestors and the writers of our sacred texts used their word for "God" as a symbol to describe *reality*. For Dowd, "God is a mythic personification of reality. If we miss this we miss everything.... Religion is about right relationship to reality, not the supernatural."[12]

Dowd is doing as much as anyone can, I believe, to find a collaborative, creative, and inspirational link between ancient thinking, modern religious thought, and the practice we need to adopt to regulate our motivations. But he glosses over a problem when he points at "reality." Reality certainly has its own authority, but something else does not hold in his explanation. This creates a problem between the figure of what is being talked about and the background context. If we say, "God is reality," then the word "God" could simply point at everything. Imagine someone pointing at everything and saying, "Well, that is what I'm talking about. That is what I really mean." That person has not actually pointed at anything at all. He or she did not communicate anything distinguishable. Invoking everything as an explanation isn't useful. Dowd's idea may have an incredible explanatory scope, but it doesn't bring the conversation to a satisfying resolution. It does not adequately inscribe the mask or the metaphor or the magic in comparison to what it might not be. And it does not point to any particular motivation as authoritative.

Human perception is not just about seeing what is real. Much of what we perceive is heavily influenced by our motivations and expectations. In the early 1900s Gestalt psychology started to explore the relationship between figure and ground in human perception. The problem psychologists discovered between what is real and what we perceive turned out to be a very old problem. Thousands of years ago, artists painted on the walls of the Cave of Altamira, attempting to represent what they perceived as real and important.

We need a figure and a ground in order to differentiate the problem and gain better insight. Hindsight can appear flawless when it comes to rationalizing explanations or telling stories. If, after the fact, we have access to all the background, we can make up a pretty good story to explain things and draw out a figure from the ground. Maybe that is a problem we have with the test of entropy—we can see what passes or fails too often with hindsight. But if we look at the stories of Agamemnon and Jephthah, we can predict a direction. Whatever motivations they assumed to be supreme, it turned out their motivations were destructive instead of authoritative. They resolved to sacrifice their daughters and thereby destroyed their families. Maybe we can at least aim at better realities.

A search for definition is like a question—a call seeking a response. The source used, and the assumptions built into that source, can frame the answer. A Canadian academic started a career as a United Church minister but found himself further compelled by literature. He was searching for "a key to all mythologies" and thought he may have found it in "the myth of God, which is a myth of identity."[13] Northrop Frye found an interconnectedness throughout literature, and that interconnectedness said something about identity. This connection between the words "God" and "identity" helps give context to the background and direction of our motivations. My own search for definition and identity led me once again to questions. Who would dare question a mystery, and doubt the identity of the West? Who would bother being possessed by such a search? And like many people who spend too much time with mysteries, I discovered other questions surfaced in response:

What compels you to act?

What is necessary for a god to be a god is that it compels action. And what is also sufficient for a god to be a god is that it compels action.

What motivates your behaviour, your choices?

Jordan Peterson, a clinical psychologist, wanted to know what made people act. He was concerned with the problem of evil. He wanted to know how normal human beings could carry out acts such as genocide. He wanted to know what made human beings follow orders from authoritarians. He wanted to know why people kill others for ideas, even to the point of turning themselves and everything around them to ruin. In his book *Maps of Meaning: The Architecture of Belief*, he examined the mythological archetypes in our ancient texts and sacred stories. According to Peterson, there are fundamental elements in the nature of experience, and these elements appear in our stories and in the psychological makeup of our identities. He developed a map between what we take as reality and what we should do about it. Regardless of what cloak or mask or language or metaphor we wrap around a god, actions, motivations, and compulsions must come from it. Whatever your god is, it is "something that controls behaviour, or at least that must be served."[14] Otherwise, how could it be a god?

Peterson's psychological examination of ancient literature and tradition illustrates a kind of trinity that is similar to many religious traditions. He refers to three main archetypes—*Father*,

Mother, and *Hero*. Instead of relying on a mystical context, however, this trinity illuminates paths connecting literature and religion, psychology and culture, science and innovation. Although Peterson's examination of this trinity provides a solid grounding for the psychological development of belief, I think it can be expanded into studying our relationship with information itself. Beyond that, we can further understand a moral community's place in today's pluralistic world through our relationships with what can be called the *observed-other*. If traditional religious spirituality is going to have any role in the future, it will have to do more than assume the authority of its texts. It is not necessary or sufficient to remain fixed on old conclusions unless they work today. We need a much richer understanding of the role of story in our lives, and a better understanding of what we do when we adopt or adapt personal identities for ourselves. We need to understand how to face, process, and embrace new information apart from our motivations, because we live in a world of faster communication technology and greater energy consumption. We need a literacy of the self, identity, and consciousness that is accessible on different levels of resolution.

In this book, I will use the word "god" as a question of what compels your behaviour; what must you serve?

But just because some thought, goal, idea, or story compels us, it is not the compulsion that makes it worthy of authority. Our compulsions can lead to just as much evil as good. For now, I will avoid using the word "god" with a capital. The capital may appear when quoting others. They may want to point toward something compelling for their stories. However, my thoughts are leading me elsewhere. And besides, who am I to name your beautiful mystery?

As mentioned earlier, this is a song to a girl.

Namastes, Plural

> The function of mythological symbols is to give you a sense of "Aha! Yes. I know what it is, it's myself." I'm calling a symbol a sign that points past itself to a ground of meaning and being that is one with the consciousness of the beholder. What you're learning in myth is about yourself as part of the being of the world.
>
> —Joseph Campbell[15]

When I was in my thirties, a new minister graced my parents' church. I noticed a change in my mother's language. She started to say things such as, "You should come with me," and "You really should listen to him sometime." When my mother began saying *should* so much, I knew she had found something compelling.

When I first met the minister, he asked if I'd like to have a coffee with him someday. He was a good conversationalist. He bought the coffee. We talked about the history of the church and the importance of cheese factories in early Ontario communities. The first thing to be built at the intersection of four farms was often the cheese factory. Then, later, the church. When our conversation turned to belief, I noticed he was fond of the phrase, "the god within." "How does the god *within* speak to you?"

My mother doesn't particularly like that kind of language. She was raised with her god outside her body. She is on a journey *to* her god. Human desires are not the source of the divine for my mother. What you strive for should be something outside your own wants, something with a higher purpose than your whims within.

Years later, my wife and I bought a house and went to a lawyer. On the front desk there was a wooden carving in the shape of an *aum* symbol. Intrigued, I asked the receptionist about it. I never dreamed there was such a thing as a spiritual lawyer, yet we discovered one in our own town.

When the lawyer came to greet us, I shook his hand, gestured to the wooden carving and said, "Namaste." He beamed at us and repeated, "Namaste."

On his wall were pictures of Jesus, the Buddha, and a few yogis. Each image had technicolor vibrancy as in the portraits of Hindu gods. After going through the paperwork for the house, we talked about spirituality.

Namaste means, "I bow to you," but it is often translated as "The divine light in me honours the divine light in you." Some people go further: "The god within me recognizes the god within you." This was our lawyer's favourite. I wonder sometimes what he would think of cultural appropriation and identity politics. Without that symbol on the front desk, I probably would not have recognized or even seen the divinities in his office. However, that particular symbol was only part of my interest because of my curiosity in world religions. Many people going in and out of his office would not have seen the *aum* symbol as anything besides something foreign, wooden, and not worth noticing. Somebody else's symbol. This is important with respect to communication. Two people can speak the same language and yet hold in authority very different references or meanings. Some people may see the *aum* and feel compelled to behave a certain way. Others, curious, may ask questions. Others may not even see it.

The *aum* symbol is sometimes translated literally as "no sky." Like many symbols, it points to many things at once. According to Hindu traditions, invoking the sound or the symbol can be a reflection on the absolute and on reality. That reality is understood as having three main elements or aspects: creation, preservation, and liberation. But again, if the *aum* symbol isn't part of your vocabulary, or even if you don't regularly think in terms of creation, preservation, and liberation, this might all look like what the author Douglas Adams referred to as an "SEP field"—somebody else's problem, something safely ignored. The observed can be compelling or it can be ignored, depending on the motivations and expectations of the observer.

My mother appreciates Karen Armstrong. She gave me one of Armstrong's books, *A History of God*, saying I should read it. One idea caught my attention because I wasn't expecting it from Armstrong. According to her, any idea of god, if it is to survive, must work for the people who develop it. Ideas of god change when they cease to be effective.

> Despite its otherworldliness, religion is highly pragmatic. It is far more important for a particular idea of God to *work* than for it to be logically or scientifically sound. As soon as it ceases to be effective it will be changed—sometimes for

> something radically different. This did not disturb most monotheists before our own day because they were quite clear that their ideas about God were not sacrosanct but could only be provisional. They were entirely man-made—they could be nothing else—and quite separate from the indescribable Reality they symbolized.[16]

Like Dowd, Armstrong seems to want to associate the word "reality" with the word "God" (her capitalization). She goes so far as to capitalize Reality. Unfortunately, the popular understanding of "reality" is very similar to the popular concept of a person-like god behaving like a human being. It no longer works for many. And capitalizing a word does not make it authoritative. Armstrong suggests the search for a new concept has begun. Such a development is inevitable, because it is a natural aspect of our humanity to seek what works. We do the same thing over and over again until we no longer get the intended result.[17]

Instead of a radical shift in concepts, we can give our thinking a nudge in the way one sibling might nudge another, directing attention toward a parent who is watching them play. Perhaps what might work is a shift from the idea of god as an individual to a god as a family. The way a family manages fears and motivations might be a more useful illustration today than how an individual manages them.

Namaste, according to my spiritual lawyer, means two divinities can meet and share respect for one another. To match the symbol with a more pluralistic understanding of the "ineffable reality that is universally perceived," my own greeting could mean something more like this: "The family within me recognizes the family within you."

There is a competition inside of me, identities struggling for recognition and rule. But they can also collaborate. For now, I will grant none of them full authority. First, let us introduce ourselves to them, in all their great and terrible aspects, and observe. Then we can consider how each mask fits and "works," in the sense that Armstrong uses for that word. Campbell said that what you learn from story is about you as part of the being of the world. That means understanding what compels your actions.

The anthropologist Christopher Boehm was fascinated with altruism. He studied human and animal societies to understand the origins of moral communities. At the heart of human nature, according to Boehm, is a fundamental conflict. Human beings are filled with resentment about being dominated by others and the environment, and at the same time we strive to dominate others and the environment. In *Hierarchy in the Forest*, Boehm examined how chimpanzees and humans can simultaneously display both dominance and resentment to dominance.

> Potentially we are all both doves and hawks, and the prudent course is to realize that our contradictory nature predisposes us to draw caricatures. The next step is to try and be evenhanded, looking dispassionately for specific combinations of nice and nasty in order to see how the two work together.[18]

The desire to live in an ordered world, to minimize chaos, gives us motivation to dominate our surroundings. At the same time, we seek freedom from the dominance of others. To find a balance, we have come up with two more responses, the first being resolution through change (or innovation), and the second being advocacy (or submission).

These four ideas—domination, the desire to be free of domination, resolution, and advocacy—create broad categories. However, these four elements appear in our oldest stories and our most recent news events. When ideas are difficult to fully express, people rely on symbols to stand in for what is meant. Boehm refers to this as a predisposition to "draw caricatures." Even when we see something as an ineffable mystery, we don't hold back from attempting to describe and define it, dominate it, or resent it. But if a symbol works, in Armstrong's sense, then even a caricature can successfully bring us to say, "Aha! Yes. I know what it is, it's myself."

The four elements can be mapped onto four important literary symbols. By association, I want to link them to psychological elements of experience as well. By recognizing them in a story or in a personal experience, the symbols point past themselves and past any possible events in fiction or history, and into the audience members' lives. The story is the artist's way of saying something about how to act when faced with life, when dealing with the experience of being in the world.

Mother—Empowering and Devouring

Sigmund Freud once said, "The great question that has never been answered, and which I have not yet been able to answer, despite my thirty years of research into the feminine soul, is 'What does a woman want?'"[19]

This quotation perhaps says more about Freud than it does about women. Freud is still considered a giant in psychology. What might have made him revolutionary in his time was that in order to explore his question, he asked questions of, and listened to, women. He studied women, recognizing them as worthy of being asked what they wanted. That shift in attention may have inspired a change over generations in how some men recognize those who are not men. Still, to find a good answer, Freud had to abandon some of the things he thought he knew about women.

The experience of conscious doubt about our beliefs, those things we hold precious as true, comes with biological changes. Our brains contain both excitatory and inhibitory neurons. Inhibitory neurons provide stop signals so that neural networks don't all fire at once. Much of our nervous system is inhibitory, and by no means does this apply exclusively to women or to men.

Whenever we experience something that doesn't fit our arrangements of assumptions, routine actions become inhibited. We slow our movements and direct full attention to the thing that doesn't seem to fit with our anticipations and our environment. When we can't predict what's coming next, we pay attention and seek new information. This also often triggers an emotional response. We feel as though we are suddenly in a new place. If we feel we must act, we can draw from our emotional power and initiate action. We can also attempt to ignore things or force them to happen as we predict and wish.[20]

The same thing happens to prepare other responses in our body. Some might refer at this point to the older parts at the core of our brains governing our fundamental responses to environmental stimuli. We prepare ourselves for the "five big Fs"—fighting, fleeing, freezing, feeding, and… well, sex. There is something far more vast and complex and interconnected at work than the mere pointing to a word or a sign.

If something is so overwhelming, either fear or fascination can simply hold us in a grip of wonder or awe. Some might refer to this feeling as the experience of being in the presence of the Great Mother.

Christianity, in modern history, has regulated and systematically confined most authoritative elements of our psyche, within and without, to a place dominated by the Great Father. The only accepted female representation or archetypal symbol was Mary. Though appropriately titled in Christian traditions as the Mother of God, she is often stripped of any authoritative role in today's religious practices. Ask for her help, let her offer guidance and grace, but don't allow her to rule. Rachel Fulton Brown, author of *Mary and the Art of Prayer*, suggests the medieval church had a different relationship with Mary. Brown has studied the medieval church and found something so compelling she dedicated her career and identity to it. The *Vierge Ouvrante* (mentioned in the Introduction) portrays Mary's presence as greater than any other element of the icon. Mary played a central role in medieval Christian life, as can be seen by the time and devotion dedicated specifically to her in prayer.

> Almost every aspect of late medieval European Christian religious life was marked—and enhanced—by salutation of the Virgin. From the invitatory sung at Matins to the threefold Ave Marias recited with the Franciscans' encouragement at the ringing of the bells at the end of the day (the "Angelus"), from the multiple genuflections made before the images of Mary to the ubiquitous altarpieces and Books of Hours depicting the angel kneeling before the Virgin in imitation of her earthly devotees, from the Mary-psalters of the twelfth, thirteenth, and fourteenth centuries to the fully developed rosary of the fifteenth said while fingering one's beads, the mystery of the words spoken by the angel was invoked aurally, visually, corporeally, and haptically day after day.[21]

From this understanding of European Christian practice, Mary contained the day and provided a divine presence throughout the day. God, as creator, humbled himself before this woman to receive her blessing and ask her to carry a child. Mary may seem closer in association to *reality* than the god in that tradition or the child born to her. Medieval church practice could be understood as a collaboration between Mary and her son. But the Middle Ages can feel so distant now. Hundreds of years of novelty and technology and change have passed. The Protestant movement in Christianity, and some modern interpretations, turned Mary from a central icon into an incidental embarrassment.[22] In the secular West, it can be difficult for people to identify with such structured devotion, except perhaps on Mother's Day.

Wm. Paul Young surprised some religious people with his book, *The Shack*. He portrayed different aspects of the Christian God as an African woman, an Asian woman, and a Latino woman. This creative and multicultural portrayal of the Supreme Being, the Holy Ghost, and the biblical Lady Wisdom got attention because such ideas were novelties to some in mainstream Western religion. This was something almost unimaginable for many Christians. Although novelty can win attention, time will rule on the lasting effect of such thinking in the spiritual chambers of people's hearts. Young's imagination and narrative reflect a deep history and a place for the nourishing and devouring mother in our thinking. What was known can become unknown, but it can resurface once again in different language.

Pope John Paul I once said in a public address that God "is our Father; even more He is our Mother."[23] This may have been a simple appeal to focus on the tenderness of motherly love more than a suggestion to reform the patriarchal structure of the church. In a papal bull in 1854, Pope Pius IX declared Mary pure of original sin. From the very moment she was first in her mother's womb, Mary was pure. In 1950, Pope Pius XII presented the *Dogma of the Assumption*, describing how Mary was taken body and soul into heavenly glory.[24] When someone can decree what was going on in a womb, or in the heavens, millennia after such miraculous events, it reveals something about the nature of authority. Still, these moments of history can be read as signs of a new beginning, or possibly a retrieval, in the Christian divine family. The feminine and the divine can be associated with each other in the modern mind and in the West. Mary may not have been divine in the sense of a deity. She can be divine, however, in the sense of compelling our behaviour with some authority. Instead of sacrificing Mary like the daughters of Agamemnon or Jephthah, we can challenge ourselves to recognize the divine in people and places we otherwise give little authority, even if it takes hundreds or thousands of years to do so.

A Song of Faith from the United Church of Canada first describes God as a "Holy Mystery." This is a call to face the unknown, to trust what it can reveal rather than shrink from it or deny its power. It is a call to inquiry. And yet, bestowing authority on the unknown and accepting the unknown as dominant over what is known can be a dramatic act of faith. It means, like Freud's challenge, abandoning personal assumptions and entering the search for good questions.

Erich Neumann, like his predecessors Jung and Freud, understood that the unconscious has a powerful influence on our behaviour. Despite our efforts at being ruled by rational decision-making, we often give behavioural authority over to our emotions. Neumann's book *The Great Mother*, details positive and negative aspects of this archetype. His intention was not to answer Freud's question about women. Instead, he suggested this unknown and lost side of our identities could not only be recovered, but it would also lead to a healthier understanding of our being in the world. Neumann suggested that denying or repressing the role played by the unknown in our selves affected the psychic health of individuals and communities.

> The development of a psychic wholeness, in which the consciousness of every individual is creatively allied with the contents of the unconscious, is the depth psychologist's pedagogical ideal for the future. Only this wholeness of the individual can make possible a fertile and living community. Just as in a certain sense a sound body is the foundation for a sound spirit and psyche, so a sound individual is the basis for a sound community. It is this basic fact of human collective life, so often ignored, that gives psychological work with the individual its social significance and its significance for the therapy of human culture.[25]

One traditional way to develop consciousness of something is to meditate with an icon like the *Vierge Ouvrante*. That Mother figure—containing the uncontainable—preserves, prepares, and presents everything within. Today, the icon may seem traditional, mundane or even too Christian for some, but it also challenges a modern conception of religious thinking in the hierarchical ordering of figures. It can suggest how a family of motivations can be brought together to transcend ideas that are no longer effective.

The Divine Mother is primordial, before culture and language. She represents those things not yet wholly understood or fully mapped, the world not yet separated into distinct categories, the world beyond the walls. She is nature acting as one. She scuttles attempts at domination or encapsulation by language. She gives birth to and then takes back in death, figuratively and otherwise, everything. She is the vessel past what we think contains us. The author Lillian Smith provided a clear and pregnant insight into Freud's inquiry: "What Freud mistook for her lack of civilization is woman's lack of *loyalty* to civilization."[26] This lack of loyalty to civilization cannot be understood simply as resentment, though it could turn attitudes in that direction. When culture and order become corrupt, different loyalties prove valuable against the tests of entropy. A mother's loyalty might be to her children, and not to whatever civilization wants to do with her children. The Christian god of the European Middle Ages attempted to answer the challenge with humility, bowing before the mother of his child. According to Armstrong, that response might have been highly pragmatic at the time. Spiritually, that answer seemed to work.

The Great and Terrible Mother is mystery, beyond complete description, both threatening and inspiring, fertile and destructive. The Oroboros serpent, with wings and claws, eating its own tail, symbolically portrays these ideas as one. *A Song of Faith* does call upon her with its initial words, but without complete recognition of her other aspects, within and without. We can look on her as divine without having to appeal to the supernatural, theologically or metaphorically. We need not be biased in our thinking and presume she represents only positive or negative aspects of the realm of the unknown either. Instead, she is both *all at once*.

Other descriptions for her in story and myth include nature, the material world, unexplored territory, the wild, the deep, a darkened cave, a forest, the sea, the water, and the flood. She has been associated with the hearth and with the throne, or places of births and beginnings. She is not just settings or events, though: she can appear as the ocean monster, a matriarch, the fertile womb, and even the inevitable mystery of death. She manifests in new expressions as well, such as the appearance of silent evidence.

All these ideas are expressed in the symbol of the Great and Terrible Mother. The symbol is often portrayed as feminine due to its fertile and cyclical associations. Some of our first formative experiences tend to be anchored to moments with a motherly figure. Neumann outlined an entire wreath of illustrations connected to this archetype.

How would an audience today identify, or identify with, this archetype? Boehm warned us that our own contradictory natures predispose us to draw caricatures. If we identify with both the nice and nasty, we can see how we must work at managing both within ourselves to find how they work together. Two aspects of the Great Mother follow, in caricature, to help us see the hawks and doves within ourselves.

1. The destructive, devouring mother swallowing life, breeding despair and fear.
2. The creative, nourishing mother giving birth to abundance, possibility, and hope.

How does this play out in the stories we tell ourselves and one another? Tension and drama can take possession of an audience when a story moves from the routine of the known to the surprise of the unknown. When a character faces uncertainty, members of the audience can speculate on how they would act in the presence of the unknown. For millennia, people have treasured religious icons, finding motivation and identity in the figures. If we pay attention while watching a movie, for example, we can take part in a similar activity and change how we understand the story. We can imagine a different relationship with what we don't know.

The Great Mother invites us to inquiry. She presents us with questions, such as "Do I welcome new experiences, seeing hope and possibility within?" or "Do I fear the unknown and strange to the point that I shut down, become overly inhibited and refuse to act or listen?"

Father—Tyrannizing and Encouraging

In 1957, the pharmacologist Arvid Carlsson and his team isolated a neurotransmitter in the central nervous system. For a decade this discovery wasn't that interesting to the medical world. But years later, other researchers used Carlsson's discovery to create drugs for addressing Parkinson's disease, drug addiction, schizophrenia, and other medical diagnoses. In 2000, Carlsson and his team received a Nobel Prize for their discovery of dopamine. Dopamine turned out to be one of the most important physiological discoveries in the last one hundred years.[27]

Dopamine is linked to salience, the difference between what's important and unimportant. We recognize the value of something in an environment by mentally "seeing" it separated from everything else. Dopamine plays a big role in initiating movement. It is also closely linked to the anticipation of rewards. Dopamine helps us to fix attention on a cue from the environment. Then it helps us work toward coordinating things around us so that, through our responses, reality becomes what we want it to be.

Dopamine is not simple and straightforward. We cannot define it as mere motivation or anticipation in chemical form. As well, dopamine levels can decrease dramatically if the satisfaction from what is desired becomes routine. My discussion of dopamine here is intended to be more symbolic than scientific. I am pointing at something within us more complicated than a mere word. And yet, the use of that word can connect a modern consciousness to an older tradition. We don't simply say dopamine is in charge of our lives, for example. There is more to our relationship with dopamine than just naming it and granting it authority over us.

When the environment provides cues for potential stimulation, and when events appear to be heading toward what is anticipated, dopamine flows nicely. And as with creature comforts and some narcotics, what initiates that flow can be great for us or terrible. Sometimes both at the same time. The nature of experience makes us predisposed to prefer environments where we know what to expect, where we understand what people or things mean, and where we have some control. One of the most persuasive motivations in our lives is what we think we *know* – the comforting routine, the safe environment of our home, our seat in the car, the chair at our desk, all set just so.

This state of being appears at the beginning of most stories, too. The main character, a focused reflection of the reader, often begins at home or in something like a hometown. An audience can quickly identify with the character or with the home environment, even if fictional or unreal, because of the power of association.

The predictability or comfort that we feel when in this environment, or in the powerful arms of this symbolic presence, is a compelling psychological state of being. It allows us to trust routines and expect normal outcomes, whether good or bad. We can do the same things over and over again and expect the same results. How often, after all, do we do something because it is the way we have always done it?

But there is a precarious side to this motivation as well. Predictability can create complacency and boredom. If nothing changes, and there is no anticipation of things hoped for, then the flow of dopamine diminishes. The inability to see something as both potentially great and terrible at once can mean we understand only part of a story. Sometimes we don't want to transcend the roles we are playing, even if the environment has changed. Agamemnon and Jephthah saw their own motivations as singular, primary, and authoritative. If they had opened up to another side of themselves, they might not have destroyed their families.

The father figure in stories appears in many different costumes. One-eyed, one-sided characters often play the role of something associated with one main drive, one goal, or one way of doing things. The ruling tyrant can be an old man, a giant grinding bones, a benevolent patriarch, or an oppressive king. Institutions and environments can represent this figure through stories that feature a government, a walled city, a person's conscience, a known world of home, a familiar neighbourhood, a culture or, previously explored territory.[28]

The association with the masculine may be a part of our long history as mammals and social animals. But it is worth remembering that mothers and babies can be tyrants and fathers can be nurturing. Violence is not exclusively masculine. But many have found the association with the masculine sufficient to let their preconceptions rule them. Instead of seeing the archetype at work in story, they see a stereotype. In mythological terms, all these ideas are expressed in the symbol of the Great and Terrible Father. Two caricatures of this archetype involve:

1. The father who eats, destroys or oppresses: social order and institutional flourishing dominate over individual needs. Anticipations are given more authority than observations.

2. The father who encourages, strengthens, and coaches: social order and institutional establishments serve the flourishing of individuals. Observations are given authority and divinity in balance with anticipations.

How does this play out in the stories we tell ourselves and one another? A producer, writer, or artist may intend to express their own values, but decoding the symbol into one or the other, Great or Terrible, is just as much up to the observer. With many religious and secular stories, the tension between *Great and Terrible* creates drama while highlighting both aspects of this fatherly figure. Examples can be found in the stories involving Yahweh and Elohim. Both names have distinguished histories and distinct natures in the Bible; wrathful and fostering. In Greek mythology, father figures like Kronos eat their young. Zeus even attempted this but then stopped himself when he found his children might be useful. In Egyptian narrative, Osiris is both wise in his rule and blind to the plans of his brother Set. In today's stories, oppressive and one-sided governments appear in popular series like *Divergent* and *The Hunger Games*.

Doctors diagnosed Anthony Burgess with a brain tumour in 1960. The diagnosis compelled him to write. He hoped his novels would provide his wife with income if he were to die before her. In 1962, Burgess published *A Clockwork Orange*. The novel focused on an urban juvenile named Alex who lacked personal restraint. He stole. He harmed the weak and poor. He raped. When the legal system caught up with him, he went to a reform facility. While incarcerated, Alex read the Bible and envisioned himself as a soldier lashing Jesus.

Burgess grew up Roman Catholic. According to Catholic teachings, development of a person's conscience is of prime importance. The ideas of free will and original sin were deeply entrenched in Burgess's own identity. For Burgess, a system that sacrificed individual freedom for a perceived public good would crumble under political and proverbial feet of clay. The reform facility in *A Clockwork Orange* featured a program, sanctioned by the government, that used conditioning to modify delinquent behaviour. When presented with a stimulus, such as an opportunity for violence or rape, Alex became physically sick to the point of retching.[29]

The government attempted to solve the problems created by the juvenile's lack of inhibitions by removing freedom of choice and controlling physical behaviour. Alex became a "clockwork orange"; a predictable function-performing subject of control. When a group used the boy to make the government look bad, the government reprogrammed Alex back to his original state.

In the early to mid-twentieth century, academic attention in psychology turned to behaviourism. Through reward and punishment, stimulus and withdrawal, discrimination and definition, psychologists directed subjects to behave according to expected goals and objectives. Burgess's fictional story was, in many respects, a direct commentary on this area of psychology.

A Russian physiologist, Ivan Pavlov, became fascinated with animal reflexes. He decided to treat the mind as an impenetrable box that could not be opened. However, behaviour could be directly examined through stimulus and response. His most famous experiment involved dogs. He noticed that dogs would salivate in the presence of food. He called this an unconditional stimulus. Over a period of days, he added the sound of a buzzer before offering the dogs food. He called this the conditional stimulus. After a period of conditioning, he realized the goal of his experiments—the dogs would salivate to the sound of the bell, whether or not food was present. Pavlov's contribution to psychology is known as *classical conditioning*.

In 1908, John B. Watson gave a lecture titled "Psychology as the Behaviorist Views It," and later published it as a journal article. In plain terms, Watson explained that psychology should be the science of observable behaviour only. If it were up to Watson, there would be no looking within. Introspection was not an essential part or method in psychology. He believed all that was needed was control. If given control of someone's life when a baby, he could make the person into anything, from a doctor to a thief. He rejected the notion of individual differences and considered emotions to be just more examples of classical conditioning.[30]

In a way, Watson's bold statement was a direct criticism of several of his contemporaries who advocated for eugenics—the deliberate control of the genetic composition of human beings. When some academics and psychologists encouraged selective breeding programs for humans, Watson was basically proposing the opposite; programs with an emphasis on nurturing.

Watson conducted a study, now known as the "Little Albert" experiment. He and an assistant conditioned a small child to fear a white furry animal. Albert would play in a closed environment. A small creature was introduced to the environment, accompanied by a loud noise. Over time, the appearance of the animal provoked a fear response in the child. Watson went further and demonstrated this fear could be generalized. Other white furry objects provoked the fear response. Watson received criticism for the ethics involved in his experiment. It was said he never deconditioned the child to remove the response, but instead left the deconditioning to time and chance. Watson left his academic career in 1920 due to an affair and sensational divorce. He worked for a public relations and advertising agency until 1945.[31]

B. F. Skinner wondered if Watson's views had been too extreme. He worked on an idea called *operant conditioning*. Operant conditioning involves giving a reinforcement or punishment after a behaviour. He experimented with rats and pigeons, placing them in a controlled space with levers and lights. When the animals performed a behaviour such as pressing a lever, they would receive a food pellet or mild electric shock. This type of laboratory device became known as the Skinner Box. In educational practices, Skinner was careful to encourage praise and discourage all forms of punishment. Nothing was more effective, according to Skinner, than praise and reward.

A student of Skinner, Ogden Lindsley, cautioned that one must remember the box is not there to keep the subject in. It is there to keep the world out.[32] One does not use a Skinner Box to understand how a pigeon flies or how a rat makes a burrow in a natural environment. The assumptions of the box allow the experimenter to reach a goal. Lindsley coined the term "behavior therapy" in his research on operant conditioning and learning theory.

In the last chapter of Burgess's *A Clockwork Orange*, the boy's love of music inspired him to change his ways. Possibly, he grew tired of being placed in a box, or possibly a physiological change took place in his motivations. Some editions omitted this final chapter. Stanley Kubrick, director of the movie that added to the story's popularity, ignored the final chapter completely.

Anthony Burgess did not die from the brain tumour. Apparently, the most sophisticated of academic boxes and medical tests can miss something important. Sometimes mistakes are made reading data. Sometimes the silent evidence means more than what is observed. Sometimes in life the unanticipated is more important than the anticipated.

Burgess's wife had her own problems. She fell into a sea of alcoholism and died a few years after the novel received so much attention. Burgess began an affair with another woman during this time and married her after his wife's death. Apparently, religious people, like those in academics, face tests of discretion. How can we predict the consequences of something so compelling as our own wine-dark anticipations?

Newer trends competed with behaviourism for the attention of people in psychology. However, reward and punishment still affect how we act, direct our decision-making, and play roles that shape our identity, just as dopamine works its way within us. Like the masks of comedy and tragedy, reward and punishment act as gods upon the metaphorical clockwork machinery of our selves. The urge to transcend the protective but isolating walls of our expectations can be just as strong as the wish to remain caged. The dominating but encouraging boxes of our culture might very well be what makes us human, but the combination of our anticipations and our potential also makes us great and terrible.

Conscious recognition of the signs of the Good and Terrible Father can help an audience or an individual question the motivations of the characters in a story. But something much more useful can occur when readers ask how they come to worship expectation and their own surges of dopamine. "Am I protecting my creature comforts, or am I addressing a change in information?" "Do my own actions serve anticipated social order or do they serve the individual?" "Have I made something into a god that doesn't deserve to be so authoritative in my life?"

SON—INNOVATING AND RETREATING

Choh Hao Li dedicated his scientific career, about thirty-five years, to a gland the size of a pea. In 1956, he helped isolate what came to be known as human growth hormone. Deficiency in this growth hormone was linked to development problems in children. The hormone could be used as part of a treatment for stimulating the growth of physically underdeveloped children. A relatively small part of our being can affect the development of the entire body. Unfortunately, Li found that only so much growth hormone could be extracted from the pituitary gland.[33]

Li didn't stop studying the pituitary or the hormone. By 1971, he and his associates determined the complete structure of the complicated hormone and succeeded in synthesizing it. In 1985, the synthesized hormone became available for use, and thousands of underdeveloped children began treatment. Li died just a few years later. Though he likely understood the potential for the hormone in childhood development, he may not have known how it would affect athletic competition.[34]

Stories of Olympians and professional athletes using growth hormones started to emerge in the 1980s. Early testing procedures could not tell the difference between natural and synthesized growth hormone, creating concerns for how to regulate use of the substance in sporting events.

Years later, other research teams from around the world started to notice something strange about the brain. Brains seemed to have special receptors for opiates such as morphine. The strange part was that the opiates were products of flowers and not found in human biology or chemistry. In 1975, John Hughes and Hans Kosterlitz published a paper that described their discovery of a small amino acid molecule in the brain of a pig. This amino acid had similar properties to opiates from flowers. They proposed that this discovery could lead to a painkiller, like morphine, which might not have the addictive properties of the plant-based painkiller. They tried out their idea. The result was a painkiller so weak and ineffective it wasn't worth producing. However, the substance turned out to be extremely addictive.[35]

The series of discoveries led to understanding something new about the pituitary gland and hormones. The gland releases internal painkillers when the body experiences stress. Painkillers such as morphine occupy the receptors in the brain in place of what is released by the pituitary. The pituitary responds by producing less hormone. This series of events started the study of *endorphins*.

Physical activity decreases stress-related chemicals while increasing natural painkillers like endorphins. In a sense, cortisol, endorphins, and adrenaline take possession of you during exercise.

Cortisol prepares the body for exertion, generates new energy from reserves, and stimulates brain function. Physical exertion can also lead to the release of adrenalin and dopamine. Adrenalin, also known as epinephrine, increases the body's heart rate while opening blood vessels and air pathways. Muscles become primed for peak performance.

The more someone engages regularly in this kind of activity, the better the body responds to stimulation. With practice, the body can do more, do things with greater skill, and do things successfully, even under stress. In turn, this accumulates into personal confidence in one's body, one's abilities, and one's identity.

When you take action, or act toward accomplishing a goal, all these parts of you participate at some level. And at the heart of every heroic journey—symbolic, fictitious, or historical—is the resolution of some goal through a series of actions. The chosen one is the one chosen to do something. At first it may be uncomfortable to be chosen, but with experiences come qualifying skills and expertise and the ability to resolve problems. Effort results in ability, meaning, and identity.

Often the hero is portrayed as masculine. Christians have a focusing point in the figure of Jesus. Egyptians had Horus. The Greeks had several heroic sons overcoming challenges and rising to rule over fallen fathers. Norse cultures and now Marvel Comics tell stories about Thor and Loki. Heroes take many forms in our stories—Frodo, Sam, and Smeagol, or Luke, Leia, and Han, as examples. Each figure participates in the quest to recover lost light, restore a lost order, or establish new freedom through skill and innovative behaviour. In the case of tragedies, heroes often fail to complete the recovery for themselves and perhaps lose battles within as much as without. However, the hero can still be an example, or counter-example, for how an individual is to behave between the realms of the known and unknown.[36]

Masculinity is not a necessary characteristic, though often that seems to be sufficient to win an audience's attention. Characters like Dorothy in Oz show that a hero can be female and can display heroic traits. Violence is also not a necessary element of the hero identity. Instead, the heart of the identity is the call to finding a problem's resolution. Dorothy's most violent acts in *The Wonderful Wizard of Oz* were more accidental than masculine or feminine. Her house landed on someone, and she threw water in someone's face. In both cases, Dorothy's intentions were anything but forceful dominance or violence. She did have to address the consequences of her presence and her choices, though. In the story, she won friends, built teams, made moral choices, voluntarily took on a journey, and learned that she had the power within herself to return home. There is nothing exclusively feminine or masculine about winning friends, building teams, or making moral choices. This is the behaviour of a hero, and not of a specific gender.[37]

Symbolic associations with this archetype in narrative include the rising sun, a star, the eye, a path, or a road. Characters might take the form of the protagonist, a skilled apprentice, a trickster, a fool, a coward, hostile brothers, competing sisters, a team leader, a craftsperson, an inventor, or an explorer. Our heroes suffer from the risk of becoming caricatures too, but they help audiences identify with different aspects of this character:

1. The individual voluntarily accepts the presence of the unknown and steps into the realm of the unknown, seeing it as potential promise and potential threat. The hero sacrifices something of his motivations, safety, comfort or dopamine level for the world. The hero resolves conflict by establishing or recreating order.

2. The individual dismisses and runs from new information or the unknown, seeing them as threat. The hero sacrifices the world to his motivations, his safety, his comfort or dopamine flow. The hero refuses and destroys the world for her idea.

How does this play out in the stories we tell ourselves and one another? The audience often identifies with main characters. The story illustrates how to act in order to come to some resolution of the crisis. The audience is almost always invited to ask, "What would I do?"

The modern world may associate this kind of identity with the innovator—in particular, the inventor of new technology, harnessing raw forces and resources into some kind of tool that allows the user a greater potential in skill, work, play, or status. The assumption is that the character addresses the responsibility of good and evil, to use religious language, and the power to act out a hierarchy of motivations. By an act of choice, one want or god is more important, more meaningful, than another. Thomas Edison's light bulb is an artifact that declares light to be more meaningful than darkness, even to the point of overcoming the natural patterns of light and dark in a day or season. The inventor of the shovel made a choice—how the user arranges rock, dirt, seed, plant, and materials is more important than how Mother Nature arranged things or how past builders structured them. Alternatively, how the user arranges these things is at least important enough to interrupt (or possibly participate in) the workings of time and nature.

In 2004, Tom Harpur published *The Pagan Christ*. The Greek word "*christos*" means chosen one, like a hero or bringer of something new. Harpur's exploration of the roots of the *christos* idea challenged the assumptions around the special significance of the figure of Jesus in Christian traditions. The chemical makeup of the smallest glands in our bodies shows us that everything within and without can be much more complicated than one story from one book. Harpur's subtitle is *Recovering the Lost Light*. He doesn't believe the so-called pagan roots of the *christos* story should be viewed as threatening to anyone's beliefs. Instead, those roots re-establish a greater and more comprehensive tradition that will create a more vibrant community. Some people may hold specific descriptions of religious, historical, or mythical figures as unassailable, unchangeable, and authoritative. But the archetypal hero at the heart of this conversation always faces the negotiation between old and new information.

Jean Piaget's mother wanted to make sure he received a well-rounded Protestant education. She worked for the humane treatment of prisoners during wartime. Piaget's father, an influential academic and lecturer, wrote a book about their town's history. Piaget grew up with books, ideas, and communal lore. In his adolescence, he came across the works of a writer named Auguste Sabatier. Sabatier used some impressive titles for his works—*Outlines of a Philosophy of Religion Based on Psychology and History*, and *The Vitality of Christian Dogmas and Their Power of Evolution*. Henri Bergson influenced him as well, with book titles such as *Creative Evolution*. The idea that religious ideas could evolve fascinated Piaget. The problem of unifying science and religion chimed like a bell throughout his career as a psychologist.[38]

Before Piaget, children were often thought of as less developed adults. But Piaget's work demonstrated that the thought processes of young children were not simplified adult processes. Something else was going on in the child's brain. The behaviourists devised ways to condition animals, children, and even psychologically disturbed individuals toward desired patterns of action. Piaget studied how concepts like number, time, causality, and justice emerged in young minds. He referred to his work as *genetic epistemology*, which sounds more like philosophical pondering than psychological measurement. Genetics is the study of biological origins. Epistemology is the investigation of the differences between a justified belief and a mere opinion. Piaget wanted to understand the origins of thinking in order to find a bridge between the logical rationality of science and the compelling beliefs of religious faith.

Piaget was fascinated by how children play. His theories identified building blocks of thought that enabled a child to form mental representations of the world. According to Piaget, the building blocks generated repeatable sequences of actions. Those actions were interconnected and managed by some core meaning or goal. Over time, the building blocks connected, creating a complicated bank of stored behaviours. Some of these building blocks, for Piaget, came from biology. Children younger than two can play by themselves but don't readily play with others. To play with another person, the child must share a frame of reference.

An example of Piaget's work comes from a test he did with photographs. He sat a child on a chair in a room. The child looked at three papier-mâché models of mountains arranged on a table—left to right, two small ones and a larger one. Piaget then showed children a series of photographs of the mountains from different perspectives in the room. He asked children to pick out the photograph that showed what a child seated across the table would see. Anyone on the other side of the table would see a flipped order—left to right, the larger one and the two smaller ones. But

Piaget found that children under six consistently picked the photograph that matched what they saw: two small mountains and the larger one. It was as if they could not imagine any perspective other than their own. The children failed to understand the visual point of view of another person.

Piaget used the term *egocentrism* to describe this situation. It was a cognitive description, not a moral one. The children seemed to have a limitation and did not see things past their own perspective. Through stages of development, however, children expanded their consciousness to include the perspectives of others. Babies are egocentric to the point that they have difficulty distinguishing physical objects from their own actions toward those objects. Preschoolers can be egocentric in terms of language and space. School-aged children begin to think about their values and perspectives in a more abstract way. Adolescents and adults can shift from their own perspective to the perspectives of others. Despite this development, previous levels of egocentrism remain with the individual. In school, "graduation" can mean not going back as much as moving ahead. But our consciousness can backtrack and even change direction as much as a ship out at sea.

Over the course of his career, Piaget realized that each stage of development included beliefs or assumptions not consciously known at that stage. When those assumptions are consciously examined, individual development can lead to another stage, but that new stage comes with its own assumptions. A child would live in *equilibrium* with its surroundings when the mental building blocks satisfied any problems that arose. However, when presented with new information or a problem, the child would experience *disequilibrium*. The child's current building blocks would not be enough for the new situation. He or she would need some innovation or accommodation in order to build a new arrangement of building blocks to manage the situation.

For Piaget, the ages for each stage were descriptive and general rather than definite. Though his main interest was far from education policy, his thinking inspired a movement in education that came to be known as *discovery learning*. Classrooms with ordered rows and columns of desks turned into exploratory activity centres filled with opportunities for children to play. Some behaviourists took Piaget's stages of development as an easy challenge. For example, children given the three mountains task could be trained to pick the correct photograph. Some studies went even further. With the right sequence of step-by-step instruction, even primary grade children could perform secondary school math computations.

As his career progressed, Piaget doubted and tinkered with his first theories, working less with structural stages. He became more interested in the biological elements of development and how an individual gained new knowledge when faced with novelty; how assumptions developed and changed over time.

The re-evaluation of assumptions may be a root chord for the hero in a story. The sound calls the hero to consciousness. Jordan Peterson illustrated this relationship with reference to the Egyptian God of Horus, the son of mysterious mother Isis and the orderly father Osiris.

> The process of voluntary engagement in the "revaluation of good and evil," consequent to recognition of personal insufficiency and suffering, is equivalent to adoption of identification with Horus (who, as the process that renews, exists as something superordinate to "the morality of the past." This means that the

capacity to reassess morality means identification with the figure that "generates and renews the world"—with the figure that mediates between order and chaos. It is "within the domain of that figure" that room for all aspects of the personality actually exist—as the demands placed on the individual who wishes to identify with the saviour are so high, so to speak, that every aspect of personality must become manifested, "redeemed," and integrated into a functioning hierarchy. The revaluation of good and evil therefore allows for the creative integration of those aspects of personality—and their secondary representations in imagination and idea—previously suppressed and stunted by immature moral ideation, including that represented by group affiliation (posited as the highest level of ethical attainment). [39]

The shape of your journey in life depends greatly on the direction you choose. Do you turn to face new information with courage and renew your world and identity, or do you turn away from that which doesn't fit your thinking? Do you value predictability, pride and confidence over adaptation? Attitudes have consequences.

The act of turning away from something anomalous is the process of labeling that anomalous thing as "too terrifying to be encountered or considered," in its most fundamental form. To avoid something is also to define it—and, in a more general sense, to define oneself. To avoid is to say "that is too terrible," and that means "too terrible for me." The impossibility of a task is necessarily determined in relationship to the abilities of the one faced with it. The act of turning away therefore means willful opposition to the process of adaptation, since nothing new can happen when everything new is avoided or suppressed. The act of facing an anomaly, by contrast, is the process of labeling that event as tolerable—and, simultaneously, the definition of oneself as the agent able to so tolerate. Adoption of such a stance means the possibility of further growth, since it is in contact with anomaly that new information is generated. This "faith in oneself and the benevolence of the word" manifests itself as the courage to risk everything in the pursuit of meaning. If the nature of the goal is shifted from desire for predictability to development of personality capable of facing chaos voluntarily, then the unknown, which can never be permanently banished, will no longer be associated with fear, and safety, paradoxically, will be permanently established.[40]

Peterson's passage explains the dynamic involved between the two sides of the Divine Hero character. However, the modern world has revealed another kind of inventory of effects. In religious terms, for example, some cultures have placed the Hero or Villain characters into otherwise unassailable positions. They are not models we embody or characters we play in our actions. Instead, they have become the actors outside of us, waging a performance for us, as if to gain purchase on our souls as well as our viewership or our attention.

One of the main stories of the West portrays a saviour willingly sacrificing himself for others and for an ideal. This has been taken as the ultimate symbol of heroic life. That character faced the wrath of his Great and Terrible Father in order to redeem us, redeem the world, and redeem all things forever after. What part does this leave for the audience to play? Many Christian denominations in the last 200 years have redefined our part in the story in order to prioritize the "desire for predictability." The weight of meaning in the Christ figure's actions are so great, according to some modern tellings of the story, that it would be too terrible for any human to bear. We have written our own characters off the stage, in the sense of what roles we play. And the sacrifice may be the personal integrity of our very souls.

Likewise, evil is too terrifying to be encountered or considered. As a result, we expel it outward. For the sake of personal ego, Satan is a character on our shoulder or the terrorist on television, and not the shadow in our own hearts. We come to terms with evil, but those terms are projected out, not observed within. We are dangerous, motivated individuals and can create good and evil through the choices we make and the things we tolerate.

Strangely enough, though, as with the terrorist on television and the hate in our hearts, we have invited dangerous guests into our living rooms. We have invited them into our social circles with social media sites. We have put a thin and fragile screen of plastic and glass between us and them, thinking this is enough to establish the separation we want between good and evil. Politics, psychology, and science redefine, recontextualize or re-describe the problem in terms of economic policy, border security, personal motivations, and neurochemical biological systems. And yet the language adopted or rituals appropriated stem from an observer's choice—what saviour, ideology, medium, right, drug, or tool will *save me?*

Those outside agents have become the subjects of our lives, the authorities we watch. The person taking in the story becomes the object. The individual adopts the identity and integrity of that larger story or culture but without actually becoming the mediator between personal order and chaos. That is done for them by the figurehead, the hierarchy of authority, as presented to an audience. When "evil" is described not as bad judgment, sick motivations, or psychotic tendencies, but instead as an "I," then the individual faces the disequilibrium of identity.

Agamemnon's desire to conquer Troy was worth more to him than his own daughter. The unintended consequences of such a sacrifice did not outweigh his ambitions as he calculated the costs. His gods made him do it. With Jephthah, the unintended consequences of his words made him carry through with his promise to sacrifice his daughter. If these heroes had been able to identify the evil within themselves and their motivations, they might have had a moment of pause, a moment when the screen that had their attention wasn't an absolute authority. By figuratively putting ourselves into our own stories, taking our eyes away from the screen, we have a chance to recognize and name a new member of the archetypal family that makes up our identities. In that situation, even our own voices may surprise us and offer new information.

Daughter—Observed and Unrecognized

In the 1990s, a group of researchers at the University of Parma in Italy wanted to know more about hand-eye coordination. They set up an experiment where a macaque monkey could reach for a piece of food and eat it. The researchers then recorded responses from individual neurons in the monkey's brain to map what movements were linked to either the firing or inhibiting of those neurons. The researchers told a story about how one of them picked up and ate a piece of food while a monkey watched. A small group of the neurons they had already mapped to the monkey's own movements fired again as the monkey watched the human being. Watching the actions of some other being, and possibly identifying with that other being, provoked a neural response as though the monkey was doing the movements itself.[41]

The scientific community took little notice of the findings initially. The researchers continued their work and proposed these *mirror neurons* played a role in hand actions, mouth movements, and facial gestures. In 2002, another team suggested sound could also initiate responses from mirror neurons.

Mirror neurons received much more attention as the thirst for interesting and novel scientific stories grew online and in the media. Mirror neurons have been linked to empathy, self-awareness, and language. Some researchers have even claimed that mirror neurons made civilization possible. These claims open exciting directions for research but are not yet fully accepted. If anything, mirror neurons have presented to us another vast realm of the unknown, both within us and between people. Like a guest we have wanted to have over for dinner, the idea of mirror neurons seems quite charming and intriguing at first. But we don't really know where the conversation might lead after opening the door.

Mirror neurons could be a *consequence* of our development as much as its *cause*. The function of mirror neurons may not be about identifying or understanding the actions of others, but about using actions from others as information toward choosing how to act. They may be as understandable as body language.

Christopher Boehm studied chimpanzee body language. Chimps and other apes display what researchers call a "fear-grin" when one chimp feels dominated by another. Fear-grins can lead to "screeches" of submission if the dominance becomes intimidating or violent. The screeches and fear-grins subside when the dominant chimp calms down or moves away. The dominated chimp then might replace the noises with "waa-barks." This sound seems to communicate resentment. Other chimps in the group that witnessed the domination may mimic any or all the sounds, depending on their allegiances.

Boehm observed as two alpha males sorted out between them who would dominate and who would submit. The interaction involved the fear-grin, but one chimp covered his mouth to hide the facial expression. Boehm suggested that although the fear-grin may have been an automatic, unconscious gesture, the chimp had enough awareness to know what it might signal to a rival. By covering its mouth, the chimp tried to withhold information from the other and maintain a dominant outward appearance.[42]

Though the chimps may not have had the language for it, they were saying "Namaste" to each other. The gods within and without each of them recognized one another on some level. The presence of one potential leader changed the behaviour of the other potential leader. That recognition, however, wasn't enough to resolve the situation between them. One would eventually lead and the other would submit, all respect and body language aside. Human beings have had to sort out these dynamic forces too. Body language rarely consults with the conscious mind before saying "Namaste" quite openly to other people. We take cues from those around us and change our posture and behaviour according to the compelling presences of others on display.

The study of mirror neurons illustrates an amazing capacity that emerges with developed brains. We have an incredible ability to suspend disbelief and take up another's frame of reference. If something is perceived as a valuable goal—as, for example, eating the food someone else is eating—then the brain takes that as a valid frame of reference. That goal appears worth pursuing. Could we be social animals without this ability? It does not matter that a frame might be fictional. What matters is identifying the goal as worth pursuing, then embodying the actions that would realize that goal. In Peterson's words: "You are using your embodiment as a computational device that can run simulations of other consciousnesses. And it does that with the body."[43]

The next development is to organize and regulate which goals are worth pursuing and what identities are worth embodying, all while sharing an environment with others. The other does hold power over how we act and what we do. Recognition of the other as the hero of his or her own journey is a theme expressed in ideas such as the Golden Rule: do unto others as you would have them do unto you. The appearance of the other can also be understood as the appearance of novelty, part known and part unknown. The role of the *observed-other* in myth and narrative tends to take the form of a stranger, a foreigner, or a guest. That often turns them into an adversary because we don't fully know what motivations might make them act. However, the other can also appear as a friend, a potential lover, or a mixture of beings both great and terrible.[44]

A common theme in many religious and mythological stories, however, is the relationship between host and guest. In these stories, there is an etiquette between the characters, and often the story progresses through consequences of the right or wrong actions taken by either host or guest. The host has obligations and responsibilities in terms of behaviour toward the guest. But the guest has obligations and responsibilities toward the host. A story in Hindu mythology captures the divine power and relationship between host and guest.

> The serpent monster, Vritra, hoarded the waters of the world and caused a drought. Indra, decided to challenge Vritra. Indra had learned to use the thunderbolt. Vritra injured Indra, but Indra killed the serpent monster with a thunderbolt and released all the rivers of the world. Everyone celebrated and crowned Indra king.
>
> Indra called for the architect Vishwakarma to build a palace. Each time Vishwakarma finished the palace and presented his work to Indra, Indra's imagination grew, and he would ask Vishwakarma to add another wall, another

garden, another canal for the water. Vishwakarma agreed until he realized there may be no end to these monuments to Indra's pride. Vishwakarma went to Lord Brahma for help and prayed.

The next day a beautiful child appeared in the palace. Indra welcomed the boy as an honoured guest and then asked what had brought him to the palace.

The boy answered, "I heard you were building a palace greater than any Indra before you ever built. And I must say, this palace is by far more majestic than anything any Indra before you has ever built."

Puzzled, Indra asked, "Any Indra before me?"

"I have seen them come and go," said the boy. "The Creator Brahma opens his eyes and speaks, and a world comes into being. And in that world an Indra comes to rule that world. But when Brahma becomes silent and closes his eyes, the world goes out of being. After that, Brahma opens his eyes and speaks, and another world comes into being, to be ruled by Indra, only to become silent, closing his eyes again and that world goes out of being. There might be wise councillors in your palace who count the drops of water in your rivers, or the ants in your gardens, but no one will count the number of those Brahmas or those Indras."

Indra listened to the boy in silence. While the boy talked, great colonies of ants came in from the garden. The boy laughed out loud. Indra asked the boy why he laughed.

The boy pointed to the ants and said, "Former Indras all. Spiritually, they began from the driest worlds. They destroy one monster only to begin building palaces around the springs and rivers of their own illumination. But another thunderbolt comes, and it lowers them to the role of the ant once again."

Indra declared the building of the palace had come to an end. He went to his gardens to meditate before the lotus flower. Indra's wife, Shachi, went to the garden and found him but could not win his attention. He had become fixated on the lotus flower. Shachi, frustrated, searched for the priest and asked for help with her husband.

The priest went to the garden and sat with Indra. The priest said, "You are Indra. You are the master of the thunderbolt. You are the one injured by Vritra. You are the destroyer of Vritra. You are the champion of the Devas. You have been crowned king of the Devas and gods. You are the manifestation of the mystery of Brahma in the field of time. You have won many high privileges. You are also the husband of Shachi."

Indra stirred and looked at the priest.

The priest continued, "The highest honour you could give, to what you have been given, is to live as though you were what you really are."

Indra went to the throne room and embraced Shachi. For the rest of his days, he ruled with one eye on the eternal, and the other on present.[45]

Vritra, Vishwakarma, the beautiful strange boy, Shachi, and the priest all influence the behaviour of the main character, Indra. They are all deities in the world of the Devas. But one important difference persists in their intentions. Vritra and Indra fight as competitors for mastery over the world's waters. Vishwakarma, the beautiful strange boy, Shachi, and the priest never compete with Indra for the position of ruler in the story. Indra, as the main character, is the ruler and hero of his life, reviving the order of the rivers and pursuing his personal interests. But the nature of that personal interest is not wholly defined by his own ego. Vishwakarma, the beautiful strange boy, Shachi, and the priest all act as guests in conversation with the host Indra. They do not rule, though they are present in his kingdom.

A fourth archetype provides for us an abstraction of the other as divine in mythological or symbolic terms. As well, we can use this archetype to better understand what our literature tells us about the audiences of our heroes and villains. And it allows us to perceive another social dimension in the psychology of our own identities. Instead of framing relationships as a dialectic of hero and villain, champion and adversary, oppressor and oppressed, the relationship can also take the form of dialogue between adventurer and stranger, host and guest, even lover and beloved.

It is hard to tell a story about something other than its main character. And yet hints of her presence can be found in the historical and literary record. Agamemnon's daughter Iphigenia, though not central to the story of the Atreides line, symbolically captures an aspect of her role, illuminating Agamemnon's motivations and tragic fate. Jephthah's daughter, an unintended victim of a hero's will and word, again symbolically focuses attention on the dynamic consequences that come from domination, resentment, action, and submission. Unfortunately, neither of these characters is considered divine, as in supernatural beings in control of some aspect of nature or humanity. From the outcomes of their stories, their presence does not seem to compel the behaviour of their fathers, either. However, both do achieve a place of honour and remembrance. Both daughters achieve a kind of divinity in what they give us to contemplate. They both hold a mirror to show us something about the potential sacrifices we make to our ambitions. They represent what the hero could have identified himself with, and what consequences come from the actions or motivations of the hero and villain *within*. The daughters, however, clearly identified with their fathers; they follow in complete submission and trust.

The audiences of these stories are expected to learn some lesson about how to act. As they identify with Agamemnon and Jephthah, some of their own mirror neurons may fire if they put themselves in the stories. But do they make the connection of how their own actions may have unexpected consequences for others? Have they thought twice before they, figuratively, sacrifice their daughters to their ambitions?

The Divine Daughter, I believe, represents the *observed-other*, the reflective audience of our actions. She, along with us, bears the consequences of our actions. She submits, follows, and helps—or ignores, obstructs, and undermines. She is Great and Terrible, all at once, just as novelty can appear as whim and wisdom together.

She is difficult to recognize because it means seeing someone else as a person, a hero of her own journey. She is an end and not a tool or obstacle for our own motivations. When the hero Hercules faced the many-headed beast of the hydra, he found that many heads grew back each time he cut off one. Iolaus witnessed the great labour and predicted Hercules would be overwhelmed by the increasing number of heads the hydra grew. He entered the fight with a torch and cauterized each neck after Hercules had cut it. Together, the two defeated the hydra.

The recognition of the *observed-other* also means seeing the observed as a divine authority, potentially worthy of as much worship as any other personal motivation. In stories, she might be any of the following: the friend, a companion, a follower, the community, a familiar, a pet, a sidekick, a witness, the fan, the reason for doing something, the sacrifice, a child, the one that submits, the consequence, one that believes in the hero, an obstacle, the handy tool, or a moment of self-reflection.

In mythological and narrative terms, these ideas are expressed in the symbol of the Great and Terrible Observed. Aspects of this character include:

1. The other the hero observes and identifies as a person or manifestation of another story. The other a hero sees as an opportunity for growth and development.

2. The other the hero does not identify as a person but as object or property. The other the hero ignores, or evaluates as an obstacle to growth, development or benefit.

How does this play out in the stories we tell ourselves and one another? The audience consciously looking for the Divine Daughter in a story may be better prepared to answer the question we seem to be asking the world as an extended, economically driven, interdependent global family: "Who pays for the consequences of my motivations?" "Am I sacrificing myself to my motivations or someone else to my motivations?"

Pope Francis used family relations to describe our relationship to the earth in his encyclical *Laudato Si'* in 2015:

> Praise be to you, my Lord, through our Sister, Mother Earth, who sustains and governs us, and who produces various fruit with coloured flowers and herbs. This sister now cries out to us because of the harm we have inflicted on her by our irresponsible use and abuse of the goods with which God has endowed her.[46]

Perhaps this was a call to move away from dominion theology as well as dominion motivations in our relationships to the global environment. Pope Francis obviously admires his namesake of St. Francis, but still puts his Christian God as primary cause. According to his beliefs, human beings and our planet are generated from a similar parent-creator. If we think of ourselves as siblings with the physical world, or children of the physical world, then these relationships take the form of a family. A family looks after its members, sharing motivations and consequences. As we know from the stories of Agamemnon and Jephthah, ignoring the relationships between family members invites the harshest tests of entropy.

A young man enrolled in the University of Wisconsin in 1919. He wanted to study agriculture. In about five years he changed his course of study to religion and then history, enrolled in theological college, and then transferred to teachers' college. In 1931, eleven years after his first adventures in higher education, he completed his doctorate. Like so many other young people left to their own interests, Carl Rogers struggled in the search for a personal identity.

Rogers studied the competing modes of thought in psychology but eventually turned away from the controlled environments of behaviourism and education, away from Piaget and structured developmental tinkering, and settled his attention on what he called "non-directive therapy." This eventually came to be known as client-centred therapy. Whereas Freud and Jung focused on the fundamental differences between consciousness and the unconscious, tracing the inner drives of clients, Rogers believed that the primary motive driving behaviour in people was the actualization of the self.[47]

Figuratively speaking, Rogers put aside the laboratory and the classroom and focused on meeting with and listening to the other person in dialogue. The psychotherapist should start only with full acceptance of the person, according to Rogers. Instead of starting with a defined goal or predetermined objective, the therapy session begins as a conversation. In this way, the client, as a full person, is free to express positive and negative feelings without judgment. The client, in this sense, maintains the position of main character, the centre of the action and journey, throughout his or her story. The therapist joins the journey but does not unseat the client's place of initiative, voluntary action, and responsibility. Like the beautiful boy or the priest who talk to Indra, the therapist does not compete for the throne.

According to Rogers, people already have a concept of their ideal selves. That image of the self, however, may not match the perceptions we experience. By supporting the actualization of the ideal self through unconditional support and a good amount of listening, a client and therapist can construct a state of congruence between a person's self-image, self-esteem, and ideal self.

Rogers's person-centred method is the most widely used approach to personal therapy in the West. His work also had an enormous impact on conflict-resolution strategies used in business, industry, and politics. Rogers supported and adopted ideas about individual self-actualization from another psychologist, Abraham Maslow. Maslow was famous for his ideas on a hierarchy of goals, which wove together a perspective on individual motivations based on the individual's environment and needs. An individual worked through the progressive steps of meeting basic needs such as survival, food, and shelter. The person turned to love and belonging, respect and esteem, and later sought out self-actualization and personal fulfillment. Together, Maslow and Rogers helped shape what came to be known as humanist psychology. Like Neumann, Maslow and Rogers had a larger vision. Psychology could heal cultures as well as individuals. Maslow thought of his work as another side of Freud's work. Maslow wrote in *Towards a Psychology of Being*: "It is as if Freud supplied us the sick half of psychology and we must now fill it out with the healthy half."[48]

In comparison, we might say the last century demonstrated some of the darkest consequences of our sick half. To fill the next century with the healthy half, our change in mind might also require a change in character. But like the change between a villain and a hero, the change within might need a healthy family, or a supporting cast, raising the main character to such a moment of awareness and choice.

Carl Rogers stated a clear description of where authority should reside for the individual: "Neither the Bible nor the prophets—neither Freud nor research—neither the revelations of God nor man—can take precedence over my own direct experience."[49] This quotation from Rogers is in the context of therapy and personal development. However, it also demonstrates the change in the West in recognizing the authority in the individual, not the group and not a religious body. The motivations and experiences of the individual figuratively broke open the waters, won the throne, and built palaces on the proverbial ruins of the past. But the work of Rogers, Maslow, and other psychologists also points, like the story of Indra, to the responsibilities of the individual in relationship with the observed.

Empathy became a guiding, authoritative principle for the work of Rogers. Jeremy Rifkin outlined a brief history of the word "empathy" in his book, *The Empathic Civilization*:

> The term "empathy" is derived from the German word Einfühlung, coined by Robert Vischer in 1872 and used in German aesthetics. Einfühlung relates to how observers project their own sensibilities onto an object of adoration or contemplation and is a way of explaining how one comes to appreciate and enjoy the beauty of, for example, a work of art. The German philosopher and historian Wilhelm Dilthey borrowed the term from aesthetics and began to use it to describe the mental process by which one person enters into another's being and comes to know how they feel and think.
>
> In 1909, the American psychologist E. B. Titchener translated Einfühlung into a new word, "empathy." Titchener was primarily interested in the key concept of introspection, the process by which a person examines his or her own inner

feelings and drives, emotions, and thoughts to gain a sense of personal understanding about the formation of his or her identity and selfhood.

The "pathy" in empathy suggests that we enter into the emotional state of another's suffering and feel his or her pain as if it were our own.

Variations of empathy soon emerged, including "empathic" and "to empathize," as the term became part of the popular psychological culture emerging in cosmopolitan centers in Vienna, London, New York, and elsewhere.

Unlike sympathy, which is more passive, empathy conjures up active engagement—the willingness of an observer to become part of another's experience, to share the feeling of that experience.[50]

The concept or feeling of empathy was undoubtedly experienced before 1872, but that doesn't mean people possessed the language to express or name what they were feeling. They might have attempted to capture the experience in a story or association. They might have related it to something they were more familiar with, such as a passage from a holy book. The new word grew in value and authority as people played with it and fit it into their identities. A term from aesthetics and art influenced history and philosophy, then moved to psychology and science. Today, writers have inserted that same term and its associated history into the field of neuroscience—mirror neurons have also been called *empathy* neurons.

Perhaps the power of empathy, in terms of the Great and Terrible Observed, transcends the gap between the imaginative and the real. Rifkin used the phrase "dramaturgical consciousness" to describe what individuals experience in the contemporary world. We are acting things out dramatically, empathizing with the identities of others more than ever before. The fears of cultural appropriation come with the hope of cultural collaborations. Mass media technology and increased individual energy consumption have influenced how we define ourselves, especially in relation to the other and the observed. As Rifkin states:

> We extend empathy to large numbers of our fellow human beings previously considered to be less than human—including women, homosexuals, the disabled, people of color, and ethnic and religious minorities—and encoded our sensitivity in the form of social rights and policies, human rights laws, and now even statutes to protect animals. We are in the long end game of including "the other," "the alien," "the unrecognized." And even though the first light of this new biosphere consciousness is only barely becoming visible—traditional xenophobic biases and prejudices continue to be the norm—the simple fact that our empathic extension is now exploring previously unexplorable domains is a triumph of the human evolutionary journey.
>
> Yet the early light of global empathic consciousness is dimmed by the growing recognition that it may come too late to address the specter of climate change and the possible extinction of the human species—a demise brought on by

the evolution of ever more complex energy-consuming economic and social arrangements that allow us to deepen our sense of selfhood, bring more diverse people together, extend our empathic embrace, and expand human consciousness.

We are in a race to biosphere consciousness in a world facing the threat of extinction. Understanding the contradiction that lies at the heart of the human saga is critical if our species is to renegotiate a sustainable relationship to the planet in time to step back from the abyss.[51]

Rifkin explains that dramaturgical consciousness flows from role-playing and experimentation. A dramaturgical perspective on human behaviour sees the "self" as no longer a private possession of an individual, but instead an identity given to an individual by the very people with which the individual wishes to share it. The self is not a thing like a material object. It is a fictional, abstracted, constructed quality validated and made real by the person and the group. According to Rifkin, we face a paradox. The tools that help us expand and ultimately play out our identities threaten social stability and put pressure on the environment. Technology extends our motivations but also rearranges the foundations that made them possible. What if it's not a game, but something much more serious? What if it turns out that everything in our environment is at stake?

A Divine Debut

Homer's *The Odyssey* is about the hero Odysseus. However, it does not start with Odysseus. Instead it starts on Mount Olympus. The gods talk about mankind and wonder why people blame them for everything, as though gods are the source of all troubles. We can look on this literary scene with new eyes if we read it from the frame suggested earlier—that a god is closer to the question, "What motivates your behaviour?" Even our own motivations shake their anthropomorphized heads in confusion at our behaviour. Why do we blame our motivations and beliefs as though they are not our own responsibility?

Zeus, the lord of Olympus, shares a similar name ending with the main character, Odysseus. However, it is Athena, child of Zeus, who sprung fully armed from Zeus's head upon her birth, that moves the conversation of the gods to the fate-stricken hero. Calypso, a daughter of the Titan Atlas, holds Odysseus captive and wishes to keep the poor Greek warrior for herself. Despite his waiting kingdom, his waiting wife and his son, Calypso wants to possess the hero and refuses to let him return home.

Why is Athena, the supposed Goddess of War, the cold, focused calculator of tactics, acting as an advocate of Odysseus? Why does she care about the fate of some mortal, quick-witted Greek warrior stranded and so far from his home?

The title Goddess of War may be a sign of the limitations of the ancient Greek vocabulary as much as a signal of what can be lost in translation. She is a formidable fighter, for sure, but she picks fights where she either feels she has an advantage or when someone has earned her allegiance or loyalty. The story is not about Athena. And yet without her, the hero would not find the heart to take up his next journey, to muster every bit of personal courage, and to apply every morsel of wit needed to make it back home. Odysseus's son, Telemachus, would never rise to his own adventure unless Athena prompted him as well. The story is in part about how she guides Odysseus and his son to take up the roles and responsibilities that come with being a hero. She whispers holy counsel so that they each can navigate the motivations and traps set for them by their opponents. Sometimes they fight; sometimes they withdraw and take a more subtle path to their goals. Finally, once Odysseus seizes control of his home and re-establishes his power, Athena's mind does not linger on further aggressions and acts of war. The final scene in Homer's epic puts Odysseus and Telemachus against their fellow Ithacans, all motivated by blood vengeance and family feuds. But Athena does not rejoice in this moment of war. She calls out to them to stop the bloodshed. Her cry is so piercing and precise that it strikes terror in everyone present.

> "Ithacans, stop this disastrous fight and separate at once before more blood is shed!"
>
> Athena's cry struck pain into the Ithacans, who let their weapons go in their terror at the goddess' voice. The arms all fell to earth, and the men turned city-wards, intent on their own salvation. The indomitable Odysseus raised a terrible war-cry, gathered himself together and pounced on them like a swooping eagle. But at this moment Zeus let fly a flaming bolt, which fell in front of the bright-eyed Daughter of that formidable Sire. Athena called out at once to Odysseus by his royal titles, commanding him to hold his hand and bring this civil strife to a finish, for fear of offending the ever-watchful Zeus.
>
> Odysseus obeyed her, with a happy heart. And presently Pallas Athena, Daughter of aegis-wearing Zeus, [still using Mentor's form and voice for her disguise,] established peace between the two contending forces.[52]

Today, we might think better of Athena as the Goddess of Strategic Thinking, or the Goddess of Strategic Representation of the Observed, or the Goddess of Cool-Headed Persistence in Pursuit of a Goal. To play with the mix of meanings even further, Athena might today be the Goddess of Just Advocacy.

In his book *Thinking Fast and Slow*, Daniel Kahneman describes two "fictitious characters" in order to explain his work in psychology. One is quick to judge, impulsive and emotional, triggering the compulsion to act. The other is more deliberate—calculating, cataloguing, evaluating—often looking for a rationalization of the wants of the first one. The two are operating processes in the brain. Kahneman refers to them as "System 1" and "System 2," although he stresses that the labels are far simpler than what's really going on in our heads. It isn't just a matter of parts of the brain lighting up or cooling off when one system goes online or offline.[53]

Similarly, we can think of Athena as the goddess of "System 2," an archetypal messenger with authority in certain situations. We should not be afraid to trust her voice in the times we need her.

Athena is an ideal exemplar of the Divine Daughter archetype, the one who participates in the hero's actions without overshadowing the main character. Her motivation is always a shared one, because she assists characters like Odysseus in realizing their goals and even stops him when he oversteps his position or jeopardizes his own fragile victories. Clear-eyed Athena often seems to find an ideal relationship with the observed.

As mentioned, archetypes can come in both great and terrible forms together. Where Athena is the ultimate advocate for Odysseus, Calypso illustrates the Divine Daughter's shadow side. Calypso imprisoned Odysseus with a stagnant existence. Imagine the lingering, self-critical voice—repeating hesitations, rehearsing doubts, mistrusting all feedback, well-intended or not. Calypso was enamoured with Odysseus and had the power to hold him. Odysseus wept over being held captive for so long, but it was not enough to change Calypso's mind.

The Odyssey is a source of incredible insight into our ancient past and into our present motivations, but it is not considered the word of a god for all time in the public consciousness of the West. It's just old literature. And for some people, it is somebody else's problem. Authority in the modern West seems to focus instead on the relationship between the Divine Son and the Divine Father. The trajectory of the West has trained our sights on ever-tightening goals and narrower points of view.[54] The benefits of that focus have come at the cost of strained relationships between other motivations. Those other benefits and relationships can have just as much relevance and authority to our well-being, if we have the ears to listen to wise words.

Figuratively, the relationship between daughter Athena and father Zeus reveals a peculiar tension and platonic intimacy. Between a community and an established cultural order describing it, there is often a family-like balance between practicality and authority. Zeus and his own father, according to myth, practised that strange, family-destroying ritual of eating offspring. Once established in power, the last thing a god seems to want is to hand over power, even to his own offspring. Where do gods get these fragile egos, anyway? Athena, however, appeared with a theatrical opening number to rival the virgin births of any divine sons. She sprang from her father's head, fully encased in armour. Zeus was so impressed he felt he simply had to get to know her. Maybe she would prove useful.

But this is mythology. The story expresses something in narrative and drama rather than rational, empirical definition. We may not yet fully understand these relationships at the rational level of resolution, but they can captivate our collective imaginations still. Athena and Zeus appear in today's movies and stories. The daughter-father bond is representative of a bond that would benefit the West today as well, when we foster our respect for the authority of Athena in our lives and in our decision-making. Eric Neumann suggested that his study of the Divine Mother was a useful cultural therapy, a way to heal the fragile world of his day. Raising Athena once again out of her father's head could do the same for today's fragile global village.

Athena never fully rivals Zeus for dominance in the Greek pantheon. She never manipulates things so that she can seize the throne of Olympus. She expresses a deep loyalty and commitment to Zeus that we don't always see between rebel sons and tyrant fathers. She seems almost wholly uninterested in her mother, Metis, and her stepmother, Hera. This may be a telling shortcoming of the character reflected in the world today as well. But what is Athena's fixation? Her love for her father is consistent but not unlimited or pathological. According to Homer and others, she occupies much of her time defending, counselling, steering, and inspiring her chosen heroes, to a point of almost dangerous rationality. But her motivation is always directed to the observed-other. She works toward achieving some sort of peace or harmonized realization between steadfast father and wayward, returning hero. Her sober second thought is, in part, an angel of our better nature.

Athena appeared in the works of Riane Eisler to illustrate a change in the ancient Greek culture. In *The Chalice and the Blade*, Eisler outlined a different story of our cultural origins. Eisler's main interest was in what she believed to be a long period of peace, prosperity, and technological growth. For thousands of years, human beings were not structuring societies based purely on male authority and hierarchical order. She used two terms to differentiate societies at the time: a *dominator model*, based on ranking individuals successively or vertically, and a *partnership model*, linking individuals in a more horizontal set of connections or networks.[55] Much of her theme relied on the work of the archaeologist Marija Gimbutas. Gimbutas experienced a turn in her own authority in the study of archaeology—many of her ideas were first accepted by peers but later rejected.

Eisler's work seems to share some ideas with Boehm's studies on the origin of human societies and morality. Boehm refers to hierarchical societies, where alphas compete for leadership to win political control over a group, and reverse hierarchies, where political power resides more in the consolidation of opinions from members of the group.[56] Again, there is a tension between our motivations. We can be ruled by our desire to dominate, to control, to get our way, but with that comes resentment—the desire to not be dominated or controlled.

Charlene Spretnak wrote an article for the *Journal of Archaeomythology* examining the strained legacy of Marija Gimbutas. In "Anatomy of a Backlash," Spretnak recounts instances where fellow academics and archaeologists challenged and buried the work of Gimbutas, only to announce their own breakthrough discoveries later, which happened to mirror conclusions from Gimbutas herself. What are we to think of someone who would denounce a competitor, only to copy conclusions later?

Still, some of the archaeological evidence from Gimbutas that Eisler uses in her book has been reinterpreted. Camille Paglia critiqued Eisler's work as "partisan sentimentalism,"[57] which could perhaps be used as a term of caution to both Eisler's detractors and supporters. These kinds of challenges and rebuttals happen in the academic world. According to Spretnak, Gimbutas rejected any label of matriarchy for the ancient cultures she studied.[58] However, my own interest isn't to defend either side's sentiments on the issue. I found Spretnak's conclusion could be taken as cool-headed advice for anyone feeling the possessive grip of partisan sentimentalism:

> Everyone who has spent any time in academia easily recognizes the difference between articles that aim to annihilate someone's status and work as opposed to articles that acknowledge what seems right and valuable in someone's work and then argue for a different, or enlarged, perspective or conclusion. The steady drumbeat of *Gimbutas must be dismissed* has now influenced an entire generation of young professors.

The more various streams of multidisciplinary knowledge enrich the perspectives within archaeology—especially knowledge of relevant ethnographic studies in anthropology and indigenous religion—the more the dismissive articles from the 1990s attacking Gimbutas' plausibility are shown to be largely underinformed or ideological and baldly competitive.

It should be noted that some archaeology professors have stood up to the backlash forces, have refused to "dismiss" Gimbutas in any way, and actually practice the virtue of multivocality, which is much touted by but oddly elusive for many [archaeologists]. [One archaeologist], for instance, taught a course on "Archaeology of Prehistory: In Search of the Goddess" at Stanford University in 2006 in which he provided a detailed, in-depth, and appreciative view of Gimbutas' work and then did the same for [others in the field]. Perhaps he is a portent of a post-backlash rebalancing.[59]

Our worship and our demonizing both have consequences; both bring intended and unintended outcomes. The stakes are high enough to suggest we could encourage hesitation and delay judgment on the observed, especially in the process of empirical inquiry. Jephthah and Agamemnon walk with us at our sides, but so do their broken families and their stories. Agamemnon's wife and Jephthah's child played their own parts in bringing down those noble families.

With this caution in mind, it is worth exploring how Eisler takes the time to discuss the mythological character of Athena. She used this figure from literature to illustrate her academic point. She used what might be called a fiction to explain something that is difficult to fully articulate or understand. According to Eisler, the way Athena was portrayed in ancient Greek literature reflects the transformation in Greek culture at the time.[60] Athena, a goddess of wisdom, wore the helmet as well as carried the spear and shield of martial dominance to show her authority. How else would she get unruly, stubborn competitors to listen to her? She had a part to play. In the ending of *The Odyssey*, for example, Athena's voice alone did not stop Odysseus. It is the combination of a dramatic flaming bolt and her strong voice that inspired the needed change of mind—sight *and* sound.

Eisler also pointed to *The Oresteia*, a Greek drama by Aeschylus. Orestes was the son of Agamemnon. Agamemnon's wife, Clytemnestra, killed the returning king in part because of his sacrifice of Iphigenia. Orestes, prompted by his other sister, Electra, killed his own mother and her lover in revenge for what they did to his father. The family may have a lot of initiative, but it is not a model of healthy relationships.

Athena held court with twelve jurors to decide the fate of Orestes. Should he be acquitted for the murder of his mother, or charged and brought to justice? The jury was deadlocked, so Athena cast the deciding vote. Athena decided in favour of acquitting Orestes. The rationalization was not based on mercy. Nor does it come from hope for the rehabilitation of this dysfunctional family. The explanation may sound not of this world to modern ears. Instead, Athena used herself as an example. She was born of no mother; only from Zeus. In her view, mothers were only nurses to their children. Orestes's loyalty in terms of lineage was to his father, not his mother.

Today, this may not seem like justice. It may not have been justice in ancient Greece, either. However, according to Eisler, Aeschylus may have been saying something, through fiction, about Greece at the time. His intention was not to recreate a true-to-life legal drama, but perhaps instead a symbolic drama of the tensions between the different authorities that rule us. The dominator model was winning out, or had won out, over the partnership model, to use Eisler's terms. The Athena character negotiated, narrated, or rationalized the change.

The partnership between mother and father in the social world crumbled just like the marriage between Clytemnestra and Agamemnon. In literature, the symbolic moment of the fall came when Agamemnon sacrificed his daughter. Athena did not intervene at that moment. Perhaps she did not have Agamemnon's ear. But then again, no one around Agamemnon intervened in that moment, either. His officers and soldiers simply kept to the hierarchical structure of command. Iphigenia raised no suspicion about her father's intentions. No dramatic flaming bolt or voice of reason made Agamemnon reconsider. Not even the goddess Artemis stayed Agamemnon's hand.

Maybe Agamemnon wanted Troy so badly, no System 2 (to use Kahneman's fictitious character) or sober second thought or guardian angel would have changed his mind. Maybe the character of Agamemnon gave little authority to Athena, symbolically, religiously, or otherwise. In Homer's *Iliad*, Athena's attention rarely followed the leader of the Achaean army. Instead, she spent much of her efforts guiding characters like Achilles. She even stayed Achilles's sword before he drew it against Agamemnon. Discretion with valour is the more heroic combination, our clichés and meeker archetypes advise us.

It may have taken generations—hundreds, thousands of years—for these kinds of cultural changes to take place. But when the cultural audience assented to the dominator model, it rationalized the cultural shift through the stories it identified with. If these models are, like archetypes, made of both light and shadow, then we might have to ask what was it that worked in the ordered, structured fostering of the dominator model. As students of both fiction and history, we have the chance to examine our own partisan sentimentalism when we chase after better articulations of justice. How do we evaluate what compels us today? How do we determine if our gods are actually worthy of worship? Have we, and our gods, changed in ways we do not yet comprehend?

Eisler quoted a line from the chorus in the play of *The Oresteia*. The Furies cried out:

> Gods of the younger generation,
> you have ridden down the laws of the elder time,
> torn them out of our hands.[61]

Things fall apart, and younger gods take over. Like the Furies, figures of authority don't like being stripped of power and then replaced with younger generations. Jealous gods are protective of their power. And now jealous gods challenge us with the test of entropy. What do we now find sufficient to win our praise and worship—novelty or wisdom?

Athena's judgment, consistent for her character in the sense that she is loyal to the hero, may have also been a symbolic gesture of releasing the audience from the responsibility of divine power. For the centuries after the Greek drama, divine sons and heroes would dominate the West's attention. Athena, as the deity of the city of Athens and not Jerusalem, turned quiet after her court ruling, as though figuratively sitting still between Apollo and Dionysus. With very little social authority in the present age, perhaps wisdom had to make way for the volatile up-and-down progression of the West.

In *The Great Code*, Northrop Frye noted Athena's role in *The Oresteia* as well. The Greek sense of a social contract, according to Frye, involved nature, the gods, and community, as much as the individual. This can be seen in the trial of Orestes, where the Furies of nature attend to the judgment with the Olympians and human characters. Frye pointed out a significant difference in the Greek sense of the social contract and the Biblical contract. In that other tradition of the West, the contract was between a monotheistic god and his people. Frye explained the difference in the contract: "If the people are as loyal to it as God is, the nature around them will be transformed into a quite different world."[62] Supposedly, justice and equity extended over both the moral order of things and the natural order of things.

Frye also suggested that *The Oresteia* can be understood as a near-clash between siblings—Apollo, standing as counsel for Orestes in the trial, and Athena, the one mediating and judging at the trial.[63] The social contract, in whatever form, may still depend on something more foundational, such as a family contract.

In Judaeo-Christian terms, the singular god is considered a Supreme Being. Earlier, I wondered if the modern problem has to do with finding a Supreme Way of Being. In the West, a god is often portrayed as personal, a person-like individual—an anthropomorphic super-being. Perhaps, for our creators and our ideals, the better metaphor for a Supreme Way of Being is *familial* instead of personal. Where the individual lives through the struggles of *being*, the family, before the religion or state, can help us with the *way*.

Leo Tolstoy started *Anna Karenina* with the sentence: "All happy families are alike; each unhappy family is unhappy in its own way."[64]

We might think Tolstoy is saying each healthy family is converging on something that is at least better than the unhappy, dysfunctional families. A family faces and manages the fears and motivations of each member—father, mother, son, and daughter—leading either toward health and empathy or toward disease and entropy. By playing with Tolstoy's insight, a comparable understanding comes to mind:

> All healthy families have found a supreme way of being in managing empathy and entropy; each unhealthy family is unhealthy in managing empathy and entropy in its own way.

The gods take comfort on distant Mount Olympus and shake their heads at us when we blame them for our own motivations. But, in moments of conscious calculation and decision, Athena may still come down to speak with us. It takes more calories to use what Kahneman calls System

2. It can take more effort to think our way out of complex problems. But, compared to the violent, jealous, and angry Furies invoked from our past natures, it is sometimes the better course of action. Athena inspires us to take measured action, but she also understands the responsibility that comes when we play out our roles in the drama. She may also hold ultimate judgment over what comes from those actions. Walking with Dionysus and Apollo, Athena provides a balanced and steady voice between impulse and hesitation.

Jyoti—Allatonce in the Family

Marshall McLuhan described the contemporary world of electrically driven innovation and communication as "a brand-new world of allatonceness"—a place of simultaneous happening. He warned us that the ways we apprehend the world—pure and serial and radically summarized—were too simple and slow to be effective in the world of electric communication.

> Unhappily, we confront this new situation with an enormous backlog of outdated mental and psychological responses. We have been left d-a-n-g-l-i-n-g. Our most impressive words and thoughts betray us—they refer us only to the past, not to the present.
>
> Electric circuitry profoundly involves men with one another. Information pours upon us, instantaneously and continuously. As soon as information is acquired, it is very rapidly replaced by still newer information. Our electrically-configured world has forced us to move from the habit of data classification to the mode of pattern recognition. We can no longer build serially, block-by-block, step-by-step, because instant communication insures that all factors of the environment and of experience co-exist in a state of active interplay.[65]

Allatonceness, like the great Oroboros, threatens the stability of orderliness and evokes immediate emotional responses in many people. But that very response is a kind of proof that there is a plurality out there, contending for our attention and our worship. For much of the history of the West, plurality has been understood as hierarchical—*Father, Son, and Holy Ghost*. Allatonceness is such a foreign idea to our thinking, McLuhan played with the spacing of the words to attempt seeing past the limits of the language.

How would authority *work*, to use Armstrong's word again, in a healthy family contract? The dynamic experience of raising a family gives us a clear illustration of how a plurality of intentions can contend with one another on a daily basis. It provides us with one of the best examples of how we manage life by shifting authority from one character to another, one motivation to another. A healthy family is not a dialectic of war and oppression. Neither is a healthy family static and unchanging. A daughter can grow up, transcending that role to become a parent and mother, growing in her understanding of her story and identity.

What rules a family? The ambitions of one parent? Not consistently. What must be obeyed? On occasion, perhaps, a child screaming in the night. What do we hope is the motivation of each member of a family? The hope, in terms of health, would be something like the love for one another. Authority is shared, voluntarily handed-over in appropriate times, and followed—sometimes grudgingly, sometimes with pride, sometimes unconsciously—toward a familiar ideal. A family finds a better way when each member in some manner serves each other. Little in our cultural inheritance, in the West at least, bestows this level of recognition or authority on the other. And yet right in the dynamics of the family the *observed-other* compels us, as much as each member of a family shares a place, a voice, a role, and a moment of ultimate importance. The problem might be in the level that we are conscious of these compulsions.

In Munirka, in December 2012, the world witnessed the sacrifice of another daughter, Jyoti, a present-day Iphigenia. Five days after the brutal assault and rape, public protests began outside India's parliamentary buildings and the official residence of the president. Demonstrations in Bangalore. Silent marches in Kolkata. Social media users adopted a black dot as a symbol to identify with Jyoti and the protesters. The government acted like an archetypal father. Police and military were used to maintain control and manage the protests. India's "Rapid Action Force" used tear gas and water cannon during some demonstrations. Metro rail stations were closed strategically to hamper the surge of protesters in certain areas. Statements were made by government representatives expressing empathy with shared values. One official said, "As a father of three daughters I feel as strongly about the incident as each one of you." But other statements betrayed apathy and a focus on other values. Another official remarked, "One small incident of rape in Delhi advertised world-over is enough to cost us billions of dollars in terms of lower tourism." Order first. Change later, and only if necessary, only if the control of order is duly threatened.[66]

It took only five days for people to become apostles of Jyoti and act as advocates for both social and political change. Judicial processing and changes to social norms often need much more time. In one interview, Jyoti's mother despaired over the sluggish progress: "My daughter asks me what I have done to get her justice. She asks what am I doing so that many more like her get justice and I wake up to realize how helpless and trivial I am."[67]

This poetic, tragic comment reveals the powerful presence that loved ones can have on us whether they are present and alive or not. Michael Dowd makes a creative distinction between the "night" language of metaphorical expression and the "day" language of what some might call more objective explanation.[68] Does the "real" Jyoti speak to her mother, or is it just an emotional presence in her mother's psyche? Regardless of any explanation an observer might cling to, what is important is that Jyoti's mother feels a compulsion to act. Her daughter, Jyoti, alive or dead, a physical being or remembered presence—the story of Jyoti in the most real sense—still has implications for her mother's being and her mother's actions.

But her frustration resembles the feelings of Clytemnestra, having lost faith in the established order. The rules of human society delivered no justice for Iphigenia. India, collectively, metaphorically, sacrificed and consumed a mother's daughter, and must stand to account for it, according to that mother. More objectively, the men who raped and killed her daughter were arrested, brought to court, and sentenced. They can no longer commit such acts. Others, however, may continue to act in such a way unless stories like Jyoti's have some bearing, some authority over their identities and actions.

BBC's *Storyville* aired a documentary titled *India's Daughter*. Despite the slow pace of social and judicial reform, the director, Leslee Udwin, said India led the world by example, by taking up the conversation of women's rights and by protesting for change.[69] In this comment, she identified the country of India as the people of India—not the ruling government or the established order. In Dowd's "night" language, the daughters of a society express or describe as much of the identity of the society as a ruling father might.

Jyoti's father commented on the BBC documentary, saying the story held a mirror up to society, showing that his daughter's struggle continues.

> "Our daughter has shown society its true face. She has changed the lives of many young girls. She remains an inspiration even after her death. She fought back those devils. We are proud of our daughter."[70]

Jephthah's daughter willingly accepted her fate. Iphigenia didn't really fight back against the devil that possessed her father. Jyoti's father offers a very different message for young girls. Agamemnon won Troy through war and destroyed his family. Jephthah became a broken man after the sacrifice of his daughter. Will the young girls of the world follow Jyoti, who fought against those who would sacrifice her to their desires and wants? Or will they find more competent fathers who prize something more?

This grieving father also said, "Every girl on the street is like a daughter" to him and his wife. In a sense, he has taken responsibility for every woman, thereby embodying or at least expressing the sentiments of a positive, great and noble father archetype. To put it another way, unlike Agamemnon, he would not sacrifice anyone's daughter in order to accomplish his ambitions or wants.

How would Athena weigh in on the trials this family went through? Reality and imagination both speak about how we regulate our motivations. For Orestes, Agamemnon's child, Athena was the deciding vote breaking the impasse of the jury. How would that armoured daughter rationalize the events and motivations involved in Jyoti's case and find a just solution for India's future daughters?

What happens to our mirror neurons, to our inhibitory or excitatory neurons, to our levels of dopamine and adrenalin, when we take in Jyoti's story? If we identify with the people involved, with the suffering of this young woman, it can inspire us to some level of response, large or small—to cry, to share, to donate, to change how we treat others, to travel to some part of the world and participate in change. However, the story itself may not move some people to do anything, for a variety of reasons. It could come from a certain inclination of personality or a political loyalty. It could come from distrust in the media reporting the story. There could be limits to a person's empathy, and good reasons for those limits.

We tend to identify with our families and the people geographically close to us more than with those outside our kin and close relations. Concepts like race, religion, and nationality helped us expand group and personal identities. But even those concepts have begun to shear from the squeeze of global familiarity and psychic boundary lines. As Jeremy Rifkin pointed out in *The Empathic Civilization*, "We are within reach of thinking of the human race as an extended family—for the very first time in history."[71] This could have beneficial but also dangerous consequences. As much as globalization, tribalization carries with it benefits and dangers today.

Sacajewa and Pocahontas are two well-known daughters of the Americas, but they were not the heroes of the stories in which they first appeared. Instead, just as Iolaus was companion to Hercules, the roles of Sacajewa and Pocahontas are that of companion or advocate, helping to accomplish the goals of some other. It took a Disney movie, four hundred years after the historical figure died, to transition Pocahontas from the supporting cast to something of a lead role in pop culture.[72] Forsaking historical accuracy, the production team invented something closer to a modern fairy tale. They borrowed from the form of fiction to create an abstraction, a message they felt was more important than promoting resentment toward the historical account. What can be said about unreal fairy tales and their popularity? If facts tell us how things are, fiction offers us ways to change our minds and become the characters that pass the tests of entropy.

If each family member has some implication for action, for motivations and for how we feel about things, then it can hardly be a mystery why we refer to gods in stories as fathers, mothers, and fellow brothers or sisters. In the social and family contracts of the West, we no longer consider daughters as objects of property, for adoration, trade, or consumption. In many parts of the world, however—and no doubt still in the hearts of some in the West—the other is still considered little more than *somebody else's problem*. How then, if host and guest sit together, will we compare mythologies, histories, and families?

The Aporia (Puzzle) of Apostles and Advocates

Two teachers left such a significant impression on B. W. Powe that he felt compelled to write a book about them. The book is about Northrop Frye and Marshall McLuhan—their academic styles, their antagonistic exchanges, their deeper fondness for each other's works, and what Powe calls their *complementarity*. One passage of *Marshall McLuhan and Northrop Frye: Apocalypse and Alchemy* refers to a conjunction useful to apply to the idea of the Divine Daughter— "advocates and apostles."[73]

Secondary characters in stories are important. Distinct from mentors, secondary characters act with the hero during the course of events, and they typically express a kind of empathy or resentment toward the main character. Athena played the role of *advocate* with Achilles and Odysseus. But what if the hero turns martyr or sacrificial victim? When the audience takes up the call to right something after an injustice, the role could be described instead as apostle. "Apostle" in simplest form can mean follower. To extend this description, we could say "follower of the way," or even "the one that continues or upholds mindfully."

In the Introduction of this book I cautioned that Agamemnon and Jephthah both sacrificed their daughters for something they found more valuable. Nothing intervened or prevented those sacrifices from happening. However, Agamemnon's wife, Clytemnestra, acting on her own sense of justice for her daughter, killed Agamemnon. No longer able to fulfill an advocate role, Clytemnestra twisted her role as nurturing mother into the role of a vengeful apostle.

According to some readings of the story, Jephthah could have gone to his high priest, Phineas, for advice. Phineas had the authority to revoke the vow or negotiate a more just resolution between Jephthah, his word, and his god. However, Jephthah's pride stopped him from doing that. It would have meant this leader of men would have to ask for help. In doing so, he would have recognized his own limitations and someone else's authority in certain matters. The title Phineas held didn't absolve him of his pride either. He could have approached Jephthah about the matter, but instead assumed it was Jephthah's responsibility to come to him and seek priestly advice. In the end, Jephthah's daughter and his family line paid the price for the pride of these two characters of authority.[74] The story initiated a tradition in which Hebrew daughters would lament the girl's fate for four days.

Ancient Greece and ancient Israel stand as foundational stones of the West. These two stories follow a series of consequences that resolve the problems of authority in very different ways. They also demonstrate the role of the other as an archetype: figurative or literal witnesses to some action, event, or story. They describe two avenues of participation the audience can adopt for themselves. As advocates or apostles, the audience can follow or reject an authority. Clytemnestra no longer identified with her husband; she identified instead with her daughter. Her new lover may have provided some motivation as well. The daughters of Israel identified with Jephthah's daughter, ritually following her in the four-day ceremony and upholding her memory.

When Anthony Burgess wrote *A Clockwork Orange*, he had no intention of inspiring boys in the United Kingdom to rape someone's daughter.[75] In fact, the clear majority of his reading audience did not commit such acts. But sometimes the outliers reveal a story worth attention. "Droogs" is another word for friends or cohorts, part of the slang Burgess invented for his characters. Alex and his droogs, Dim, Georgie, and Pete, had their own language and their own morality. The droogs acted as an audience to Alex's ambitions and desires. Alex's world reflected that of Christopher Boehm's chimps. Individuals in the group competed for leadership, formed alliances, and displayed fear or submission when in the presence of one another. Georgie failed to usurp Alex. The droogs later betrayed and abandoned Alex and his dangerous leadership when he committed manslaughter. Alex went to a reform facility. Dim became a police officer. Georgie died pursuing a life of crime. Pete found a girlfriend and left the droog life for what could become a family life.

The droogs are hardly a good model for a lasting society. And yet, the dynamic between them felt familiar or at least spoke to a number of Burgess's fans. Some in his audience identified with it so much that the story became a voice of authority in their lives, a compelling god. The fiction resonated with a few readers to the point of informing their personal identities, even if temporarily. Instead of understanding the author's message and accepting it as authoritative, a group of boys in Lancashire, for example, acted on the desire *to be* Alex and his droogs. They adopted the language and acted out scenes, physically embodying the story and characters. A daughter in Lancashire was raped when boys embodied Alex and his droogs. It was not the only case of what has come to be known as copycat crimes. And it came from fiction.

The test of entropy offers us something to measure our motivations against, outside of the stories we tell ourselves. Acts of religious faith, psychological practices, initiation rituals, neuronal responses, and hormone levels can be measured against the test of entropy. This test is the relation that develops between our actions and the observed. Whatever language we settle upon, whatever language we declare authoritative and follow, the healthy progress or entropic decline that comes from it helps us remain aware of our responsibility to what works.

In *You Are Not Your Brain*, Jeffrey Schwartz analyzed psychological conditions such as obsessive-compulsive disorder (OCD). According to Schwartz, our sophisticated, amazing brains have the power to work in our favour but also against our best interests. He coined the term "brain lock," in which authority is given to a particular idea. The brain initiates a loop, reinforcing that thought again and again. It becomes a compulsion that must be served. However, as the title suggests, even if the loop locks our consciousness temporarily, we don't have to identify with it.[76]

Schwartz has successfully treated many people with OCD by training them to think about themselves from a distance. His treatment involves adopting the perspective of a caring but impartial spectator—our own Athena. This perspective takes the form of a wise advocate. From another point of view, the impartial spectator can refer to an empathic spectator. But the key is that this approach encourages healthy development and gives individuals a way to change personal decline.

The treatment does not make the client or patient an object. Instead, clients participate in their own therapy, playing both the subject analyzed and also the advocate observing or initiating change. Reward, punishment, and responsibility do not rest on the shoulders of someone else. By observing ourselves as the other, we gain insight into what voices, angels, authorities, or compulsions are worth listening to. From the perspective of the audience, we are given the power to worship the motivations we believe most worthy.

Schwartz refers to this technique as finding an impartial spectator or wise advocate. If we turn our gaze from ourselves to someone else, we can use a similar technique to connect with our empathic spectator. When we watch others in distress, we don't always care about their situation enough to act. Even if we witness violence or terrible events, it might register as someone else's problem. We don't always recognize the gods we share with others, in the sense that gods are those things with implications for behaviour, those things that must be served. But even inactions can be measured against the test of entropy. This change can make the difference between managing a tragic event and ignoring malevolent acts.

In ancient Greece, Athena wore a helmet and armour in order to be heard above the fighting between her father and brothers. Once she took up the spear and shield, she became practically estranged from her mother. But as Aeschylus, Riane Eisler, and Jeffrey Schwartz suggest, the wise and cool-headed Athena can still cast the deciding vote. And because she favours the fair and heroic individual, she could grow into a formidable parent. With Jyoti, the memory of a daughter tests us. What kind of suffering will come if her voice has no authority over our compulsions?

Reflection

In 1897, Joseph J. Thompson experimented with a vacuum tube and found that magnetic fields affected the paths of cathode rays. In 1906, he was awarded a Nobel Prize for his discovery of the electron. In 1925, Edwin Hubble wrote a paper on astronomy for the American Association for the Advancement of Science. The paper explained the discovery and movement of galaxies outside our own Milky Way. About one hundred years ago, what we considered *real* changed because of discoveries into the very small and the very large. Through a systematic process of studying the observed, we changed our most basic beliefs about the universe and about the principles of matter. The role played by scientific observation in public policy and in family life has increased dramatically in the last century. It changed our language and reference points.

One of the most popular and distributable recording devices for thousands of years was the book. Perhaps this is how sacred texts still claim authority upon so many people today. Things change, but they don't have to fall apart. Form and content can adapt to a different medium. A change of key can lift the theme of a piece of music like a turn in a philosophical argument. New information calls on religious beliefs to change, too, like a guest at the door.

Samir Selmanovic is a minister known for his work in interfaith dialogue. His community, Faith House Manhattan, is made up of Christians, Jews, Muslims, and atheist humanists, all coming together to share in a ritual life and a devotional space. Their goal is to foster commitments to justice in the community and to heal a hurting world. They want to share a common journey even if individuals within the community choose different paths. Selmanovic has referred to religions as "God-management systems."[77] If we couple his idea with the question of what a god is, then we can see there is a place for religion in pluralistic, modern, and future communities. The hawks and doves of our natures may need to take as examples for behaviour the lions, wolves, and lambs of some of our oldest texts. The popularity of today's dating apps tells us something about our compulsions. We still seem to need enough character within us to manage our desire to lie down with the other and the observed in healthy ways.

Mother, father, son, and daughter are all archetypal roles in the family. I deliberately avoided using testosterone and estrogen in the four symbolic character descriptions above. The presence of both testosterone and estrogen in our own bodies and in the bodies of others does compel certain behaviours. Hormones can be powerful forces within us, with implications for our actions. They can possess us, but we can also find better authorities, and better methods to manage our motivations.

If we are willing to take responsibility for the language we use, like taking responsibility for the things that compel our behaviour, we can find common grounds of being. The four archetypes can be just as usefully understood as *known, unknown, observer, observed*. As archetypes, they point not just to ideals but to dangers as well. According to Erich Neumann, any image or representation can be symbolic, archetypal. It only needs to be given value by the person experiencing it. Northrop Frye believed that an education into the archetypes and symbols of literature gave readers the opportunity to achieve a heightened awareness, enlightenment, or better understanding of our part in the being of the world. And in doing so our imagination could triumph over the injustices and slights between us. We could even resolve the misunderstandings within ourselves. An educated imagination could responsibly manage and respond to any call from reality.

Marshall McLuhan noticed a dramatic change in cultural archetypes in the middle of the twentieth century. Electrical technology reconstructed how we tell stories and how we recognize ourselves in the stories of others. Literature was one of the few sources of study that examined how we communicate with one another in his time. His thoughts and teachings helped give birth to media literacy. When confronted with the mass audience and modern innovation, the rigid literary archetypes given authority from religious texts and social inertia were turning into clichés before his eyes. He wrote a book on the topic titled, *From Cliché to Archetype*. McLuhan suggested that the power to turn a symbol into an archetype, or into something more authoritative, did not rest in any kind of objective existence of the thing described. A writer or an audience could raise a shared idea from cliché to archetype, or reverse that process.

Richard Dawkins coined the term "meme" in his book, *The Selfish Gene*. The internet community has since adopted the term to refer to what's shared over social media. Today's memes often combine a visual image with text that either plays on words or tells a joke.

Our popular accounts of reality have journeyed from religious symbols to literary and psychological archetypes to common language clichés to quick regenerations of shared memes—all in a very short time. Authority over language and ideas has changed hands in less than a lifetime, possibly less than a generation. Compare these statements:

> God—the real reason anyone does anything.
> Love and Fear—the real reasons anyone does anything.
> Cultural Socialization—the real reason anyone does anything.
> Motivation and Identity—the real reason anyone does anything.
> Dopamine, Serotonin, Endorphins, Neurons—the real reasons anyone does anything.

Why is it that we have assigned or at least associated value, authority, and divinity to roles such as son, mother, and father, and not to daughter? Perhaps the language of divinity in the West didn't have a story that lifted a daughter to such a level. The mythologies of Greece, Rome, Northern Europe, and the Celtic traditions all appeal to male, female, and androgynous incarnations of the supernatural and the divine. In his work, Neumann associated feminine—mother and daughter together—as different elements of one archetype. Standing on his shoulders, and on the shoulders of past traditions, we can differentiate between such aspects and embrace insights that help us with the tests of today. For Aeschylus, justice was measured out in the presence of the gods, the community, the individual, and nature. Frye suggested that the Biblical social contract was between God, individual, and community. If the proper relationship developed, then nature would follow. The individual who spoke and acted in truth, embodying the *logos*, could redeem the world. Today, the social contract and the stories we tell ourselves might involve the entire family of archetypes. The individual pursuing a proper relationship with the *observed-other* might in addition pass the test of entropy and transcend the differences between past, present, and future.

The stories of Agamemnon and Jephthah illustrate the West's struggle to articulate an association between a child in a family and the authority a child might have over our actions and motivations. The West has associated the child and hero as different elements of one archetype. However, many new and novel developments have emerged in the modern era. The scientific revolution has given us a new love of inquiry, a new enthusiasm for innovation, and a new respect for the observed, as apart from our motivations and actions. We can model the relationship between observer and observed spiritually on the relationship between lover and beloved instead of user and object.

The world is experimenting and reimagining nature's role in the social contract as well. The constitution of Ecuador, for instance, grants inalienable rights to nature. According to that document:

> Nature, or Pacha Mama, where life is reproduced and occurs, has the right to integral respect for its existence and for the maintenance and regeneration of its life cycles, structure, functions and evolutionary processes. All persons, communities, peoples and nations can call upon public authorities to enforce the rights of nature.[78]

Constitutions are like new beginnings, declarations of the actions and observations that are meaningful for a nation. Does this mean the environment and ecosystem, in some figurative sense, could be recognized as part of the citizenry and identity of a nation? How do you commit nature to a contract or relationship? Perhaps this gives us a chance to adjust our understanding between what is our reality and what is our story.

Many today consider religious traditions to be out-of-date, superstitious fictions. What is gained by recognizing yet another deity or using religious language? Is there a way to suspend judgment, like the way we suspend disbelief when absorbed in a story? I believe how we manage fictions will prove important in the new consciousness. However someone uses the words, "real" and "unreal" stories alike do influence our thinking and our motivations. The world has witnessed an incredible bloom in the authority of fictional stories, especially in terms of how they inform our identities. Like children at play, people temporarily adopt the identities of their favourite characters from movies, television shows, graphic novels, and epic literature. Like play, fiction allows us to experiment. We try different things until we find what we want. In the process, we explore our motivations and better understand what works. Fiction also provides a bounded field, so that we can be conscious of the limitations of authority in a particular arena.

Two examples of the phenomenon illustrate the global change. J.K. Rowling's Harry Potter books brought together an entire generation of young readers from across the world. Despite being a clearly fictional story about an orphan wizard, children in Asia, Australia, America, Argentina, and Albania could all relate to one another because they all enjoyed the same story. Instead of belief or language, fiction brought them together, an inspirational story from the imagination.

Another popular example looks to a world of aliens and space travel. An orphan boy struggled to find meaning, skill and identity in the face of the greatest evils in the universe. He learned the evil within is just as great as the evil without. Luke Skywalker of *Star Wars* comes from nothing other than the imagination and hopes of a storyteller, and yet people across the world identified with this character.

Fiction matters because fiction holds an authority over us. Imagination is just as powerful a force on people as the reality that surrounds them. But, we can break the spell of a fiction that no longer works in the time it takes to get out of a costume or remove a mask. Fiction addresses two key questions:

1. How do I control my fear?
2. How do I manage my motivations?

Readers and viewers understand that Harry Potter and Luke Skywalker are fictional. And yet we identify with them and take up the costumes in play. We also take up their behaviours and attitudes as models for handling fears and motivations in our own lives. We embody the roles and become the heroes. But in terms of managing our motivations and fears, stories also open us up and prepare us to recognize ourselves when we are not in the role of the hero—when the urge to dominate possesses us, or when freedom calls out, or when our role is to be the audience to someone else's growth.

Traditional religions often call on the divine for help with these questions. However, the stories expressed with traditional divinities managed our fears and motivations only to the point that got us to this moment. We know more about our relationships with the planet and with our own impulses. We can use new tools in imaginative ways. However, we need something with authority and value, something with psychological weight to compel our actions. Today's consciousness recognizes fiction as both imaginative and authoritative. Without relying on superstition, we understand how something can be symbolic and important—even divine.

Harry Potter relies on the help of friends, family, and mentors to reach his goals and to manage his fears and motivations. In the end, he is not the sole victor over the evil forces of that imagined world. The triumph lies in the collective efforts of everyone participating in the problem. Likewise, for Luke to take up the heroic journey, it takes the spark of fascination in his own sister, a stranger. This fascination is further kindled by the lessons of a mentor in Obi-Wan Kenobi. His own rise to personal identity and strength requires a virtual galaxy of events and characters all working together. The fight eventually spreads out over vast and complicated worlds, both within and beyond himself. Luke sees the good remaining in the dark mask and machinery worn by the man that is his own father.

Perhaps the West never found it necessary to consciously worship the *observed-other* until the scientific method reached the popular mindset. Embedded as we are in today's advanced tribalism, the idea that authority could be found outside a person's cultural tradition is difficult to comprehend, even if we're quick to adopt the newest electronic device or foreign food. Perhaps the West never had the words to do such a thing until technology, language, and communication grew to embrace a new kind of consciousness, a love of the empirical method of inquiry. Peering into the very small and very large, we have come to reflect on our own identities, our own families, our own citizenship, our own fears and motivations. And in doing so, we found new relationships with the world around us, and we found new wisdom.

How can we recognize the unrecognized? With a paradox—a fictional deity as part of a family that respects the contexts of traditional religions while holding us accountable to managing our fears and motivations. In this way, we can create a relationship with the *observed-other*, like a host with a guest.

If we invite guests into our home, then we must prepare the house for visitors. The next chapter examines four environments as architectures of meaning and authority in relation to the divine family.

2

Settings and Structures

We tend to view the "environment" as something objective, but one of its most basic features—familiarity, or lack thereof—is something virtually defined by the subjective. This environmental subjectivity is nontrivial, as well: mere "interpretation" of a phenomenon can determine whether we thrive or sicken, live or die. It appears, indeed, that the categorization or characterization of the environment as unknown/known (nature/culture, foreign/familiar) might be regarded as more "fundamental" than any objective characterization—if we make the presumption that what we have adapted to is, by definition, reality. For it is the case that the human brain—and the brain of higher animals—has specialized operation in the "domain of order" and the "domain of chaos." And it is impossible to understand the fact of this specialization, unless those domains are regarded as more than mere metaphor.

—Jordan B Peterson
Maps of Meaning: The Architecture of Belief

*The house of a god
was a place the
individual ego met the infinite*

Children of the Sun

Marshall McLuhan once said of Northrop Frye, "Norrie is not struggling for his place in the sun. He is the sun."[1] This comment reveals something about the motivations behind academic work and the associations we use in understanding authority. The sun, the source of all energy, the initiator of the primary economy of photosynthesis, the revealer of information with its light, symbolizes for some people everything that can be overwhelming and life-changing and great and good and worth worshipping. Even a mild-mannered, mumbly-voiced, woolly-haired professor from a northern country might be identified with the revelations of the sun. That association becomes all the more clear to a student dependent on the approval of the teacher, or to a fellow-admiring professor.

Northrop Frye came from eastern Canada, spent a short period of time as a United Church minister, and despite never earning an official PhD, secured a lengthy and stable tenure at the University of Toronto. His work changed our understanding of the relationship between literature and religion. Marshall McLuhan came from western Canada. He earned his academic stripes at Cambridge University, converted to Catholicism, began teaching at the University of Toronto in 1946 and, with others, started the field of media studies.

Both McLuhan and Frye described themselves as *apocalyptic* thinkers. Today's ears might think this word theatrical or antiquated. Perhaps the word "apocalyptic" sounds boring and religious to some. We tend to use more modern words now. The original meaning for them came closer to the word "revelation"—new information comes to light, a moment of awareness fills an experience. Through a change of perspective, the sun no longer orbits us, but we orbit the sun. A different centre of gravity now informs our orbit, to play with the metaphor. What I have depended on before, what I knew and gave authority to, no longer holds. The current situation calls for something beyond my current understanding. I must think and act in new ways. There's no going back, but there may be a way forward.

According to Frye, all knowledge became personal knowledge informing identity, and the "spiritual" always aimed toward peaks and transformations of consciousness. When we perform a religious ritual, or take on the pursuit of a personal hobby, or take up the mere act of reading, it is to prepare ourselves to be ourselves *consciously*, associating our being with what we do in the moment and our being across time. Adopting a story, and participating in the roles in a story, helps a person transcend who they are and become the person with which they want to identify. But the environment or setting of a story can play its own part too.

Sam Harris linked peaks of consciousness to a kind of ethical high ground in his book *The Moral Landscape*. Harris asked what the basis of morality could be other than the well-being of conscious creatures. In another book, *Waking Up*, Harris asserted that investigating the nature of consciousness—and transforming its contents through training—is the basis of spiritual life.[2] Geographically, peaks can be the first places illuminated by a rising sun, the first places where transformations can be observed.

Harris has little interest in giving authority to religious traditions that don't stand up to modern scrutiny, but he does grant spirituality an important role in our lives. He encourages meditation, for example. Meditation offers the best training for reaching peaks in consciousness without reliance on unnecessary claims or beliefs. At the heart of spirituality, according to Harris, we need not find leaps of faith, but instead better practices of managing consciousness. If we relax into a pose where we can recognize gods as motivations for behaviours, we can see our ancient texts and stories differently. Story makes the experiences of consciousness richer in terms of communication, but not always more accurate in terms of description. Story and myth can be the objects of our observation and attention. New revelations on our own motivations present themselves when we study, as Frye once noted, the myth of God, which is a myth of identity.[3] The first chapter examined the faces and characters we might see in a god. This chapter explores four different houses in which we might find a god.

In her study of symbols, Susanne Langer came to think of architecture not so much as the craft of making spaces, but as the creation of ethnic domains, a translation of a place for perceiving.[4] The architecture of a location directs our attention, leading us to behave, believe, and value things in certain ways. Since we are living more and more in coded environments framing our perceptions with mediated screens, it becomes even more important that we recognize how these environments are constructed.

"Choice architecture" is the deliberate construction of different ways in which choices can be presented to consumers. In *The World Beyond Your Head*, Matthew Crawford points out that audio in social spaces is often present without a negotiation between an authority and the individuals in an environment. Imagine a room in which Muzak plays over a sound system. Perhaps it is a waiting room in an office or a food court in a mall. Someone believed that Muzak solved a problem, but they didn't consider it necessary to give people in the space any authority over the Muzak. They can't turn it off or adjust the volume, for instance. By default, the Muzak is on. The offended or unimpressed individual must take the initiative to *ask* for it to be turned off.[5] Choice architecture is controlled architecture, guiding our perceptions and assumptions, the very sights and sounds that arrange the relationships between dominion, nature, innovator, and other.

We have examined characters in story. Our attention now turns to the settings—the places and ways, the peaks and transformations.

Concerns, Cultures, Monuments, and Meditations

Frye used four archetypal settings to discuss recurring symbols and images that communicated spiritual ideas in the Bible. In particular, he focused on the *Furnace*, the *Cave*, the *Garden* and the *Mountain*. In his book, *Words with Power*, Frye prefaced his discussion on these settings by saying he organized each one with respect to a primary concern, or what we might consider a primary motivation. Primary concerns include:

- the concern to escape from slavery and constraint (freedom),
- the concern to sustain oneself and assimilate the environment (dominance / anticipation),
- the concern to love (acceptance), and
- the concern to make and create (innovation).

Secondary concerns, according to Frye, arise from the social contract. He lists examples such as loyalty and religious beliefs but links these secondary concerns to what he considered ideologies.[6] No hard boundary lays between the primary and secondary concerns except for how one views the problem. In Frye's words, "a famine is a social problem, but only the individual starves."[7]

The Protestant religious writer Paul Tillich attempted to communicate his understanding of theology in a way consistent with the new information of the modern era. He wrote:

> The object of theology is what concerns us ultimately. Only those propositions are theological which deal with their object in so far as it can become a matter of ultimate concern for us.[8]

One of Tillich's premises was that faith is the state of being ultimately concerned. For Tillich, a person's faith was that which takes hold of them such that no condition can usurp its importance. What if we read those words of Tillich, "ultimate concern," with their simplest, barest meaning? What is that idea in your life that registers with you as absolutely unconditional? In that unconditional, you find the ultimate reason for living. As well, you find that any split in identity between the self and that unconditional disappears.

Marshall McLuhan cautioned his readers about the difference between what is invisible and what is not perceived: "The present is always invisible because its environmental. No environment is perceptible, simply because it saturates the whole field of attention."[9]

Humans tend to take the visual presentation of information as primary. We have incredibly well-developed visual capacities. And yet, our sense of vision is the sense least attuned to understanding the role of the invisible in our lives. This is no mere spiritual play on words. In a material sense, every other sense is in communication with the invisible. And like the reflective echoes that bounce and provide us with different information, our other senses can help us be conscious of the way our environments captivate our attention and act as authorities upon us.

Other fields of study besides theology can help us navigate our ultimate concerns. Science has developed methods to investigate the invisible, the very large, and the very small. McLuhan's cautionary words provide a meditation that can bring us back to conscious control over our motivations, ultimate concerns, and even environments: "There is absolutely no inevitability, so long as there is a willingness to contemplate what is happening."[10]

Frye and Tillich both concentrated on the written text. McLuhan saw the text as only one medium in an environment filled with change. The electronic age gives authority to the image, the action, and the sound as well as the word. We need to contemplate all these concerns, all at once. According to Tillich, a person can be concerned ultimately with just about anything. A hierarchy develops from our concerns. Frye's distinction between primary and secondary concerns suggests a hierarchy too. To consciously determine what is worthy of our attention and worship, we need to examine the choices in our surrounding architectures and beliefs. What are they preparing us for? What people need to pursue life more abundantly may not coincide with the observed, the culture, or the natural world around them. Innovation has worked over our environments completely.

Frye examined the furnace, cave, garden, and mountain to show how these biblically significant settings influenced Western literature. Today's audience lives in a plurality of backgrounds. The electric and urban environments of pop culture arrange our concerns into relationships that don't always map onto ancient concerns or pastoral pursuits. Today's social environments are not constructed to reflect the nature of the world. Instead, our most familiar environments today seem to be what our social institutions want to make of the world, and what they want to make of us. A secular architecture has shaped the world we experience and navigate.

Marshall Berman attempted to find an understanding of the modern environment in his book *All That Is Solid Melts into Air*. He examined progressions in art, architecture, and city development, hoping to get a sense of where we were taking ourselves in the modern world. We have given such authority to progress, for example, that our values have become invisible—mere assumptions in the landscape. Attempts to manage our changing motivations have their own consequences. In Berman's words:

> We want culture to be a source of nourishment for ongoing life, rather than a cult of the dead. If we think of modernism as a struggle to make ourselves at home in a constantly changing world, we will realize that no mode of modernism can ever be definitive. Our most creative constructions and achievements are bound to turn into prisons and whited sepulchres that we or our children will have to escape or transform if life is to go on.[11]

Berman used illustrations of creative achievements from architecture, such as prisons and sepulchres. For some, to be modern might mean to be a builder. However, our spiritual thirsts are not always quenched by monuments. Creative achievements can also come from crafts and traditions, such as singing, dancing, and wine-making. Crafts can adapt to changes over time. A monument does not adapt.

Though the symbols of the furnace, cave, garden, and mountain may hold symbolic weight in terms of that long chain back through Western history and literature, the plurality of the world's contemporary generation must also be addressed. Today's audiences have found themselves experiencing moments of consciousness not tied to or depending on these spiritual traditions and textual devices. Our symbolic or archetypal expressions are not just on the page. Now we construct three-dimensional spaces—or spaces with virtual dimensions in electronic media—to form our beliefs and institutions. We arrange, and then are mastered by, the landscape of progressive civilization. Once the environments are constructed, we discover we have to live with both the intended and unintended consequences while the constructions fade into background invisibility. If someone receives social media updates automatically, in real time, throughout the waking day, then the social media platform might as well be invisible to consciousness because it *is* the environment. Contemporary generations continually light upon the symbolic relics of old tribal fears and expressions, but they may not feel the same "ultimacy" from stories of great and terrible giants in the past.

Later in his career, McLuhan and his son Eric described four laws of media as the new science. The McLuhans formulated a model of how things like the telephone, television, and now the internet change our identities. Similarly, these innovations also come to assume authority over our motivations. They come to shape our ultimate concerns. The intention behind the four laws was one of education—communicating to the natives of the electronic environment how to understand the world around them. Media literacy—understanding what video and audio information does to us, understanding how people use technologies to influence behaviours and attitudes—helps us to participate consciously in the world of media rather than being chained within it. After all, if we become part of the environment ourselves, we risk becoming an assumed and invisible part of the background of our own lives.

Today, we need another kind of literacy to navigate the constructed environments that have worked us over completely. To represent these environments, I describe below four figurative settings. Each of the four archetypal family members discussed earlier plays a part in these environments. The structures themselves cast our characters into roles—the hero, the known, the observed, and the unknown. The four symbolic settings are the pyramid, the panopticon, the theatre, and the agora (marketplace). The figurative settings hold a problem similar to the one McLuhan warned us about; namely, forcing something old to do the work of something new. This time I want to step backward, deliberately moving against the tide of thought over the last two centuries. This is a chance to retrace our steps through the academic halls in an attempt to find a home in the world instead of a cult of the dead. From there, we might make cautious progress.

I want to heed Berman's lesson and avoid turning my own precious achievements into prisons that younger generations only want to escape. To that goal, the figurative settings are presented as useful, symbolic descriptions—heuristics. I do not want to suggest they wholly inscribe the modern reality or point to some utopian ideal. Today's audience, I believe, is more intimately familiar with these four settings, though they may play within them unconscious of the effects. What's more, the symbols of the West's past do not work, in Armstrong's sense, if the next generation does not recognize them. We can train ourselves to be conscious in these architectures, as Langer suggested, and see the translations each place is making on our perceptions. In a plural world, there may not be a shared or prescribed ultimate concern dominating all aspects of group and personal identity. But we may be able to at least communicate and describe our ultimate concerns and construct a story in which we all can play a part. To manage everyone's ultimacy, we have constructed and institutionalized a plurality of environments. Now the task is to breathe and meditate—recognize our parts on these stages and pay attention to how these settings work us over. These symbols, these architectures, may draw us up to a peak experience of consciousness, shine a light for us and produce an echo off the walls, bringing us back to our own moments of choice.

The Pyramid—Derrida and Competition

Malidoma Patrice Somé grew up in the Dagara tribe in Burkino Faso, in western Africa. He lived with his family in a close-knit, semi-nomadic village. In his book *Ritual*, he recalls a time he took an elder to the city of Ouagadougou. The elder looked upon a multi-storey building for the very first time. Somé described the event:

> The poor man was so shocked that he was speechless for a while. When he finally spoke, he said, "Whoever did this has some serious problems."[12]

Such a simple story shows us how much can be assumed in the constructed environments of the West today. Somé's elder was raised with people who did not prize such innovation. To them, power used toward building up in that way would be a sign of a problem, a sign that someone had not been properly initiated into the identity of the tribe. To the Dagara, motivations that would lead a person to do such a thing would be considered inappropriate. But to others, such a motivation models the very drive of advancement and progress, a (supposedly) self-justifying god worth pursuing ultimately. Why would anyone question the assumption of progress as it obliterates the traditional?

The culture of Somé's elder was not a modern one. Innovation to archaic ways would have been resisted. The expectation was that elders passed on the customs, while sons would continue to behave and manage motivations as their fathers did, with similar tools and skills. Daughters would not seek out different lives from their mothers but instead fulfill the roles given to them by generations past. Yet, despite his trust in the old ways, Somé's elder did have a confrontation with something outside his customs and traditions. The old ways didn't prepare him for the sight of a multi-storey building. This elder's relationship with the observed brought him face to face with a test of entropy.

When Peter Sloterdijk learned of the death of Jacques Derrida in 2004, he wrote a book about the legacy of the French writer. Many know Derrida as the father of deconstruction, and some would consider him a patriarch of postmodern thinking. Sloterdijk entitled the book *Derrida, An Egyptian*.

One of the most striking symbols of ancient Egypt is the pyramid. Architects and tourists alike still marvel at the great pyramids. The structure of a pyramid gives it incredible resilience. If a pyramid were to somehow wear down or fall apart, its overall form and shape wouldn't change much. Remove a block, and gravity would work with time to settle the material into a similar form.

Ultimately, the pyramid is a construction that imposes and rewards certain actions, and therefore establishes meaning. Many living creatures, from the lobster to the mountain ibex to the human being, live in hierarchical groups. This not only establishes a type of order, but it establishes progressions or goals within the population. The mountain, as an ecosystem of populations, is not an agent with an agenda in a personal sense. The scrub brush, bacteria, mouse, ram, and snow leopard can all occupy the same levels of elevation. The snow leopard may be a predator but suffers the same vulnerabilities that come with gravity and time.

Christopher Boehm's studies of ape and human cultures gave him insights into how individuals compete for status within these societies. While watching chimpanzees, he took part in friendly wagers with other researchers. They would attempt to predict which individual chimpanzees would win leadership of a group. The researchers observed which chimps made alliances, which ones were aggressive toward current leaders, and which ones had more persistence in their ambitions. The largest or strongest chimps did not turn out to be safe bets. The researchers found that male chimps often gained leadership because of support from key friends in the group. Alphas that maintained their power longest were not always the most brutal or powerful. Long-lasting alphas tended to show interest in protecting relationships and fostering the young. Once in power, the ultimate concerns for the long-lasting alphas seemed to be maintaining the health, balance, and growth of the group.[13]

Discussions about competition for leadership don't always highlight the number of individuals engaged in competitions in relation to the rest of the group not actively competing. In the case of chimpanzees, a small group of males usually keeps an eye out for a chance to rise in the ranks. Many males do show dominance behaviour as part of growing up. However, the subgroup actively pursuing the top spots is only a small percentage of the entire group. The motivations of the few dictate the constructed environment of the many. We focus on that behaviour and think we perceive a pyramidal structure in the social makeup of the group, yet that does not seem to be the solitary motivation for every individual. There is a plurality of concerns and personalities. The most successful alphas seem to be led by this insight.

According to Boehm, one response to the human social pyramid is for individuals to differentiate between leadership control and leadership influence. Boehm and Riane Eisler both suggested that certain cultural groups went through a period of development in which the dominance hierarchy in the social environment was, in a sense, flipped. Instead of simply following whatever leader happened to hold control at a given moment, people would manage leaders with both hope and caution. Boehm used the term "reverse dominance hierarchies."[14] Groups adopting this very different environment of relationships would come to decisions based on a system of consensus—a new game, with different rules. Unless aggressive individuals played the game properly, they would not receive recognition as authorities. Competitive personalities would not necessarily be rewarded with status. These kinds of motivations would be controlled with group inclusion or exclusion, with status or shame. Status and authority were not necessarily *taken from others through force but given by others* based on evaluations of skill and value of gifts shared. This developed the need for a different kind of communication within the hierarchical social structure. Instead of a leader's personal motivations holding supreme authority, the group's motivations gained authority. Group behaviour was determined by consensus rather than the will of the dominant individual, even if the individual was an esteemed leader. This decentralization of power meant that competence in group-favoured qualities could be rewarded, while excessive dominant behaviours could be prevented, shamed, or redirected. Competence earned rewards. Competition earned regulation. Something in this change helped us pass the test of entropy for a few generations in our history.

Boehm suggests that a period of time, perhaps more than one thousand generations, would be enough to make a notable difference in the behavioural nature of a species.[15] If reverse hierarchies, to use his phrase, maintained a human society or group for an extended period, then individuals would be selected for their success in that kind of environment. It must be noted, however, that this change would not be a replacement for our hierarchical tendencies. It would be the emergence of one more development, bounded in with all other aspects of human nature. For human beings, a thousand generations could be equivalent to 25,000 years to 50,000 years, roughly. The human being we know best has been around for 100,000 to 200,000 years. Our ape ancestors emerged around 6 million years ago. The earliest mammals appeared 200 million years ago. The last few hundred years of social change and scientific development can look like a young David compared to the giant Goliath of our biological history. Perhaps David would appreciate it if his sisters Athena and Sophia stood by his shoulders.

Pyramids are built bottom-up, working layer upon layer until a multi-storey structure reaches a pinnacle and makes a lasting impression on those who stand witness. In a hierarchy, attention is focused on goals, the vision of what's ahead, the next block in the structure. The structure itself arranges place, position, and dominance as ultimate concerns, as a kind of contest to competence. Time fears the pyramids perhaps because even after corruption, even after throwing a sacrificed daughter's body down the steps, the pyramid can appear unchanged, ordered, majestic.

Sloterdijk's use of "Egyptian" was not to suggest anything literal about the genetic lineage of Jacques Derrida. He wanted to express something about Derrida's way of thinking—the point Derrida was trying to make in his writings and the legacy he pursued. Derrida's reputation with students and rivals reveals possible motivations behind his work as well. In academic squabbles, Derrida earned a reputation for getting the last word. He accomplished this not through winning his opposition over to his arguments, necessarily. How often do arguments ever win over an opponent? Arguments are made to defeat opponents, but just as often they are made to win over audiences. Derrida outlived many of his critics by out-questioning them. His style of writing involved wordplay, puns, and creative spelling to assert his position as an academic authority. He held mastery over the language, making it do and mean what he wanted, when he wanted. His approach was not scientific—collecting data, analyzing it, and then presenting his conclusions in a scholarly article so that peers could replicate experimental results. It was a high-stakes game about the use of words.

Despite all his games and questions, Derrida still admired and respected the traditional progression of Western thought. Gary Olson interviewed Derrida for the *Journal of Advanced Composition*. When asked about using deconstruction in a classroom to throw literary texts into disorder, Derrida seemed to reverse the trajectory of his own practices:

> I call my students in France back to the most traditional ways of reading before trying to deconstruct texts; you have to understand according to the most traditional norms what an author meant to say, and so on. So I don't start with disorder; I start with the tradition. If you're not trained in the tradition, then deconstruction means nothing. It's simply nothing....
>
> I think that if what is called "deconstruction" produces neglect of the classical authors, the canonical texts, and so on, we should fight it. I wouldn't be in favor of such a deconstruction.[16]

From this interview, Derrida can appear more concerned with the process of inquiry and questioning than with his own creations or their effects. Derrida used poetry and argument interchangeably in pursuit of his goal—he wanted to be the top French academic of his time. Perhaps he wanted to be the top academic of the West. To do that, he couldn't simply mimic the learning of past generations. Derrida's writings look very much like the multi-storey building that gave Somé's elder such a shock. To the person playing one game in academia, Derrida's work is a sign of someone with a serious problem. And yet he would have assured his elder that, despite his persistent questioning, despite the complex monuments he wrote, he respected the traditions of the tribe. To the person playing with the rules to win a game, it is innovation. Still, it is worth evaluating the authority of innovation. Innovation can initiate climbing up the pyramid or the corruption of the entire structure. The climbing game can be a pursuit of dominance or it can be a pursuit of competence, truth, and knowledge.

When we recognize this kind of behaviour in a person—always seeking the last word or pushing the next question—what can we hypothesize about the person's motivations? Persistence may suggest a passion for the work, even a desire for the truth. But it also points at something else. If the ruling motivation in a person is to win, to always come out a step ahead, then the person's actions may serve only to keep one step ahead of the competition. The person's ultimate concern, in the bare meaning of those words, and in the context of the chapter you are reading, is the pyramid.

The environment of competition often takes the metaphorical form of a hierarchy. Games are played to decide a winner. Awards are earned with increasing value. We rise above our rivals, stepping up throughout our career to grasp the highest rung possible on the corporate ladder. Almost every institutional structure adopts pyramid architecture. It took less than 200 years for the early Christian church to adopt a hierarchical structure. Little wonder that almost all businesses follow a similar pattern. A president, CEO, and board are the top bricks. New hires usually enter at the bottom. Sometimes this is a matter of competence, but the environment is also structured to regulate and harness the power of competition. The corporate world has institutionalized and now serves the architecture of the pyramid.

Dominance hierarchies are very old, reaching back millions of years in our cultural and biological development. In our stories, the relationships between characters is often influenced by the environment. In a competitive, pyramidal environment, the other cannot help but take a role, in the eyes of the individual, as an opponent or adversary. Even in moments of collaboration, there is a chance the other could be motivated to get ahead of us. Given the hierarchical assumptions of the pyramid, it is difficult to understand that the other may be motivated differently. How can the other possibly participate in climbing the pyramid *without* being motivated by competition, winning, and the desire to lead? And yet like the apes studied by Boehm, often the few set the stage for the all. The few dictated the architecture of the environment based on the assumption that all individuals were playing one ultimate game.

Capitalism is often described as "creative destruction." Through the push of innovation, old things are destroyed, old successes surpassed. Words like "pivot" and "adapt" are the mantras of the business world. The established pyramids are under constant threat of deconstruction because something could come along that is more persistent, more hungry, more inventive, more efficient, or better priced. Admiration for the innovator is part of the modern soul. In the constant deconstruction and reconstruction of innovation, competition establishes disruption in the place of balance. We worship inventive and winning heroes, not just in our economic stories but in politics and even in spirituality.

Ayn Rand worshipped the innovator. She used narrative to express an ideology of individualism and objectivism. Her views have influenced the West for decades. What was Rand's ultimate concern in Tillich's sense? She would say, "I swear by my life and my love of it that I will never live for the sake of another man, nor ask another man to live for mine."[17] She believed in trade between individuals over the use of coercive or political power. She believed in a hierarchy of values and the supremacy of reason. Rand wanted to clear away the older pyramids and, in their place, erect one based on self-interest and the productive work of each individual. But she was also conscious of the potential problems with hierarchical environments. In *Atlas Shrugged*, she wrote:

> The man at the top of the intellectual pyramid contributes the most to all those below him, but gets nothing except his material payment, receiving no intellectual bonus from others to add to the value of his time. The man at the bottom who,

left to himself, would starve in his hopeless ineptitude, contributes nothing to those above him, but receives the bonus of all of their brains.[18]

According to Boehm's work with hunter-gatherer societies, those who contribute to reverse hierarchies are esteemed, but they do not earn authoritarian power. Special consideration is given to the suggestions of those who have demonstrated skills and competencies. The group listens to them and even praises them, which are precious rewards for a human being. But even the most competent do not become rulers unless they can influence an audience's motivations. Today's market societies may not work in the way hunter-gatherer societies work. Today, markets ultimately frame social values. Markets measure public education systems, religious practices, and ironically, even not-for-profit projects. In just a few generations, we have moved from the family economy to the market economy to the market society.

In the creative destruction that is capitalism, disorder results in gains for those playing the opportunity game. Nassim Taleb tried to find a word to describe this and settled on "antifragile." Imagine something that gains from shocks and doesn't require more and more energy to maintain.[19] In mythological terms, it might take the form of a hydra that grows two heads in place of one. Hindus tell a story of Raktabija and Durga. Raktabija possessed an incredible ability—each drop of his blood spilled onto the battlefield would create a fully-grown recreation of himself.

Capitalism may be able to grow in destruction and reincarnate itself with little more than the building blocks of inventiveness and ambition. However, as each creative validation ratchets up the legacy of capitalism, our consumption of energy increases as well. To adapt Frye's words quoted earlier, a drop in the market is an economic problem, but only the individual loses a job and a home. Alfred North Whitehead warned:

> It is the first step in sociological wisdom, to recognize that *the major advances in civilization are processes which all but wreck the societies in which they occur* [my emphasis]—like unto an arrow in the hand of a child. The art of free society consists first in the maintenance of the symbolic code; and secondly in fearlessness of revision, to secure that the code serves those purposes which satisfy an enlightened reason. Those societies which cannot combine reverence to their symbols with freedom of revision, must ultimately decay either from anarchy, or from the slow atrophy of a life stifled by useless shadows.[20]

The Willis Tower in Chicago uses more electricity in one day than a town of 35,000 inhabitants.[21] That is just one of the monuments to progress in just one city, and an example of what is needed to maintain it. Depending on the definition, there are almost a thousand skyscrapers in the United States alone. By extension, just those buildings might consume the same electricity of 10 percent of the country's population. The amount of energy consumed to maintain the tall buildings of the world would add up to something almost mythical, an astronomical number. Yet, somehow, we've been able to stifle the shadows for now and keep the lights on.

According to the Bible, it was not the materials that failed in the story of the tower of Babel. What collapsed was the trust and communication between people.[22] Each time we figuratively build up, we test our ability to manage complex and fragile infrastructures. The myth of consumer capitalism may very well take the form of a hydra or Raktabija, a "serious problem" our ancestors may never have faced or resolved. The labourers who built the tower of Babel were able to walk away. In the global village we have cobbled together, walking away no longer seems like a viable option. When our towers fall, they come down on our daughters and neighbours.

Sisyphus, the guest of Hades in the underworld, was punished with a most difficult task. He had to roll a large boulder up a hill. His work was never finished. Inevitably, the boulder would roll back down. Sisyphus was lucky to avoid being flattened. But that was part of the punishment and predicament he had won for himself.[23]

The myth of Sisyphus has a lesson for us when we pursue progress as an ultimate concern. The punishment of Sisyphus took place on a hill, but we can understand it as a particular kind of pyramid. Instead of pushing a boulder up a hill, it might be better to understand his hill as an accelerating line, curving up steeper and steeper. The pinnacle creates an impossible goal. It either reaches to infinity or creates an infinite slope. Even if one were to reach the topmost point, there is no place on which to rest the burden, no place to stand other than a figurative geometric point.

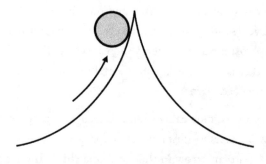

If Sisyphus could have seen the curve of the hill from an impartial observer's perspective, he might have better understood the futility and punishment that comes from worshipping ultimate progress. It takes more and more energy to reach the goal until maximum energy is used to bring the boulder to the peak. To add to the punishment, it's impossible to balance the burden we bring with us once we get there. Nevertheless, like Sisyphus, we feel tethered to our rock because our traditions tell us to keep doing the same things over and over again and keep expecting the same results.

Biblical stories address the idea of escalation, progress, hierarchy, competition, and son-inspired innovation as early as the book of Genesis. Cain killed his brother in a moment of dominance and resentment, only to have his god step in to make him aware of the escalation. Offences made against descendants of Cain received payback equalling seventy-seven times as much as any original offence.[24] The adventures of Jacob illustrate what could happen when a competitive son worships the wrong motivation in the wrong places. Jacob first followed a god promising him the first-born share in the family. This voice compelled him to the point where he willingly drove himself out of relationships with his parents and brother. He was more concerned with his status as an individual than his identity as a member of the family. There may have been an unfair hierarchy between Jacob and his older brother, but Jacob did not address that problem. His motivation was bent on something else, on his own trajectory up the local pyramid.

After running from his family, Jacob spent a night in the wilderness and dreamed of a great ladder into heaven. This time his god sat atop the hierarchy, commanding messengers up and down the steps of the structure. Jacob then found this god worthy of worship. He worked to build up his own position, to construct an environment where he controlled and commanded like the god in his vision. Jacob had to leave his next home because his father-in-law got tired of playing games with him.

Eventually, Jacob set aside both these motivations and recreated his relationship with his brother. He had to wrestle with his god to reach a moment of peak consciousness. In the end, he found his own place and his own way, but it was difficult and without the guidance of his family.[25]

Raktabija's creative, destructive power made him so dangerous that Durga, the highest symbolic form of feminine expression, could not defeat him easily. Durga, in her frustration, found new form. From her forehead emerged Kali with a combination of new knowledge and righteous anger. Kali's motivation did not spring from the same source as Raktabija's. Whereas Raktabija was a creature of the battlefield motivated by competition, Kali (Durga) and her husband, Shiva, shared a bond of love. This turned out to be something so powerful it could threaten the universe as well.[26] But it could also serve the universe and inspire growth, the battlefield and the pyramid notwithstanding.

On the pyramid, the hero can be either good or terrible, building order or initiating collapse. The father figure almost always appears archaic, something to be surpassed rather than copied, though some apprenticeship may occur. The observed, or the other, takes a role as competitor or collaborator, but rarely has the same authority as the actor and climber. The unknown, the mother figure, can be a source of both hope and threat for the hero on the pyramid. As a result, her authority can be respected or ignored, to the peril of the hero.

Pyramids litter the landscape of the contemporary world, to the point where we don't perceive them, let alone question their effectiveness or longevity. We find it hard to remain conscious of them and conscious of their effects on us. But observing our human nature can suggest we are motivated by something else as well. We have reversed the hierarchies in order to differentiate dominance from competence and manage the potential rise of resentment toward tyrants.

Malidoma Somé suggested that we can consciously examine progress instead of assuming it is an unassailable good. When we worship progress, we sacrifice something that may have had an unobserved value. But consciousness allows us to expand our frames of reference, so that we can consider more and more information and manage the risks of collapse or the promises of transformation. Somé's words bring us closer to the realization that our assumptions may not give us the firm foundations we anticipated: "Progress is the invention of someone who suffered immaturity and who craved to be initiated."[27]

Unquestioned progress is a kind of competition with time, an attempt to triumph over death. By speeding things up with machines, we can satisfy our temporary motivations, distract ourselves from the inevitable. This comes at the cost of not actually understanding the relationship—how the machines work us. Alfred North Whitehead captured the issue: "Civilization advances by extending the number of important operations which we can perform without thinking about them."[28] The advances he addresses also all but wreck civilizations exactly because we are too distracted to think about them. Perhaps we are too fixated on searching for peak experiences of stimulation instead of consciousness. The exponential accumulation of all this not-thinking-about-them has helped us adopt, for example, economic systems blind to the effects of externalities in a business or market. The natural environment, as an example, became a source for material but little more than an externality not measured in the ledger. And if it isn't in the ledger, it isn't worth thinking about; it's someone else's problem. From such assumptions, we have built economies as dumb as trees.

The zoologist and religious critic Richard Dawkins compared economic policy to forest growth. From an observer's perspective, tree trunks could be monuments to futile competition. In the race for solar energy, plants stretched skyward, moving the ground-level meadow up on stilts. The energy used to grow the stilts is, in his sense, futile, because the solar energy would have reached the ground as much as it hits the raised canopy.[29] Yet, individual trees cannot ignore the competition. Perhaps a better re-statement of the point in the context of this chapter is to say that our own motivations (and our own levels of consciousness) haven't become much more sophisticated than the motivations of plants.

This illustration could be taken as a critique of narrow ideological thinking. Does competition create efficiency on stilts or complicated, fragile niches? The rise in the canopy has also fostered biodiversity, creating opportunities for adaptations in animals and plants living in the layered ecosystems of the forest. Competition creates consumption. But maybe that's the ultimate concern of a market society.

For millions of years, natural processes of evolution ran the economy; photosynthesis was in charge. For the last several centuries, we thought we were rational actors building a world economy in the form of market societies. Now, when we begin to understand that we are merely biased prospectors, we put alpha apes in charge of economies and follow policies hardly more rational than trees. And yet we still rarely see an ultimate relationship between photosynthesis—creating value and energy—and the economy. We don't see the other side of competition because when the pyramids become corrupt, they still look like pyramids, treasured hills to climb. The innovative spirit, as Whitehead suggested, doesn't just build better pyramids—it threatens to turn all the progress of civilization to ruin.

How do we then initiate the hard work of transformational consciousness in pyramid-like environments? Without taking the time to hold a conversation with our motivations, having a mature relationship with our motivations, we can fall prey to their assumed authority on us. As a comparison, a teenager may be motivated to be the first in her group of friends to have sex. The car and the phone may help speed up her pursuit of that goal and her climb up her social pyramid. The condom may help her regulate some of the biological consequences of that motivation. A conversation with loved ones—or more importantly with herself—about what it means to be conscious of hormones and responsibility, lets her enter into a respectable relationship with the god-like impulses of her compulsions. We can find higher purposes, within and without, and learn to be smarter than the pyramids and the trees that surround us.

At the end of his life, Derrida wondered what would turn out to be his legacy. It is said he believed his work would receive two paradoxical fates. He believed that his name would be forgotten the moment after his passing. However, he also believed that some part of his work would survive in the cultural memory. Perhaps he understood that if one brick is removed from the pyramidal structure, the structure still remains.

Derrida's prediction of a dual and paradoxical legacy parallels the legacies of those who rise and fall in political office. Power and position, themes of the pyramid environment, can be the most temporary and fleeting of attainments. One national leader can practically sweep away the legacy of the last with a few signatures. The pharaohs of Egypt are now little more than dust in the cultural memory. Their political manoeuvrings, triumphs, and policies are dead. But the artwork of the culture still captivates and fascinates us. The leaders burn out, but the pyramids have hardly faded away. Perhaps we can take Derrida's legacy, the pyramid, and even the growth of trees as reminders to dedicate ourselves to something other than dominance.

Like Somé's elder staring at a multi-storey building, we can understand serious problems may emerge if competition and hierarchical position are the ultimate concerns we grant authority. Relationships, trust, ideas, and tools all benefit from the process of practice and revision. The work and craft involved in group performances with music or dance suggest collaboration can be as meaningful as competition. Like well-crafted glasses of wine, the arts are not mere decoration or distraction. They can be understood as attempts to express something transcendent, revealing something beyond the sensory stimulation. The experience offers a shared consciousness, bringing a sense of life, identity, and meaning to the performers and the audience, something beyond the fleeting desperations of politicians and pyramid climbers.

Recognition of the pyramids that shape our behaviour is one step to greater consciousness of our own motivations and the environments that surround us. With that perspective, regardless of where we might stand on those pyramids, we can regulate our motivations, dedicate ourselves to competence, observe our behaviours, and better decide what is worthy of worship.

The Panopticon—Foucault and Anticipation

Jeremy Bentham wanted to build a better prison. For Bentham, better meant more efficient. He had an idea. One guard could oversee many prisoners and manage their behaviours, all at once, if the prison itself was constructed in a way to give the guard complete oversight. With the right vantage point, simple observation—the sense of being observed—could establish control over the behaviour of the prisoners.

Michel Foucault saw in Bentham's panopticon an expression of how an environment can be constructed to generate uniform, homogenized behaviour in a group. The panopticon is observation, anticipation, and expectation realized in architecture. Foucault went beyond the prison system and beyond brick-and-mortar constructions. Control, examination, and classification of the behaviour of an audience all operate within the relationship of power established by the constructed environment of the institution. This architecture was not just for use in physical space, but in mental space and political policy. One of Foucault's famous questions reveals the motivation behind the use of the panoptic structure in contemporary institutions: "Is it surprising that prisons resemble factories, schools, barracks, hospitals, which all resemble prisons?"[30] It is worth adding "churches" and "shopping malls" and "laboratories" and "websites" to Foucault's list to understand the architecture of beliefs constructed in these environments.

Why are so many traditional portrayals of paradise, heaven, and the ideal state made in the image of a walled garden, where within the enclosure almost all behaviour is predictable and standardized? This must say something about people's ultimate motivations and fears. Consider the typical business suit. Even the things we don't think much about, like dry dog food, demonstrate our desire for the homogeneous and the uniform, the efficient totalizing solutions to otherwise complicated situations. The walled and constructed environment of the institution demands to be taken as total, denying or at least limiting the influence of externalities. Inside, regulation frames the experience. Behaviour is noticed, measured, recorded, and compared to expectations.

Matthew Crawford examined what he called "choice architectures" in *The World Beyond Your Head*. In the context of a supermarket, for example, a choice architect constructs an environment of aisles and shelves so that shoppers are nudged toward optimal purchasing behaviour.

> The studies that inform behavioural economics investigate an individual in the artificial setting of a university psychology lab, where the whole point is to isolate and control every variable.
>
> When we are in the supermarket or any idealized consumer space (for example, alone with one's laptop and a credit card), don't we in fact resemble the isolated subject of a psych experiment? As such, we are ideal raw material for the architects of mass behaviour, and we do well to be aware of the fact so we can choose our architect.[31]

Mass behaviour can also be understood as homogeneous, anticipated behaviour. When I sign into a social media account or a shopping website, I am given news, updates, and special deals, all presented in such a way just for me. But just for me to do what? What is the ultimate concern in that environment? Do the architects construct this presentation with a primary motivation of what's best for me, or what's best for making me consume through a particular channel? Crawford suggests that awareness of the constructed experience is key. When we are conscious consumers, we can act on our choices rather than someone else's choices.

Where the pyramid assumes worship of the hero that climbs it, the panopticon assumes the obliteration of the innovator's individual behaviour into the behaviour of the ideal customer who flows through the purchase funnel correctly. The ruling force is the controlling dominance of the orderly father figure, what is known and anticipated. Authority is top-down and behaviour conforms to what is anticipated. A culture of consumption ultimately must come from a relationship between those who want to sell and those who want to buy. But when those who want to sell control the environment, the constructed demands and engineered paths make our choices for us.

Another example of the panoptic environment is the traditional classroom. Teachers instruct and monitor students, measuring behaviour and performance based on a curriculum set by the larger education system. The classroom demonstrates both the terrible and encouraging faces of the father figure. In one case, conformity to a group's goals can be praised. Skills are nurtured that eventually benefit the freedom and strength of the individual. By working through the system, the individual can become a just and competent member of society, even a leader. By revolting against the system, disruptive individuals find another way, potentially great and terrible as well.

Community groups face similar challenges. Alcoholics Anonymous has helped many people through their struggles with addiction. The twelve-step model has gone from one-time innovation to archetypal self-help program to cliché. Step 1 involves a person admitting to being powerless to a problem or addiction. Step 2 directs the person to "believe that a Power greater than ourselves could restore us to sanity."[32] The original organization came out of the Christian tradition and relied on the Christian conception of the world. Over the decades, some people found the specifically Christian underpinnings of AA difficult to accept.

Jim Christopher attended AA meetings but found he was uncomfortable with the twelve-step method. After committing to his own recovery, Christopher interviewed two thousand others like him. His research led him to question the religious foundation of the twelve-step model. Why would he replace a fearful and guilty alcoholism with a fearful and guilty sobriety? Turning one's life over to a higher power, as defined by the Christian underpinning of AA, addressed only one part of the psychological side of addiction, for Christopher. As well, it recognized virtually nothing of its physiological side. Christopher wrote an article entitled "Sobriety Without Superstition," which in turn led to four books and to the Secular Organizations for Sobriety (SOS).[33]

Christopher's group, SOS, quickly gained recognition across the world as a viable, effective alternative to AA, helping people maintain sobriety through personal responsibility and self-reliance. Christopher gave a radio interview in 1987 about the organization. After the interview, one of the producers confronted him. She screamed at him, telling him that AA had saved her life. How dare he offer something different from AA?

AA didn't have to change. The people in charge of AA had no real desire to recognize new information and no mechanism to update how it could affect the institution. Other solutions and groups arose for people looking for different paths, different panopticons. Christopher's goal was never to obliterate AA. Neither did his work invalidate the radio producer's journey through the institution of AA. But his ideas somehow deregulated the producer's emotions to the point where she felt her identity was being challenged. She felt compelled to act on her emotions. Her charged reaction suggests she was in a place she had not fully anticipated. Because Christopher's story was outside of her expectations, she turned to a verbal assault to reassert her journey in her own panopticon.

Though this example is quite mild compared to full religions or belief systems, it does give us a glimpse into the potential violence lurking behind the walls of the panopticon and the wrath behind an otherwise benevolent personality. When whatever is anticipated is not fulfilled or confirmed, the power to use force to make things happen as expected can be very tempting. The panopticon gives authority figures the licence and means to exercise power and restore order—the anticipated. That's what has ultimacy in such settings. Prisoners are not punished when they follow the rules and behave as directed. When they do not follow the rules, they are watched more closely. Social interaction is restricted. In extreme cases, solitary confinement imposes severe restraints until the prisoner's behaviour can be fully anticipated.

What was Jim Christopher doing with his own behaviour outside the orderliness of AA? What was leading him, or what was the authority he was listening to, if it wasn't the authority of AA? He simply paid attention to and investigated something not already addressed in that system. He offered another way, another path. This helped some people successfully regulate the addiction beyond the confines of AA. Institutions of any kind—personal habits, government departments, corporations—all build their own panopticons to regulate the behaviour of their audiences and consequently set limits on the identities of people submitting to the anticipations of the institution.

Utopian and dystopian literature addresses the consequences of panoptic societies. In *1984*, George Orwell led the hero, Winston Smith, through a systematic process of personal obliteration and submission to the state. Winston became a regulated audience—an advocate, witness, and supporter of the state. He was reborn out of the head of the state as an ineffectual Athena with no armour, doing only the will of Big Brother, serving no Odysseus. Winston ended up unable to act even on his own behalf. He became a mechanized child of the state without the thrill of any independent journey or self-direction. Orwell addressed the use of specialized language with the society's *Newspeak* jargon. Language itself establishes a kind of panopticon. The government organizations in the novel saw to it that the environment itself imposed language and behaviour to serve state goals. The manipulation of media ensured consistent, homogenized behaviour on the part of the audience.

What was the ultimate concern in this constructed environment? Anticipated behaviour. The known, the regulated, the hoped for. In the panopticon, the relationship with the other is based on knowing what the other is supposed to *be* and *do* at any given time. The overseeing state coordinated elements of the environment to bring out the desired behavioural outcome.

What the wardens of the panopticon don't want is revolutionary disruption or translation of what is happening. The hero, Winston Smith, is regulated to be nothing exceptional, simply a member of the larger audience, and given as little authority as possible. The appearance of novelty brings Winston more anxiety than hope. Other nations are demonized and used to confirm the biases of the system within. The mother archetype receives little recognition. The natural world beyond the political walls plays a part in only a few scenes of the story. The audience enters into a relationship of subjectification.[34] The known, father archetype that governs the panopticon, can be either benevolent or tyrannical, but his intention is always to bring forth what is anticipated.

Like many constructed environments, the pyramid and panopticon can be neatly embedded within each other. To embed a pyramid within a panopticon, simply structure a ranking system of officers and subjects. Status and shame regulate behaviour within a culture's figurative walls just as surely as reward and punishment in a laboratory with caged white mice. The West has gained innumerable benefits from panoptic structures—increases in health and lifespan, institutional responses to environmental disasters, and decreases in physical violence between individuals. But when control rises as complete authority, when it is a matter of control for the sake of dominance, the panopticon establishes the anticipated as a god, an authoritarian ultimate concern.

Communist ideology offers a method for redistributing resources according to each person's ability and needs.[35] In order to realize that slogan, judgment is needed from an authoritative, anticipating, and measuring authority. The authority may believe it has enough information and the correct rational processes to determine the ability and needs of individuals. But carrying out the necessary measurements can create physical and metaphorical walls around a community, based on the top-down observations and anticipations of those in charge.

Walls frame the popular image of the Garden of Eden. Walls also frame Ezekiel's holy city in the Bible. Buddha's parents constructed a beautiful walled garden to protect him from the information of the outside world. In Hindu mythology, the tyrant king Kamsa received a prophetic vision—the eighth child of his sister Devaki would kill him. Kamsa placed his sister and her husband, Vasudeva, in a dungeon so that he could take all their offspring and regulate their behaviour. Kamsa's desire to control his destiny reduced Devaki, her husband, and all their children to the role of passive, sacrificial others. They no longer jeopardized Kamsa's interests. Devaki's child Krishna escaped Kamsa's control. As so many stories tell us, there is always something beyond the walls, outside our current beliefs and anticipations. There is always something not contained within our ideologies.

Walls can create great and terrible spaces. They can foster growth and inhibit it. Sacred rituals act like panopticons in one sense—they create symbolic spaces to regulate our desires and behaviours. As Kamsa's story illustrates, the thought of death is a powerful motivator. To enter into the unknown of death is painful for the human ego, but the threat of being forgotten is just as unbearable. The desire to influence the factors that lead to death can be sufficient justification for building the walls of a panopticon, or, for that matter, ascending the blocks of a pyramid.

Entrance into a panopticon acts as a kind of initiation. But its construction acts as a kind of substitute—something more permanent than myself will continue, something without my limits will still serve my anticipations. In the face of the complexity, randomness, and threat of what's outside, some walled space must be established to separate unknown from known. At least temporarily, until you put down this book.

Malidoma Somé discusses the funeral rituals of the Dagara in his book *Ritual*. In the face of Western influence, elders concern themselves more and more with traditional ceremonies. Elders "interpret people's refusal to get initiated as the first sign that death is being evaded."[36] The modern world, according to Somé, sees death as the end. Traditional cultures tend to see death as a transition—a threshold to something else. The concern of the elders for proper funerals demonstrates the motivational pull of anticipation, and the desire to have perceiving places (mental or physical) governed by rules and walls.

In the West, entrance into many of the established panoptic institutions is legally enforced. Children, for example, must attend schools or otherwise receive education in some regulated way. Building projects require approval to ensure adherence to safety codes. Traditional rituals gave communities methods to regulate emotions through the big transitions of life and death. Today's panopticons regulate our relationships with what is now granted authority, sometimes even over the primary concerns of the individuals within them.

Somé explains that the purpose behind a ritual is the driving force, and the same can be said for a panoptic institution. His elders said, "Ritual is like an arrow shot at something. When the intended target is not there, the arrow invents one."[37] Somé's elders and elders of the West like A. N. Whitehead understood both the power and danger of an arrow. The panopticon's architecture invents a target. The audience only needs to be in the path of the arrow to be initiated.

The ultimate concern of the keepers of the panopticon is the heart of the audience. Whether that concern takes the form of Cupid's dart or the executioner's bullet depends greatly on the intention of those in authority.

The Theatre—Levinas, Lonergan, and Responsibility

In the world of the theatre, performers give the audience a nickname, and it is God. Where the pyramid is a competitive, innovative economy and the panopticon is a centralized, walled economy, the theatre is an economy of attention. People don't just vote with their feet or think with their stomachs. They settle the scores of their purchase with captivated imaginations.

The success of a theatrical production does not necessarily depend on making things correspond to some "reality." In the environment of artistic performance, the imagination of the audience has authority. Actors are successful when they win attention. Not just disbelief, but psychic distance is temporarily suspended. When the audience identifies with the performer's thoughts or deeds, the separation between observer and observed fades to virtually nothing.

The theatre holds up a mirror to both the panopticon and the pyramid, but instead of just proving a reflection, it can also change the relationships of authority. Whereas the audience was watched in the panopticon, the audience now watches. The audience can bestow kinship, success, approval, or love. In a concert hall or ancient Greek theatre, the audience might look down on the performance. Whereas the other was a competitor to beat out in the hierarchical pyramid, the audience in the theatre has something more like a seat of judgment. In a pyramid, the audience looks up. Together, the theatre and the pyramid form different kinds of arenas, such as places for sporting events or game shows.

In this environment, communication takes the form of performance. The audience in a theatre environment asks: Will you make me care? The ultimate concern in a theatre environment is to satisfy this request and hold attention. The hero, regardless of the amount of "strutting and fretting," asks a corresponding question: Did I make you care?

A group of French officers spent the last part of World War II in a German concentration camp. As military prisoners of war, this group underwent hard labour at the command of their prison keepers. They assembled each morning and marched away from the barracks, performed different tasks under the scrutiny of the Nazi camp administrators, and returned late to the barracks. A stray dog happened to appear outside the fence by the barracks at one point. For a brief period of days, this dog greeted the prisoners each morning as if it cared about them. It would bark and move about in attempts to engage the attention of the prisoners. In the evenings, the dog would appear again as the prisoners returned to the barracks, like a welcome home if the environment had only been more domestic. The troop gave the dog a name—Bobby.[38]

One of the prisoners was a Ukrainian-Lithuanian Jew who had studied in Germany. He came to live in France before the war. He worked as an academic and teacher and signed up to fight with the French army. After the war, he published a number of books and articles but rarely referred directly to his experiences in the concentration camp. He did recall Bobby in one of his essays. He struggled to come to an understanding about the differences between this dog and the Nazis. How was it that a dog, with the somewhat limited canine awareness, could so easily recognize the existence and presence of the prisoners as living beings, *human* beings, while the Germans at the camp could not?

Emmanuel Levinas's status as a military prisoner of war ended up meaning his survival. Orders in the camp were to kill Jewish civilians but not military personnel. The uniform was like a costume for a role that gave him an identity in this very different, absurd theatre. He spent the rest of his life aware of how a combination of mere circumstances had saved his life, and how his individual wartime suffering, bad as it was, had turned out so small compared to the tragedy of the Holocaust. Theodicy is the attempt to answer why an all-good god permits evil. For Levinas, the experiences of World War II and the Holocaust put an end to theodicy.

After the war, Levinas took up a challenge of revising Western thought from its base assumptions. Socrates started many of his investigations with a question: "What is…?" The West has made "what" and "being" the central questions of inquiry. But this approach implies that the audience goes to a theatre to see the props and not the sequence of events that occur between characters. Meaning, for an audience, does not come from the matter taking up space on the stage, but from what is expressed as important by the actions and characters that make up the story.

Levinas went back to that question from Socrates. He wondered about the nature of questioning itself. If a speaker like Socrates asks a question, would that not mean some other was present, or at least called to answer? A question is like a call, but only a call before a response. Before dialogue, before dialectics, before determining what constitutes "this" or "that," there is already a relationship to an unknown that is beyond our ego. Levinas suggested this relationship, or call to the other, is even more primary than the discrimination of material objects that surround us. We cannot even recognize those objects until we call to that which is beyond us. Even a question asked of oneself is articulated outward, sent out as a request to some other part of one's self, asking if it will give the question consideration, attention, response.

Levinas laid one main criticism at the feet of Western philosophy, something few in the tradition seemed to understand and to which fewer have responded. Many theories from the West are attempts to totalize—attempts to reduce matters to some prime assertion or belief and then press this identity onto *all* matter. In the tradition, there is a strong desire for reduction: inscribing a circle around a subject, putting a container around a mystery, or constructing a wall around a garden. For Levinas, if Western philosophy was based on attempts to understand *being*, it would be incapable of talking about transcendence after formulating or articulating a totality.

Levinas thought of the Western tradition as a "philosophy of the same." What is the same throughout? This approach is extremely powerful in terms of seeking and understanding patterns. However, concentrating on what stays the same can make us blind to the existence of the things that don't confirm the expectation. Whatever is not the "same" is put into a category practically similar to what is "not."

Totalization found its own horizon in the materialism, determinism, and absurdity of today's post-mythological perspectives. The materialism of the West transforms our planet from a home in which to dwell into mere raw material awaiting organization and consumption into the same. Levinas suggested the thinking subject is transformed in moments face to face with the other—the unidentified, not-yet-fully-mapped guest to our consciousness. According to Levinas, Western philosophy prefers to totalize rather than address what's outside the horizon of a theory. It does not sit down and share a meal between ideologies of different premises, like host and guest. A dialectic is a confrontation within an already walled arena, for example, contained but not in dialogue with what is outside the arena itself. Illustrations of this can be seen in the modern and postmodern economic experiments with panopticons and pyramids.

And yet, after the concentration camps, after the devastation of the atomic bombs on Hiroshima and Nagasaki, after more than two wars that threatened civilization as we know it, technology in the West retrieved an old addiction—theatres, performances, and displays. The coliseums of Rome and the open-air theatres of Greece now govern the physical and mental architectures of the West again. Some might say the Greeks gave birth to Western philosophy to dethrone opinion, to challenge the constant threat of tyrannical totalizing.[39] A displaced Jewish academic and survivor of the twentieth-century concentration camps reminded the West of this challenge.

In 1945, a Jesuit priest from Quebec offered a university course entitled "Thought and Reality" to his students. Bernard Lonergan wanted to articulate what he saw as a generalized empirical method.[40] This method is a map of the architecture of human inquiry. The course led to a book, *Insight: A Study of Human Understanding*. Lonergan's book is another response to the problem that worried Levinas. For Lonergan, an insight could be thought of as a discovery of something not the same. Insights come to us as part of the process of inquiry and from the tension we feel when faced with a problem. And often enough, insights come with a feeling of joy and discovery and interest.

The spirit of inquiry, especially for creatures as curious as human beings, is the opportunity and desire to transcend the present limitations of what we know. A lot of energy and attention in the history of philosophy was spent on concepts, according to Lonergan, without giving insight much of a role in the process. Insights can be understood as the pivots between concrete experiences and abstract judgments, the flashes of understanding where perceptions change. A pattern seems to emerge from the sensory information, suggesting a coherence or correspondence toward something more.

Lonergan believed the goal and process of this generalized empirical method was "self-appropriation." Self-appropriation involves individuals identifying themselves as inquirers, not concept-holders, and taking up the self-correcting and self-expanding journey of learning. Appropriation is the process of making something one's own. This means paying attention as the self observes something in the background become foreground, or when things in the foreground become background.

The person who identifies first as an inquirer pays attention in the moment of an experience. In order to develop knowledge from the encounter, the next step is to find an understanding of what is happening through that attention. Questions come to mind and call out to the horizon of our understanding, looking for the responding information that arranges data into an intelligible pattern. Next comes a kind of judging, deciding if the self-as-inquirer has correctly understood the experience of attention. Facts are not mere sensory experiences, after all, and need some verifiability to be considered true or real. The fourth step involves valuing, as in acting on the judgments that came from understanding the attention given to the experience. Each step is an opportunity to transcend the one before, as well as transcend the limiting or totalizing of past knowing.

Lonergan expressed the steps as invitations on how to perform or act in any moment of living:

> Be attentive in experience
> Be intelligent in understanding
> Be reasonable in judgment
> Be responsible in decisions[41]

The result of this repeating process, for Lonergan, is an inquiring self, with an authenticity that better prepares the self for further investigations and experiences. The self is in love with the form of being that has been appropriated, in love with the questions that arise, and in love with the act of asking questions with the observed.

What is the lesson we can take from Lonergan and Levinas? Engagement with the other, and with inquiry, gives us opportunities to embrace and release Western thought, appreciating but also transcending our past performances.

The theatre is a very old environment, and it could be argued that its foundations are in biology. Beings, as thinking subjects, present themselves to their audiences. This can be seen in the mating dances of animals, the coats of birds, reptiles, and mammals. Living things developed intricate displays of fitness, readiness, and desire, all in the pursuit of the other, the intended, the beloved. Body language reminds us daily, if we are conscious of it, that we inhabit a theatre as much as a pyramid or panopticon or some other environment.

We can see the power of this different authority in the time we spend in front of screens, as the audience for those others who perform for our attention. We now worship novelty, new information, new stimulation. These things grab our attention, but may not invite us to be intelligent, reasonable, or responsible. We have unconsciously dismissed any fear of this new god. If novelty compels our behaviour, we must understand its terrible and great aspects, if only to know ourselves appropriately. If the West were to learn anything from the horrors of World War II, should it not be the value of measuring our motivations, compulsions, our precious and ultimate gods with both fear and doubt?

Levinas wanted to dislodge the unique, authoritative position of "the same" in our thinking, and this can come from a transcendental push or pull. Lonergan wanted to give his students a method of engaging in the process of self-appropriation. If the what of reality involves me and what is beyond me, then personal perceiving places cannot be reduced to just one type of environment. The ground model involves a pluralism, a relation between the same and the other—what we give attention and what we do not.

When Levinas wrote of Bobby the dog and his time in the concentration camp, his thoughts took him to biblical passages that reference dogs. He referred to a quotation from Exodus about knowing the difference between Egypt and Israel.[42] Israelites escaped the rule of the pharaohs and pyramids. However, they may have brought something of Egyptian culture with them in that escape. The Jewish tradition developed a culture that wrestled with dignity for individuals and justice within a community, and how the two could dethrone each other. They created a society and mythology where prophets could both contest and advise kings without initiating revolt or usurping the dignity of those kings. The stories of the Biblical prophets portray human dignity equal in importance to the pursuit of justice before the law. Even dogs can attest to the role of the other and the wisdom of recognizing the other, according to Levinas. Levinas and Lonergan suggest that transcendence can appeal to the mysterious without appealing to the supernatural. Transcendence might be thought of as a spontaneous responsibility for another being, experienced in moments of change and recognition and inquiry.

Levinas searched for the better names of places and things in his ideas, almost as though he worked his thoughts through Lonergan's invitations to be attentive, intelligent, reasonable, and responsible. To the inquiring mind, the world is a place of invitations, a place offering sensations even before establishing objective reductions. The world is a place of enjoying experiences as much as a place to put possessions and property. We see objects as tools or obstacles, but Levinas maintained that we live from these things as "nourishments,"[43] potential parts of ourselves that we can celebrate and take in before we even perceive discrete objects. A baby feeds from a mother's breast without differentiating between world, mother, milk, and mouth. We take what is other and make it become a part of ourselves. This is an environment like a theatre. Something makes itself present before an audience, nourishing the soul and senses with meaning. Before consciously articulating what it does, we feel how it fills our selves or gives shape to our identities. Unlike the contents of ideas, sensations are discovered or revealed as though by a curtain drawing back, given in performance and presentation, not invented in the viewer's abstractions or evaluations.

In the theatre of attention, a court of law can look like a place to repair wrongs, a place to impose fairness or a place to implement the interests of those in power, depending on interpretation and point of view. Today, the court of law may appear more like a pyramid due to the back and forth of dialectical competition. It may appear like a panopticon due to the framed, institutional, homogeneous processing of cases.

Levinas used something else, however, to illustrate justice between the same and the other. The family and the home, institutions common to all of humanity, drew the attention of Levinas as informed models of justice.[44] This is not the same as a model from state-administered court systems. Justice in a family involves a different kind of sharing of responsibility when compared to the justice of the state. Each member of a family shares and shapes the identities of the other members, in love with some ideal abstracted out from the family as much as in love with the actual family members. Rights of belonging and responsibilities of service co-exist in shared roles and shared spaces. When a guest appears, the idea of rights of belonging and responsibilities of service take a different shape but inhabit both guest and host family alike. Like many world traditions, the Jewish tradition involves stories based on the meeting of a host and guest.

In the environment of the theatre, the hero grants the audience a level of exceptional authority, perhaps more than is due. If the individual is divine and must bear the role of hero in his or her own life, then it is the individual who decides what ultimately compels or rules. But in the theatre, that decision is made by the audience's reactions. All the preparation, production, and conscious coordination is done to stir the audience to action, to celebrate and advocate for the ideas expressed, or to identify with the story presented. When we care, we show our compassion, our solidarity, our choice of sides. The reward of the work comes when the reflective self, family, or community, says, "That's me! That's what I want to identity with!" and rises to celebrate or act on that moment of identification. The audience holds a kind of authority for good and for evil.

Marshall McLuhan coined the term "global village."[45] William Shakespeare's plays were performed in the Globe Theatre. When we think of the importance of entertainment in our lifestyles, it shouldn't be much of a surprise to find a theatre in the centre of today's figurative village the central concern of our attention. With the amount of text, video, and audio information captured and shared with digital devices, the boundary separating the stage and the audience is incredibly thin. We carry the theatre with us as we participate through media platforms and gaze ever more enraptured into today's intimate screens.

In *The Empathic Civilization*, Jeremy Rifkin categorized different forms of consciousness in history according to energy consumption and communications technologies. According to Rifkin, we have entered an era of what he calls "dramaturgical consciousness." We are expected to play different roles, but we are prepared to do so:

> Role-playing is no longer just some therapeutic technique (or something done by the comic book costumed geek) but, rather, a form of consciousness for Generation X and the Millennial Generation.[46]

We are wired to experience another's plight as if we are experiencing it ourselves, even in cases where the plight is a fiction. But just as important is the way in which we identity the other.

Mammals have been around for about a hundred million years. Compared to reptiles, the care of infant mammals involves much more attention from parents. If we apply Langer's thoughts on architecture to evolution, we could speculate that human beings have adapted to perceiving places unique in terms of relationships between parent and child. Christopher Boehm suggested that a thousand generations could be a sufficient span of time to influence the established nature of a species.[47] Over the course of our development, the human nervous system appears to have adapted to the mother-infant relationship as well. The other is just as important to our survival as the self.

Human infants are particularly vulnerable. Attending to that vulnerability creates vulnerabilities for parents. Breastfeeding is an important activity shared between mammal mothers and babies. But as every parent knows, infants need constant care through day and night. The expression of distress from a baby in the first year of life is compelling stimulus for a parent. It hardly matters if the infant is in peril or not. The parent *must* respond, as though compelled. The parent must also be extraordinarily sensitive to the environment. The emotional demands can be high. How could such a relationship not influence adaptations over time to support the most useful behaviours and attitudes a parent would need toward a child? The parent's very survival depends on it. The survival of a human community depends on the success of that relationship.

When, however, a baby does not receive attention, it takes that as a sign of danger. The stress system is activated. Normal development includes ups and downs as stress systems activate and then deactivate. In an environment empty of attention from an other like a parent, the stress systems can remain on, slowing or stopping the connections between neurons that occur with the ups and downs of normal development. Lack of attention and interaction means that a child does not receive the stimulation required to develop some of the most basic architecture of the nervous system. A child exposed to very mild inattentiveness may develop self-soothing skills and initiate independent exploratory behaviour. Chronic or severe neglect—witnessed in both family homes and in institutional care organizations—takes children to a place they are not biologically prepared for.

The brain goes through a rapid growth spurt in the first three years outside the womb. But that growth depends on calls and responses from the environment. Smiles and praise reward the child. This drives the child to rapidly build synaptic power in the brain for repeat rewards and increased skill development.

Children raised in orphanages have been known to have higher death rates than children raised in family environments. In the 1940s, a psychiatrist named René Spitz wanted to know why even sterile environments like hospital-run orphanages could cause such problems for the health of children. Spitz was a student of Freud. Freud placed much of his attention on the study of adults, but Spitz wanted to know more about the development of infants.

He conducted a study of children in two different environments—one group in isolated hospital cribs, and one group raised by their mothers in prisons. As many as 37 per cent of infants in the hospital cribs died. None of the children in the prison died.[48]

The general practice in the hospital orphanage was to remain distant from the children. Nurses were discouraged from picking up the children or playing with them. Spitz catalogued and filmed cases of infants, babies, and toddlers with very slow development in their bodies, language abilities, and motor skills. To solve the problem, hospitals started a new practice based on Spitz's findings: hold the child. The child's life depended on it.

Prisons, supervised housing services, and assisted-living institutions are panoptic environments used as substitutes for the more familiar environment of the parent and child. Decades of study have shown that institutional, panoptic alternatives create listless, lethargic babies who grow up to be individuals unable to easily build meaningful bonds with others. Children raised in institutions were ten times more likely to end up victims of trafficking, prostitution, and crime than peers raised in family environments.[49] For all the limitations and faults of families, we are better adapted to live and grow in that dramatic environment rather than in the most well-meaning panoptic one.

The widow, the orphan, and the stranger are all examples of the other used by Levinas.[50] Each one is identified by the lack of something—a spouse, a parent, or a home. Each one is practically defined by an absence. Interestingly, each of these others also presents a potential burden to a community as well as an opportunity for benefit. Religious traditions and secular stories often use each of these as symbolic types, characters that the community has an ethical responsibility toward. The widow or widower can be a spouse or a caretaker. The orphan can be adopted and loved. The stranger can become a guest, a neighbour, or even a family member. But each one can also, potentially, generate danger and distress.

Marriage rituals do not merely involve two people getting married. Even civil ceremonies require witnesses. Traditional and modern weddings alike often include a celebration afterwards, with food, drink, music, and dancing. A marriage is more than joining two people in identity and commitment. Ideally, an entire society surrounds and supports the union in order to help that couple live happily ever after. A marriage is the union between the individual and the other, a declaration that each individual is now giving equal presence and consideration in their identity to their chosen other. In the hatching, matching, and dispatching of religious rituals, wedding ceremonies reflect, nearly perfectly, the story structure of what Frye noted as a "happy ending comedy."[51] Life becomes art in the story of the two people sharing an identity. The ceremony brings together an audience larger than the couple itself to uplift that artistic endeavour. And the audience gives its consent, its gifts, and its well wishes. The ending, happily ever after, is just a beginning, the other side of a threshold, a transition in identities.

When Malidoma Patrice Somé was young, he learned from his grandfather a story about the name Malidoma. The grandfather had given it to him before he was born. It means "He who is to make friends with the stranger."[52] In the Dagara language, the word "stranger" and the word "enemy" are similar. And yet to be a friend to the stranger, the one without a home, is to act as host honouring a guest. This kind of relationship can be difficult because it means creating a temporary home for a potential enemy. In letting the stranger identify himself, we show respect for the very being that is not the same as us. The theatre experience is very much like this because any environment that presents and exposes something new or other invites both anxiety and hope.

When Somé went to the United States, he was surprised by the funerals. From his upbringing, Somé believed the living must feel and express sincere grief to free the dead. The expression of grief has power and as such comes with responsibility. It not only heals the hurt of loss in loved ones, but it also gives the dead power to leave this world and reach the next, the place of one's ancestors. The dead change homes, and are temporarily strangers without a home, without the power to move on to their next perceiving place. In Somé's words, "Tears carry the dead home."[53] Tears are not just a physiological reaction but an embodied communication of identity.

But when he came to the West, Somé could not understand how people could be so inexpressive. People appeared to pride themselves for showing no emotions at the loss of significant others. A community of people who cannot, or will not, shed tears together is like a time bomb, dangerous to themselves and to the world. In his home village, Somé witnessed expressions of grief every day. It was a constant reminder of how life was preparation for death, rather than a long stretch of avoiding death. But every expression is a kind of performance, an attempt to best communicate the truth of the individual performer. A performance that is given without full effort, one that is stifled and expressed with half a heart, can be inauthentic to an audience. The performance is not compelling because it is not a true reflection.

The Dagara funeral ritual involves musicians, mourners, a group to contain the mourners, and the assembled community. The entire event may take two or three days. A priest makes a circle of white ash around the house of the deceased. The musicians and singers improvise, but their task is to recreate in song the history of the family up to the death. The singers might chant and repeat important moments to guide the emotions of the mourners and community. The deceased is seated in ceremonial cloths a short distance apart from the others, as observer of the event. Elderly women may sit on either side of the deceased. Family and friends, in step with the rhythm of the music, express their grief and spiritually heap the power of that grief on the deceased.

The theatre can be a place of participation and not just passive observation. One of the problems of the twentieth century might be the development of the passive theatre environment over almost all aspects of participatory culture. In the West, material objects are passively consumed, metaphorical meanings passively received. The silent audience watches the performance, invested but not involved.

In the 1890s, the Lumière brothers set up a theatre in Paris for a short film, *L'Arrivée d'un Train en Gare de La Ciotat (Arrival of a Train at La Ciotat Station)*.[54] The Lumière brothers had screened similar short films before. Moving images were still a novelty at the time and socialites came to the theatre to take in the new experience. The film was about fifty seconds in length, shot from one vantage point on black and white. It showed people waiting on a train station's platform. The tracks created a perspective of depth in the film. When the train approached, its image became larger and larger. According to legend, people in the audience were moved, literally. Some accounts suggest the projected images created such a panic that people got up out of their seats and moved out of the way of the oncoming train. As with many stories, exaggeration blooms over time. Still, the story does say something about how desensitized we have become to projected information. The theatre has trained us well to not react to stimulation. It is as though we are numb to novelty. If all the world has become a stage, it seems like the audience members have come to believe that all the world performs for their attention.

In this environment, the authority granted to an audience over the hero, over what is known, and even over what is unknown, could be misplaced and dangerous. The theatre environment promotes a too-easy comfort: we can arrange our newsfeeds, our movie libraries, our music playlists, our social groups; making sure that we are not confronted with anything that challenges our assumptions. We end up confirming only what we know, seldom changing our minds. As a result, we lose the skills that must accompany any tools of inquiry.

Just as the hero has a twin—the villain—the benevolent, supportive audience has a malevolent or destructive twin as well. If we do not understand the *plural* nature of gods and motivations, we cannot be sensitive to what is worthy of our attention and worship.

The Agora (Marketplace)—Nietzsche and Trade

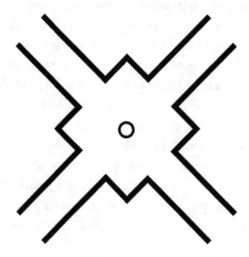

Philosopher Friedrich Nietzsche's madman did not run to a theatre to proclaim his announcement. He did not climb the steps of a corporate bank. Nor did he run to a high-walled church. In his desperation to communicate with people, Nietzsche's madman lit a lantern in the bright morning hours and ran to the marketplace.

"I seek God! I seek God!"

As many of those who did not believe in God were standing around just then, he provoked much laughter. "Has he got lost?" asked one. "Did he lose his way like a child?" asked another. "Or is he hiding? Is he afraid of us? Has he gone on a voyage? emigrated?" Thus they yelled and laughed.

The madman jumped into their midst and pierced them with his eyes. "Whither is God?" he cried; "I will tell you. We have killed him—you and I. All of us are his murderers. But how did we do this? How could we drink up the sea? Who gave us the sponge to wipe away the entire horizon? What were we doing when we unchained this earth from its sun? Whither is it moving now? Whither are we moving? Away from all suns? Are we not plunging continually? Backward, sideward, forward, in all directions?

"Is there still any up or down? Are we not straying, as through an infinite nothing? Do we not feel the breath of empty space? Has it not become colder? Is not night continually closing in on us? Do we not need to light lanterns in the morning? Do we hear nothing as yet of the noise of the gravediggers who are burying God? Do we smell nothing as yet of the divine decomposition? Gods, too, decompose. God is dead. God remains dead. And we have killed him."[55]

Derrida deconstructed as though in some playful, competitive arena of the text, but Nietzsche disarticulated and then decomposed. Though he was a forceful critic of Christianity, Nietzsche recognized that Europe and the West had shared a morality because one institution regulated and influenced people's perspectives and motivations. The cultural shift away from this shared morality would have consequences. His madman did not simply accept the demise of God and set up shop in the marketplace beside his neighbours to make a profit out of the proverbial blood in the streets he saw coming. Instead, he tried, perhaps in vain, to start a conversation. He took his message to the streets and implored people to engage in the crisis he predicted. Like Socrates at the crossroads by the marketplace, the madman confronted people about the things they did not consider worthy of their attention. In the agora, conversation is not some idle way to pass the time. It is reflection and preparation, bringing all the past to bear on the present in order to be ready for how things may be different in the future.

For the committed student of Darwin, nature holds an almost mystical and consuming authority, and for good reason. Is nature reality, or something more? How do we understand nature in today's constructed and technologically biased landscapes? In its undifferentiated, all-consuming, all-nourishing, hard-to-totally-conceptualize presence, nature is that which *selects*.

Despite all our human efforts, it is nature, the mass of the known and vast unknown together as one, and not the individual will of human pursuits, that ultimately selects. Nature is not one of our own constructs, but the source of our emergence. Even iconic institutions perish, as Nietzsche suggested. To prove our worth, we climb pyramids, build panopticons, and perform in theatres. However, nature plays the final measure, resolving all the unforeseen effects, ignored externalities, and silent evidence.

The ultimate concern in such an environment is selection—survival, growth, establishing a niche, finding a balance with the environment, and reproducing to serve life. But the realization of such a concern is not under our complete control. This is, after all, the environment of the all, the unknown and known intermixed asymmetrically. No human conceptualization or institution or theory or work of art can fully stand as a reflection of all nature. But we have created places where mixtures of motivations thrive in the presence of one another. The agora—an open public space where we meet the other, where an other meets another—can stand for a place of trade, for a station at the beginning of a journey, and for a place of conversation.

Though some may think of the agora as a marketplace, the laws and motivations of commerce don't hold final authority. In ancient Athenian culture, the markets did not dictate the regulation of all values in the society. The agora was an open place for assembly as much as a place of commerce. It was a place to muster arms and launch a march. It was a crossroads for travellers. It was a space of political discourse and rhetoric as much as an arrangement of important buildings. The market economy was but one tool among many used to build the identity of Athenians and their agora.

Hurricane Katrina did more than shut down businesses in New Orleans. It changed the geography and the community. Hillary Guttman ran a shop called the Laurel Street Bakery. In the weeks that followed the flooding, there were practically no places to get groceries. Safe drinking water was an ultimate concern, much more important than regulated or monetized economic exchanges. Six weeks after the storm, she opened her doors once again while still waiting for electricity to be restored. She was able to get supplies from Baton Rouge, eighty miles away. At that time, it wasn't just the locals who came to her bakery. "Just the National Guard alone could have kept me open," Guttman said in an interview.[56] In that situation, a bakery became a community centre, not just for residents but for aid workers and military personnel as well.

Ten years after the event, the commercial corridors of New Orleans such as Magazine Street, Bayou Road, and Desoto Street were not heavy with franchise outlets or chain restaurants. Despite being a poor investment for big brand stores, the city of New Orleans had to address concerns that were simply more important than the corporate bottom line. According to Roberta Brandes Gratz, author of *We're Still Here Ya Bastards: How the People of New Orleans Rebuilt Their City*, it wasn't the oversight of officials and authoritative planning that made the difference. The storm may have caused the destruction, but the government policies promoting disaster capitalism helped turn the crisis into a greater tragedy.[57] According to *USA Today*, in 2009, four years after Katrina and Rita hit the Gulf Coast, two-thirds of the federal aid, $3.9 billion, remained not spent on relief and reconstruction projects. The problem wasn't just the pace of the bureaucratic process. FEMA, the Federal Emergency Management Agency, and officials involved, seemed to have no real assurance of how the money was going to be spent responsibly.

For many in New Orleans, it must have felt like things were going backward, sideward, forward, up, down, and in all directions. When the panoptic institutions of governments fail, when the competitive pyramids of business don't fix problems, when theatrical performances remedy nothing, community becomes the ultimate value. People work alongside each other as in the agora, to revive the order and relationships of the community.

What did help to rebuild New Orleans turned out to be people in the public spaces working together. Vera Warren-Williams owned a bookstore and hair salon. After Katrina, her businesses shared a phone line and a copy machine with a daycare centre and a restaurant. The business owners even shared labour, working for one another as the need arose.[58] This wasn't work done in a market society, but the work of a community where market economics was one tool in the box of resources.

In a video interview, Jordan Peterson used the events that led up to the devastation of Hurricane Katrina as an illustration in perspective:

Power corrupts. So, you make your kingdom. You make your empire and it's serving its proper purpose, but you let it get corrupt. Things are going to fall apart. I can give an example of that.

What caused the flooding in New Orleans? Hurricane? No. No. Corruption.

If the dikes would have been built properly, as everyone knew they should have been built, if all those millions of dollars hadn't gone into the pockets of corrupt politicians, there wouldn't have been any flood. In Holland they build the dikes for the worst storm in ten thousand years. In New Orleans they built them for the worst storm in a hundred years. Well, everyone knew that was insufficient. Why didn't they do something about it?

If you get corrupt enough God will send a flood, like it's an old story. The question is, "Who is God?"

Well, I would say that the ancient Israelites never said who God was. They just said look the hell out for him. You deviate from the path, man, you're going to get flattened.[59]

Before Katrina, Louisiana had no statewide building code of standards, but only local area guidelines. This created a loose system of practices, not just for contractors and insurers, but for members of government as well. A standard is different from an authority. Where an authority declares, a standard can be measured against. Where an authority holds a position, a standard creates a responsibility and goal, with the opportunity to review practices for fitness and for corruption. Louisiana Governor Kathleen Blanco, the state business community, government groups, building inspectors, trades professionals and municipal mayors came together to develop a statewide building code. More than a hundred special interest groups, all with their own motivations, worked together on the project. Lawmakers acted in unison, and the building code passed unanimously.[60] Regulating and maintaining the building code brought its own challenges, such as staffing, training, and inspection practices.

This kind of community action is reminiscent of the ancient Greek contract that came after Athena's judgment of Orestes. Everyone involved came together to find a way in which the environment, law, community, and individuals could all begin again.

In the agora, communication takes the form of a conversation, an exchange between one person and another. Connections share content; all four archetypal characters or motivations—the action, the known, the unknown, and the observed—share authority. The ultimate concern in the agora is not framed by competition, dominance, or attention, though of course they play their parts. The conversation in the agora is an exchange between people, a trade of ideas with a mix of all conceivable motivations. In the end, what is selected is what works, the trade or exchange that turns out to be worth repeating.

What comes from a conversation with the unknown? The story of New Orleans involved a devastating storm. The Biblical story of Job involved a reckoning with a whirlwind. Camille Paglia wanted to start a conversation about the limited roles of young women. She was tired of women having only two choices of identity—virgin or whore. Both these identities can be considered economic. The identity is defined by a commodity—catalogued, prized, bought, or sold. Paglia proposed two other symbolic identities young women could choose from. As the title of her book suggests, women can also be *Vamps and Tramps*. Women can be defined by something other than the market, including, perhaps, their own personal whirlwinds within. Paglia wrote:

> The street is nature, the open savanna with its long sightlines and the raw, exuberant energies of hunt and pursuit. Communication is African call-and-response, loud because it must cover great distances.[61]

James Gleick examined the use of African drums in his book *The Information*. European travellers were amazed at how the hunter-gatherer tribes could communicate over long distances with the simple beat of a drum. Long before the Western technologies like the telegraph, Africans had mastered the art of long-distance calling. The secret turned out to be a special characteristic of African languages not shared by the Europeans. In many European languages, a rise or fall in pitch may affect the nuance, but it rarely changed the meaning of words.

In some parts of Africa, pitch could make the difference between talking about a bird or someone's father. Drums that mimicked the pitch intervals allowed the Africans to beat out full sentences. Gleick explained how one group could invite another across the plains to dinner.[62] The drum was an extension of language, a medium that fostered a socially vibrant continental village long before electronic media imposed a global village.

In the story of Job, friends of the unfortunate man sat down with him after he had lost his herds, his family, and his health. In typical friendly fashion, they offered him comforts while seeking to help find some rational account of his disaster. They argued with him. They told him what he should have done, and they gave him attention in his lowest moments.[63] Job's friends could have learned something from the small business owners in New Orleans. Rationalizing, quibbling, and competing for attention didn't put Job back on his feet. Job's despair was tragic because he and his friends looked at the situation as something needing rationalizing. They sat among the ashes of his burned-out estate and talked as though it were just a place to meet. It could have been a place to change their minds. By the end of the book, however, it no longer is just a meeting place but, in fact, a crossroads for the character. The ashes marked the spot where Job took the first steps in his next journey.

To be able to see this shift in setting, Job had to shake off the assumptions, framed at the beginning of the story, about his own identity as well as the identity of his god and his reality. What appeared at these crossroads, ultimately, was a whirlwind. And what can Job do in that moment other than hold a conversation with the whirlwind? He traded words with the whirlwind but did not receive the comforts or rationalizations he was expecting. Mysteries remain, even after words. Yet something in the exchange gave Job the hope and presence of mind to take his next steps.

Marshall McLuhan found himself confronted with similar conversations when he talked about the coming storm of novelty and stimulation from electric media. We have a much more intimate relationship with the sea of overwhelming information today with the internet. That relationship may swallow us whole, like a leviathan or a maelstrom consuming a ship caught in a storm. McLuhan suggested that we turn and look right into the whirlpool of information to find what it tells us—engage the conversation. Voluntary confrontation and conversation with the unknown may require courage, but that is often exactly what is needed for survival and growth. When memory no longer serves, when knowledge and guidance come up blank, the individual as inquirer must ask for further information in order to participate and ultimately prepare for further selection.

To examine economics in a new light, Jeremy Rifkin looked to the world of nature and the world of Darwin. Nature might have developed competition, dominance, and attention, but the kernel of any living thing's relationship with nature suggests a kind of trade economy with something much larger and more powerful. Before any social hierarchy was ever established between living things, an elemental relationship of trade began, even if the form of that exchange involved changing plant material into stored energy. Without that trade, that chemical transition of materials and spaces, nothing else really works. We can have a similar relationship with nature now. If we adjust our view of dominating nature with our economic system, and instead chart a new partnership between our motivations and our environments, there would be places for competition, dominion, attention, and fair selection. We can create an agora with even the most predatory or dangerous elements of the natural world, just as we must come to terms with the predatory motivations within ourselves.

In India's state of Gujurat, prides of lions live close to human villages. Livestock is preyed upon from time to time. Transportation along roadways and fields can be interrupted by lions passing. But the solution wasn't to hunt and destroy them. Instead, a kind of trade is kept up because the lions also have a role to play in regulating the environment. The wild world bumps up against domesticated agriculture, creating a strange mix of relationships and opportunities for selection.[64]

This does not create a "safe space"—a controlled environment dominated by rules where freedom is sacrificed for comfort. The people of Gujurat have what can only be an unwritten agreement with the lions. And that exchange can easily be strained and tested with each loss of cattle or with one attack on a person. But for all its shortcomings, the code satisfies more than just human motivations and assumptions. The agora is an open space, potentially an interface with the leviathan and behemoth. It creates a metaphorical holy place, a perceiving place, where the rules of commerce pale in the sight of a lion's stride and a villager's relationship with the wilderness.

Socrates was known in Athens for walking in the marketplace and engaging people with questions. According to Plato, his teacher sought out exchanges of words more than exchanges of goods or services. Socrates practised his trade in public spaces. Hecate, the daughter of Titans in Greek mythology, was considered a goddess of crossroads. Often, she was depicted as holding torches or as having three heads, overseeing the traffic at intersections. Socrates would go down to Hecate's crossroads and intersections to involve himself in conversation. He challenged people in power like an advocate or apostle, but his aim was not to win political power. Like Elijah in the Bible, Socrates wanted to hold leaders accountable to something other than the pyramids, panopticons, and theatres they kept constructing in their thoughts.

The death of Socrates is a cautionary tale about the consequences of challenging people's consciousness. The Athenian government found him guilty of corrupting the youth. However, his death was like the last stroke of a brush on a piece of art. People today study Socrates more than they study the assembly of men who judged him.

The agora does not elicit happy endings to every story or dole out justice in equal measure. This might be one reason why some people's apprehensions can rise at the thought of negotiations. Whether in a parked car at the side of a Gujurat road waiting for lions to pass, or in a bank office waiting for approval of a mortgage, trade means both parties experience opportunity and danger.

The danger in the agora is real, in the sense that it is important enough to be an ultimate concern. Chance may hold more authority in environments like the agora than we feel is fair. As a result, we have built many other types of environments and relationships to manage the risk. Still, the risk is real, and it doesn't simply go away. The other and the unknown will always carry their own kinds of authority over us in different environments, but the agora waits for those of us willing to step up and take part in the conversation.

Matthew Crawford used a similar trade-and-exchange illustration in *The World Beyond Your Head*:

> Consider the case of a motorcycle mechanic. In handing a labor bill to a customer, I make a claim for the value of what I have done, and put it to him in the most direct way possible....
>
> Here, in a microeconomic exchange, lies the kernel of ethics altogether, perhaps. In presenting the labor bill, I am owning my actions. I am standing behind them retrospectively. And this requires making my actions intelligible to the customer.... It is the confrontation between the self and the world beyond one's head that one acquires a sharpened picture of each, under the sign of responsibility.[65]

The agora presents us with a challenge and invitation. It is a chance to stand and test not only our assumptions but our competence and merit. It gives us a chance to become conscious of and realize what we are responsible for when the stakes become real. Nassim Taleb, a writer and critic of economic policy, proposed a number of financial solutions in his books after the economic collapse of 2008. He believed that too often high-stakes bankers and investment leaders gambled with other people's livelihoods instead of their own. He used a phrase to suggest a better approach to future financial regulation—make it so that those taking the risks have their own "skin in the game."[66] How would they manage things if the risk turned out to cause them their own demise, metaphorically, financially, physically, or otherwise? Like Agamemnon and Jephthah, many of us would rather sacrifice daughters than sacrifice confidence or advantage. If we can learn something from the Dagara in Africa, we might see initiation into environments like the marketplace as taking ownership of responsibilities. Putting ourselves at risk is one game. Sacrificing someone else is another.

Many cultures have rituals for boys coming of age. In many traditions, men would wear masks. The masks took on important significance. One tribe caught Joseph Campbell's attention. The boys in this tribe had been brought up to fear the masks, which represented the powers that structured society. The boys would suffer a dramatic experience; they were taken out of the known world and forced to fight one of the masks. The man behind the mask would let the boy win, only to put the mask on the child. The boy would transcend his childhood and with the mask represent the metaphor that structured society. The best response to the call of the unknown—the response with the best chance of selection and survival, according to that tribe—was confrontation. Facing up to the thing feared is better than cowering.

In the modern world, confrontation has become more verbal. And yet, initiation in any form, even into the unknown, begins with an exchange of communication. Communication can involve body language, artful expression, or even acts of force. The form of communication ultimately shapes much of the exchange. The agora between two people, or two places, is an opportunity for conversation. The meeting between a stranger and a host is a meeting between two unknowns. But if the stranger is potentially a symbol or gateway to all that is unknown, potentially evil and good, how can these two meet?

In the past, the solution was often obligatory rituals, where the stranger was accepted as a welcomed and invited guest. The guest was offered food, shelter, and respect. The host treated the guest as though the guest were *selected* for survival instead of preyed upon. Guests had similar obligations, such as graciously respecting the gifts given, and proving themselves worthy of selection by not disturbing the host's order, grace, or attention. The hope was that everyone could participate in good conversation and community.

Echoes of this kind of ritual behaviour can be seen still today. Tickld.com created a video for social media about how a mother initiated her children into the Santa ritual of Christmas giving. Though the action taken up by the boys in the stories may be quite different, a comparison of Campbell's story of the initiation ritual and the mother's story below is striking. The mother initiates each member into the spirit of Christmas by having the child who is ready for it become Santa Claus. That is, they buy and secretly deliver a gift to an unsuspecting individual.

> We have the child choose someone they know—a neighbour, usually. The child's mission is to secretly, deviously, find out something that the person needs, and then provide it, wrap it, deliver it, and never reveal to the target where it came from. Being a Santa isn't about getting credit, you see. It's unselfish giving.
>
> My oldest chose the "witch lady" on the corner. She really was horrible — had a fence around the house and would never let the kids go in an[d] get a stray ball o[r] Frisbee. She'd yell at them to play quieter, etc.—a real pill. He noticed when we drove to school that she came out every morning to get [the] paper in bare feet, so he decided she needed slippers. So then he had to go spy and decide how big her feet were. He hid in the bushes one Saturday, and decided she was a medium. We went to Kmart and bought warm slippers. He wrapped them up, and tagged it "Merry Christmas from Santa." After dinner one evening he slipped down to her house, and slid the package under her driveway gate. The

next morning we watched her waddle out to get the paper, pick up the present, and go inside.

My son was all excited, and couldn't wait to see what would happen next. The next morning, as we drove off, there she was, out getting her paper—wearing the slippers. He was ecstatic. I had to remind him that NO ONE could ever know what he did, or he wouldn't be a Santa.

One year, he polished up his bike, put a new seat on it, and gave it to one our friend's daughters. These people were and are very poor. We did ask the dad if it was ok. The look on her face, when she saw the bike on the patio with a big bow on it, was almost as good as the look on my son's face. When it came time for Son #2 to join the ranks, my oldest came along and helped with the induction speech. They are both excellent gifters, by the way, and never felt that they had been lied to — because they were let in on the *Secret of Being a Santa*."[67]

In a similar way, we must develop recognition of these constructed settings that act as arenas for our actions. These perceiving places are now the environments of the stories we and our children act within, pursuing our conscious and unconscious motivations. We need to meet in the agora, with all its risks and dangers, and talk about what motivations, what institutions, and what arenas of engagement are worthy of our very lives.

In *Ritual*, Somé explained that practically everything in the daily life of the Dagara takes the form of a ritual. Each act is an embodiment, as though preparing to stake your life and your meaning on what you intend to do.[68] His grandfather prepared Somé to shake hands and make friends with the enemy, the stranger. Somé went to America to engage in conversation with others in the marketplace of ideas. Like Socrates, he went to the crossroads, navigating the pyramids, panopticons, and theatres that possess Western thought, with the intent to engage and exchange what he found meaningful, important, and real.

Carl Jung considered himself a doctor and scientist. One of his ultimate concerns was the problem of the death of the Christian god that Nietzsche's madman brought to the marketplace. He recognized that Nietzsche's madman was not initiating a call to celebration. The death of the god of the West was not a triumph of the rational will. Nietzsche developed a concept of the *Übermensch* or *superman* as a way to address the philosophical problem.[69] In place of the mythological ultimate peak of a religious supreme being or godhead, human leaders would have to rise to that position. These leaders would formulate their own values and their populations would live or die with the consequences. Jung was not satisfied with Nietzsche's answer. For Jung, it was the responsibility of the individual to dive into the unknown depths and revive the supreme way of being, or in other words, blend father's order and son's impulse to action. Jung's vision was not a Christian project, in the traditional sense, though informed by the history of Egypt, Israel, Greece, and the West. Jung felt that the Christian foundational trinity was better formulated as a quaternity—relating four divine characters made of light and shadow.[70] Erich Neumann, working after World War II and following Jung's lessons, thought that a better relationship between consciousness and the unconscious might temper the ambitions of the modern-day Agamemnons and Jephthahs and help us survive the tests of entropy. As he suggested, it was time to "integrate Christianity and antiquity, China and India, the primitive and the modern, the prophet and the atomic physicist, into one humanity."[71]

Unfortunately, the past has never really been enough to handle the call of the present. The dignity of doing the same thing as the figurative father did, over and over again, will not produce the same results today as it may have in the past. The innovations of the figurative son help overcome the problems of the present, but they also invite the escalation of fragility and entropy. It would seem we would rather chase stimulations than be perfect or whole. We worship rapid progress and turn away from the externalities and unintended consequences of such behaviours only until things fall apart from the tests of entropy. If we see this today as a time of a new consciousness, as Jeremy Rifkin explained, success will depend on sitting down with the whole family, face to face, and having a conversation. Not just psychic integration, but communication itself—fully articulating the individual needs and concerns that affect the order and development of each other—provides another answer to family wellness.

Despite the intellectual stature of Nietzsche, Jung, and Neumann, these giants may have suffered their own kind of bias and chauvinism. Critics today, with the blindness of hindsight, have labelled Jung as racist, homophobic, and misogynistic. He had a reputation for being an imperfect husband as well. But it could be noted that Jung's own legacy may have depended most on the women advocates and students taking up his work and carrying on his conversation. He published works on psychology with his wife. He had four daughters and a son—his daughters became scholars and writers after him. Whatever may come of the judgments upon him and defences on his behalf, Jung never fully developed in his own archetypal family a name and place for a divine daughter wholly other from the mother figure.[72] Neumann was father to one daughter who became a distinguished professor. Nietzsche had no children. He may not have ever fully understood the journeys shared between child and parent.

Ultimately, the conversation in the marketplace will decide if trading with the other is a worthy exchange. The idea might be difficult to hear through the shouts and calls of the busy street. The guest—the stranger in the distance, the *observed-other*, partly known and partly unknown—could potentially be divine, as in compelling. That relationship of trade might prove profitable for everyone involved. It might also give us better insight into the constructed settings that make up and possess the stories of our lives.

Malala—I'm Fine with My Crooked Smile

Ziauddin Yousafzai participated in a TED event as a guest speaker. The title of his talk was "My Daughter, Malala." Yousafzai believes in the power of education. One of his lifelong goals was to open schools for children in the Swat Valley of Pakistan. Though his talk is an important statement on the relationships between fathers and daughters in general, it also illuminates the importance of the environments, or constructed settings, we find ourselves in.

> When [my daughter Malala] was four and a half years old, I admitted her in my school. You will be asking, then, why should I mention about the admission of a girl in a school? Yes, I must mention it. It may be taken for granted in Canada, in America, in many developed countries, but in poor countries, in patriarchal societies, in tribal societies, it's a big event for the life of a girl. Enrolment in a school means recognition of her identity and her name. Admission in a school means that she has entered the world of dreams and aspirations where she can explore her potentials for her future life.
>
> I have five sisters, and none of them could go to school, and you will be astonished, two weeks before, when I was filling out the Canadian visa form, and I was filling out the family part of the form, I could not recall the surnames of some of my sisters. And the reason was that I have never, never seen the names of my sisters written on any document. That was the reason that I valued my daughter. What my father could not give to my sisters and to his daughters, I thought I must change it.[73]

Earlier, I grouped the classroom with other panoptic environments as a setting for creating homogeneous behaviour. This means it can also be a place of development, as Ziauddin Yousafzai and his daughter, Malala, have demonstrated to the world. It is a place where an individual is recognized and given opportunities to prepare skills, resources, and mental abilities. He mentions not being able to recall the surnames of some of his sisters because he had never seen their names in print. Another implication can be drawn from what is known about the lives of women from places like Pakistan. His sisters may not have left the house or visited with him much after being married. A woman's place was in the home, in a place of homogeneous and anticipated behaviour for women. By educating his daughter in a classroom, he gave her a way to access and succeed in the various kinds of other environments outside a family's home.

In that same talk, he gives an example of the other side of controlled environments:

> Dear brothers and sisters, we were striving for more rights for women, and we were struggling to have more, more and more space for the women in society. But we came across a new phenomenon. It was lethal to human rights and particularly to women's rights. It was called Talibanization. It means a complete negation of women's participation in all political, economical and social activities. Hundreds of schools were lost. Girls were prohibited from going to school. Women were forced to wear veils and they were stopped from going to the markets. Musicians were silenced, girls were flogged, and singers were killed. Millions were suffering, but few spoke, and it was the most scary thing when you have all around such people who kill and who flog, and you speak for your rights.[74]

The Taliban started projects in the valley that seemed positive and for the benefit of the community. But as it became more militaristic and confident, it also lost the ability to respect anything other than itself. In 2007, the Taliban moved into the area and started to punish people not living up to traditional Muslim practices, as interpreted by the them. The community's markets, meeting places, and businesses served the Taliban interests. Political adversaries were killed.

In 2008, they broadcast a warning—all female education had to cease. Around this time a journalist talked with the Yousafzai family and suggested that Malala start a blog diary as an anonymous Pakistani schoolgirl. Panoptic environments such as classrooms were shut down or made to serve the Taliban. What was a working community became a place of devastation. Malala Yousafzai described the Swat Valley in her book *I Am Malala* as a beautiful and nourishing place with a reputation for producing doctors and teachers. But it became a dangerous place for everyone, irrespective of their allegiances. Malala has memories of playing in sight of old Buddhist statues, a nearly lost part of the history of Pakistan.[75] But the Taliban defaced and destroyed and tried to eradicate that history. They had no place for it in their zealous totalization.

Ziauddin Yousafzai spoke out publicly against the Taliban. He would speak at crossroads and market squares against the violence and against the forced closures of schools. Malala, now a young teen, spoke publicly as well. They spoke in open public spaces to their supporters and to members of the Taliban. The Taliban escalated their attacks on the family. In October 2012, Malala walked out of her school and entered a small bus to go home. Not far from the school the bus was stopped. A man boarded and asked for Malala. He pointed his gun and fired three times, hitting Malala and two of her friends. She spent the next six months in hospital. Nine months after the shooting, she spoke to a very different crowd in an international agora—the UN headquarters. A larger, international audience selected Malala so that she may speak and so that many more would listen to her desire for education. The man who shot her will likely never get such a chance to articulate his desires with such an audience.

Ziauddin has a story of when Malala was in the hospital. She suffered pain and headaches due to the damage the bullet did to her facial nerves. When her mother and father looked at her, Malala recognized the pain on their faces, the worry and concern that can wrack a parent forever.

> She used to tell us, "I'm fine with my crooked smile and with my numbness in my face. I'll be okay. Please don't worry." She was a solace for us, and she consoled us.[76]

Malala's recognition of her own family as audience is more than just a comment on her maturity. She had a choice of what roles she could play in that moment. She was prepared to show her face in any setting, and even turn a terrible circumstance into a lesson of heroic endurance. In that moment of parental concern, in the very height of their attention to her, she could tell her story. Her ultimate concern in that moment was to be the hero taking responsibility and reviving order in the family, instead of playing a victim, blaming others, and adding to her parents' sorrows.

In the confrontation between Malala and the man who shot her, a bullet almost decided the conversation. But instead, doctors and government workers from around the world stood with her. They fought against the violence of the bullet so that she would not just survive but live to ask again for what she believes in. The man who shot her was willing to sacrifice the little girl in front of him, someone who could have been his own daughter or sister. And yet so many others around her were not willing to see her sacrificed.

Reflection

Can people change the roles they find themselves in? Can we re-evaluate our surroundings and find the paths that lead our stories to better endings? Our most treasured narratives and historical accounts tell us people can respond to the call of change. Many myths are about individuals overcoming obstacles and modifying their identities. What is often needed, however, is an insight or revelation, a moment of consciousness.

One of India's most ambitious conquerors eventually turned out to be one of its greatest and most philanthropic administrators. Approximately ten years into his reign, in about 260 BCE, Ashoka Maurya conquered a province called Kalinga and united much of the subcontinent. His desire for conquest caused thousands of deaths and deportations along with great upheavals in the lives of his subjects. Legend says that he grew sick when he witnessed the destruction caused by his victory, and over the following years he converted to Buddhism. Many monuments to the life of Gautama Buddha arose in the empire after Kalinga was conquered. Ashoka changed his identity from conquering hero into a nurturing leader, in part because of the realization of the consequences of his younger ambitions.[77]

Some may suggest he saw in Buddhism a cultural foundation that could unite his kingdom under a shared identity. Emperor Constantine in the West may serve as a useful mirror to Ashoka: Constantine dreamed of something useful in Christianity as a shared identity across the Roman Empire.

The Western world knew little of Ashoka until British historians and archaeologists took interest in India's long heritage. In the mid-twentieth century, researchers found a rock inscribed by Emperor Ashoka from approximately 258 BCE in present-day Afghanistan. The inscription turned out to be unique in that it bore writing in three ancient languages—Sanskrit, Aramaic, and Greek.

Ashoka, the changed man, came to realize his own audience went beyond his personal ambitions. After witnessing the consequences of his actions, he wanted a different kind of legacy. According to the inscription on the rock, he found a connection between such distant worlds as India and Greece. He might also provide us with an example of how to begin again, even with such momentous tasks as rebuilding the relationship between East and West.

Three very old stories illustrate transitions characters make in managing the four figurative landscapes. As the relationships between characters change, their roles and surroundings change as well. Each story says something about our concern for justice, and our different conceptions of justice.

A city suffered under a willful king in the story of Gilgamesh. A woman seduced Enkidu, a wild man, and inspired him to challenge the leadership of Gilgamesh. The two battled in a public square. Gilgamesh bested his adversary. Remarkably, Enkidu respected Gilgamesh's victory, taking it as proof of Gilgamesh's right to lead. Enkidu went from revolutionary hero to Gilgamesh's friend and advocate, serving the king. After the fight, Gilgamesh wanted to build a legacy for himself, and changed how he treated his people. The wrestling match that started as a pyramid-like competition turned out to be a conversation in the agora, albeit a violent one with serious consequences. Both Gilgamesh and Enkidu changed their minds and their roles after that competition. The hierarchy and the vision for the society were rebuilt from the encounter.[78]

In the story of Ramayana, Rama was unfairly banished from his father's kingdom. Though the prince was treated unfairly, he voluntarily obeyed and went into exile. Sita, his wife, went with him. Sita demonstrated that Rama was more important than the comforts of the walled world she knew. In the events of the story, he rescued his wife from a demon and returned home to be crowned rightful king.[79] The relationship between Rama and Sita illustrate the expectations we place on those close to us, and how we value loyalty and commitment.

In one story about Elijah, King Ahab killed a neighbour and took possession of his vineyard. Elijah visited Ahab in order to change the king's mind. Huston Smith, a religious scholar, believed this story was the first in the world's literary record where an advocate confronted a king in the name of justice.[80] Elijah never challenged Ahab for leadership. He changed the setting from a pyramid to a theatre, focusing the king's attention toward what ultimately mattered.[81] After Elijah's words, Ahab's reforms fostered a less corrupt panopticon for the kingdom. In terms of executive power, Elijah had no real position other than that of critic. Outside the pyramids of will and power, Elijah's words carried authority.

In each story, the other compelled behaviour through competition, collaboration or conversation. In each case, the main character sensed a kind of unnamed divinity in those who journeyed with them.

In Zen Buddhism, a series of pictograms and poems illustrate the path toward enlightenment. The series came to be known as the "Ten Bulls." The Ten Bulls have also been described as a pictorial representation of the inquiry into what it is to be alive. The bull, a headstrong, dangerous, but also treasured animal is a symbol for the practice of meditation. The ten steps are as follows:

1. In Search of the Bull
2. Discovery of Footprints
3. Perceiving the Bull
4. Catching the Bull
5. Taming the Bull
6. Riding the Bull Home
7. The Bull Transcended
8. Both Bull and Self Transcended
9. Reaching the Source
10. Return to the Marketplace[82]

The pursuit of mindfulness involves a return to society. Even the monk comes to the marketplace and interacts with others. Without the metaphorical photosynthesis, trade, and conversation of the marketplace, no other constructed environment passes the tests of time.

When Northrop Frye talked about Sophia, Lady Wisdom of the Proverbs in the Bible, he suggested we should not just see her as a gracious and mature woman who gives advice. She does not have to be our lawyer giving us prudent counsel. Frye associated Sophia with another image entirely—the playful young girl.[83] Children have their own kind of wisdom that can enchant and baffle their elders. They ring bells for us, returning us to different places of perceiving. Play creates an environment where the limitations of the rules generate possibilities and we share a frame of reference with others. Play is a matter of doing different things in different ways until a desired goal is achieved. Such a mode of behaviour fosters human dignity just as much as traditional rituals and educational institutions. Children thrive from play. And in play lies another divine consciousness that involves inquiry, adventure, and discovery of new insights. According to the book of Proverbs, this daughter was there in the beginning, before the works of the creator god in that tradition. Though she may have been no more than a twinkle in her father' eye, she gives us an opportunity to think about how we construct a home for what we love, how we manage our own delights and fears in the presence of something new.

The four environments described in this chapter impose directions upon us. Our motivation toward competition and action develops in us a sense of status and goals. Our motivation to dominate our perceiving places gives authority to our sense of anticipation and confirmation. Our desire to inquire and care about what we observe rubs against our sense of identity, distinguishing what wins our attention and what does not. And our motivation toward freedom cues us to moments when we are presented with novelty or opportunity.

The actions we take on a journey can move us between different settings and places. Once we cross the thresholds from one environment to another, we often notice a difference in acoustics and authorities. One landscape may produce no echo, whereas another might be filled with auditory reflections. Those echoes could be just the thing to take our attention away from the shining surfaces of our obsessions and help us find a better path home.

Next, I will discuss four models of story and change. One model focuses on goal-directed behaviour between the realm of what is and the realm of what should be. Another model involves a journey from home into the abyss of the unknown and then a return to re-establish home. A third model involves an allegory of reality, beginning in the darkness of a cave. The subject is guided into the light of day and then returned to the depths of darkness. The final model opens the circle into a U-shaped pattern associated with the spiritually significant events of a community through time. The differences between the models further prepare us for the changing roles we play in managing our motivations.

3

Story Arcs and Social Circles

Tragedy is the shattering of forms and of our attachment to the forms; comedy, the wild and careless, inexhaustible joy of life invincible.

—Joseph Campbell
The Hero with a Thousand Faces

*The path of a god
was a path toward
an expansion of consciousness.*

Narcissus and the Self-Correcting Process of Inquiry

Ovid wrote a series of tales called *Metamorphoses*. As the title suggests, the stories are about how the characters face change. In one, a mother was so worried about her son she asked for advice on how to keep him protected. Her son was beautiful. He caught the attention of every young woman who saw him. But his mother still worried about how he would live long enough to reach old age. She searched for wise counsel and came to Tiresias. Tiresias was considered the most wise because he had lived as both a woman and a man. He gave cryptic advice. "If your boy ever knows himself, surely he will die." The mother seemed to take this advice to heart because she raised her boy, Narcissus, to never know his own image or his own face. She protected him but never prepared him. As a result, he was not ready to know himself when presented with his own reflection in the world.

When he was sixteen years old, Narcissus looked into a pool and saw his reflection. He became obsessed. He was so infatuated with what he saw he wanted to go into the surface of the pool and unite with the vision that captivated him.

> To the cold water oft he joins his lips,
> Oft catching at the beauteous shade he dips
> His arms, as often from himself he slips.
> Nor knows he who it is his arms pursue
> With eager clasps, but loves he knows not who.[1]

Narcissus didn't understand that the reflection depended on his gaze. The reflection no longer existed if he simply moved away from the watery screen. As Narcissus became more conscious of his situation, his infatuations turned into realizations. Unfortunately, the awareness of his mistake led to his ruin. Instead of a moment of embarrassment or transcendence, a lesson learned to help him grow, Narcissus experienced resentment and bitterness. He turned himself into a victim for not being able to kiss, seduce, and possess something, even if it was his own face. Consumed by his reflection, unable to correct his attention, Narcissus transformed into a green stalk with a yellow blossom.

Marshall McLuhan used the story of Narcissus as a cautionary tale for the age of electric information.[2] When the boy gazed into the mirror of the water, he thought he saw someone else.

To play with Bernard Lonergan's term mentioned in the last chapter, Narcissus suffered from a lack of "self-appropriation." He could not tell the authentic self from the inauthentic self. He wasn't asking the screen good questions. He found himself unable to transcend his inattentiveness, his limited competence, his sense of reason, and his irresponsible fixation. Insight, the daughter of your attention, helps navigate the figures and grounds of experience. A similar experience occurs each time someone becomes too absorbed by the stimulation of a story or a screen. Like Sautuola in the Altamira cave, we sometimes need another voice or an echo to draw our attention up.

A theme running through Ovid's *Metamorphoses* is that the change in each character depended on their attitude. If the characters voluntarily accepted the experience of change, they transcended their limitations. However, not being ready brought destruction. Narcissus lacked the moment of insight, leading to a loss of identity instead of the emergence of love he could have shared with someone else.

Stories ultimately depend on these kinds of patterns. Civilizations depend on them too. They depend on processes in which characters go through changes and events. The relationships between observer and observed, viewer and viewed, user and interface determine the drama and resolutions of the stories we tell ourselves. Stories help us temporarily or psychologically embody characters and events in preparation for when we face change in our own lives. We are thrown into the limitations of being with existence. Our attitude toward this *thrownness* could mean the difference between tragedy and comedy.

We can draw a similar insight from Agamemnon and his daughter. *The Oresteia* by Aeschylus tells the story of Agamemnon's family falling apart. In describing the sacrifice of Iphigenia, Aeschylus plays with a similar exchange of information, from sight to sound. Agamemnon purposefully gagged his child to stop the power of a child's voice from changing his mind.

> A father's hands are stained,
> blood of a young girl streaks the altar...
> Yes, he had the heart
>   to sacrifice his daughter...
>
> "My father, father!"—she might pray to the winds;
> no innocence moves her judges mad for war.
> Her father called his henchmen on,
>   on with a prayer,
>   "Hoist her over the altar
> like a yearling, give it all your strength!
> She's fainting—lift her,
>   sweep her robes around her,
>   but slip this strap in her gentle curving lips...
>   here, gag her hard, a sound will curse the house"—
>   and the bridle chokes her voice.[3]

Agamemnon cursed his own house by refusing to hear the cry of his child. A sound from her voice might have brought a new kind of consciousness to him. Instead, he acted in a way that only accelerated his family's tragedy.

Jeremy Rifkin outlined a series of eras in the development of consciousness in his book *The Empathic Civilization*:

> Stages of consciousness reset the boundary line between the "we" and the "others." Beyond the walls is no-man's-land, where the aliens reside. For mythological man, the alien is the nonhuman or demon or monster. For theological man, it is the heathen or infidel. For ideological man, it is the brute. For psychological man, it is the pathological. The alien domain is shrinking as globalization accelerates and the empathic impulse begins to encompass the totality of life that makes up the biosphere of the planet.[4]

Agamemnon could very well be called a monster, heathen, brute, or psychopath. We can identify him as embodying behaviours that do not stand up to the test of entropy, regardless of the type of consciousness we might use. He willingly sacrificed his daughter in place of changing his mind, his desires, or his process. Despite the differences in words, this consistency can be a foundation for optimism and pessimism. To pass the test of entropy ourselves, we need to recognize Agamemnon in ourselves and in the behaviours of others. The measuring stick works through each stage of consciousness because the measuring stick is the relationship between the observer and the observed.

The development of the relationship between guest and host, we and others, has its dangers and opportunities. A lover may not know if feelings will be requited. A narcissistic psychopath can cause as much damage as a political tyrant or a religious terrorist. And each can appear as a stranger or even a welcome guest in need of attention. To invite them in may signal empathy and compassion, but it can also lead to ruin. Clytemnestra did not pass the test of entropy either when she took justice into her own hands and murdered her husband, Agamemnon. She wasn't the one to set her family in order. She didn't even transcend her own resentment. Jephthah, too, may not have sacrificed his daughter had he welcomed the counsel or the mere presence of his priest into his heart. Ovid's Narcissus, though a mere fiction when compared to the biology of a plant, demonstrates that transformations in ways of thinking can be just as powerful and life-saving as transformations in ways of material being. It is no wonder the virtues of a host can be honour, grace, and suspicion, together at once.

Rifkin suggested that we are unique among the animals because we are the only ones we know of, in our limited competence, to tell stories. We live by narrative. Stories organize our roles and identities. Concepts like the past, present, and future are all introduced to children through narrative. Narrative becomes critical in conflict resolution and problem-solving, because it gives us a map for transforming distress into engagement, crisis into resolution. As a result, we build ourselves out of the stories we tell about ourselves and the stories others tell about us. But we can even go so far as to put meaning above our survival. Like Narcissus, we can become so obsessed with what we see that we wither without action, and in the process lose our own identities. But if we hear the call, we can respond and pass the tests of entropy. Voluntary transformation, by way of working through a narrative of events and changes while participating in our responsibilities, can bridge meaning and survival.

Rifkin called the new era of development a time of "dramaturgical consciousness." Screened media has become an authority in our day-to-day behaviours. The development of character in an individual has come to mean we value and encourage a theatrical self in individuals. Rifkin explains:

> The new dramaturgical consciousness shows early signs of propelling a younger generation to global cosmopolitanism and a universal empathic sensibility. The problem is that the same communications technology revolution that is paving the way toward global consciousness has a dark side that could derail the journey and sidetrack the Internet generation into a dead-end corridor of rampant narcissism, endless voyeurism, and overwhelming ennui....
>
> Although, in a sense, this ought to be regarded as pathological behavior, even delusional, we have come to accept it as quite normal. The important point to emphasize is that even more so than novels of the eighteenth and nineteenth centuries, movies, radio, and TV allow millions of people to suspend disbelief and slip into roles and try on new personas.[5]

The idea of playing a part creates a problem for Rifkin because it can be difficult to know if a person actually believes or is just pretending. Nevertheless, we act out our beliefs and concerns. The dramaturgical consciousness can be thought of as reawakening or reviving the role of participation in ritual. In ritual, a person spiritually carries out the actions of the ideal way of being in a moment or situation, according to the person's culture and identity.

A Kiss That Was Just a Kiss

In 1968, a science fiction television show broadcast the first interracial kiss between fictional characters on American network television. A group of aliens had visited ancient Greece on Earth long ago. Later, on their own planet, they established a republic based on principles they learned from ancient Greece. The USS *Enterprise* visited the planet in an episode called, "Plato's Stepchildren."[6] In the episode, James T. Kirk kissed Nyota Uhura.

Whoopi Goldberg remembered watching *Star Trek* for the first time as a child. When she saw Uhura, she excitedly shouted for her mother: "Come quick! Come quick! There's a black lady on TV, and she ain't no maid!"[7] Racial borders and mental barriers were opening up for a new kind of consciousness. Some of the crew on the show worried an interracial kiss would seem apocalyptic to audience members. After the episode aired, the production offices received a lot of mail. Almost all of it was positive. Not only did the audience identify with the story and the characters but approved and supported the storytellers. The love affair and relationship between the heroes of the screen and the advocates in the audience grew even stronger.

A kiss can be a dangerous thing for both the observer and the observed. The lover and the beloved both bring promise and anxiety, potentially leading to a war-torn tragedy or a loving comedy. Agamemnon and Jephthah never allowed their daughters the chance to find someone worthy of a kiss. If we take tragedy and comedy as extreme directions in which a story can lead, we can find guiding questions, a method to help us better navigate the decisions that affect our own families.

In this book, I have used the words "mystery," "mask," "metaphor," and even "monument" to examine what is involved in a Supreme Way of Being. The next word I want to consider is "map." If the path toward knowing oneself in the world, self-appropriation, takes us on a journey, then what kind of maps can we use? What signposts, sequences of events, patterns of actions, can we use along the way? What will help us be more conscious of our progression from one situation to another, and lead us to better and better kisses?

Bernard Lonergan's work provides us with a general method. We can remain conscious of our intentions and fix our focus on the path through the mystery:

> Experiencing—Am I paying attention to, or am I ignoring, what is important?
> Understanding—Am I developing competence, or desiring dominance, in an area?
> Judging—Am I being discerning enough to correct myself, or proclaiming judgment and confirming that judgment?
> Deciding—Am I taking up a responsibility or am I laying blame?[8]

For Lonergan, success can be understood as having achieved a state of being in love with the contents of the inquiry and the process of inquiring. The last question then becomes: Am I ruled by love—in love with the mystery of a beloved, or am I ruled by fear—acting on fear and mystification of the unknown?

Jordan Peterson practised his own skills of empirical inquiry while studying how anomaly affects us. Anomaly comes upon us as a novel event, filled with new information for us, like a voice in the night or a smile from a stranger:

> Anomalous events share capacity to threaten the integrity of the known, to disrupt the "familiar and explored." Such events, while differing in their specific details and manner of manifestation, tend to occupy the same natural category. Threats to the stability of cultural tradition emerge in four "mythologically inseparable" manners: through rapid natural environmental shift, "independent" of human activity; through contact with a heretofore isolated foreign culture; through application of… episodically mediated critical skill—the inevitable consequence of increasing ability to abstract, learn and communicate; and as a consequence of revolutionary heroic activity.[9]

Peterson described four categories of events as "mythologically inseparable" because they are emotionally equivalent. A person *sees* each of these as not fitting into what is familiar and already explored. We radically summarize, even to the point of judging first and distinguishing later. However, by changing perspective, suspending judgment, and paying attention to the relationship between observer and observed, one can become four. As Lonergan suggests, we can move from experience to understanding first before taking comfort in judgments. Our capacity to consciously distinguish which one of the four manifests in our experience can help us avoid the fate of Narcissus—literally planted in the ground, beautiful but unable to move independently. Narcissus made up his mind before understanding. He wouldn't let loose his judgment, and he became fixed in place because of it. Peterson's four threats align with the four different archetypal motivations described in the family of four characters.

The Great and Terrible Father	The Great and Terrible Mother	The Great and Terrible Son	The Great and Terrible Daughter
Protective/Tyrannical Known	Abundant/ Threatening Unknown	Hero/Villain	Observed/Other
Episodically Mediated Skill	Rapid Natural Environmental Shift	Revolutionary Or Innovative Activity	Stranger/ Person from a Foreign Culture

Our cultural inheritance prepares us to bestow authority on past knowledge, such as traditional skills, cultural practices, and social prejudices developed and shared over time. We bestow a kind of authority to natural environmental shifts as can be seen by our migrations and responses to disasters. We bestow authority on the revolutionary hero, as demonstrated by following leaders and adopting the inventions of innovators. In mythology, religion, literature, and political practice we have "deified" each of these three categories in some manner. After the rise of the scientific method and the industrial age, Neumann, Jung, and Nietzsche each suggested a different configuration of these archetypal figures that could help heal the relationship between culture and individual in the modern age. However, the closest we have come to granting authority to the observed, or the other, in any symbolic or narrative sense, might be seen in the relationships between lover and beloved, hero and friends, representative and citizen, scientist and data, or host and guest.

Without metaphor, literature and art might as well be incomprehensible. The art of a civilization might be the only thing that survives past a culture's collapse. Leaders rise and fall in short counts of years. Legal policies may last many decades or centuries. But as Sautuola and his daughter discovered, art persists. Metaphors are often thought of as comparisons between two things, such as characters, qualities, objects, or places. But metaphors can be used for comparison between sequential processes—successions of events. Story and narrative act as maps of action.

The nymph Echo followed and watched Narcissus in his despair. She wanted to win his affections and share a kiss. She also wanted to help the boy. Unfortunately, Echo was cursed with a problem. She could only repeat the sounds of someone else's actions and words. If we are to avoid the fate of Narcissus, we need some way of recognizing when to shift our attention and change the direction of our infatuations. We can learn when to listen to the reflections of our own echoes, not to confirm the bias of our judgment but to correct our ways of thinking.

Camille Paglia wanted to rescue the long chronology of art and culture, the process of history, from the contemporary trends in the academic world:

> We have available to us two great Western traditions of skepticism and disputation, the Hellenic and the Judaic. Our educational and legal systems have been heavily influenced by Greco-Roman philosophy, rhetoric, and oratory, partly transmitted through the Catholic church, whose theology was born in the Hellenized eastern Mediterranean.
>
> The Jews know there is a story in history, for they have suffered it. Those who deny there is meaning or order in events have their heads in the sand.
>
> Injustice cannot be remedied by injustice.[10]

Paglia's words put in plain language the lesson from Clytemnestra's unjust actions. To pass our tests, our words will have to remedy the injustices of past events with the quality of mercy rather than add more violence in the present. There are four narrative maps that can be traced out of our history, through our evolutionary and storytelling development. Like translucent layers, these metaphorical maps can be stacked on one another as filters over the lenses we use to navigate experiences in the world. Separately, they bring different aspects of experience into focus for the individual. Together, they give the individual a chance to pry open another eye to the processes and infatuations that influence beliefs and actions. They might also provide a clue about how to escape the visual fixations that undid Narcissus. They may even give us opportunities to better appreciate the caring, warning voice of Echo.

If Lonergan's "generalized empirical method" does ultimately lead someone to being in love, as he suggested, then an individual identity can be transcended by trusting the process of inquiry and the insights that come from it. Each of the four maps offers a unique lesson to help us focus our attention, develop competence, correct our judgments, and decide to follow the values that draw us away from tragedy and into the happier endings of comedy.

PETERSON AND THE LINE IN THE SAND

In 2016, a University of Toronto professor recorded a series of videos. He was concerned about what kind of place the campus had become. He was worried about Bill C-16, a piece of legislation initially intended to protect the rights of identified minorities. The bill and the professor's videos would also make people much more conscious of the role of language in our thought-processes. The professor plainly stated that he would not use certain words just because others forced the words on him—not under threat of losing his job or under accusation of performing a hate crime. He considered the motivations behind the idea ideological, or potentially resentful, rather than beneficial. Compelled speech, for Jordan Peterson, wasn't a solution to social problems. If anything, it merely created more problems with authority and authoritarianism. For Peterson, it is dangerous to consider it a hate crime if someone refused to use certain words.[11]

Within months, the number of reply videos, comments, interviews, and further discussions multiplied across the internet. Many people, viewers and media personalities alike, quickly and radically summarized the issue as one of justice—intolerance for marginalized people versus the rights of free speech. But the finer details of the issue persisted. Despite the desire to make things simple and polarized and emotional, more and more people watched and thought about it and attempted to find a meaningful thread through the labyrinth of opinions and reactions.

Almost twenty years before the videos, Peterson published *Maps of Meaning*. In the preface he described his formative years in northern Alberta. In adolescence, he became disillusioned with the implicit Christian religion of his upbringing. That led to a disillusionment with politics. His description of his experiences hints at something familiar and revealing to many of us struggling to negotiate between the cleverness of the contemporary world and the antiquated wisdom of the past:

> No one really opposed my rebellious efforts, either, in church or at home—in part because those who were deeply religious (or who might have wanted to be) had no intellectually acceptable counter-arguments at their disposal. After all, many of the basic tenets of Christian belief were incomprehensible, if not clearly absurd. The virgin birth was an impossibility; likewise, the notion that someone could rise from the dead.
>
> Did my act of rebellion precipitate a familial or a social crisis? No. My actions were so predictable, in a sense, that they upset no one, with the exception of my mother (and even she was soon resigned to the inevitable). The other members of the church—my "community"—had become absolutely habituated to the increasingly-frequent act of defection, and did not even notice.[12]

He involved himself in political work at a young age but again discovered a problem. He found he did not admire many of the people he worked with, though they supposedly believed the same things as he did. This led to a disillusionment in utopian thinking and in ideological systems in general. He came to a point in his life where he began to critically examine virtually everything he said and believed—about himself, others, and the world. The vague but heavy fears of the Cold War brought him to a daunting question: What could possibly justify the threat of a totalizing destruction? The problem of evil, the capacity of people to do evil, and the problem of how to act in an absurd world all persisted, despite these layers of disillusionment. Threatening dreams started to haunt him. He was left with confusion and existential dread over how ideas can lead people to cause suffering in others. How can people put motivations before the well-being of others or the well-being of the world?

Instead of following a path to nihilism or some kind of fundamental totalitarianism, Peterson kept pushing himself against these ideas. He kept attending to the problem of evil, focusing his efforts on understanding the psychology of blame and resentment. The results of his pushing took him away from any kind of moral relativity or materialist reduction, but instead revealed to him a different conception of reality. He ended the preface of his book with a summary of his work:

The world can be validly construed as a forum for action, as well as a place of things. We describe the world as a place of things, using the formal methods of science. The techniques of narrative, however—myth, literature, and drama—portray the world as a forum for action. The two forms of representation have been unnecessarily set at odds, because we have not yet formed a clear picture of their respective domains. The domain of the former is the "objective world"—what is, from the perspective of intersubjective perception. The domain of the latter is "the world of value"—what is and what should be, from the perspective of emotion and action.[13]

The poet Muriel Rukeyser once wrote, "The universe is made of stories, not of atoms."[14] Rukeyser's claim is a call for the second perspective, portraying the world as a forum for action. But however poetic this view of the universe might be, it can sound strange to the rational, scientific, and materialist view of the universe that comes from the modern world. It takes a moment of insight to move past a fixed point of view and toward another plane of potential. One perspective presupposes characters make decisions. The other presupposes objects are ruled by physical laws and natural mechanisms.

Peterson's work negotiates between the two perspectives to answer the questions that motivated his book. He used diagrams to illustrate what a world might look and feel like abstractly if portrayed as a forum for action. Although simple in their initial construction and appearance, Peterson's diagrams map motivation and narrative to behaviour and reality. They also help us move toward understanding how we manage information. In such a world, goal-directed perspectives and behaviour influence what takes shape; what draws an individual's attention.

Beliefs influence perception and draw attention to an emergent figure from a background. As a result, we do not live in or perceive only the world *as it is*. The very act of observation attaches formative values. The act of observation colours our motivations and defines the limits of objects in the settings of our actions. Our attention goes to our goals, creating a realm of *what is* and a realm of *what should be*. What bridges these two domains? We act. Peterson drew a line representing the behaviour that could take a person from one domain to the other, from what is to what should be.[15]

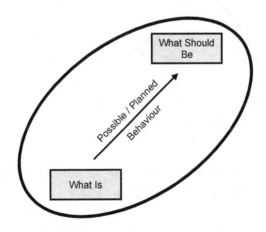

We act and choose, consciously or not, how to behave with hope or anticipation that something in our actions will bring us closer to what we think will be the domain of what should be. This simple diagram brings together three of the most common and universal archetypes, three of the proposed divine family. Culture, the known and anticipated, the archetype of order, is represented by the domain of what should be. Nature, the never fully known, the archetype of the encompassing cosmic all, is represented by the domain of what is. Between them, the individual actor, the archetype of the hero and the way, is represented by the behaviour that connects the two and travels from one to the other.

Evolution depended on goal-directed behaviour. Single-cell organisms move toward environments they perceive as abundant in food and move away from toxic environments. Our own behaviour ultimately comes from how we perceive the world and what registers with us as valuable to our concerns. Our bodies are constantly acting to transform what is into what should be. This can be as automatic as breathing. The exchange of oxygen and carbon dioxide from different bodily systems is just one example of how our bodies perceive the world as made up of not just what is, but also what should be.

Peterson did not end there. He intended to find more than a reduction of reality to a basic diagram. Instead, he wanted to map out how we find meaning from information and action. What happens when the action, the journey from what is to what should be, is not a straight line? What happens when behaviour is interrupted, when anticipation goes unfulfilled? What if we do the same thing again and again but don't get the desired result we expect? In a further step, Peterson addressed *novelty*.

Novelty, according to Peterson, presents itself as either promise or threat. Promise leads to hope, since it suggests the behaviour chosen is producing desired effects. Threat leads to anxiety, in the sense that the behaviour chosen is either delaying resolution or creating more distance between the hero and the desired goal.[16]

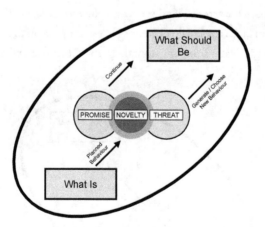

Depending on how the hero faces novelty, he or she can either rise to the benefits of success or fall into a realm of unbearable disorder. What matters is how one pays attention.

Peterson continued with his maps, linking myth, literature, and drama from our collective histories with today's modern thinking in psychology and science. He does not introduce more archetypal members to the family because the constituent elements of experience, as he put it, are the known, unknown, and the knower.[17] The knower is a mixture of both known and unknown, yet not fully of either.

Literature wrestles with these elements to illustrate meaning. A main character may move from the known to the unknown or from the unknown to the known, seeking a resolution to a problem, a change in status, an adjustment of attitude, or a new understanding of an environment. But along the path, the main character meets up with others. "Solipsism" is the word used to describe the idea that the self is all that can be known to exist. Many writers have struggled with the idea of solipsism—how to know there is an other, and how to act in the presence of the other. The modern experiment has given us incredible power over the objective world, the world of material things. But as another consequence, it has created a culture obsessed with rationalizing the "I" to the point of sometimes sacrificing the other.

Why is novelty, not fully of the realm of the known or the unknown, not part of the divine family? Perhaps it is possible to have an experience without the presence of novelty. In the domain of narrative, the other three archetypes can take form as a character, setting, or object. Novelty, as the observed, partially identified but still partially unknown, does the same. It may appear as a mixture, potentially either ally or obstacle to the main character. Novelty can be a bump in the path or a shortcut. Like the three constituent archetypes, novelty requires evaluation because it may be positive or negative. It competes for our attention, and its presence can potentially mean tragedy or success. In each moment of our lives, is anomaly worthy of some authority and responsibility or can we safely leave it *unnamed*?

In the book of Genesis, the problem of the other and the presence of novelty appear as early as the stories of the Garden of Eden. But one of the most revealing narratives about recognition of the other can be found in the comparison of how two characters accept guests. In Genesis, Abraham looked up to find three men in his presence. Immediately, he bowed to these strangers and welcomed them to his tent. He offered to have their feet bathed and to have food prepared for them. He sees in them something divine, as though they come from his Lord. The men, after being treated as welcome guests, wish to repay the hospitality. They tell the aged Abraham and his wife, Sarah, they will have a child.[18]

As incredible as this "blessing" upon an aged couple from strangers may sound to a modern audience, Abraham's initial behaviour is still a story, or at least a suggestion, on how to act when faced with a guest—or, in more general terms, with novelty.

Lot, who was related to Abraham, lived in the city of Sodom. Strangers came to the gates of Sodom and Lot welcomed them, suggesting they should not stay on the street during the night. Like Abraham, he offered to prepare them something to eat. In the evening a gang in the city came to Lot's door, demanding he send out his guests so the mob could have its way with them. This mob of Sodom, in a narrative sense, suggests another way to act toward a stranger, a striking contrast from Abraham's example. Lot recognizes this way of acting toward strangers is wicked or evil. His resolution to the problem of a mob at his door, however, compounded the problem:

> I have two daughters, which have not known man: them will I bring out now unto you, and do them as seemeth you good: only unto these men do nothing; for therefore came they under the shadow of my roof.[19]

What kind of father offers his daughters to a violent mob in this situation? Even in the most generous context of the situation, this is no triumph against the test of entropy. Many have used this difficult passage to evaluate the entire library contained in the Bible. If a book has such a passage in it, then all of it must be morally suspect. This kind of evaluation can be a projection, judging the whole by the passage. But if we have any faith in inquiry, this could also offer us a chance to ask what is getting our attention. This passage calls us to understand, through illustration and narration, how even a well-meaning character can be morally lost. Lot is given a chance to redeem himself, his family, and his city. Instead, he shows a weakness in character and serves as a negative example for the reader—how not to act. Lot cannot perceive his daughters, though of his own family, as worthy of being identified as divine, as recognizable as individuals. They are not even identified as part of himself, or as others worthy of the welcome and protection given to guests.

What we give attention, and what we ignore, pushes and pulls at the figure and ground of our perspectives. This is a story of Lot—the one not participating in the mob, the one not adopting the full identity of the city. He is a marginalized character in Sodom but the main character in his own story. In the sense of narrative, Lot tests and proves the problem addressed by the story. And Lot's character only half-heartedly rises to the challenge of being a hero. Lot's fate is not doomed because he failed to honour strangers as guests. He certainly acted as a gracious host to them. Instead, he attempted to appease a mob with a kind of scapegoat or substitute.

Lot's guests, as messengers of the Lord in the story, told him to gather his extended family and escape the city. His guests, as outsiders, told him they would destroy the city. The mob of Sodom broke the relationship with the other, with the surprise guest, with the appearance of novelty. Can a city, family, or individual for that matter, sustain itself by raping guests? Can a city, family, or individual sustain itself by a giving in to mob rule?

Lot, his wife and daughters were reluctant to leave. Though he was not born in the city, Lot built his work, life, and identity in Sodom. Lot's wife, born in Sodom, looked back and was lost, turned into a pillar of salt. Whether this passage is taken literally or figuratively, the idea of a pillar of salt implies something about character and the consequences of choices. Lot and his daughters attempted to re-establish themselves in another city but ended up living in a mountain cave. Living in the depths of personal despair in a cave, a broken and destitute man, Lot felt he could no longer live in the presence of others. Even the responsibilities he had for giving his daughters a better life did not appear as motivations worth addressing. As a further descent into unsustainable relationships, his daughters turned desperate. They broke one of the most important covenants between a parent and child. They gave Lot wine to drink and then initiated incestuous relationships with him. There may be no bottom to the problems that breed and multiply whenever an individual loses all recognition of how to behave in the presence of novelty, as represented by the guest, the observed, the stranger, or the other.[20]

In *The Hitchhiker's Guide to the Galaxy*, Arthur Dent woke up looking forward to a morning cup of tea. He found several bulldozers outside, about to smash his house down for a new expressway. That was unexpected, for Arthur and the reader. As soon as he woke up, novelty appeared, and his morning became a place of chaos.[21] What do you do when you are still in your pyjamas and your home is about to come down around you? What should you do?

Arthur tried lying down in front of the bulldozers. That is not the typical behaviour to expect from an English gentleman in his pyjamas. His friend Ford came along at that point and told him they had even bigger problems. The whole planet was about to be bulldozed for an intergalactic expressway. Arthur didn't know what to do. He could no longer predict outcomes, couldn't really direct his behaviour normally. Where could he turn? He listened to his friend Ford. And as ridiculous as it seemed to Arthur, Ford had a way to survive the coming disaster.

In just the first few events of Arthur's story, we see how the power of anomaly can be found in today's literature, preparing us for the most common experiences and most unlikely of circumstances. Also, we see an example of how important it is to listen to a friend, a second voice, the observed other.

Plato's Disillusionment

A bright, noble idealist watched his beloved city of Athens fall apart before his eyes. When he was about sixteen, oligarchs started a revolution and assumed control. After the city subdued that uprising and restored the democratic constitution, a new brand of state-run terror gripped the city. In his early twenties, the oligarchs regained power and brought eight more months of bitter tyranny. The city's democratic legacy won out again, but the citizens of Athens harboured a new, deep resentment against political extremes and civil dissent.[22]

In these years of turmoil, the young man met a teacher. This teacher believed that if you could not say what you mean then you could not possibly mean what you say. This teacher infuriated others with persistent questions about knowledge and ethics. He was infatuated by, and ruled by, the desire to articulate the meaning behind beliefs and actions. He loved questions and inquiry. In Athens, this teacher gained a reputation for uncompromising honesty. That kind of reputation can leave someone with few political friends. But maybe there are better legacies than political ones.

Before the young man's thirtieth birthday, the city executed the teacher on charges of impiety and corrupting the youth. His teacher's death became an experience of disillusionment for the young man. He couldn't forgive his city. He felt so jaded against the ambitions of politics he created a school to train a very different kind of politician. He wrote several dialogues featuring his teacher as the main character. In one of his dialogues, his teacher, Socrates, tells a story about disillusionment. It is an allegory of reality, an illustration of two opposing realms. One realm represented the physical appearances and common perceptions of the changing world around us. The other realm pointed to the eternals, the unshakable, reliable absolutes that make up knowledge and truth.[23]

The allegory takes the form of a circle, a journey out of a cave and into a sunlit world, with an eventual return to the depths of the cave. Imagine subjects or prisoners physically bound in a row and facing a tall flat wall at the back of a cave. Behind them a fire casts shadows on the flat wall. Performers walk before the fire and carry props or objects to create shadows upon the wall. The audience watches with no other reference to reality other than their own shadows and the shadows that play on the flat screen of the cave.

A guide decides to unbind one of the subjects and show him the fire and the performers. What's more, the guide then takes the person by the hand and walks out of the cave. The subject stands before a reality he cannot fully understand except in reference to the shadows on the cave wall. He experiences tension between what he thought was real and the experience of a new reality, as revealed from following his guide. The guide directs the entire process of inquiry, until the unchained prisoner is given a brief independent moment in the presence of the light.

The guide does not let him stay, however. After he points toward certain things, differentiates and compares objects he deems important, the two of them return. The guide leads the prisoner back into the cave. The subject returns to the row before the high wall, bound once again to watch the shadows. The shadows have changed in meaning for him. When he tells the other members of the audience of his experiences, they seem to only understand him in terms of the shadows they know.

In a sense, this circle is a map of mediated learning, or the development of skill in the presence of a teacher or master. Through episodes of exposure, the student gains perspective and skill. Plato showed us something about the limits of the knowledge we get from our perceptions. But the story is all the more remarkable in what it does compared to mythological stories. Though

Plato's story of the cave is often described as an allegory for society, and not a strict, real account of actual events, it has influenced policy-makers and political leaders throughout history. Some readers have granted Plato's thoughts authority.

The story focuses on the objects of reality. In the process of inquiry, attention and understanding are governed by the guide. The subject, passive, is led away from his chains, up past the fire and shadows and out to where the light shines upon him. The treasure of his return is supposedly the knowledge of the truest forms of things, but he seems to never master it or stay in the presence of that knowledge. He is only allowed a quick vision, the briefest of kisses, before being delivered back to the chains of his initial perspective. He is observer more than actor. This is an object-oriented, or concept-oriented, model of reality. The story of Plato's Cave, after all, is named for the setting of the story and not the characters. This story is symbolic of the pursuit of knowledge and concepts.

Plato wanted to make good and fair politicians. He wanted his students to stand tall and uncorrupted by the everyday while walking with an understanding of both the light and the shadows we cast. Plato hoped his students, future politicians with critical minds exposed to the light, would act with a firm grip on the forms of truth and their love of philosophical inquiry.

Plato's Cave is a story of top-down authority. Imagine the communication of a preacher in a church, teacher in a classroom, or prophet in a public square. Think of seeing things as a state, with an overview that goes beyond this moment in time or space, measured by something other than pure individual motivation. The guide directs the prisoner's attention toward what is considered important to see, what to think. The overseeing person or group in power directs all action and controls aspects of the environment. The entire metaphor of the journey from cave to the outside world of wisdom is primarily a visual experience—shadows, objects, fire, and light. Student and guide point toward objects of examination in the visual nature of this map.

The character Winston Smith in *1984* thought a lot, but he initiated very little action. His love interest, Julia, approached him and offered him hope of a relationship. In the middle of the book, Winston was given a book to read, a kind of essay on the structure of class struggle and political changes in his world. Winston treated the book as something to observe and think about. Figuratively, it was a philosophical moment out of the cave and in the light. However, the information caused no real transformation in the character; no call to adventure. He was caught and rehabilitated by the state. Everything in the chain of events in the plot happened *to* Winston. In the last events of the story, Winston sat, chained as if in the cave of his society once again, swallowed by the state as though surrounded by the psychic machines of loving grace.[24] Readers of *1984* experience an opportunity to reflect on how to make sure to avoid the fate of Winston for themselves.

But like most archetypal characters, settings, and processes, the cave can be understood to have plural meanings. We could apply this map to the life of the Buddha as well. Buddha had teachers who brought him into the light, only to leave him unsatisfied and seeking further lessons. In his personal moment of enlightenment, Buddha considered a choice—step into the light or return to the world. He reasoned his own ascension would be incomplete unless he returned and taught others about what he had found. To the Buddha, the other and the community had some authority or participation with his peace and enlightenment. His own identity wasn't separate but made one with everything.[25]

When we find ourselves in the cave, we can choose to work toward Winston's fate or toward the Buddha's. It does not need to matter what is fact or fiction, hard realities or imagined stories, when we think of these two characters. We can recognize the Buddha's answer to the test of entropy as we experience the sequence of events in our own moments of achievement, isolation, or community.

Joseph Campbell's 10,000 Hours

In 1929, a young student withdrew from graduate studies. He rented a shack near Woodstock, New York, and set a goal for himself—nine hours of reading each day. For the next five years, he read and thought about the course of his life. And that's about it.

He became a professor in 1934 and taught for the next thirty-eight years. In 1949, he published *The Hero with a Thousand Faces*. He believed that every story borrowed from a pattern, retracing a circle, a journey. He called this the "monomyth," or the "Hero's Journey." Joseph Campbell's ideas came from hours of reading almost everything he could find. The idea of a hero cycle was not new at the time. For example, Otto Rank and Lord Raglan both puzzled over why heroes were so often born royal orphans only to die dramatically on hilltops.[26] Campbell also wondered about this and studied Jung's work in psychology to better understand the pattern. Jung considered myths as narrated abstractions emerging from forms located beneath consciousness. Although Campbell learned a lot from Jung, he wasn't satisfied with myth just rising up from the unconscious. Campbell saw the mythical forms in a more idealized way, as though each myth participated in something from above, transcendental as though from the "energies of the cosmos."[27]

Campbell and his lessons continue to receive both praise and criticism. The monomyth may not be a modern, rational explanation of the cosmos, but it has greatly influenced the storytellers and audiences of today. George Lucas, the creative spirit behind *Star Wars*, cites Campbell's work as a major inspiration for his reinvention of mythology. Many of Disney's screenwriters used Campbell's teachings for storytelling structure in their stories. The Wachowskis played with the pattern in Neo's journey for *The Matrix* movie series. Many of the stories produced in the West today depend on ideas from Campbell's monomyth. We have all been mutely indoctrinated into a new kind of religion that quietly walks hand in hand with many of our Western beliefs.

Campbell's monomyth can be used as a kind of Procrustean bed. Procrustes was an innkeeper who believed each of his guests, no matter their size, age, or shape, could fit into his guestroom bed. To prove it, he would lay them out on the bed. If the guest measured up too short, Procrustes would stretch the guest to fit. If the guest's legs hung over the end of the bed, Procrustes would cut them off.

This is a cautionary tale about what we might call today confirmation bias. For some people, a rule can become more important to prove than the evidence that tests it. Nassim Taleb used the illustration of the Procrustean bed in his writings as a warning to everyone, but especially to academics, economists, and politicians.[28] The warning applies to religious groups, too, especially when faced with the modern challenges of plurality and moral authority. Plato's cave can be thought of as another Procrustean bed. When it comes to knowledge, human beings have a long history of making beds and then wanting to lie in them.

Campbell could tuck any story into the bedsheets of his monomyth. Like Peterson's diagram of the constituent elements of experience and Plato's guided tour of the cave, the monomyth stands as another map for action: "We have only to follow the thread of the hero-path."[29] The Hero's Journey usually begins in a setting that can be called home. This is culture. This is the walled, protected garden or city where things are predictable and understood—how things should be. It can be perfect or imperfect, but at least it's what is known. Often in this setting, events are well anticipated and order rules the day. A disruption occurs—some change or threat that doesn't fit with the known world, like the presence of novelty. The limits of the culture appear in a crack or vulnerability, exposing home to the outside world and its natural forces. In other words, *mother* pays an unexpected visit and brings *daughter* along as well.

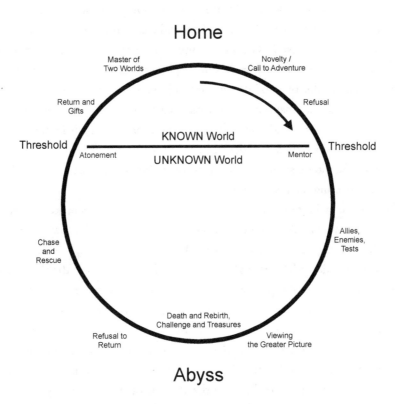

The appearance of novelty is also a call to investigation and adventure. There is a threshold where something grabs the hero's attention. The hero is given a choice—ignore the anomaly or initiate the process of inquiry. The hero who chooses to step outside the once predictable but now questioned home begins a journey that could threaten the hero's very existence. The hero is letting mother reign over the new situation and acting in a new world, acting upon the new and unprocessed information. A mentor appears, often a surrogate or substitute father figure or a potential lover who can act as a teacher with new information. Events, tests, and friends move the character and prepare the hero for a confrontation with the unknown. These tests are opportunities to build skill, competence, and knowledge. Beyond home, there is the abyss—chaos, the unpredictable. Beware: there be dragons.

Surrounded by the unknown, the hero faces another choice: find a path between what is real and not real, what is important and not important, and then act. From the abyss comes a gift, treasure, or piece of knowledge that can help restore the balance that first threatened home. The hero faces another choice—stay in the abyss or return. The decision ultimately depends upon what the hero loves. Upon crossing the threshold back from the unknown and to the known, the hero then uses the new gift to recreate the order of home and rebuild identity. Campbell's circle illustrates a map of revolutionary change and problem-solving, from the perspective of mythological consciousness.

This is an action-oriented model of reality, a goal-oriented model of reality. As the name suggests, the Hero's Journey is about what the hero does and decides, and the consequences of those actions. Though Campbell lived in the twentieth century, the monomyth is not about modern thinking. He plumbed the depths of stories older than Plato, and likely from more expansive sources than Plato could have imagined possible. Campbell jumped from one giant's shoulders to another.

The abyss, the true nature of the world, is not a place of fundamental order that we observe easily. It is not a place of discrete and determined objects. It is everything in vast and raw complexity, unfiltered by rational mappings, predictable patterns, or observed bits of evidence. It is overwhelming to the witness. And this feeling of being overwhelmed is important because it is a common experience we intimately understand as limited beings. The abyss holds treasures for the one who carves out some small part from the overwhelming, consuming maw and makes a new world from it, passing the test of entropy.

Campbell wanted to make good students of life. He wanted to give them access to the wisdom of the past, so they could act when overcome with uncertainty. Campbell's journey is a story of bottom-up problem-solving. Imagine the communication from a coach toward a performer. Individuals play roles and discover talents. The individual decides on how to act given the circumstances of the situation. The environment holds power, but the hero navigates some aspect of action within the environment and acts as a model of action for the audience. The metaphor of the Hero's Journey is, comparatively, an auditory experience—the call to adventure, advice spoken and shared, the murmurs and roars of the wild unknown, the pronouncement of a return and resolution.

One of the most successful and enduring stories of the last century is J. R. R. Tolkien's *The Lord of the Rings*. Three of his characters illustrate the struggle of the hero as it plays out within the psyche and through relationships. Frodo stood between Sam and Smeagol, deciding the fate of his journey, his community, and his world. In the most dangerous furnace of Middle-earth, Frodo faced the toughest opponent he would ever encounter—his own will. Sam, the faithful servant, carried him to the point of decision. Smeagol writhed under the torment of his own twisted motivations. By the end, Smeagol tried every kind of politeness, submission, and treachery imaginable to take that decision away from Frodo.

Of the three, Sam turned out to have the best attitude through the journey and the most successful answer to the tests of the furnace. Smeagol perished along with his precious fixations. Frodo came out alive but withdrawn, as though there was little left of him but a weakened spirit. Sam made it home a whole person, ready to marry his love and care for a family of his own.[30]

Northrop Frye Made Waves

In 1929, a young man from New Brunswick went to Toronto to compete in a national typing contest. While in Toronto he applied to be a student at the university. He studied literature and theology and then journeyed out as a student minister for pastoral charges in the vast farmlands of the Prairies. Though ordained in the United Church of Canada, the flat plains of Saskatchewan did not win the young man's heart. He returned to Toronto and married his love, a woman by the name of Helen. He married another one of his sweethearts when he returned as well: he committed himself to the pursuit of academic life and changed how people across the world approached literary criticism. Northrop Frye was one of the first to suggest that criticism, appreciation, and commentary on the written word could be organized, systematized, unified, and understood under a general theory. When it came to the written word, Frye was an exceptional perceiver.

Frye knew that discussions about the Bible, or religious texts more generally, often started with a common question—are these writings histories (with facts and interpretations of actual events) or fictions (with stories and opinions on what is valued)? As a student of the West, Frye decided to address the problem by looking at the Bible and literature. He found that when this question is asked about the Bible, as a library of texts, the work is unique to an extent that the problem cannot be decided at all. A different understanding needs to be found. The question needs to be asked in a better way for the inquiry to lead to better insights.

Frye also found an important and reoccurring pattern in the text that spoke of something besides history or fiction. The ebb and flow of the text had a recurring shape, a suggestive principle. This narrative pattern can appear in history or fiction. This pattern involved events or characters starting in a kind of steady or ideal state. An interruption, in the form of infidelity or corruption, destabilized the society or family. This interruption moved the action of the group into a condition of war or slavery. A return follows, usually associated with a deliverer of some kind. After, there is a restoration of freedom or recreation of order. Whereas Joseph Campbell mapped the journey of a hero, Frye expanded the level of perception to the family, group, or society. Whereas Plato framed his analogy in terms of a guiding teacher and student prisoner, in Frye's scheme, change came in the form of the observed other—a deliverer able to bring about a new way of seeing things, prompting a community to follow. Whereas Peterson looked to the evolution of living things over adaptations and environments, Frye looked to societies travelling through time as much as through geography. Instead of a circle, Frye used a repeating U-shaped pattern.[31]

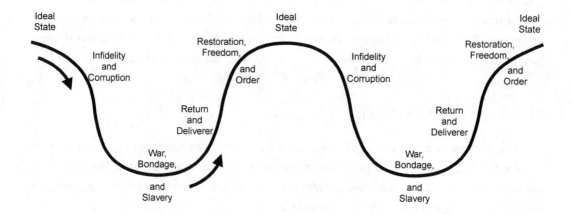

According to Frye, the narrative structure of the Bible has a conception of time different from other sources—away from a cyclical pattern and instead toward a pattern of sequential events. A closed loop suggests a kind of mechanization like gears or motors—a return on cycles and a denial of historical development. We can look at time as a circle, but we can also look at time as an arrow. With this U-shaped pattern, a narrative establishes a beginning and an end, a sequencing of experiences with priority given to emerging developments instead of repetition. This is not a matter of doing the same thing over and over again, expecting the same results. Instead, through the progressions of the pattern, an increased level of consciousness, freedom, or transcendence can be achieved through each dip and swing. But it isn't just about individual elevation. The individual, the community, the culture, and the environment all participate in the journey. This is a family or social contract involving everything, including time and space and experience and perception. Frye's use of the wave-like, U-shaped pattern demonstrates how a shift in point of view can change a circle on a map into a line of progression through time. Mathematics students might recognize the wave as a circular pattern mapped out graphically as a function.

This pattern had "spiritual" significance for Northrop Frye, but he used that word in a limited way for his students. In his lectures, he would explain that the word "spiritual" must be understood the same way we would use the word "metaphorical." If something is to be considered spiritual, it is to be considered *in the spirit* of something. In this way, an event in the present can be in the spirit of an event in the past. Spiritually—that is metaphorically—the Garden of Eden can be the Promised Land, the walled city of Ezekiel, Jerusalem, and a Messiah character, all at once. The word "is" turns out to be much more complicated than signifying an exclusive identity or simple equation. Frye's wave pattern repeats several times through the Bible. But the characters, settings, and symbols change, as though the elements of stories themselves are taking up roles and playing parts, leading to an anticipated, future resolution.

Associative thinking developed long before logical syllogisms or the scientific methods of inquiry. Frye saw in the metaphor a foundational linguistic statement, on par in significance to the basic equation in mathematics. But he also had a sense of caution and humour when it came to metaphorical thinking. Logic states such things as "A is A" and "A is never B." However, the metaphor transcends the rules of logic. In a metaphor, *this is that*. A metaphor can state "A is B" and remain coherent if the audience assents to the association. According to Frye, "Nobody can take a metaphor seriously except... the lunatic, the lover, and the poet."[32]

However, this is exactly what we do every day, consciously or unconsciously, when we use language. Analogous learning is fundamental to understanding categories, for example. A tree in a garden can be thought of as all the trees in a garden. It can also be a symbol of strength, individuality, a source of nourishment, a branching family, or all these things together. In the course of our lives, the influence of our families and the influence of our beliefs can simultaneously make us lunatics, lovers, and poets. One of the most difficult passages in the Biblical text reads:

> Their corpses shall lie in the streets of the great city, which spiritually is called Sodom and Egypt, where our Lord also was crucified.[33]

The great city is spiritually called Sodom and Egypt, and also Golgotha or Calvary. This makes little sense if these places or events are understood as separate historical facts and spaces. But in a metaphorical sense, these distinct figures of story are interchangeable in meaning or symbolic referent, in the spirit of each other. Together, metaphorically, they point beyond themselves and through to something else. This kind of association can span across characters, objects, and settings. Nor is this reserved for sacred texts. The *Harry Potter* series is steeped in metaphorical references and the developmental cycles of the school year. It makes little sense unless understood and enjoyed in that spirit. For children, each school year is an adventure, a reflection and expansion of similar themes and echoed meanings. Competence, increased skill, and graduated responsibilities can shape the identities of an individual, a family, an organization, and a population. In this process of further expansion, the individual and the group can both be better equipped to face new information, turning tragic stories into heroic triumphs.

Does this mapping of narrative transcendence grant the Bible some authoritative status for all time? Or does this mean we must take all associative thinking as authoritative? To every authority, there is a season, a place, a time, and a reason to be cautious. There is an inextricable danger to poetry, lunacy, and love. Frye was both careful and optimistic, pointing out that an apocalypse was not the end. Instead, an apocalypse, in its original meaning, pointed to a revelation. It signalled the end of seeing things in an old way. If Narcissus had turned his attention to Echo's call, he could have corrected his fixations and stopped seeing his reflection as the object of his affection. An apocalypse is an opportunity to cast off what no longer works and ask questions leading to a new way of being—the next peak or trough of consciousness and experience.

Lonergan attempted to map out the relationship between progress and decline as well. His examination of historical dynamics associated progress with things like intellectual development and bias with decline. However, he proposed another dynamic that can be understood as differentiated from progress and decline—recovery. Recovery adds the sense of correction or restoration to the process of history, either for the individual who has a change of mind or a community that has a change in tradition. Recovery is a chance to either retrieve something from the past that was meaningful or let go of something that no longer serves the historical development.[34]

If we examine our relationship to the observed other in this process, the discovery of anomaly might prove to be another useful differentiation between progress and decline. Like recovery, discovery acts as a vertex or inflection point, bringing to light a change in direction. Discovery can take the form of something present but unnamed, such as experiencing a moment of corruption or finding an opportunity for further inquiry.

The serial nature of radio, television, and movie productions meant a show's cast would routinely be put through the troughs and crests of iterated and reiterated story-lines. The original series of *Star Trek* presented episodes as successive layers on characters and settings. The audiences followed along with the steps of exploration, descent, bondage or war, to redemption and restoration of stability. With the show's success over two generations, new shows emerged—spinoffs with entirely different characters. But again, the flow of the wave continued as though through ever-expanding stages of plot, theme, and consciousness.

A bond between two very different characters created the core foundation of the original series. Captain Kirk and Mr. Spock came from two different worlds, but they shared an unlikely friendship and goal in exploring the unexplored. In their relationship, one was not just observer to the other observed, but a sibling in shared consciousness. Through each episodic adventure, each challenge, they found a way to face the dangers of the galaxy and save each other, again and again. The reboot movies of the story have gone back to the first characters with which the audience fell in love. Different actors have taken up the roles, adapting the characters and the bonds between them to new situations, sparking both bitter resentment and favourable curiosity from the audience.[35] But some of the old wisdom and storytelling magic lives on. As Frye's teachings suggest, each wave or episode or production offers us a chance to begin again, expanding the breadth and depth of our own character and consciousness as we take up the roles of our lives. Also, as observers we can make the associations between story, pattern, and behaviour to inform our own relationships with novelty and wisdom.

Wisdom, in the Biblical context, is considered an essential part of the creative act. Wisdom is also considered the Daughter of God, present at the time of creation, or the beginning of the narrative. In the Christian tradition, the Christ figure is sometimes referred to as a bridegroom, the individual. The congregation is metaphorically, or spiritually, the bride of Christ. In the book of Revelation, the bride is identified with Jerusalem and Israel, as city and land. But Wisdom is also a female personification present in books such as Proverbs. Counsel from this figurative Lady of Wisdom seems to take two basic forms—love for the consistency, prudence, practice and participation in the law holding together a society, as well as the love for growth in skill, continuity, and transcendence of the past. In Frye's words,

> Wisdom as continuity of institutions goes back to the fact of a social contract, to the fact that we belong to something at least nine months before we are anything.[36]

The individual and the family or group can emerge out of the mechanical repeat of the past and play with new ideas that bring advancement. If our psychological development involves the integration of both light and shadow, then another dimension of our identities involves finding a balance between novelty and wisdom. By falling in love with both consistency and with adaptive change, as in consciously recognizing their aspects in our lives, we might better weather the ups and downs of the world's history. Wisdom speaks as a woman in Proverbs:

> Then I was by him, as one brought up with him: and I was daily his delight, rejoicing always before him; Rejoicing in the habitable part of his earth; and my delights were with the sons of men. Now therefore hearken unto me, O ye children: for blessed are they that keep my ways. Hear instruction, and be wise, and refuse it not.[37]

Frye pointed to this passage in his lectures, suggesting the word "rejoicing" is a poor translation. The original Hebrew makes more sense if the female Wisdom is "playing throughout the earth." Frye compared the Greek goddess of wisdom, Athena, to this playful Hebrew image of wisdom, or Sophia. Athena wore armour and carried a shield. The Biblical daughter might as well have had a skipping rope or a swing, according to Frye. Athena sought to win a victory as in a battle. Sophia expressed her energy for the sake of achieving a feeling of being alive, in the moment, and in the flow of accomplished skill and ability.[38]

Frye commented in his lectures that the difference between superstition and religion is this element of apocalypse or revelation. Superstition is doing the same thing over and over again and expecting the same results. Religion, for Frye, meant doing the same thing over and over again until it no longer achieved the desired results. Some people today make the quick association that "religion is just superstition." This criticism may seem unfounded or offensive to those initiated into religious traditions, but it also may be a call for devout religious people to examine Frye's distinction. Has religion today, or at least the popular understanding of religious practice, become superstition, in the sense that doing the same things over and over again no longer brings desired results? Can we integrate the clear-eyed lady Athena with the playful child Sophia, and love them both as they deserve? This question needs more and more attention in a world of technological progress and social fragility. Jeremy Rifkin also looked beyond the theological aspects of the Hebrew tradition and its contribution to the development of a consciousness between individual and community:

> To be a Jew is to engage in an ongoing personal conversation with the Lord Almighty.... Every individual, regardless of their stature in life, has access to the Lord of lords. No other previous cosmological story had ever elevated the individual in this manner.... The new Hebrew narrative was as much about the emergence of the self from the collective as it was about the advent of monotheism.[39]

It is a common expectation in the West that every child should know how to read. This expectation only emerged in the last couple of hundred years. Perhaps in this age of science and reason, we can hope for a new expectation where each individual engages in a personal, conscious conversation with their motivations and behaviours. We may be lunatics, lovers, and poets after all, but we play out these roles in conversation with our families, our communities, and with all of being. Frye's wave diagram is not just the ebb and flow of the Hebrew society and the initial developments of the Christian religion in an old text. It can also be thought of as a map of the spiritual relationships and responsibilities around the divine individual, the observed other, the community, and the unknown. The longer those relationships are steered by something like love instead of war, the better prepared we will probably be against the eternal returning tests of entropy.

Circles and Lines, Emergence and Responsibility

Alex, in Anthony Burgess's *A Clockwork Orange*, experienced a striking series of training sessions in the spirit of the shadows in Plato's Cave. After he was sentenced for murder, Alex served time in a correctional facility—a prison-like panopticon. He volunteered for a government experiment that would make him good. The training involved strapping him down in a chair and fixing his head to look only toward a movie screen. The assistants kept his eyes open mechanically so that he had to watch the selected films. The films displayed scenes of violent acts and criminal behaviour. At first Alex enjoyed the show. Burgess's modern twist on the cave, however, came when Alex started to feel uncomfortably sick the more he watched the films. The government and the assistants conditioned Alex to react in a physiologically predetermined way. His body, once compelled toward violent acts, no longer enjoyed the stimulus. Instead, he rejected it the way a body might reject a spoiled chicken dinner.

Alex made it through the therapy and later demonstrated a complete inability to do anything wilfully violent upon other people. Deemed no longer a threat, the correctional institute released him. However, society did not simply absorb Alex as a functioning member. He no longer defended himself against violence or manipulation. He was labelled as "good" by the authorities but not given the means to play a part in the world at all. In this state, he did not find a role for himself. He was observer, not actor. Other characters used him for their own motives. In the beginning of his story, he acted more like a wolf after prey than a child preparing for adulthood. After the treatment, Alex became a sheep led by others rather than a lion with responsibility.

Alex's story can be understood as an adventuring line between the what is of his world and what should be. He followed his interests. Along the way he met anomaly and novelty. The story can also be mapped as U-shaped iterations of his descents of behaviour and rises into further consciousness. He committed crimes. He lied to his social services officer. He controlled his friends. He volunteered for therapy. In each scene, he made decisions on where to direct his attention and what motivations will direct his actions. Through the process of trial and correction, he finally came to a choice about his interests and responsibilities.

Plato's teacher in the cave is the one who initiated the journey out of the darkness. The teacher, as authority and guide, undid the prisoner-student's restraints. The teacher showed him the fire and the shadowy puppet show. The teacher led the subject out of the cave. The subject, compelled to follow, submits completely to the decision-making and initiating steps of the teacher. This type of process is institutional. Traditional schools model this process with highly structured classrooms, lecture-focused transmission of information, and authorities holding the reins throughout the experience. Rituals are fixed and set into observances more than actions.

Plato's story of the cave has survived longer than any actual European government. Something about this model works, in that it brings individuals into alignment with group identity and the processes of culture. It is a modern story about our relationship to information. The modern thinker intimately understands how light brings information. We view the stars through a mediated screen more than we view them by looking up to the night sky. The modern world also relies on a deep assumption that underneath everything, there is a predictable order to things, and our understanding of reality keeps closing the gaps between mystery and model. We believe the truth that the fundamental underlying order of nature can be observed with effort and sacrifice. Knowledge builds upon itself in progressive steps, to something brighter and more accurate each time one steps out of the cave and into the light.

In Campbell's monomyth, the mentor seems to appear only when the student is ready. Even though destiny might play behind the curtains of the process, the hero, conscious or unconscious of it, has a choice. She can choose her path—hero or victim or villain. Whatever the hero feels compelled to do, she participates in some fundamental way with the initiation of action or decision-making. The hero voluntarily steps out of the boundaries, or beyond the walls, of home. She decides what is compelling enough to initiate action, moving her into a sequence of events with anomaly and unpredictability. This leads to something potentially better than what she leaves behind.

Campbell's first concern was not the state, but instead the workings of story in relation to personal experiences. When the West places rights on an individual or makes the individual sacred before the law and authority, we recognize in some way that an individual's initiative, decisions, and actions are fundamental to lived experiences. The authority of our leaders, the law, and circumstance are all weighted to the authority of the individual. An audience has a choice of where to invest its attention—emotionally compelling stories or authoritative lectures. Lectures are for the converted or at the very least symbolically chained. Narratives are for initiating people to take up the way presented. The choice we have in our own relationships depends greatly on the journey we are creating with the other—conversing or preaching. Over time, through participation or observation, the individual collects a series of these experiences—descents and elevations—and a store of responses to the calls of the environments. From those experiences of integration, disintegration, and reintegration of identity, the individual emerges more prepared for inquiry, adventure, and further expansions in consciousness.

Bernard Lonergan was a Jesuit priest. His life's work can be seen as an attempt to reconcile the long history of our world and the religious beliefs that came from that history. He wanted to understand evolutionary processes and close the gaps of traditional theology. In his efforts, he came to his own formulation of a test of entropy. In his words:

> The challenge of history is for man progressively to restrict the realm of chance or fate or destiny and progressively enlarge the realm of conscious grasp and deliberate choice.[40]

For Lonergan, the mystery of his god revealed itself in a world process based on what he came to express as "emergent probability." Our understanding of natural or scientific laws comes from specific circumstances abstracted to some correlation or function between those circumstances. But when these laws are applied to further events, deviations emerge between actual and ideal results. Statistical laws and statistical methods of inquiry anticipate that some data will not conform to the more systematic laws of discovery. The two methods, scientific and statistical, complement one another and reveal something dynamic, leading to further inquiries. The inquirer experiences progressive levels of conscious understanding and participation. Emergence, survival, recurrence, and disintegration play around each other in this process. As an example, single-celled organisms went through a process of development in certain environments that brought about multi-celled organisms. Lonergan agreed with Charles Darwin in that probability played a role in the selection processes of evolution. However, Lonergan did not want to reduce those processes to mere random chance. The impulse toward greater levels of complexity, and the success of some chances over other chances, suggested to Lonergan that selection was not a phenomenon that could be understood by mere reductive materialist thinking. The interplay between construction and repression exercised by intelligence and choice through history suggests a path to both sense and imagination. Lonergan states:

> Man, then, is at once explanatory genus and explanatory species. He is explanatory genus, for he represents a higher system beyond sensibility. But that genus is coincident with species, for it is not just a higher system but a source of higher systems. In man there occurs the transition from the intelligible to the intelligent.[41]

Lonergan's ambition was to find a way to bring scientific investigation and religious practice together under love. The more we pay attention to the process of inquiry, which enlarges the realm of consciousness, the less of a role chance will play in our existence. Put another way, we might avoid the tragic decisions and fates of Agamemnon and Jephthah. With better maps through our experiences, we too can recognize the moments we come to thresholds in our lives. And with that recognition, we enlarge the realm of conscious grasp and deliberate choice.

Thresholds, Decisions, Observations, Actions

In the process of inquiry, we often need to recalibrate our attention, our skills, our thinking, and our commitments. The relationship between apprentice and master is an important one for creating a developmental transition from irresponsibility to responsibility, between ignorance and intelligence. The relationship fosters a corrective dialogue taking place between ideal and actual, serving the needs and direction of the difficult craft of living. In the transition of responsibilities, the master must negotiate a love for the craft with the instinct that prefers being in control. The profession of education shares something with lunacy, in that the process involves doing the same things again and again but expecting different results. If a teacher presents a lesson and the student does not learn, the teacher can blame the student or present the lesson again. Development of skills requires repetition and practise, refining results, limiting the role of chance, and favouring deliberate choice in each iteration.

Both encouraging mentors and inhibiting powers cluster around the thresholds between known and unknown worlds. In story, they might be personifications and characterizations, or simply mechanisms of the environment—tools or obstacles. Where Plato's teacher led with complete authority and directed knowledge, the mentors in Campbell's monomyth assist with skilled expertise or wise information (incomplete, and possibly even incorrect or ambiguous, but still more information than what's in the hero's possession). Authority remains in the hero and her motivations, as steered by many influencing factors from the environment. Whatever compels her onto this path, it is not solely the teacher. With this personal compulsion comes responsibility.

Within both the story of the cave and the monomyth, thresholds act as symbolic shifts of authority from one archetype to another. The figurative known (or anticipated) tends to hold a place of authority in the cave or in home. This can be extended to the realm of what should be in Peterson's diagram or the steady state of Frye's wave. However, the manifestation of the unanticipated demonstrates to the individual that what is known is incomplete. The map doesn't map everything we always want it to map. Campbell described this optimistically as the call to adventure. This call can be refused or accepted. In either case, the presentation of unanticipated information marks an opportunity for the individual to follow another archetype besides what is known. The individual can fall in love with the process of asking further questions or hold to past information and stall the process of inquiry.

The Hero's Journey addresses this idea of transition between a master and apprentice differently than Plato's Cave. Responsibility always rests upon the hero and individual rather than the state or teacher. This process is perhaps not as efficient or linear as Plato's guided instruction, but it may be more common to personal experience. The pursuit of conscious grasp and deliberate choice in lived moments, to use Lonergan's words, provides us with the transition from the intelligible to the intelligent within ourselves. If the individual is sacred, according to law or religion or scientific language, then perhaps these maps could help us pass the tests of entropy and recognize our responsibilities to the individual in the other.

For mythology and narrative, the abyss as marked in Campbell's circle tends to be the place where the figurative unknown holds authority. This is a place of uncertainty, where both void and the all are not differentiated into discrete known objects. The individual cannot fully anticipate consequences of actions. However, in that significant moment, the hero, as an actor taking responsibility for her actions and decisions, challenges the authority of the archetypal unknown by focusing attention on one particular thing in that formless vortex and seeing it in relation to a motivational goal. Something in the all can serve the hero's purpose or motivation and bring an insight toward innovation or new information.

Plato's circle treats this moment not so much from a place of action but instead a place of observation. Instead of an abyss, this is a place of light and ideals for Plato. After a lengthy initiation with the individual, the teacher releases the individual to observe the world as illuminated by the light of the natural world outside the cave. In this place of light, the unknown is still ordered, according to Plato, with fixed forms in contrast to the temporary shadows of the cave. Quickly after this moment of observation, the student returns to the authority of the teacher.

The two circles present two very different aesthetics, two very different relationships with information, and two very different relationships with authority. As well, the two circles present two very different relationships with the other. In Campbell's Hero's Journey, the walls of identity dissolve. Opportunities for what Lonergan calls self-appropriation emerge. The hero may change or reshape her self, her own identity, and even identify with the observed other, whatever it may be. In Plato's Cave, the subject comes to a final revelation:

> The thing he would be able to do last would be to look directly at the sun itself, and gaze at it without using reflections in water or any other medium, but as it is in itself... he would come to the conclusion that it is the sun that produces the changing seasons and years and controls everything in the visible world, and is in a sense responsible for everything that he and his fellow-prisoners used to see.[42]

Even in this highest moment of conscious experience, responsibility ultimately lies in the authoritative hands of the light. The subject observes and understands something still true to us today 2,500 years later. As an echo to this, why would a story referencing the sun appear at the beginning of a chapter in this book? But the student of Plato's guide does not act. Like Newton and the creation story of the concept of gravity, the role of observation takes centre stage rather than action.

In Campbell's Hero's Journey, the hero's encounter with the abyss leads to another threshold moment in which the hero must often rely on someone else. In the story of Theseus and the Minotaur, the hero, Theseus, defeated the beast in the labyrinth. However, this victory was not enough. He then found himself still in the encapsulating environment of the labyrinth. Ariadne, the daughter of King Minos, fell in love with Theseus and gave him the tools to find his way out of the maze. In this short description of the story we see the relationships between four archetypes—Theseus as acting Hero, Bull and labyrinth as manifestations of the realm of the unknown, King Minos as a tyrannical aspect of culture, and Ariadne as daughter and observed other. Ariadne did not just provide Theseus with the string to use so he could retrace his steps in the labyrinth. She also compelled him to return. Theseus could have taken the Minotaur's place as dominion master in the labyrinth. But Ariadne gave him reason to return. Theseus freed the other Athenians who came with him to the labyrinth of King Minos, a second audience for the hero to identify with. Theseus could have also challenged Minos for the kingdom, but another audience compelled him—his family back in Athens. He readied a ship and sailed for home.

Plato also wrote about the subject's eyes taking time to adjust to changes in light. The return to the darkness of the cave would leave a person blind and bewildered for a while. The change from disillusionment to reintroduction to illusion generates important questions. What is the value of the trip and why are the subjects so bound and controlled? Who benefits from all this? Good leaders, in Plato's eyes, had to experience both the light and the shadow, and steer their communities toward the upward progress of the mind into more intelligible, conscious realms of living—no easy task.

With the Hero's Journey the return brings the hero back home, proverbially, where he performs one last deed. In some way the hero brings a restoration of order, so the individual and community can flourish once again. The community benefits through the resolution. If lucky, the hero achieves a reward, often taking the form of a spouse, a level of status, or a treasure. But he might just as likely die on a hill. However, death can restore or reveal a hero's identity quite clearly for an audience. The community may bestow a spiritual authority on him and possibly even return the hero to life, symbolically or otherwise. In adopting the gift, the new story, or the restored order, the audience takes up the identity. They also prepare themselves for the next fall and rise of Frye's wave pattern. Ultimately, the hero acts out a supreme way of being, rather than observes a supreme way of knowing.

Peterson's line and Frye's wave suggest an arrow of time. In this sense, there is always a threshold on the horizon or in the future, an unrealized other or unknown to meet with the proper attitude. For both Plato and Campbell, the journey involves a return, bringing back or at least communicating something to others. In each case, the community can then hear, share, adopt, and build identity either through adopting the model of the individual or receiving gifts from the individual. In this sense, there is a bridge between hero, story, community, and reader. The progressions of the traveller on Peterson's line and Frye's wave suggest something about goal-oriented behaviour, novelty, corruption, and the fragile state of our perceptions. However, like the two circles, there is a clear importance given to the ability to adapt to new information. Anomalies will emerge in our experiences. Our relationship to the process of inquiry can make the difference in how we respond to that call. If we face anomalies with the attention, understanding, competence, and responsibility that leads to love, we can participate in a self-correcting process. In doing so, we can avoid the static domination of the state or institution and respect the raw flux of the unknown. Frye's U-shaped pattern suggests that we will experience repeated chances to play our roles better, to fall in love with inquiry again, and expand our collective consciousness.[43] Progress, discovery, decline, and recovery can all be understood within the processes of love.

In the larger circles of story, audiences compete for the hero's attention and approval. According to some sources, Athena, the daughter of Zeus, bent the ear of Theseus. She persuaded the hero to leave Ariadne on the Minoan shore. Today's Western audiences may think Theseus more a coward than a hero for leaving Ariadne behind. But Athena was not a goddess of love, and especially not a goddess of sexual infatuation. Ancient Greek moralities and sensibilities do not exactly correspond to today's sensibilities. Family held a more important place of authority in people's heads and hearts than romantic relationships. Perhaps the lesson for today is that the health of family relationships may often come before the pursuit of sexual relationships. Theseus and Ariadne had a brief, exhilarating infatuation. They worked together for a common goal they could identify with. Theseus unchained his fellow Athenians as well, saving them from the labyrinth. He also had the means to act on his compulsion to help his family and his home city. At least Theseus could act with some personal responsibility even if he did not fall in love with Ariadne.

In a religious context, many people have felt it a heroic act to step outside the congregation and find the light on their own. The confines of the authoritative institution keep individuals in some level of shadow because that confirms the structure and authority of the institution. However, this also robs the individual of all responsibility as well as cements past superstitions. It reduces the subject to a tool or object instead of a person with dignity, respect, and integrity.

In Jordan Peterson's words in *Maps of Meaning*:

> Recognition of the essentially ambivalent nature of the predictable—stultifying but secure—means discarding simplistic theories which attribute the existence of human suffering and evil purely to the state, or which presume that the state is all that is good, and that the individual should exist merely as subordinate or slave.... The Great Father is protection and necessary aid to growth, but absolute identification with his personality and force ultimately destroys the spirit. Culture, career, and role do not sufficiently exhaust the possibilities of the individual.[44]

What is known and desired does hold authority, but it is not absolute. This holds for spiritual journeys, personal development, the management of our fears and motivations, and exposure to new information through media.

Using four maps for a journey could bring about confusions and further questions. How do we know we are heading in the right direction? How do we know when we reach our destination? In the larger story of the life of Theseus, the hero faced other challenges and tasks. If the trip to Crete can be thought of as one adventure over a period of time, then it would be one U-shaped pattern in his life. In other adventures, the hero Theseus met up with the innkeeper Procrustes. Procrustes wanted to treat Theseus the way he did many of his guests. Procrustes felt his bed was the ideal and all his guests should fit perfectly into it. As the diabolical intentions of Procrustes became evident, Theseus found an imaginative resolution to the dangerous motivations of the tyrant. Theseus put Procrustes in the bed and made the innkeeper fit into it. Procrustes never tortured another guest after that. The labyrinth and the bed became metaphorically similar—dangerous settings to overcome. Theseus as hero acted with responsibility in each instance toward his life and toward what he thought should be.

We can prepare ourselves for a change in mind, for the next stages on the path, with a process of inquiry, measurement, and evaluation, fixing our eyes and ears on love. In the process we will expand our current consciousness and become more adaptive to the tests of living. As well, it is important to cultivate a level of consciousness in each moment and hear the echoes that tell us when something no longer works. There are times when superstitions must be tested, defended, abandoned, or transcended to restore both the freedom of deliberate choice and the dignity of order that comes from consciousness. The individual, the institution, and the community all need to recognize when it is time to adopt new modes of behaviour and when something no longer works.

Birth, Death, and a Doctor's Love of Inquiry

A Viennese hospital in the 1800s established two maternity clinics. Across Europe, people struggled with the problem of infanticide with illegitimate children. Many communities set up free maternity institutions offering to care for the unwanted or soon-to-be abandoned infants. Underprivileged women and prostitutes would give birth in a maternity clinic. Midwives and doctors in training would receive experience from real mothers giving birth. If the woman survived giving birth, she would leave the maternity ward and her child. The child would stay in an orphanage service. Male doctors in training worked in the first clinic. Female midwives in training worked in the second clinic.

The reputation of the two clinics grew in Vienna. If given a choice, pregnant women preferred going to the second clinic. Instead of using the first clinic, some pregnant women gave birth in the streets and then handed over their children for the offered child-care benefits. What did they know? More women died after giving birth in the first clinic than in the second. Many of these women were dying of what was called childbed fever.

In 1846, a young medical doctor won a position with the first and second clinics at the Vienna General Hospital. The reputation of the first clinic worried him, but as a man of science he believed in investigating the data. The reputation turned out to be well founded—statistically the maternal mortality rate in the first clinic averaged two to three times the mortality rate in the second clinic.[45] The doctor grew frustrated with the situation. Why would there be a difference? The frustration continued when he found the frequency of deaths in women from the doctor clinic was higher than deaths occurring with street births. What protected those who delivered outside the clinic? What could be safer about a street birth for a pregnant woman?

We don't usually connect scientists and their work to mythological stories, but the story of Dr. Ignaz Semmelweis figuratively traces to all four of our maps of experience and initiated a new beginning for the medical community. He found an anomaly and he fixed his attention on it in order to gain further insight. He went past the threshold of his regular hospital routines and anticipations to learn more. In terms of Plato's cave, Semmelweis's teacher wasn't the senior doctor above him but the method of scientific investigation itself. He checked the numbers and kept meticulous, systematic notes, moving closer to the light of the answer. Through a series of experiments, Semmelweis began a process to eliminate all differences between the wards to find the variable that would deliver a solution and the path to a better way.

Some of his early investigations tell us something of the stage of medical practice at the time. Each variable was a chance to give attention to novelty, an invitation for insight to emerge from the investigation. He dismissed overcrowding first. The second clinic was the more popular of the two, yet the mortality rate was lower. Both wards had the same climate conditions. Women in the second clinic would often give birth on their sides, as part of the midwife practices, whereas in the first clinic women would give birth on their backs. He ordered doctors in the first clinic to keep women on their sides. This led to no change in the death rates.

Even religion entered into the investigation. Semmelweis noted the common practices of a priest who would come in to the ward when someone died of childbed fever. Maybe the priest's solemn walk through the ward and his attendant's bell ringing terrified women to the point they would experience fear, develop a fever, and contract the sickness. Semmelweis suggested the priest walk a different route and keep the bell out of the ceremony.

The scientific method unchained Semmelweis and allowed him to gaze past the elusive shadows. Step by frustrating step, he rose out of the cave of ignorance until he was able to make a connection and point toward a brief glimpse of the light of new knowledge. Each variable was also a potential redeemer or deliverer, freeing Semmelweis of the tension of his inquiry and freeing the pregnant women from the bondage of their potentially fatal situation. One of his colleagues, a doctor, had fallen ill and died after pricking his finger while performing an autopsy on a female patient who had died from childbed fever. Semmelweis, after studying the doctor's symptoms, realized the man had died from the same illness as the woman. How could a man die of childbed fever?

Semmelweis used this finding to discover another difference between the two wards. Doctors performed autopsies. Due to the amount of time involved in childbirth, it was common practice for doctors in training to attend autopsies between childbirths. Midwives in the hospital never took part in autopsies and rarely took part in any kind of surgery. Semmelweis came to a conclusion not considered part of the medical establishment's body of knowledge at the time. Passing a threshold held by past authorities, Semmelweis proposed the idea that particles or elements of the cadavers remained on the hands of doctors after the autopsies. When a doctor delivered a baby, those particles would then infect the women who would develop the fever and die.

Semmelweis went into the vast unknown, armed like a hero with the equivalent of a "vorpal sword"[46] and found a hidden treasure, a useful piece of information, to bring back to the medical institution. He ordered his doctors to wash their hands in a rinse of chlorine and lime. But Semmelweis wasn't satisfied until the authority of the statistics showed its own approval.

The mortality rate of the first clinic in 1847 reached staggering proportions. Doctors started methodically washing their hands and instruments the next month. The mortality rate dropped quickly from almost one in five women to one in twenty. The clinic achieved a zero death rate for two months at one point following the discovery. Semmelweis had taken what was and through his actions performed a figurative transmutation of reality into what should be.

Plato's story involves a return to the shadows and chains. Frye's wave also involves a return where a community takes up and follows the insights of a redeemer figure. Within Campbell's monomyth, the hero sometimes dies. At the time, the medical establishment believed diseases came from many different and wholly unrelated causes, affecting each human being differently. The idea that many problems could be addressed with a simple commitment toward cleanliness seemed to some doctors like a threat to their practices and authority. They were comfortable in their authority and dominion. When the insight emerged of their own role in the deaths of the pregnant women, many doctors resented the assertion.

Word of Semmelweis's work circulated over Europe. Some of his students lectured on the topic of handwashing between patients or published the findings, but Semmelweis himself did not immediately seek to broadcast his findings formally. Much of the medical community on the continent dismissed the news as nothing new. Doctors cited over thirty distinct causes of childbed fever in response. Though simple handwashing solved the problem, it did not provide a thorough explanation. Without a solid theory, the solution didn't fit with the medical establishment's lines of procedure. They quite literally didn't know how to handle the information. At the time, there was no real practice or policy in place for granting authority to an unknown but positive outcome. They could see the observed other and watch her die from disease, but not hear her voice.

Semmelweis continued his work in the clinics but other hospitals did not adopt the new practices, even in the face of statistical information. The known, habituated, anticipated, and comfortable were all more important than solving problems like the deaths of pregnant women. Dopamine and serotonin, not to be discovered for over a hundred years, seemed to hold a powerful authority over the thinking of the medical community at the time. The inertia of established order resisted change even in the face of new information. Semmelweis grew more insistent about his findings. He left the obstetrical clinic after being replaced with someone less revolutionary. His successor did not enforce the new practices and doctors returned to their old habits. The death rates in the first clinic rose once again.

He repeated his work in another hospital and instituted his handwashing practices. Again, more women lived through childbirth. Over the next decade he wrote open letters, books, and articles imploring others to adopt his practices. He berated his critics when he could and denounced them as irresponsible murderers. In some respects, he identified with the pregnant women dying in his clinics more than with the authoritative traditions to which he now found himself subject. Pregnant women, however, had little authority in the conversation since they were medical subjects, or in a sense, objects to be studied. The women had no voice to broadcast their feelings and as a group may not have even had the vocabulary or representation to make an appeal. Before the insight of Semmelweis, women simply voted with their feet. They went to the second clinic or gave birth on the street.

Semmelweis figuratively joined his fellow doctors and the women of his community, chained and staring at the shadows on the cave wall. And when he tried to explain the insights he had gained from his trip outside the cave, the unfortunate authority of the audience and the established tradition beat him down. The worth of his innovation didn't hold authority until after his death. In 1865, his family admitted him to a mental institution. He refused to stay and was severely beaten. Days later he died of an infection from his wounds.[47]

Michael Shermer explained the problem Semmelweis faced, though in a slightly different context, in his book *The Believing Brain*: "Aren't scientists supposed to be open to changing their minds when presented with new data and evidence? The reason for skepticism is that we need both replicable data and a viable theory."[48]

Spiritual wisdom can be interpreted as guidance for knowing when to change one's mind. Scientists, in theory, may have one of the best methods to do just that, involving replicable data and viable theory removed from, or at least conscious of, personal opinion. Instead of holding arguments and wordplay in authority, scientists find and serve a measuring system independent of their own motivations. If a scientist can't replicate the data and articulate a supporting theory, more inquiry is needed. Science, in an ideal form at least, involves falling in love with inquiry. This may be due in part because, in the face of what we want to see, so much of the data often says, "No."

Shermer also suggested, "The invisible and the nonexistent look the same."[49] This quip shows a bias toward visual sense data. That said, science has created tools to both examine the invisible to understand what's found there and differentiate it from what simply isn't there. But as an audience, Semmelweis's medical community had already adopted a dominant, ordered position. Despite the replicable data, Semmelweis had no theory. He brought to their attention something invisible but existing, in a sense. Unfortunately, in that kind of culture, the invisible corresponded to the nonexistent. To adopt his innovation of a clean or sterile environment, the medical community at the time would have needed a very different set of authoritative motivations ruling over them. They needed a way to address novelty besides rejection. They needed a way to invite that unexpected guest in for a visit, not as a mob but as a gracious host. They needed a better way of seeing, or hearing, the observed.

The legacy of Semmelweis could reflect the legacy of some dead but renowned artist. The value of the works of many esteemed artists only increases after the artist perishes. But like many artists who suffer for their work, Semmelweis may have chosen a style of communication with little influence on traditional authorities. Classical heroes often die in service to their cause, and Semmelweis seems to fit that model. The medical establishment of the time made him a bed to lie in, but then grew indifferent and even hostile when he found new information that did not fit well within it. They tortured him, along with his new way, cutting his legs out from under him and stretching him so thin he practically lost his mind. Their own audience of the women giving birth in their clinics continued to suffer as well until a germ theory of disease gained popularity in the years that followed.

In a final twist of fate, the medical world now openly pays homage to Semmelweis for his pioneering efforts in antiseptics. In Semmelweis's final, declining years, Louis Pasteur and others explained the pathology of childbed fever.[50] Medical facilities adopted the practices of sterilization and handwashing, but not with great enthusiasm. A new term emerged—the Semmelweis effect—to describe the behaviour characterized by reflex-like rejection of new knowledge on the grounds it contradicts entrenched norms or beliefs. The effect plagues every institutionalized authority. Every traditional bedrock of accepted knowledge faces a challenge with new information. Anomaly knocks at the door, threatening to shatter the old forms, but also inviting us to turn toward the light once again.

Lonergan's idea of self-appropriation, if expanded to institutions, could address this problem with what might be understood as a "novelty-management system." Instead of reverting to behaviour like the Semmelweis effect, a community or organization could adopt a reflective policy. What is winning our attention and what are we ignoring? Are we being competent or dominant? Are we correcting our errors or confirming our biases? And are we being responsible? In the process, we might be better prepared to adjust our sights on our goals and still hear the calls of love.

Ayaan—When Your Daughter Becomes Her Own Woman

Ayaan Hirsi Ali grew up in Somalia, Saudi Arabia, and Kenya. Her grandmother tested Ayaan and her siblings to make sure they knew by rote the family lineage and the names of men in the extended families. They would recite generation upon generation of the past, connecting them with centuries of family history. Her grandmother also told fairy tales and stories. But Somalia is not a country of the West. Stories from grandmothers in Somalia have themes that may sound strange to Western children. Hirsi Ali recounts one of these stories in her book *Infidel*.

> There was once a young nomad who married a beautiful wife, and they had a son....
>
> The rains didn't come, so the nomad set out to walk across the desert, looking for pasture where he could settle with his family. Almost as soon as he began walking he came upon a patch of green young grass. On it was a hut made of strong branches, covered with freshly woven mats and swept clean.
>
> The hut was empty. The man went back to his wife and told her that after just one day of walking, he had found the perfect place. But two days later, when he returned to the pasture with his wife and baby, they found a stranger standing in the doorway of the hut. This stranger was not tall, but he was thickly built, and he had very white teeth and smooth skin.
>
> The stranger said, "You have a wife and child. Take the house, you're welcome to it," and he smiled. The young nomad thought this stranger was remarkably friendly, and thanked him; he invited the stranger to visit any time. But the wife felt uncomfortable around the stranger. The baby, too, cried as soon as he cast eyes on this man.
>
> That night an animal sneaked into their hut and stole the baby out of his bed. The man had eaten well and slept heavily; he heard nothing. Such misfortune. The stranger visited the nomad and his wife to tell them of his sorrow. But when he spoke, the wife noticed that there were tiny pieces of red meat between his teeth, and one of those strong white teeth was just a little bit broken.
>
> The man stayed on with the couple in the house. For a whole year, the grass stayed green and the rains came, so there was no reason to move on. The wife had another baby in that hut, another beautiful son. But again, when the child was barely one season old, an animal came in the night and grabbed the baby in its jaws. This time the child's father ran after the creature, but he was too slow to catch up.

The third time, the nomad caught up with the creature, and struggled with it, but the animal overpowered him. Again, it ate the baby! Finally, after her third baby was eaten, the wife told the nomad she would leave him. So now that stupid nomad had lost everything!

"So what have you learned?" my grandmother would shout at us. We knew the answer. That nomad had been lazy. He had taken the first pasture he found, even though there had to be something wrong with it. He had been stupid: he had failed to read the signs, the signals, which the baby and the woman had instinctively felt. The stranger was really He Who Rubs Himself with a Stick, the monstrous being who transforms himself into a hyena and devours children. We had spotted it. The nomad had been slow of mind, slow of limb, weak in strength and valor. He deserved to lose everything.[51]

Why would a grandmother tell this story to children? Suspicion of the stranger, in Somalia and in many parts of the world, could be considered a virtue, a strength, a skill to be developed. Hirsi Ali continues:

In Somalia, little children learn quickly to be alert to betrayal. Things are not always what they seem; even a small slip can be fatal. The moral of every one of my grandmother's stories rested on our honor. We must be strong, clever, suspicious; we must obey the rules of the clan.

Suspicion is good, especially if you are a girl. For girls can be taken, or they may yield. And if a girl's virginity is despoiled, she not only obliterates her own honor, she also damages the honor of her father, uncles, brothers, male cousins. There is nothing worse than to be the agent of such catastrophe.[52]

The cultivation of suspicion as a virtue helps us to remain conscious of the shadow side of the relationship between a host and guest. The other is a mixture of known and unknown, like the hero, and as such can be a source of positive and negative change in a person's life.

Hirsi Ali's father and mother were Muslim. Her father dreamed of making Somalia a strong nation. He put all his energy into political and revolutionary work for Somalia. Her father drew inspiration from America. The United States rose from a collection of colonies into a world power and a beacon of success. If such a nation could be built in North America, could it not happen in Africa? What could an ambitious man with clear vision do, even in a place torn apart by politics like Somalia? His story matches the paths taken by Agamemnon and Jephthah. He loved his children dearly, but his own daughters were no match for his ambitions and drives.

Her father spoke out against the dictatorial regime in power. He also tried to help organize resistance against the militaristic government of his beloved home nation. He was arrested and detained. Meanwhile, young Ayaan went to school. She was taught to memorize the holy book of Islam. She was told what a good girl was and was not, what a good girl should want and not want. In a sense, her grandmother and her teachers had only a panopticon-influenced vision for her role in the religious community. As the audience in that environment but hero in her own life, she struggled to balance her known and unknown worlds while identifying with the traditions around her. She struggled to identify with how women were treated. And she came to witness the political corruption that affected each country of her childhood. Those moments of insight took her to personal thresholds, where she would redefine her identity in the process of self-appropriation.

She also learned English. Girls in her school shared English books. How did these non-sacred books compare to the Koran? She found an identity she wanted for herself in the common heroines of children's literature. She found she cared for the characters. They had opportunities to make their own identities for themselves, or at least participate in directing their own lives and interests.

> Most seductive of all were the ragged paperbacks the other girls passed each other. [My sister] and I devoured these books in corners, shared them with each other, hid them behind schoolbooks, read then in a single night. We began with the Nancy Drew adventures, stories of pluck and independence. There was Enid Blighton, the Secret Seven, the Famous Five: tales of freedom, adventure, of equality between girls and boys, trust, and friendship. These were not like my grandmother's stark tales of the clan, with their messages of danger and suspicion. These stories were fun, they seemed real, and they spoke to me as the old legends never had.[53]

Her own story and spirit brought about an added suspicion—doubt of the tradition and religion into which she was born. Her father arranged a marriage to someone living in Canada. The flights from Africa to Germany and then to Canada also brought an opportunity for Hirsi Ali to escape. She was on her father's path, but on that path his daughter found places where she could change her story. For Hirsi Ali, the path laid down before her felt like a descent into a terrible state of bondage, a place where she might never be allowed to be an individual. The novelty of the plane ride gave her an opportunity to choose a different course of action.

She went to Holland and asked for refugee status. Holland presented to this Somali woman another way of shaping her own identity. It took many years, and a remarkable thirst for information from Hirsi Ali, but she fell in love with her new life and personal responsibility. Like the ragged paperbacks of her childhood, the insights of her education drew Hirsi Ali to question what she cared about and what she wanted to identify with. The process took about ten years, but over that time she found something in which she wanted to participate.

She received refugee status, earned a university education and Dutch citizenship, helped with translation between Dutch service workers and other refugees, and even became a Dutch politician and activist. Later, her criticisms of Islam and her calls for reforming the traditional treatment of women created a backlash. Under threats of violence, Hirsi Ali made plans to leave Europe.

The Dutch government had an open and welcoming attitude toward refugees. Many individuals and families from Africa, for example, found a chance to start again in the Netherlands. Tolerance was presented as virtuous in the political world of the nation. Like Abraham and Lot, the Dutch nation wanted to treat its guests with hospitality and care. But tolerance has its own consequences.

Hirsi Ali recounted stories of female genital mutilation—a common practice in parts of Somalia. These practices continued in refugee families in the Netherlands. Hirsi Ali stood between the two cultures and watched as a well-meaning host turned a blind eye to the violent actions of a stranger and guest. As a politician and activist, she wanted to bring attention to this problem. She believed integration was missing from the immigration process—changing the fixed viewpoint of refugees who refused to step into the light of a new environment and culture. In the story of Lot, it was the mob of Sodom that brought disorder and destruction. For Hirsi Ali, a small but notable portion of the immigrant population wasn't living up to the responsibilities of the guest. They were eating their own children like a hyena in a grandmother's story. The very ways that may have been responsible for the need to escape their home countries now threatened the order of their new community.

Sacred books did not direct her on such a path. Even in the early days of her time in Holland, she believed the Koran was the most real book in the world. She read the paperback fictions knowing they were not real. Yet, it was fiction that made a difference. A set of figurative circumstances allowed her to peek into a world that *could be*, just as an audience peeks into an artist's imagination. When she stated that the English paperback stories "seemed real," one can just as easily translate that into "seemed important" or "seemed like what I wanted for my own identity."

Hirsi Ali, as the individual and hero of her own life, found a way to integrate her past and present with an identity of what seemed most important to her. She worked toward bringing a better sense of integration into the process of refugee immigration in Holland. This idea of integration is a political manifestation of the recognition of responsibilities between host and guest. It might be one of the most difficult relationships to put into practice, but it also may be one of the most important challenges we face today. Young children, especially infants or toddlers, have little control over the toys presented to them or the food prepared for them or the homes made for them. But if they are cared for, given proper attention, and even given space in a safe setting, they can find practically spontaneous delights all their own. They can invent games and even delight in the rhythm found in skipping down a path or the rush of a ride on a swing. In the spirit of the imagination, they can invent stories that take them anywhere they wish. If they are given the chance to be Sophia, instead of Iphigenia or Jephthah's unnamed daughter, they will have the chance to find stories to live by.

Reflection

No map is as detailed or true as the journeys and places it describes. However, if these maps are to work, in Karen Armstrong's sense, then we can see them as sheets on the bed of Procrustes. It is important not to mistake the sheets for the bed. This chapter is intended to make it possible to figuratively change the sheets in our heads when its time to clean our rooms.

The four maps represent four different attitudes toward the process of going through change. But these two circles and two lines can also be used to represent the relationships and applicable domains of authority. Peterson's line between what is and what should be portrays events in terms of goal-directed behaviour. Plato's cave models the relationships involved in developing a skill or gaining experiential knowledge. Campbell's monomyth gives us a sense of the individual's struggle in finding innovative resolutions to problems and reviving order. Frye's wave suggests a pattern to the ebb and flow of responsibilities between the individual and the community. Each diagram acts as a figurative description for how and when to bow to each of the four archetypes and say, "Namaste." Conscious recognition of what kind of change is needed can help the individual choose an appropriate map, embody the actions and choices needed, and then find the best way home.

The hero or main character in a story, as actor and observer and decider, must build relationships or allegiances with each of the other archetypes. We are constantly negotiating, re-establishing, leading, championing, or fighting. But we can also offer gifts. Each time we read a story or take in new information, we follow along and figuratively participate in those relationships and allegiances. This investment can become a mystical one if the reader grants so much authority to some aspect of the story that it becomes a defining part of the reader's personal identity. The process of falling in love with inquiry, falling in love with self-appropriation, involves the creation of a story with characters, settings, and maps. Whether real, constructed or just imagined, these stories can be enough to influence how the reader or user manages their fears and motivations.

In psychology, the voluntary exploration of new information can be one of the most important aspects in finding a therapeutic resolution to a problem. Likewise, a motivated student tends to learn the material of new lessons more quickly and thoroughly than an unmotivated one. The role of choice at the thresholds of these four maps is one important difference. According to Jordan Peterson, "action presupposes valuation."[54] This holds for goal-directed pursuits, institutional learning, spiritual journeys, and social groups, even in the worlds of screened media and entertainment. This chapter is about choices, and the consequential journeys that come from our choices.

Parenting styles fascinated Martin Hoffman. He studied parental discipline techniques and wondered what was the better way to raise morally responsible children. What happens if a parent withdraws love from a child behaving negatively? What if a parent asserts power such as withdrawing privileges or physically controlling the child behaving negatively? Hoffman found these two strategies were not terribly effective, though in common use with the families he studied. He set his work on another path in which parents would use "inductive discipline" to communicate with the child.[55] The parent would first explain the need to behave differently because of potential harmful consequences. The parent would then appeal to the child's sense of pride, the desire to master a skill, or the wish to be treated as a grown-up. These can be important motivators for a child. The parent would make the child conscious of a goal but first put that goal in the context of consequences for the child and for others affected. The language used by the parent would focus on relationships to others, their feelings, and how they were now injured because of the behaviour.

With effort, a child or client can develop a point of view outside of personal obsessions or motivations for an expanded sense of consciousness. Hoffman's technique seemed to have some influence on the moral identity of children. Adolescents raised with inductive discipline from parents, when asked to describe themselves, tended to use moral qualities more often than non-moral qualities, compared to children raised in other disciplinary settings.[56] Instead of raising narcissists, parents had a chance to put children on the path toward worthy goals with healthy strategies.

As many parents come to understand, studies on discipline in academic towers don't always translate to solutions in the trenches. Parents often adopt many discipline styles because over time children build up creative playbooks for different behaviours. Hoffman's work, wherever it may stand after years of academic scrutiny and popular parenting trends, helps point parents toward discipline methods that strengthens a child's moral identity and consciousness. Hoffman's technique, though focused on parental discipline, shines a light into other aspects of our lives. His work calls our attention to the journey children must take in developing awareness of their own motivations and their own relationships with others.

It may be important to consider, at this point, that neither Agamemnon nor Jephthah were disciplining delinquent daughters. Their actions came in direct relation to their own goal-directed behaviour. They both came to face novelty in the path of their pursuits. And that novelty, made of both potential hope and threat, presented them with a threshold—a chance to make a choice of what path to take. If, in that moment, they had some other voice as counsel, or heard some faint echo of even their own zealous commitment to their goals, they might have recognized the responsibilities they had toward their own daughters.

In the Hero's Journey, the cycle of a story is not complete until the hero returns with a treasure to rebuild or re-enter home. In some cases, the treasure is the story, communicating and offering a map through the dangerous environments the hero experienced. In other stories, the treasure may be just a kiss. Concerned fathers, knowing what kissing leads to, might be justified in measuring optimism with caution. In Plato's cave, the student is left with fellow audience members, chained and imprisoned in the theatre of shadow. Frustration can come from the inability to communicate. Frustration can lead to an escalation of emotions and the urge to use violence in order to assert identity. If we use Frye's map as an influence through our process of self-appropriation, then there is some hope that with each iteration there is a chance to transcend the past repetitions and find new peaks in consciousness. Redeemers, deliverers, and heroes often share a characteristic—their journeys bring them to moments where they have a choice. Do they live in truth and speak in truth, or do they use words and actions as instruments of motivations? Do they risk themselves or find a scapegoat? Instead of communication motivated by a love for the truth, communication can turn to manipulation in service to a goal. The next chapter examines four modes of language or expression based on the intent behind the words.

4

Speaking in Tongues:
Sales and Services, Sacrifices and Solutions

> You who build these altars now
> To sacrifice these children
> You must not do it anymore
> A scheme is not a vision
> And you never have been tempted
> By a demon or a god
> You who stand above them now
> Your hatchets blunt and bloody
> You were not there before
> When I lay upon a mountain
> And my father's hand was trembling
> With the beauty of the word
>
> —Leonard Cohen
> "The Story of Isaac"

> I did my best, it wasn't much
> I couldn't feel, so I tried to touch
> I've told the truth, I didn't come to fool you
> And even though it all went wrong
> I'll stand before the Lord of Song
> With nothing on my tongue but Hallelujah
>
> —Leonard Cohen
> "Hallelujah"

*The voice of a god
was the measure
of your intention.*

Canadian Poetics

Philosophers and critics (those who have come after deconstruction) often struggle to locate [Northrop Frye and Marshall McLuhan] in a European or American context. I propose something more robust and radical for them and from them: they have authored themselves, creating a new line—subtly insistently part of the new that is Canadian and yet (paradoxically) universal. They are their own tradition. While well-schooled in Western literary traditions and what I will call the ancient wisdom, they paid almost no heed to what was emerging in European intellectual circles in the 1960s on. *One of their boldest acts is to put communications (media, literary studies), rather than ideology, at the heart of their thought* [emphasis mine]. They initiate and ignite; their conjunction features a decisive turning away from an enslavement to others' systems of thought in order to seek their own sources of perceptions and ideas, in a championing of poetics.

—B. W. Powe[1]

Does ideology work anymore? What would we think of a tool box if it only contained hammers? How would we prune the vines or collect the harvest if we only had hammers?

If politics involves the development of policies about borders, then psychology can help us develop strategies in negotiating thresholds, and art can help us recognize the relationship between the figure and the ground of our thinking. One of the great challenges facing the West today might be the implementation, management, and evaluation of evidence-based social policies and programs. This challenge, of course, presents a question about the authority of the observed as separated from our motivations: who gets to decide what counts as evidence? Data, when sufficiently tortured, will confirm anything asked of it.[2]

In the last chapter, I laid out four maps of plot progressions in relation to spiritual development in the individual and in the group. For the most part, the four maps were related to narrative and story and action. But in the early decades of the media age, Bernard Lonergan suggested the empirical method of inquiry itself was an essential process in the development of our spiritual identities too. Religious tradition would have to face and embrace the tides of change from science, technology, and innovation. Earlier, I wondered about the difference between a Supreme

Being and a Supreme Way of Being. Have we refined things further now in search of a Supreme *Method* of Being? If the study of art teaches us how to move our consciousness between figure and ground, then modern science can be thought of as a refined and accelerated extension of this skill, narrowed to fine variables and evermore controlled conditions. If the craft of wine-making could be considered a *way*, then we have progressed to a *method* of distillation in search of stronger and better spirits. Are we ready to stomach the consequences?

One person's perspective on evidence can presume certain sequences, settings, or roles as authoritative, while another person may want to tell a very different kind of story. An adversary's solution might appear to be a threatening apocalypse rather than a welcoming opportunity to entertain a change of mind. When faced with a choice of changing one's thinking or proving there is little reason for a change, as John Kenneth Galbraith pointed out, "almost everyone gets busy on the proof."[3] What kind of language can be used so that people do not feel their very personalities need defending? Is it possible to communicate without such heavy influence from ideology? How can we practise conscious restraint and limit our rhetoric to better focus on the tasks of problem-solving?

B. W. Powe, in the quotation above, suggests something could replace ideology as an ultimate concern. Powe's perceptive praise of his two teachers challenges some of the usual associations that come to mind when we think of big thinkers or great influencers. Can a leader be driven by something other than ideology and political will? Political agendas seem to shape our daily news, our government structures, our economic regulations, and the material comedians use to express our grievances. The mere suggestion that communication can come first, before politics or economics, may be hard to grasp. Yet the transmission of information and the forms of information transmission become important, fruitful topics of study in today's media-influenced landscape. Art and media can teach us something about managing politics, just as the empirical method can help us with our spiritual development.

This chapter examines four intentions behind communication, four modes of expression. Conscious identification of when and how these four modes are used helps a listener identify the sequences of events, settings, and roles informing a speaker's communication. When speakers use these four modes, their use suggests an imposition, limiting or framing their communication, in relation to their intent.

Canada has strutted and fretted through most of its history on the international stage as a small, strange mosaic in search of its own place in the sun. In a poetic sense, Canada has known what it is like, according to T. S. Eliot,

> To swell a progress, start a scene or two,
> Advise the prince; no doubt, an easy tool,
> Deferential, glad to be of use,
> Politic, cautious, and meticulous;
> Full of high sentence, but a bit obtuse;
> At times, indeed, almost ridiculous—
> Almost, at times, the Fool.[4]

Powe described the Canadian difference as "more concerned with communication than with conquest, more concerned with revision and reforming than with overpowering or obliterating the other."[5] Canada has its share of historical prejudices and blunders, but the country also has a unique creation story. Many historians may cite internal political deadlock or pressure from an ambitious neighbouring country as reasons for Confederation. One certainly cannot ignore the colonial history and expansionist ambitions that initiated the country's beginnings. But another story shows a different side of the nation's identity. Canada became a country after a drunk said he wanted to change his ways and prove himself worthy of marriage.[6] On some level, John A. Macdonald understood the challenge well—becoming the father of a nation meant committing to the responsibilities of a relationship, a marriage, and a family. In that story, there seems to be no motivations for ideological revolution or violent war. It would be a story of communication with and not dominance of a spouse—measuring up through building something together. Perhaps Canada took the challenge of metaphor seriously, attempting in some way to embody the lunatic, the lover, and the poet.

What would Agamemnon or Jephthah say about such motivations, and such an identity? Was it a worthy pursuit? Would such a legacy satisfy the ambitions of such giants? For 150 years, Canada has been suspect of its own level of might and power. But the country is rich in resources. The nation has a history of duct-tape connections over formidable geography. The Canadian landscape is daunting and beautiful. As a result, Canada is in a unique position to ignite and insist on a new consciousness grounded on communication instead of ideology. A curious symbol of Canada stands above the Toronto skyline. The CN Tower wasn't constructed to sell luxury apartments or display military power but to put up a media antenna.

The first prime minister of Canada, John A. Macdonald, had to resign from the position in 1873 due to evidence of his own corruption. He offered work contracts on the national railroad in exchange for bribes and support. Our second prime minister, Alexander MacKenzie, established an office for the Auditor General—an attempt to keep a better measure on the government and the politicians. Five years later, the Canadian citizenry re-elected that same first prime minister Macdonald. Outrage, punishment, correction, forgiveness—Canada embodied all four in the first decade of the nation.

In 1885, Canada tried Louis Riel for treason and organizing a rebellion. Against Riel's wishes, his lawyer defended him by saying he was insane. At the end of the proceedings, Riel stood up and gave a speech that effectively dismantled his own lawyer's defence and made a clear-headed case for why the rebellion was justified. It could be said that Riel articulated a Canadian *logos* and was sacrificed because of it. The jury found him guilty but asked for clemency. Riel was executed by public hanging. Today, Canada recognizes Riel as a father of our Confederation, practically as high in importance and possibly more fitting to the popular heroic model than our first prime minister. Somehow, Canada has found a way to create a national identity of prudence, heroics, suspicion, and naiveté, all at once.

After his experiences in World War II, Emmanuel Levinas returned to his academic interests. He began his first major published work with an examination of what compels people to descend into war for their ideas. In the beginning of his book, he captured a sentiment that could be used as a lens through which to study the history of the twentieth century:

> It is of the highest importance to know whether we are not duped by morality.
>
> Does not lucidity, the mind's openness upon the true, consist in catching sight of the permanent possibility of war? The state of war suspends morality.... War is not only one of the ordeals—the greatest—of which morality lives; it renders morality derisory. The art of foreseeing war and of winning it by every means—politics—is henceforth enjoined as the very exercise of reason. Politics is opposed to morality, as philosophy to naiveté.[7]

In the early years of Canada, many Lithuanians and Ukrainians travelled across the globe to establish new homes on the prairie frontier. It is unfortunate for Canada that Levinas's family line did not rise to that call. He might have found himself at home in this land of double visions. He might have appreciated our own efforts to give attention to communication over ideology.

Before we establish political allegiances, hierarchies of status, shared goals, or antagonistic competition, communication connects us. The communication of information from one to another is primary. Communication, whether with the world, with an environment, with another, or with ourselves, is the photosynthesis of self-knowledge. Potentially, it is communication and not ideology that calls us to moral consciousness.

According to Powe, Frye and McLuhan championed poetics over political agenda. They lived in poetics, steeping their careers in the cultural brews of literature and media. They cut themselves into the chronology of academia, not to tear down the old and sanctimonious ivory towers. Instead, they built bridges between the architects of the past and the students who would have to bear the weight of the present. Frye and McLuhan were continuing, in their own ways, the academic conversation about consciousness and motivation that began well before the modern era.

The Critical and the Kerygmatic

Marshall McLuhan received a PhD for his studies on Thomas Nashe, a playwright, satirist, and pamphleteer from the 1500s. In the introduction to his dissertation, McLuhan prepared the reader for something more than a study of Nashe's contribution to English literature: "There is finally no way of studying Western society or literature which does not consider, and constantly reconsider, the entire tradition from its Greek inception."[8]

McLuhan then moved to works of Zeno, Cicero, Quintilian, and Augustine. He wanted to better understand the evolution of grammar and dialectics—roughly associated with the relationship between form and content, structure and message. St. Augustine mentioned a story in his *Confessions* of visiting a teacher and finding the teacher reading silently.[9] Augustine wondered about why someone would do such a thing. At the time of Augustine, only a small minority would be trained in reading. In the 1800s, one in ten people might have been able to read. Today in the

West, one in five might be considered illiterate.[10] We have flipped the expectations. Today, we want every child to practise and master the exercise of silent reading. Parallel to this, we expect individuals to be responsible for their actions, whatever histories or demons they might bear.

McLuhan enjoyed exploring paradoxes and clichés. But for him, it wasn't a matter of solving a puzzle and quarantining the resolution. Instead, like the problems that come with motivation, evil, and fear, the process involves returning to the conversation again and again—consider, and then constantly reconsider. The problems we face today had their inception in the beginnings of civilization. The present makes more sense if we look at the past and the future with more questions rather than more theories. McLuhan enjoyed the puzzles that reversed the figure and the ground: What if today's chicken is just the egg's way of making another egg?[11]

One of his first publications for a general audience was a study on advertising. For an academic versed in a long, chronological perspective of literature, what drew the attention of this man to the transient messages on country billboards, store walls, magazine pages, and television commercials? This turn of his attention is a manifestation of taking his own advice—consider, and constantly reconsider. He grasped a shift in the grammar, in the modes and forms of communication. The written word, as the primary form of authoritative communication, had an upstart competitor for the audience's attention. He realized that marketing messages and moving images held the power to compel people. The new messages were taking possession of people, as if we were guided by new spirits, both benevolent and malevolent. But how conscious were we about this shift in divinities, in the compelling forces over our behaviour? And was this the dawning of an age of a healthier regulation of our motivations and fears? Or could we be enslaving ourselves to new idols and glittering images? Was there something in our past that could help us sort through the entrenched problems that antiquity considered, and reconsidered, but never fully resolved?

McLuhan singled out the long Greek genealogy of thought that anchored Western literature at the beginning of his studies, but he understood there was another root as well. Northrop Frye turned much of his attention to another family line in the West. Frye loved the written word, and that love took him down the long chronological paths of literature to understand why certain words had such power. He taught a course at the University of Toronto based on "The Bible and Literature." Before that, however, he wanted to teach students about Milton's *Paradise Lost*. He encountered a problem very quickly. His students couldn't access the depths of *Paradise Lost* because they lacked any real grasp of the narrative arcs in the Bible. However, Frye didn't want to teach a religious course on the Bible. After a great deal of inquiry, Frye articulated his goal:

> Provide for students, whether their main interest is literature or not, some knowledge of the cultural traditions that we've all been brought up in and which we are all conditioned by every time we draw a breath, whether we realize it or not.
>
> The narrative unity of the Bible... was something that I stressed. And that concern for narrative seems to me to be distinctive of the Bible among other sacred books.

The second way in which the Bible is unified is through a number of recurring images: mountain, sheep, river, hill, pasture, bride, bread, wine and so on. They echo and re-echo all through the Bible and are repeated in so many ways as to suggest that they have a thematic importance: that they are actually building up some kind of interconnected unity. The present course is really based on this conception of the unity of the narrative of the Bible and the unity formed by its recurrent imagery.

[The Bible is one book] that has been decisive for western culture through the Middle Ages and Renaissance to our own time.[12]

Frye's introduction to students may seem indifferent to cultural traditions outside the West. But his goal was not to convert students to doctrine. He had a teacher's goal. He wanted to teach. A piece of literature like *Paradise Lost* can seem opaque, even meaningless, to uninitiated students, unless those students can identify the narrative unity of the Bible. I use the word "uninitiated" with the caution that Malidoma Somé suggested—uninitiated can mean attempting to evade something important. Frye offered his students a glass of wine, only to find they had no way of appreciating the craft and care and time that went into making it.

Frye was a critic. Part of the critical tradition meant looking for things that can act as foundational. This was not a criticism of destruction or deconstruction, but a contribution toward resiliency, a preparation for challenges and growth. Like teaching itself, or empirical investigation, fine criticism can compel someone toward refined skill, deeper stories, and better wine. Criticism can appear in two different forms. One attitude of criticism evaluates a work of art, for example, in terms of its vulnerabilities and weaknesses to understand how the work compares to an ideal. Another attitude of criticism evaluates something for what it may have that works. Where other critics earned their reputations for having a cutting tongue and sharp eye, Frye built a reputation for being thorough, expansive, and generous.

Frye also told his students that half of the course was based on classical mythology, by which he meant roughly Mediterranean, Mesopotamian, Greek, and Roman mythology. The purpose of the course was to bring students to some conscious understanding, through the root literature and traditions of the West, of why the West is the way it is. Chronology played a prominent role in Frye's teaching methods, underscoring some basic assumptions about time and cause and effect—what happened yesterday informed today, whether we are conscious of it or not, whether we want to give it authority or not. In that same course, Frye addressed another issue with the text of the Bible:

The narrative sequences in the Bible that I was speaking of are of a type that make it very difficult to answer the question, *are they histories or fictions?* In fact, it might be said that what is distinctive, almost unique, about the Bible is the fact that that question cannot be directly answered at all.

> Every sequence in words, just by virtue of the fact that it is a sequence, is a verbal structure in which the words have their own patterns and their own forms. It is impossible to describe anything with definitive accuracy in the outside world by means of words, because words are always forming their own self-contained patterns of subject and predicate and object. They are continually shaping reality into what are essentially grammatical fictions.
>
> And I suggested that it doesn't matter whether a sequence of words is called a history or a story: that is, whether it is intended to follow a sequence of actual events or not. As far as its verbal shape is concerned, it will be equally mythical in either case. But we notice that any emphasis on shape or structure or pattern or form always throws a verbal narrative in the direction we call mythical rather than historical.[13]

Frye understood the limitations of language and communication. He wasn't content to resolve those limitations with ideological assumptions. As well, he understood that no satisfaction would come from some brute enforcement of the literal correspondence of words to the material world. Instead, his interest was to make his students conscious of how myth, history, and fiction have not been separated by form. Instead, we need some understanding of the differences in the *intent* or *purpose* that initiated an expression of words, phrases, patterns, or statements. What's more, we have a method to investigate the intent and purpose. Critical analysis, for Frye, was more than an exercise in finding talking points about public figures. It was more than an opportunity to interpret writing and art through an ideological lens. For Frye, the history of literature, and the human pursuit of communication itself, provided a call to peak experiences of consciousness. From such experiences and insights, we could find motivations and purposes worth pursuing.

In keeping with the numerical theme of this book, I want to examine four general categories of language—Instrumental, Descriptive, Prescriptive, Imaginative. Knowledge of these modes of language can help us reach everyday consciousness in how words work us over completely. As heuristics, these modes can help us to better understand the intentions behind what we communicate. These categories can overlap, frame, or support one another. McLuhan and Frye both give us a chance to hesitate—if we are not conscious of what lies behind some form of communication, we cannot appreciate why it is the way it is. From simple observations, we can make choices as to what kinds of communication we give authority; which ones steer our thoughts and actions. The expression of information from someone presents identity and intention at once, be it honest, guileless, mediated, misdirecting, or hypocritical. With one mere act of communication, we say something about our relationship to what we think we know, what we don't know, our willingness toward mediating between the two, and our attitudes about our audience.

Frye formulated a kind of spectrum of communication, modes of expression useful for examining the language of texts. On one end, Frye placed what might be considered "realistic" language. On the other end of his dimension he placed "imaginative" language. Between the two poles he used a set of categories for further discriminating what lay behind the words of a text.[14]

Realistic <--> Imaginative				
Descriptive	Dialectic	Rhetoric	Poetic	Kerygmatic
Factual accounts with as much ideology or motivation removed as possible.	Logic and evidence used to frame an argument in order to understand what is factual. Some readers may suspect the fingertips of ideology starting to tip the scales already.	Emotional appeals and evidence intermixed with a goal to show, persuade, or create an authoritative account.	The literature and fiction that may draw from the real, the factual, and the argumentative evidence to register some emotional identity between the reader and the material in the text.	Visionary writing that may draw from the other categories or may be imaginative; written as a kind of proclamation inspiring readers to discover stories to live by. Readers may invest their personal identities in these kinds of text.

Frye's teaching tool, though useful for understanding texts and the intentions behind them, is somewhat one-dimensional. His categories mix together language used to describe and language used to persuade. As he cautioned, we cannot look to the grammar of sentences to tell the difference between history and fiction. Language offers little direction on how to distinguish between when a writer uses language as an instrument to achieve an end and when a writer uses language to express an imagined or prescribed end.

Frye's approach suggests there are no separate dimensions for what is and what should be. He coordinated both along just one axis. It may be true that in our naive, day-to-day experience, we live in both realms at once. But there is a benefit to situating these two realms in different dimensions. And there is a method. David Hume and others provided us with a meditation on the leap we often take in our thinking—*no ought from an is*.[15] These words are invoked with the trust that they can bring about some peak experiences of consciousness or transcendence. Levinas warned us that we can be duped by even our most basic assumptions and our own morality.

Another approach would be to draw Frye's initial modes of expression, realistic and imaginative, as one plane aligned horizontally. This plane of investigation gives us a way to discriminate between information that is meant to correspond to the material world (*realistic*, to use Frye's word, or perhaps a more fitting word for my purposes would be *descriptive*), or information that is meant to express something not of, or not yet in, the material world (*imaginative*, to use Frye's word).

Another dimension can be added as a vertical. This dimension measures the intention behind the actual presentation or delivery of the information—what is believed to matter in the world. For my purposes in this chapter, this plane would counterpose instrumental language use and prescriptive language use. The distinction is to show a difference between a speaker's intentions. Do authors use the information as a means to create an end—how they can get what they want from the audience or observed other? Or do they use the information to communicate some kind of prescribed, ideal end—what is it that the audience or observed other ought to do?

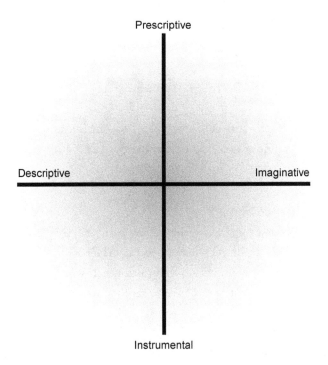

To understand the West, McLuhan and Frye went back through time, putting together a chronological view of their subjects of study. As long as we pay attention, we can train ourselves to become more conscious of how information is presented and what intentions or assumptions frame that information. For each of the four categories of expression, I focus on an example of a portrait from recent art history. Levinas considered the face-to-face encounter to be the foundation of not just morality, but practically all thought and development. His use of the idea of the face was not literal. Today, however, the act of looking into the face of the other is so common it might as well be a meditation, a lost art, a useful practice. Through the face-to-face encounter, we recognize that there is something beyond our own perspective—a being, or perhaps a way of being, distinct from our own. The presentation of the face involves form and content. How can we examine the content in terms of the use of realistic and imaginative language? How can we decode and grasp the use of instrumental and prescriptive language in media, in art, in our identities, and in the faces of others?

Instrumental

> Read my lips: No new taxes.
>
> —George H. W. Bush

> I've never broken any state laws, and when I was in England, I experimented with marijuana a time or two. And I didn't like it, and I didn't inhale, and I never tried it again.
>
> —Bill Clinton

Some politicians have refined the art of truth-telling so much, they overwhelm us with their performances. We cannot always detect when the form of their sentences obliterates the content. One needs an equally prepared skill in order to measure their words. Politicians can tell truths; however, it may be just as important to recognize what they are telling the truth *about*. It may not be the content the listener expects.

There is a kind of hope in asking a question, a call looking for a response. It is hoped the reply will address the matter in the question. The question creates a frame, an expectation. But the response can nudge the frame and speak to something else entirely. Unfortunately, the nature of communication doesn't give us direct and clear clues each time. It is not just history and fiction that may share the same sentence and content structure. The difference between the truth in a person's statement and the lie in a person's statement falls into that ambiguous place where we need to read between the lines and find the intention. But if the audience consciously compares the question and the answer, the expectation and the realization, the call and the response, then certain clues can reveal themselves.

George H. W. Bush directed people to read his lips, encouraging the audience to focus on his conviction rather than what those lips might say afterwards. Bill Clinton directed people to think in terms of his legal innocence, without plainly answering a question put to him. These utterances and language constructions have been called "performatives"—utterances that do something rather than describe something.[16] Some performatives prepare information for an audience, without trusting the audience itself to have the authority of interpretation or evaluation of meaning. This is an instrumental use of language, where the motivation is not to simply state a factual answer. The information is embedded in intention. An audience taught to recognize and call out political performatives could decrease the babble of ideology in our public discourse. We could instead demand more from policy-makers. At least, we could hold public figures more accountable to how they say what they say, and what they mean when they speak.

Harry Frankfurt wrote a paper with the title "On Bullshit":

> The bullshitter may not deceive us, or even intend to do so, either about the facts or about what he takes the facts to be. What he does necessarily attempt to

deceive us about is his enterprise. His only indispensably distinctive characteristic is that in a certain way he misrepresents what he is up to....

The fact about himself that the bullshitter hides... is that the truth-values of his statements are of no central interest to him; what we are not to understand is that his intention is neither to report the truth nor to conceal it. This does not mean that his speech is anarchically impulsive, but that the motive guiding and controlling it is unconcerned with how the things about which he speaks truly are....

The bullshitter... is neither on the side of the true nor on the side of the false. His eye is not on the facts at all, as the eyes of the honest man and of the liar are, except insofar as they may be pertinent to his interest in getting away with what he says. He does not care whether the things he says describe reality correctly. He just picks them out, or makes them up, to suit his purpose.[17]

Instrumental use of language has the remarkable quality, as Frankfurt explains, of being hitched to nothing but the speaker's motivation. As a result, correspondence with the material world has no real measure against it. The measure of this kind of language can only be the results intended by the speaker and the behaviour it compels from the audience.

Performatives in language give us a quick signal of the possible presence of instrumental expressions in communication. But instrumental language does more than influence the political arenas of our lives. Marketing, advertising, public relations, and branding all inevitably process the contents of their messages through this form of communication. The advertiser is asking the audience to adopt information, intentions, and directions as authoritative, as worthy of compelling behaviour, regardless of any correspondence to some reality outside the advertiser's intentions.

A restaurant chain renovated a commercial building in my hometown. The building was used in the past by at least four different restaurants over a period of about twenty years. One day as the preparations neared completion, I noticed in my mailbox a flyer from this new restaurant. The wording of the flyer caught my attention:

THIS IS YOUR EXCLUSIVE INVITE TO THE GRAND OPENING.

I looked up and down my street. My street was not filled with affluent families. Some homes across the street at the time were public housing—owned by the city and rented out to families not financially independent. We have about four walk-up apartment buildings along one end of the street. The total population of the municipality is about 50,000. How many of these invitations did the restaurant print and deliver to the public through the mail service? What did they mean by the word "exclusive" if potentially thousands of homes received the invitations? Maybe it served some other purpose than to mean restricted or limited access to this opportunity. Or maybe the franchise and the owner wanted to direct my thinking about the invitation. They chose their words carefully as to create an effect on my neighbours and me.

In his book *The Mechanical Bride*, McLuhan began an analysis of a Coca-Cola advertisement with a look at the all-American girl:

> Now, the American girl as portrayed by the Coke ads had always been an archetype. No matter how much thigh she may be demurely sporting, she is sweet, non-sexual, and immaturely innocent. Her flesh is firm and full, but she is as pure as a soap bubble. She is clean *and* fun-loving.
>
> In short, she is a cluster-symbol which embraces at one extreme Abe Lincoln's "All that I am and all that I hope to be I owe to my darling mother," and, at the other, Ziegfeld's dream of the glorified American girl as a group of tall, cold, glittering, mechanical dolls. The gyrations and patterns assumed by these dolls in a revue is intended to convey, if not the Beatific Vision, at least Jacob's ladder of angelic hierarchies linking earth and heaven. We are pictorially encouraged to meet and mingle with these divine creatures in a sort of waking sleep, in which the male is not emotionally committed and in which the innocence of the doll is as renewable as a subscription to *The American Home*.[18]

In one quick set of sentences, McLuhan dashes between displays of vampish sexuality and practical puritan virginity, then graciously bows to political references and perfectly choreographed Broadway dancing troops, only to run up the steps of a poetic expression for the metaphysical structure between earth and heaven. And all of it comes thanks to the mythology of the American dream and the pursuit of soft drink happiness.

Part celebration, part deliberate framing, soft drink advertising continues today to work us over with this brand of archetypal magic. And it is not exclusive to one nation or one modern mythology. Advertising reflects the audience to itself, as the audience wants to see itself and see its pursuits. Advertising validates wants and motivations with pictorial and textual encouragement, making the pursuit appear satisfying, engaging, consequence-free, and ideal. The appetites that gave rise to the pursuit are as renewable as a magazine subscription.

However, the consumption of a soft drink is not just a simple act of enjoying something clean and fun-loving. The sugar rush is not just a quick refreshing way to energize the body for a good run up and down a stairway to heaven. Advertising, in a culture of screens and daily flyers and monthly magazines, does not just have the advantage of renewability. Instead, this magical influence works by repetition. The constant reminders have a cumulative effect. The product and message become part of the environment, part of the presumption upon reality. And each affirmation and consumption of the soft drink brings that confirmation, satisfying the want but also ratcheting up the unintended consequences every time.

In 1882, Edouard Manet painted a picture of a girl in a bar. After serving in the merchant marines, Manet spent six years studying and working in an art studio. Old masters in the art tradition greatly influenced him, but he found he did not want to simply revive the past in his own works. Paris in the latter half of the 1800s went through a modernization—city planners and engineers widened streets and business owners gave more thought to store front designs. The goal was to make Paris modern and beautiful.

Early in his painting career, Manet received a lot of criticism for painting nudes in the midst of all the modernization and development.[19] Instead of mythological figures, Manet painted modern people. He gave the observed a sense of respect, dignity, and even divinity. Two examples of his work at the time include *Dejeuner sur l'herbe* and *Olympia*. Manet's style caused an uproar among the conservative art patrons of Paris. He had a way of bringing the viewer into the content of the painting, as if implicating the person. He closed the psychic distance between art and audience so that no gap remained. His nudes look directly at the viewer, assessing the viewer as much as the viewer assesses the painting. His work influenced other artists of the time, such as Pierre-Auguste Renoir and Claude Monet. The period of the Impressionists brought a new perspective, a new way of seeing things, to the world of art.

One of Manet's last works, *Bar at the Folies-Bergère*, shows a serving girl leaning forward on a bar counter, as if waiting on a customer. Manet went a step further in this piece, however, by suggesting there was a mirror behind the serving girl. On the right side of the piece, we can see the back of the girl and the customer in front of her, wearing a top hat and suit. The serving girl was known by the name Suzon.[20]

The placement of her flower corsage, directly in the middle of her chest, could be instrumental in understanding the potential transaction between Suzon and her customer. Even with the progress and modernization and cleaning up of Paris at the time, the most base motivations and oldest professions still flourished. The placement of the corsage was a way a girl could advertise. Art galleries were a place for the bourgeoisie of Parisian society in the late 1800s. Manet's suggestion in his painting is that the materially successful man in the mirror might be looking to buy a drink, some company, and a good time. If that is the case, the girl might be goods-for-sale. It would appear the girl seems to have something that compels the man's behaviour, but she might not be observed as any more divine than the spirits in his hand. Manet's works made his audience more aware of the nature of the ongoing relationship between the man with money and the girl in his economy. In the bar, in the boudoir, on the street, and in the art gallery, perhaps it was better to measure material progress on a separate plane from moral progress.

Art provides us with a mirror and a chance to reflect. What if we adopted Manet's method of reflection and audience implication? If there were a mirror before you, like the one behind the bar at the Folies-Bergère, how would you *see* yourself in front of your Suzon? What would appear to be your intention, your relationship with this observed daughter?

Advertising grants what is presented a divine authority over our behaviour but does not give the ignored a similar recognition. McLuhan's and Manet's perceptive reviews, however, give us "exclusive invitations" to think about how the relationship between communicator and audience is worked over. Advertisers, teachers, speakers, and writers might use instrumental language to communicate what they want from their audiences, regardless of what the audience actually asks for.

One way to stay conscious of the intentions behind a communication is to change the focus of attention. Instead of looking at the figure, look at the background, or look at the audience. Instead of looking at the content, look at the form. As with any flirtation, it can be fun to play along, if it doesn't mean falling into a trap. We can ask more questions about the intentions and the message. In asking more questions, the true form of the politician or the advertiser may be revealed. We can fall in love with the process of inquiry and not have to fall into the snares of bullshitters.

Robert Hare wanted to know more about the minds of psychopaths. He interviewed psychopaths incarcerated in criminal institutions to recognize the methods they use to manipulate people. He experienced something remarkable in the interviews. In the process of their narrative, he believed them. He listened and understood completely the frame of information they constructed in the interviews. If any personality type has mastered the art of instrumental language, it is the psychopath. Psychopaths are possessed by their goals to the point of not caring about the social or legal costs.

Afterwards, while reviewing videotapes and listening to audio recordings, Hare realized their "magical" influence had diminished.[21] On reflection, he was able to take their authority apart and see their use of instrumental language. He was no longer participating in the action of the moment, but instead observing. This says something important about the way to deal with the speaker of instrumental language. They are competing for authority over your attention, deliberately directing and manipulating perspective. But distance, time, and reflection can all restore your ability to choose what to think about them. It may take a change in sensory perception, a turn to a different setting, or a mere adjustment of attention, from content to form, from figure to frame. Hare was in the moment when conducting his interviews. The audio and video material allowed him to focus later on the data rather than engage in the event. This ability to detach and pay attention may be one of the best and only defences we have against our users.

Descriptive

> The contemplation of things as they are,
> without substitution or imposture,
> without error or confusion,
> is in itself a nobler thing than a whole harvest of invention.
>
> —Francis Bacon[22]

Dorothea Lange worked for the Farm Security Administration (FSA) in the United States during the 1930s as a photographer. Lange placed the quote from Francis Bacon on the door of her darkroom. When given a contract, she would travel the highways with her camera equipment, attempting to document the conditions American farmers faced through the Great Depression and the Dust Bowl. Farming families in Nebraska, Oklahoma, New Mexico, and other states in the southwest became migrants. The land no longer grew enough to sustain a family or an economy. The families would pack up belongings in a vehicle and head to California in search of a better life. In one photograph, Lange was able to capture a family who had rolled up a piece of kitchen linoleum flooring. They had kept the rolled-up flooring for the three years they had spent on the road. The family had been without a home for three years, finding temporary work when opportunities came up, but finding no place to settle and establish themselves.[23]

One day, Lange came across an encampment of pea-pickers by Nipomo, California. Families had stretched canvas sheets over the backs of their vehicles to create a temporary shelter for their children and possessions. Lange introduced herself to one woman, Florence Owens Thompson. According to her notes, some of the families had as many as seven children. Often tents or vehicle tires were sold in order to buy food. Lange proceeded to photograph Thompson. During the visit, the woman held her youngest, still a baby, and even breastfed the child. A series of the photographs from that day became known as the *Migrant Mother* collection.

The motivation Lange brought to her documentary-style photography was to show what is, even though the medium of black-and-white photography may not correspond ultimately to what we consider real. Similarly, our impressions from the daily newspaper may not correspond with the real, even when we agree with the opinions of the writers. Jörg M. Colberg, a professor of photography at the University of Hartford and writer at cphmag.com, analyzed Lange's photographs. The conclusion he came to suggests something important at the heart of any expression. The relationship between artist, medium, and viewer can often sway our understanding of the information presented:

> Portraiture makes the viewer's task particularly tricky, because it often seduces
> us to see things that aren't actually there. A photograph of another person

never is that other person. It always "only" is a photograph, made with specific devices and (usually) intent. To understand how portraiture works, one needs to look at the use of the devices, to possibly infer a little about the intent, and to learn a lot about what we bring to the table when looking at a photograph of another person.[24]

Lange's intent, according to the quotation from Bacon, might have been to contemplate things as they are, despite the form and limitations of her medium. Her *Migrant Mother* depiction can be a study of how difficult it is to act as impartial observer with the other. Did Lange pose the individuals in some of her photographs, looking to construct an effect for the final composition? It can be just as valuable to ask how much the image was constructed as to ask what our own assumptions might be when we now deconstruct it. If Lange's motivation was to communicate something in a descriptive, realistic way, to show this migrant mother as she was, why choose the medium of portraiture photography? We may not know from the photograph what Lange thought this mother should be, or what she imagined this mother could be, or even what she herself wanted the mother to do. But if we suspend our suspicions and believe that the quotation from Bacon compelled her, the intent behind what she communicated in her work would be, in a word, description.

Lange was not trained as a journalist. The Farm Security Administration asked photographers to use a "scientific" approach. Subject's names were not recorded. Photos were often categorized by socio-economic description or geographic region. Compared to today, it might seem a primitive science in terms of controls and variables. Lange sometimes wrote down notes after a day's photography sessions to keep track of what people said. Those notes became condensed, quick impressions and key phrases to help her remember context. As a result, the accuracy, precision, and objectivity we might associate with the scientific method today were perhaps not part of Lange's artistic agenda or practice.

Roy Stryker, one-time head of the FSA and the one responsible for hiring Lange, later considered Lange's *Migrant Mother* as the symbol for the whole project and the organization. He stated of Thompson in the photos: "She has all the suffering of mankind in her but all of the perseverance too. A restraint and a strange courage. You can see anything you want to in her. She is immortal."[25]

It is quite an accomplishment for an artist to make a portrait in which the observers might see anything they want. The iconic photographs may not have done much for Florence Thompson, if one were to reduce things to direct financial measurements or levels of social power. Lange showed her photos from that day to an editor of a San Francisco newspaper. The editor informed federal authorities and published an article with the photos in the paper. Something in those images and that article compelled action. Thompson sits in the centre of most of the photos. In one, a child with a dirty face rests his head on her shoulder. Her baby rests on her lap, wearing a knit booty on one foot, a child-size sock over the other.[26]

Was it the power of the press that made a difference? Or was there something real in Lange's photo for the audience? Imagine a newspaper reader at the time identifying with this mother's situation. The government rushed a shipment of 20,000 pounds of food to the camp. John Steinbeck included the photo as one of the inspirations for his novel, *The Grapes of Wrath*. Lange earned a reputation as a photographer and artist. She worked for the government on other projects and had an exhibition of her life's work at New York's Museum of Modern Art in 1966.

According to Thompson, she had moved on with her family before the government aid arrived. The relief affected the lives of other families, but not hers. Thompson was not linked to the photograph until the late 1970s. In 1983, she developed cancer and heart disease. Her family was able to use her identity to help fund her medical care. Her family put on her grave marker, "*Migrant Mother*—A legend of the strength of American motherhood."[27]

Derivatives of the image appeared in many forms. People copied the poses, changing the nationality, class, or race of the family. The recurring circulation of the original photo, in the public domain from the government, elevated the photo and its elements into a kind of archetypal form, expressing hardship, nobility, and endurance.

Lange and her fellow FSA photographers were instructed to use a scientific approach to their work, collecting descriptive information for the agency's reports. In a 1974 commencement speech at the California Institute of Technology, theoretical physicist Richard Feynman explained just what it meant to use a scientific approach. He began by summarizing the historical development of how we study things. The goal of his speech was to inspire graduates to avoid applying their academic learning in an instrumental way. Instead, he wanted them to fall in love with inquiry. He wanted them to commit to the investigation of what is:

> During the Middle Ages there were all kinds of crazy ideas, such as that a piece of rhinoceros horn would increase potency. (Another crazy idea of the Middle Ages is these hats we have on today—which is too loose in my case.) Then a method was discovered for separating the ideas—which was to try one to see if it worked, and if it didn't work, to eliminate it. This method became organized, of course, into science. And it developed very well, so that we are now in the scientific age. It is such a scientific age, in fact, that we have difficulty in understanding how witch doctors could ever have existed, when nothing that they proposed ever really worked—or very little of it did.[28]

Feynman grounded the scientific method in a kind of playful, rigorous process of trial and error. The criteria, however, depended on the idea of what "worked" or what "didn't work." He also understood that the process of inquiry had its own chronology worth understanding. Beginning before the scientific age, the process started with motivations and goals embedded in it, as Feynman's phrase "it worked" suggests. He used an illustration involving the cargo cult phenomenon where Pacific islanders would mimic the actions of people of the West:

> During the war they saw airplanes land with lots of good materials, and they want the same thing to happen now. So, they've arranged to make things like runways, to put fires along the sides of the runways, to make a wooden hut for a man to sit in, with two wooden pieces on his head like headphones and bars of bamboo sticking out like antennas—he's the controller—and they wait for the airplanes to land. They're doing everything right. The form is perfect. It looks exactly the way it looked before. But it doesn't work. No airplanes land. So, I call these things Cargo Cult Science, because they follow all the apparent precepts and forms of scientific investigation, but they're missing something essential, because the planes don't land....
>
> There is one feature I notice that is generally missing in Cargo Cult Science.... It's a kind of scientific integrity, a principle of scientific thought that corresponds to a kind of utter honesty—a kind of leaning over backwards. For example, if you're doing an experiment, you should report everything that you think might make it invalid—not only what you think is right about it: other causes that could possibly explain your results; and things you thought of that you've eliminated by some other experiment, and how they worked—to make sure the other fellow can tell they have been eliminated....

> In summary, the idea is to try to give all of the information to help others to judge the value of your contribution; not just the information that leads to judgment in one particular direction or another.
>
> The easiest way to explain this idea is to contrast it, for example, with advertising. Last night I heard that Wesson Oil doesn't soak through food. Well, that's true. It's not dishonest; but the thing I'm talking about is not just a matter of not being dishonest, it's a matter of scientific integrity, which is another level. The fact that should be added to that advertising statement is that no oils soak through food, if operated at a certain temperature. If operated at another temperature, they all will—including Wesson Oil. So, it's the implication which has been conveyed, not the fact, which is true, and the difference is what we have to deal with.
>
> We've learned from experience that the truth will out. Other experimenters will repeat your experiment and find out whether you were wrong or right. Nature's phenomena will agree or they'll disagree with your theory. And, although you may gain some temporary fame and excitement, you will not gain a good reputation as a scientist if you haven't tried to be very careful in this kind of work. And it's this type of integrity, this kind of care not to fool yourself, that is missing to a large extent in much of the research in Cargo Cult Science.[29]

Feynman was a scientific idealist. But he was appropriately conscious of the many things that could potentially influence the results of a scientific investigation. The role of science, for Feynman, was honesty in description, to get at the material composition and direction of events and objects. Feynman used examples involving advertising and consultation with political figures. Marshall McLuhan would have been proud of Feynman's perceptive eye.

In *The Mechanical Bride*, McLuhan examines a Quaker State Oil advertisement from a magazine. In the way Wesson Oil was "honest" about its cooking oil and food in the 1970s, Quaker State was "honest" about its motor oil and "Freedom…American Style" in the 1950s. McLuhan chose an ad that displayed a nuclear family enjoying a pastoral picnic, thanks to the freedom that came with their car and their lifestyle—and their choice of motor oil. According to McLuhan, "The writer of the ad, in short, takes a dim view of the capacities of his readers, especially when he makes his final gesture of including, as it were, a can of motor oil in every picnic hamper."[30]

Both Feynman and McLuhan caution their audiences about the dangers of language that may first appear descriptive, objective, and even casual or humorous. Who is going to think very long about advertising? Who has time to pay attention? Feynman and McLuhan provided methods for pursuing descriptive information, and recognizing the bait and switches in language used for other purposes:

> If you've made up your mind to test a theory, or you want to explain some idea, you should always decide to publish it whichever way it comes out. If we only

publish results of a certain kind, we can make the argument look good. We must publish both kinds of result. For example—let's take advertising again—suppose some particular cigarette has some particular property, like low nicotine. It's published widely by the company that this means it is good for you—they don't say, for instance, that the tars are a different proportion, or that something else is the matter with the cigarette. In other words, publication probability depends upon the answer.

Supposing a senator asked you for advice about whether drilling a hole should be done in his state; and you decide it would be better in some other state. If you don't publish such a result, it seems to me you're not giving scientific advice. You're being used. If your answer happens to come out in the direction the government or the politicians like, they can use it as an argument in their favor; if it comes out the other way, they don't publish it at all. That's not giving scientific advice.[31]

One of Feynman's final illustrations had to do with a researcher's investigation of rats in a maze:

In 1937 a man named Young did a very interesting one. He had a long corridor with doors all along one side where the rats came in, and doors along the other side where the food was. He wanted to see if he could train the rats to go in at the third door down from wherever he started them off. No. The rats went immediately to the door where the food had been the time before. The question was, how did the rats know, because the corridor was so beautifully built and so uniform, that this was the same door as before?

Obviously, there was something about the door that was different from the other doors. So, he painted the doors very carefully, arranging the textures on the faces of the doors exactly the same. Still the rats could tell. Then he thought maybe the rats were smelling the food, so he used chemicals to change the smell after each run. Still the rats could tell....

He finally found that they could tell by the way the floor sounded when they ran over it. And he could only fix that by putting his corridor in sand. So he covered one after another of all possible clues and finally was able to fool the rats so that they had to learn to go in the third door. If he relaxed any of his conditions, the rats could tell.

Now, from a scientific standpoint, that is an A-Number-One experiment.... [However,] the subsequent experiment, and the one after that, never referred to Mr. Young. They never used any of his criteria of putting the corridor on sand or being very careful. They just went right on running rats in the same old way, and paid no attention to the great discoveries of Mr. Young, and his papers are not referred to, because he didn't discover anything about the rats. In fact, he discovered all the things you have to do to discover something about rats. But not paying attention to experiments like that is a characteristic of Cargo Cult Science.

It is very dangerous... to teach students only how to get certain results, rather than how to do an experiment with scientific integrity.[32]

Young's motivation in Feynman's story wasn't a matter of mere confirmation of outcomes and beliefs, ticking off a box due to witnessing an anticipated response. Feynman's respect for Young's persistence says something about his own motivations in pursuing science. He was not content to be fooled by what he wanted to see, or what he thought should be. Feynman and Young were in love with the process of inquiry. They gave authority to what is, no matter how many personal motivations had to be put aside, no matter how many conditions had to be consciously addressed.

What does this mean for the person trying to navigate through the wash of information we live in today? The search engine has become the new rosary, the ritual we rely on for trust, hope, and guidance. But the answers that come from the search engine do not have to correspond to the reality of what is. They are constructed out of the popular matches of other searches, your browsing history, and your own geographic information. The web browser reads you and the words you type to initiate the search, framing things for your particular lens. Do you look beyond the popular return? Do you ask more than one question or reword the question? Do you look for material that contradicts your own interests or supports another point of view? How do you make sure you are not simply buying the metaphorical or spiritual equivalent of snake oil?

Frye cautioned his students to look for better questions, even in the face of spiritual matters. We cannot immediately spy from the grammar or form of information whether it is fiction or historical fact, truth in journalism or fake news sensationalism. The sanctified texts of holy traditions present us with this problem just as much as any secular source. Appeals to authoritative sources can make us feel "confirmed," in either the religious or psychological sense. Once an authority confirms our understanding of things, it grants us the opportunity to no longer think about it. This stops inquiry. Questions or doubts might even feel rude. But Feynman's story of Young working on his rat maze can remind us of just how persistent we must be before we take any comfort in our integrity, before we believe we sufficiently understand what is. There might always be another variable to address. Young kept looking at the problem, and not from just his initial perspective or motive. He deliberately sought out other ways to investigate the situation. This meant questioning how the different senses played a part in the rat's ability to negotiate its environment. He controlled for sight and smell and sound and touch in his attempts to perceive what was really happening with his rats.

In Greek mythology, Proteus had the gift of prophecy. People would seek him out for valuable counsel. Proteus worked for the sea-god Poseidon, herding his sea creatures. He would only come out of the sea and bathe on the rocks at midday, when the sun was highest. He would sleep surrounded by the monsters of the sea. Anyone daring enough to try and catch him would have to brave these obstacles. And even if Proteus was caught, he had the power to assume every possible shape—animal, stone, water, or fire. If his captor held on through all those changes, all those variables, only then would Proteus speak the truth.[33]

The commitment to use language in a descriptive sense, a realistic sense, motivated to perceive and then communicate only the reality of things, demands such perseverance. In a time or environment of instrumental language use, we have to muster the willingness to see beyond the forms conjured by this old god of the sea. The sacrifice of personal motivation could well be worth it, however, since the reward was always a more accurate understanding of what is, and a greater chance of prophesying what was going to come. That sacrifice also prepares us for the tests of entropy.

Before trusting information from any source, we can ask if the person's intention is to say something about how things are. Have they contested with Proteus? How many of the forms of Proteus have they wrestled with to settle with the information? We can also ask whether they have given all the information, or just the information that leads to bias and oversight—judgment favouring a certain direction. What conditions and clues have they left uncovered and uncommunicated?

The prophet Elijah was a critic of kings and priests. He became ostracized for his pursuit of stripping away what he believed were the veils of corruption in his society. Isolated, alone in the wilderness, Elijah climbed a mountain in his despair. He wedged himself into a cave. He held himself fast in place so that his actions and reactions would not interfere with his observations. A wind came up, breaking rocks loose and changing the face of the mountain. But this didn't satisfy Elijah's pursuit to observe the truth. After the wind, an earthquake shifted the landscape. But this didn't compel Elijah to stop his observations either. A great fire tore through the area. Again, Elijah refused to end his search. After these dramatic events, Elijah heard a soft still voice. The voice called him to examine what he was doing there in a cave on the mountain, alone.[34]

The story of Elijah can be read as a cautionary tale for the vigilant investigator as much as a piece of religious scripture. The trials and the pursuit of knowledge about what is can lead to isolation and even personal devastation. The natural world may hurl everything against us. Such stimulation can be a great distraction, confusing us with what really lies at the bottom of our motivations. But change is possible in the presence of the observed other, even if that other is simply another idea. If we voluntarily hold our motives down and stare into the changing faces of the storms, we will have an opportunity to know ourselves better, tame our own compulsions, and see things as they really are.

Prescriptive

> Never has there been a time when men have so desperately needed a projection of things as they ought to be.
>
> —Ayn Rand[35]

In the introduction to the twenty-fifth anniversary edition of *The Fountainhead*, the author Ayn Rand explained her motivations for writing the book. She didn't want to show how things are, but how things ought to be.

Words like "ought" and "should" come with a sense of necessity, as though how things are supposed to be might be more important than how things are. Prescriptive expression presupposes an obligation to a goal or an ideal—a *should* over an *is*.

Rand explained her writing was the fictional projection of an ideal man and the portrayal of a moral ideal. Rand was a severe critic of religion. She said her book identified the ideal of life, dramatized as "man-worship."

> The man-worshipers, in my sense of the term, are those who see man's highest potential and strive to actualize it. The man-haters are those who regard man as a helpless, depraved, contemptible creature—and struggle never to let him discover otherwise. It is important here to remember that the only direct, introspective knowledge of man anyone possesses is of himself.
>
> More specifically, the essential division between these two camps is: those dedicated to the exaltation of man's self-esteem and the sacredness of his happiness on earth—and those determined not to allow either to become possible.[36]

Rand was born in St. Petersburg, Russia, in 1905. As a student in high school, she witnessed the Kerensky Revolution and the Bolshevik Revolution. During that time, she was introduced to American history and saw in it a way of life absent of the political turmoil and chaos of her homeland. She graduated from university in 1924 and watched as the Communist movement completely dismantled all free inquiry and academic dialogue in the Russian education system. In 1926, she arrived in New York City. Her first published novel, *We The Living*, was based on her time in Russia. Three characters form a love triangle and attempt to sort out their lives through the starvation, picket rallies, and ideological forces tearing apart a regime. Reviews of the book suggested it would appeal to readers wanting to know what life was like in 1920s Soviet Russia and to those who still believed in the importance of the rights of the individual. Despite the oppressive political climate of the story, the events of the book do end with a positive message—the pursuit of purpose makes life meaningful.

Rand's criticisms of religion coincided with her criticism of collectivist ideologies. Where religion puts the highest moral concepts beyond the reach of man, in the realm of something supernatural, authoritarian ideologies allow the ruling controllers to put their values above examination. Rand believed each individual should be able to pursue his or her own interests without the state imposing moral obligations or the church declaring judgments.

It is a common argument from the religious that the pursuit of ethics is impossible without religion. An earlier Russian writer, Fyodor Dostoevsky, asked if there were no God, in the capitalized sense, then wouldn't everything be permitted?[37] Moral transgressions in the face of a god have been replaced with corruption and crime in the face of the rule of law. The threat of damnation has been replaced with the threat of incarceration. Rand believed, however, that religion's monopoly on the language of ethics was just an assumption. She was fond of giving the advice, "Check your premises."[38] She believed she could find a rational and uplifting account of ethics within the individual self, without transcending a personal frame of reference. Rand's writing is the articulation of what she believed was a supreme way of being without a supernatural supreme being. And some of her readers have found her ideas kerygmatic—Northrop Frye's word for stories and words to live by.

Prescriptive differs from instrumental expression in the belief of the speaker or writer. An instrumental expression doesn't need any tether or leash to the real world, as long as the information moves the audience toward fulfilling the goal of the speaker. Prescriptive expressions are used to influence or move the audience toward some goal as well, but the speaker or writer believes the content does have some connection to how things ought to be. A doctor, for example, writes a prescription to fix a patient's medical problem in a way that is tied to the patient's problem and biochemical processes. A car mechanic uses prescriptive language to give repair advice for the functioning of your car. The goal is to make sure the car works for you. A car mechanic might, however, use instrumental language in giving repair advice in order to gain your money without any consideration of the functioning of your car. To satisfy financial goals, an unethical doctor might use instrumental language so that more patients take a certain drug.

Advertisers use prescriptive expressions from figures of authority to inspire further trust in their message. A doctor who informs you about a drug has a different level of authority than a mechanic. An individual pursuing a goal can feel conviction and certainty when information is delivered from an authoritative source.

When should one person's goal be authoritative over some other? What motivations decide the ideal when individual and other stand face to face? The utopian state for a community is an extension of idealist goals. Despite the addictive qualities of idealism and utopian thinking, every attempt to realize a utopian state has produced measures of real hell in proportion to any intended heaven. Denial of what is for the goal of what should be distorts perceptions to the point where a person no longer understands how to listen or speak.

Ken Levine created a video game inspired by Ayn Rand's writing. *Bioshock* takes place in a world where a man named Andrew Ryan built a self-contained society in a constructed environment on the sea floor. The Ryan character called the society he created Rapture. He used a Rand-inspired slogan to summarize the philosophy and goal of his project: "No Gods or Kings. Only Man."[39]

Bioshock is an "immersive first-person shooter"—a common format for video games. The player acts as hero, working from a first-person perspective. As the word "shooter" suggests, weapons are a key element in such games. Part of the lower screen typically displays the weapon the player carries ready at the moment.

The first impressions a player has of Rapture involve city architecture and Art Deco iconography on a tremendous scale. On the city streets, however, the player witnesses protest, revolt, and murder, all leading the story to a crisis. Andrew Ryan, the visionary leader of a society where individuals are given free rein to create their own supreme way of being, becomes a tyrant unwilling to voluntarily give up power. A scientific innovation has given citizens of Rapture the ability to modify their own genetic material. They can build themselves up with superhuman powers with the use of a substance called "Adam." The citizens have gravitated to this, compelled by the personal gain offered by the Adam substance. Unfortunately, the unintended consequences turn out to be just as important as the intended ones. The genetically modified residents have turned into rampaging mutations. The hero of the game is charged with a mission—save a family from the growing chaos and escape the self-contained world of Rapture.

The player faces a moral choice. The Adam that produces the genetic modifications comes from a biological process only in the bodies of certain little girls. The girls, known as Little Sisters, have been bred to host a symbiotic sea slug that generates the Adam. Every Little Sister comes with a protector known as a Big Daddy.

In order to build up the strength needed to withstand the challenges of the environment, the player can gain superhuman powers through collecting the Adam substance. But collecting the substance involves killing a Big Daddy and then dealing with a Little Sister. The game doesn't allow negotiation or trade: the player must kill the Big Daddy first. Only then can the player make a telling decision—kill the Little Sister as well and collect a full sample of the Adam substance, or extract the slug, which leaves the child alive but yields only half as much Adam.

Although not a direct criticism of Rand's philosophy, *Bioshock* can be read as commentary on utopian thinking in general. Some of Rand's most insightful writing concerns trade between individuals.[40] But the creators of *Bioshock* seem to be saying something about the limits of human motivations. Andrew Ryan began a project to create a society without gods, kings, or panoptic governments, but he became obsessed with maintaining his position at the top of the pyramid he created. He restricted trade with the outside world, causing citizens of Rapture to take up underground smuggling in pursuit of their own self-interest.

Later in the game, players are given a chance to doubt the story they have been given. The story gets muddy. Pieces of information suggest that Andrew Ryan may not have been a tyrant after all. Certain residents may be responsible for bringing down Rapture instead.

The assumptions of weaponry, violence, plot twists, and brute action may be the figurative walls in the architecture of the first-person shooter games. Perhaps the only way to direct the attention of the players to the moral choice, and the persistent problem of motivation, is to nest that choice in potential violence toward a Little Sister. Still, it is symbolic that the choice comes in the presence of somebody's daughter. An old saying suggests that children should be seen and not heard. When we think of the things we grant authority over our attention, it is worth noting how much easier it is to turn our gaze away from something that doesn't interest us, compared to not hearing something that doesn't interest us. Both sight and sound help us come to moments of awareness. The repeated cries of a child for a parent can be compared to how Echo's voice affects Narcissus or the murmurings in the dark of the underworld. It may very well be the calls of a child that *should* be heard, taking our attention away from the screens, distractions, and motivations that possess us.

Children do not play an important role in Rand's novels. They are practically never seen or heard. Rand explained this by stating that her novels were about adults and relationships between adults.⁴¹ If this is so, then for Rand the ideal adult world was free of children and the concerns that come with them. But an adult world, no matter how ideal, cannot be sustained without the presence of children, without respect toward the role of children in a family. An ideal adult human world, using whatever aesthetics or rational accounts as ultimate, must recognize a place for children. Otherwise, the society fails.

As an exaggerated comparison, human beings are mammals and not reptiles. Generally, reptiles are not social creatures in the same way mammals are social creatures. A reptile family does not rear young the same way mammals do. There is nothing more rational than a crocodile in pursuit of its prey and holding practically no bonds to its young. In the case of human beings, we cannot bury our eggs on the beach. We cannot trust that the strong will hatch, dig themselves out, race to the water, and survive the attacks of birds. Even if the young do make it to the adult environment of the ocean, only a small fraction of them survive long enough to reach mating age. Our very survival depends on creating environments where children are given the time, respect and presence in our lives to develop into our future generations. To work, using Armstrong's word again, our utopian visions must reflect down to the children within as much as shine up and out, to whatever adult ideals and motivations possess us.

Dostoevsky used a news story from Russia about a little girl who was abused by her own parents to draw people's attention to a similar moral choice as the one in *Bioshock*:

> There was a little girl of five who was hated by her father and mother, "most worthy and respectable people, of good education and breeding." You see, I must repeat again, it is a peculiar characteristic of many people, this love of torturing children, and children only. To all other types of humanity these torturers behave mildly and benevolently, like cultivated and humane Europeans; but they are very fond of tormenting children, even fond of children themselves in that sense. It's just their defenselessness that tempts the tormentor, just the angelic confidence of the child who has no refuge and no appeal, that sets his vile blood on fire. In every man, of course, a demon lies hidden—the demon of rage, the demon of lustful heat at the screams of the tortured victim, the demon of lawlessness let off the chain, the demon of diseases that follow on vice, gout, kidney disease, and so on…
>
> Tell me yourself, I challenge you—answer. Imagine that you are creating a fabric of human destiny with the object of making men happy in the end, giving them peace and rest at last, but that it was essential and inevitable to torture to death only one tiny creature—that baby beating its breast with its fist, for instance—and to found that edifice on its unavenged tears, would you consent to be the architect on those conditions? Tell me, and tell the truth.⁴²

Dostoevsky used other stories as well, such as a boy chased and mauled by a pack of dogs. The dogs were released by a nobleman in the presence of the child's mother. These passages from Dostoevsky focus on deliberate abuse of children, but the sentiment could be carried to unintended abuse of children as well. The moral choice many people face in building their own utopias comes down to a question of who must be abused to realize the ideal. Who should be seen and heard and who should never be allowed to stand and speak? Who is considered a person and who is considered an unobservable other? But if our consciousness is growing more and more toward the idea of a global family, then perhaps we should stop fixing our sights on utopian visions. Instead of engineering a perfect state, we can direct our attention toward preparing better families. If we can get the relationships right in our families, then the politicians and advertisers and authoritarians would have a weaker hold on our children. Do we want the next generations to be turtles, sheep, or lions?

A utopian vision that grants no particular rights or attention to children appears to tunnel out and ignore even the most basic biological reality of humanity. We have not created a lasting utopian society through our ideals, ever. However, one thing that has consistently remained true and necessary through the iterations of civilization is the presence of children. No society can last unless children are recognized as primary even to economic motivations. This means the divinity of the observed other in the form of a child could be a necessity to the survival of the global village. The voice and presence of a child must compel us, even if we don't normally look to children for authority over our actions.

Our confusion between descriptive expressions and prescriptive expressions continues to frame many of our social problems. We would have much better conversations and debates if we could keep in mind the difference between "is" and "should." Without conscious effort, we can slip easily from what is to what should be in our thinking. We can quickly confuse the distance between a statement like "This is important to me," and "This should be important to everyone." If we want problem-solving dialogue to emerge from our politics, we need to understand the difference between statements of description and statements of prescription. Perhaps if the unknown and the other were given as much divine attention as the known and the individual, there would be enough time to measure the gap between what is and what should be. Perhaps the archetypal tradition of a host honouring a guest was one way of initiating the conversation between individual and observed other. In that meeting, both guest and host could tell their stories and speak of what is important, instead of jeopardizing the neighbourhood. A conversation between neighbours can become a heated exchange, but at least it isn't such a programmed relationship as those in our video games. We need not feel boxed into fixed moral choices like the one between the *Bioshock* player and the Little Sister.

Advertising often plays upon our personal relationships with the ideal in order to compel and direct our consuming behaviour. Marshall McLuhan examined a magazine advertisement for "proportioned girdles" from a company, Nature's Rival. The ad featured a row of women in their undies. The copy for the ad described a method for a woman to find her own look and conform to idealized feminine proportions. McLuhan titled his essay "Love Goddess Assembly Line."

> FOUR FIGURES—all different, but with one common factor... the waist line! This new Nature's Rival "Proportioned" girdle is available in four variations of each waist size to really give control with comfort at and below the waist line.

> The secret is in the varying hip measurements and varying lengths you may choose from to suit your proportions.[43]

McLuhan used this advertisement to explore the difference between the goals individuals pursue in embodying the ideal and the pressure individuals feel to all look the same. The suggestion in the ad is that women reading it *should* desire the common factor and the ideal waistline, regardless of who is saying this and why. The case could be made that viewers can give the ad no authority and simply turn the page. But things may only be that simple in an ideal world. In McLuhan's words:

> Just as success and personality know-how consist of recipes and formulas for reducing everybody to the same pattern, we seem to demand, in harmony with this principle, that love-goddesses be all alike. Perhaps the impulse behind this self-defeating process is the craving for a power thrill that comes from identity with a huge, anonymous crowd. The craving for intense individuality and attention merges with the opposite extreme of security through uniformity.[44]

No civilization has ever fully cinched and tailored the tension between the individual and the group, or between what is and what should be, for that matter. These changes in our figurative hemline come with the growing pains of adolescence and the growing into individual responsibility. McLuhan's title suggests the beauty industry has a lot in common with the machine industry of technology. The metaphor, extended for today's society, looks something more like a factory than a family. The belief in the quest for imposing the uniform ideal on others is a Procrustean bed raised to the level of society. The Procrustean bed can become a Prescriptive bed, if we are not careful with the power of words. Procrustes had such a focus on what should be, he was willing to deny and destroy what is. Reality had no authority for his words or actions compared to the ideal in his head.

When children do eventually grow up, they tend to become less and less interested in being told what they should do. It may be no wonder why the instrumental use of language seen in advertising has replaced prescriptive use of language in religion as our words to live by in the West. Perhaps one of the reasons fewer and fewer people identify with traditional religions is the close association between religious practice and loaded words such as "should." The preacher who relies on his or her prescriptive exhortations from the Sunday pulpit will not be as compelling as the lights and sounds from our novelty boxes and electronic screens. It is little wonder the word "should" is used less and less in advertising, replaced with temptations like "benefits," "guarantees," "proven results," "safe," and "new." People don't want to hear what they should do from authorities they no longer trust. If pushed into a constructed moral choice between just the two, people are going to prefer *offers* to *pressures*. People want some level of self-direction in their lives instead of the imposition and assumption of a spiritual assembly line.

One method to manage this persistent messaging is to tune out the barrage of prescriptive and instrumental uses of language. What others think we should do may become, more and more, noise no longer worthy of our attention. The public audience has become so overstimulated with advertising messages and authoritarian environments that people quickly dismiss anything beyond their personal interests and goals, despite the dangers of entropy. With a world of information arriving in less than one second, our attention spans have constricted to mere seconds. But on occasion, a rare image might appear that cannot be easily ignored.

In 1985, *National Geographic* magazine used a portrait of a twelve-year-old girl for one issue's cover. The girl was a refugee from Afghanistan. Photojournalist Steve McCurry toured the Nasir Bagh refugee camp in a province of Pakistan. He found a makeshift, temporary school in the camp. McCurry took photos of the students and the camp but did not record the names of everyone he photographed. It was the first time the girl had ever been photographed in her life. The picture was first entitled *Afghan Girl* but became known by many other names—*The First World's Third World Mona Lisa, Young Woman with Eyes Like the Sea*, and *The Most Beautiful Girl in the World*. She became an ideal, what a beautiful girl should look like. But at the same time, the West had a relationship with the image, and not with the actual living child. It took another seventeen years to put a name to the face that so captivated the attention of the West—Sharbat Gula.[45]

Sharbat Gula was a refugee because of the Russian invasion of Afghanistan. The Russians, inspired by the utopian imperialist vision of the Soviet Communist Party leaders, bombed Afghan villages into destruction. Her parents died in that invasion when she was very young, possibly six or seven. She came from a Pashtun community. Pashtuns have a fierce reputation. Some say that Pashtuns are only at peace when they are at war. The name given to Malala Yousafzai, a daughter mentioned earlier, comes from a story of a Pashtun woman warrior. Sharbat's eyes, and the story of her life, challenges the folk stereotype. In McCurry's photo, Sharbat hardly looks like she is at peace.

McCurry returned to the Pakistan-Afghanistan border in 2002. After a lengthy investigation, he was able to meet her again. She recalled being angry when he took her photograph, though she permitted him to take it. She was shy, torn from her home and family, and facing a complete stranger with a camera. If she were a child of the West today, she might have been labelled with post-traumatic stress disorder. The intensity of the stare brings to mind the frozen emotion of something being preyed upon, and the resolve to survive. According to Cathy Newman of *National Geographic*: "They are haunted and haunting, and in them you can read the tragedy of a land drained by war."[46]

Sharbat Gula did not know about the cover or the story in the magazine. She did not know that millions had seen her face and marvelled at her piercing eyes. The magazine *American Photo* described the image as an "unusual combination of grittiness and glamour,"[47] which is perhaps itself telling of the ways the West perceives portrait photos in magazines. People of the West have told McCurry that her face alone on the magazine compelled them to aid refugees. McCurry received letters from couples asking about adopting her. Men who were interested in marrying her contacted him.

Some part of that aid may have reached Sharbat herself. She left the refugee camp in the mid-1990s, returning to the rural life of her home. She was arranged to be married just years after the photo was taken. According to the 2002 follow-up article in *National Geographic*, she had given birth to four children. Three of them, Robina, Zahida, and Alia, were alive when she met with McCurry again. Her children were the centre of her life. She hoped her daughters would be able to find and receive education, though it was unlikely to happen in her remote circumstances. In 2015, Pakistan newspapers reported border officials seized a Sharbat Bibi trying to enter the country illegally. The name was different, but there were reasons to believe this most beautiful girl in the world had become a refugee again, an unintended sacrifice to the utopian movements and political battles of figuratively noble leaders.

In the throes of an entire life defined by war, Sharbat had some fleeting hope that education might rescue her daughters, or at least give them a chance at a better life. But educational efforts require stability. They also require a commitment from adults to recognize the role of children in the adult world. The adult world depends on the development of children. Dostoevsky's challenge, even today, seems to clearly articulate the intentions of many idealists striving for a world based on shoulds. This is as evident in our time as it was with Agamemnon and Jephthah. People are more than happy to sacrifice and torture their own children and other people's children for the sake of an ideal, or an ideology, for the whim of a motivation, or the pursuit of a personal goal. Agamemnon and Jephthah failed their tests of entropy. Perhaps if we see "the most beautiful girl in the world" in every child, we may be brave enough to let her speak and hear her words. We can be brave enough to grant her some authority over our motivations.

Imaginative

> "A long time ago in a galaxy far, far away..."
>
> —George Lucas

In the beginning of each *Star Wars* episode, the industrial light and magic of moving pictures invite an audience into stories that are as distant to us as could be imagined. With one poetic line, the authority surrounding our perceptions of both time and space is obliterated. The audience metaphorically rises out of their physical reality and into another place comparable to a sacred state of mind, a spiritual state of being.

Life today is a maelstrom of imagery, swallowing and washing away form and content and meaning. As a teacher of art and art history, Camille Paglia dedicated her career to training new artists how to see as well as how to think. But she worried about the larger public audience as well. She felt compelled to help people engage with the artworks that have truly changed our perceptions. She wrote a series of essays titled *Glittering Images*, designed to take the reader on an odyssey from ancient Egypt to the present day. Chronology and development play such important roles in Paglia's studies because she understands that scope and sequence are fundamental to the education process. In the last essay of her book, she asked:

> Who is the greatest artist of our time? Normally, we would look to literature and the fine arts to make that judgment. But Pop Art's happy marriage to commercial mass media marked the end of an era.[48]

Artists who spend their efforts on statements that merely criticize just don't cut it, according to Paglia. Great art needs to change how people perceive and live. Great art demands a constructive change of consciousness, like a call from the desired unknown stirring a response from the audience to cross a personal threshold. And that spiritual call to peak moments of consciousness, for Paglia, wasn't happening in art galleries. It certainly wasn't happening in religious cathedrals or temples. Of all places, she found an answer to her question in the movie theatre. Something as common and commercial as a science fiction serial grabbed the imaginations of people. This is not trivial. People have taken up these stories to the point of abandoning traditional ways of being. They embody, almost literally, the characters and narratives through the costumes, dialogue, and beliefs of fictional characters.

Northrop Frye and George Lucas may share complementary perspectives toward criticism. Frye looked for foundations, for things that could withstand academic sleight-of-hand tricks and ideological hand stamps. Lucas approached his work not to simply criticize or lay blame or even demonstrate superiority. Instead, his figurative muse compelled him to tell stories to live by. As Paglia says:

> No one has closed the gap between art and technology more successfully than George Lucas. In his epochal six-film Star Wars saga, he fused ancient hero

legends from East and West with futuristic science fiction and created characters who have entered the dream lives of millions. He constructed a vast, original, self-referential mythology.[49]

Paglia's praise is not some mere follow-up to popularity. Lucas created new industries and new technologies. He didn't dream of tearing things apart under a judging eye. Instead, Lucas discovered, and uncovered in his storytelling, a foundation on which to build something solid, inspiring, and kerygmatic, in the sense that the movie followers do live by them with zeal and seriousness and devotion.

Lucas himself creatively compared the combat scenes of his films to the vision of a dance: "I wanted to see this incredible aerial ballet in outer space."[50] Dance is anything but a text-based approach to creating peak moments of consciousness. And yet music and dance play at the heart of even our most subdued Western celebrations. One of the most incredible collaborative triumphs of cinematic history may be found in the musical scores of these movies. Lucas worked with composer John Williams. Each lead character had a recurring melody or theme to announce their appearance and role in a scene. These musical themes point, emotionally and figuratively, to the gravity of the scene. In the final production, the audience is served dimension upon dimension of spiritual nourishment through sensory complementarity.

Star Wars fans, with full knowledge of the fictional origins of the stories, simply don't care about what is real or what is imaginary. That is how different the contemporary experience is to the religious ceremony of a Sunday service. They have found something worth embodying, worth fighting for, in the frenzy of the narrative. Lucas built layer upon layer of sensory information to support a temple of the human spirit—what we could be. The millennia-long conversation of how to regulate our emotions and manage our motivations is manifested in a mere two-hour epic of pure fiction and fantasy.

Paglia compared Lucas to Leonardo da Vinci. *Star Wars* is famous for the memorabilia and merchandising that has flourished from the series. Along with toys and drinking glasses, the series has inspired spin-off stories and cross-section books. The cross-section books are like notebooks from technicians. They examine the made-up animals, plants, gadgets, and machines of the *Star Wars* universe:

> In genre, the Cross-Sections books are anatomies, analogous to Leonardo da Vinci's notebooks, with their medical dissections, botanical studies, and military designs for artillery, catapults, tanks, and then-impossible submarines and flying machines.[51]

In da Vinci's notebooks we found impossible machines for his day—flying gyro-copters and submarines and more. Students and fans of Lucas have already had their imaginations filled with the vision, further teased by minute details of completely imaginary things. Now the advocates and apostles of that galaxy pursue the realization of that dream and that technology, even if it is not real today.

As if the comparison was not enough, Paglia explained how Lucas has fostered an environmental consciousness with the themed landscapes and colours that have become a cinematographic signature for the *Star Wars* stories.

> Environmentalism is implicit in Star Wars' lavish array of planetary ecosystems, fertile or ravaged; the color green always signifies good, as in the lizard-like skin of the ancient guru Yoda. Lucas professes a multicultural interest in world religions, with their diverse conceptions of God and spirit, and calls himself a "Buddhist Methodist." Divine power in Star Wars is the Force, an energy field around objects and living beings. As in 1960s occultism, gifted individuals, like the Jedi Knights with their samurai warrior code (Bushido), have a mystic power of telepathy and telekinesis. In its preoccupation with good and evil ("the dark side"), Star Wars often resembles 1950s Bible movie spectacles. Indeed, a poster of Cecil B. DeMille's The Ten Commandments hung in the main office of ILM, which rescued and retrofitted DeMille's wide-screen VistaVision cameras for Star Wars. Finally, Star Wars takes a cyclic view of history, seeing democracy defeated again and again by fascism and imperialism, from Caesar to Napoleon and Hitler.[52]

Lucas, a self-labelled Buddhist Methodist, called up a complex and coherent mythological value system that pays attention to today's contending plurality and pressing issues. And as the preoccupation between dark and light might suggest, the plurality can create an epic dance. Lucas doesn't just attribute emotions and traits to nature and inanimate objects, such as the literary device of pathetic fallacy. He orchestrates a dance integrating tone, setting, plot, and characters together in a scene so that they all speak to make a statement. This is full immersion into a mythology. People are still gripped by the problem of regulating their emotions and managing their motivations. The work of Lucas lays something bare for us in narrative. The tribal and the modern can co-exist and thrive and fight side by side for good or for evil. The engineer and the sage can share a drink, embrace, and tour the stars together.

This phenomenon is not exclusive to the *Star Wars* universe. *Star Trek* and *The Matrix* series present very different aesthetic versions of what could be, and people have found them to be much more compelling illustrations of ways of being than the traditional ideas of heaven or hell.

Part of this might be due to the changes in media. Preachers have a few thousand years of writers on which to draw. They can plumb the vertical depths of the text tradition for ancient words, old songs, and still-life paintings to live by, to use Frye's phrase again. The movie producer has a few thousand work hours spread horizontally across a collaborative team for a project. The ability to combine story, music, and moving pictures together creates a feast for the imagination. As we sit as guests in the theatre, it is hard not to feel gratitude toward the host of such imagery. It is virtually impossible not to grant novelty divine and authoritative control over our attention in such an experience.

No matter how compelling a traditional preacher might be, Lucas found in the *Star Wars* universe someone so compelling she was able to awaken the hero from a dry, deserted dreamland. He cast a young spirited girl named Carrie Fisher to play the part.⁵³

In one of the first visions an audience sees of Princess Leia, she fires a weapon. She wears the white dress of a princess and a surprise of a hairstyle. She looks young and tiny—almost out of place in an adult world. And yet she is fighting for her life and her cause. When brought before the imposing dark figure of her part-man, part-machine adversary, she stares right up at him, bold, defiant. We learn that she is a politician, the youngest-ever representative in a republic's senate. She is a passenger aboard a starship with a mission. This is no simple nice girl, seen but not heard. She will make you listen, with either a blaster she picks up in battle or with a direct confrontation of unmixed words. She is a rebel. She is resourceful. She acts. In Paglia's word, the lady is a "tramp"— "The tramp is a rover, exploring the wilderness outside the status quo."⁵⁴

Leia leaves a message in one of her droids, hoping it will get to a relic from the past, the knight Ob-Wan Kenobi. Instead, a restless farm boy first intercepts the message, possibly as a ploy from the sentient and perceptive droid. Luke, another restless child, becomes entranced by her, compelled to act because of her. As despairing princess, Leia takes on another persona—the "young virgin" and unwilling sacrifice.

Another movie in the series shows another side of her. The crime lord Jabba has taken her prisoner and makes her wear a slave girl costume. Apparently, Fisher had quite a time preparing for these scenes. She went on a diet. She worked through all the competing thoughts about sexism and feminism. She also mustered the courage to be on display, vulnerable and exposed, but still Princess Leia. In the minds of young adolescents across the West, she became a sex symbol, something so compelling the costume became an iconic part of the fantasies of the culture. Boys and girls alike came to look up to her with awe, wonder, and imagination.

After the release of the movie, an action figure came out of Princess Leia in the slave costume. A father of two daughters expressed his shock to Fisher that such a sexually charged figure would be for sale to children. What should a father say to his two daughters? Fisher responded: "Tell them that a giant slug captured me and forced me to wear that stupid outfit, and then I killed him because I didn't like it. And then I took it off. Backstage."[55]

The *Star Wars* universe embodies and expands the limits of technological possibility. However, in many respects, any sexuality in the series has remained purposefully, defiantly, and even joyfully adolescent. If anything, there is a celebration of first, feisty, epic, and confused loves, all while trying to save the galaxy. Exuberance and eagerness couple figuratively with daring simple tricks and nonsense. In the adult world of sex and suggestion, potential trade and shifting principles, some may think that censorship and sensitivity should rule. But time and time again, protection in safe spaces doesn't measure up, or cover up, the onslaught of transgressions. Tyrannies put people into slave costumes. Individuals need to learn how to get out of them. *Star Wars* presents another strategy for consideration—prepare young daughters for the monsters that may appear. Princess Leia killed her captor, and in doing so brought forth the side of her character that could be called the "vamp." In Paglia's words:

> Vamps are queens of the night, the primeval realm excluded and repressed by today's sedate middle-class professionals in their orderly, blazing bright offices. The prostitute, seductress, and high-glamour movie star wield woman's ancient vampiric power over men. That power is neither rational nor measurable.[56]

One of the most valuable lessons for adolescent girls and boys to learn is that girls can hold power over life and death. This makes the relationship even more elevated while also making things abundantly clear: it's more than just your skin in that game.

In the seventh episode, *The Force Awakens*, Leia shows another face as an "older mother" character. She is a military leader estranged from her child. Gripped by the realization that her child took up a path away from mother's expectations, she becomes a model of someone ready to forgive and welcome a prodigal child home. Though emotionally crushed by personal doubts and wrinkled with experience, Leia still carried a desperate hope that she can somehow heal her family.

In one character, Fisher portrayed an entire cycle of admirable and archetypal feminine heroes, all the while standing about five feet one inch tall. Although Leia is not the main character of the tale, the farm boy would not have risen to his own identity and destiny without inspiration from her call and message. All the angels in the metaphorical landscape of heaven pale in the illumination of her grandeur. Fisher helped chart a new narrative path beyond the clouds and into the very stars, and it may be our only hope to follow.

Fisher's portrayal of Leia blended feisty with feminine. McLuhan's fascination with pop culture kept him circling back to the dominant pattern coupling sex and technology in advertising. The development of feminism has created waves of revolutions. Like art or technology, feminism has made us change the way we look at things, the way we perceive the relationships between assumptions and motivations. In one of his explorations in *The Mechanical Bride*, McLuhan considered and then reconsidered feminism in relation to technology and to the business world of the 1950s.

> Technology means constant social revolution. So much so that Marx argued that the machine would win all his battles without political assistance. A century ago the socialists began their attack on the family unit.... Their arguments really came to one, namely, that the family cost too much. By the end of the nineteenth century, industrialists and businessmen had already adopted this argument in practice by offering jobs to women. Why should half the population exist in a semi-leisured state when it might be put to work and thereby bring down the scale of men's wages? That, we can now see, was the economic logic in feminism. The woman of leisure might wear long skirts, but the working woman was put into adolescent short skirts and told in big press campaigns that the age-old tyranny of men was at an end. Today she is told every few months to shorten or lengthen her dresses in accordance with market exigencies, and she obediently does so.[57]

McLuhan's probe in this paragraph brings into question the motivations behind revolutions. The economic progress of society replaced the family unit as an ultimate concern. The economic revolution turned motherhood into something subservient to economic pursuit. The age-old tyranny of men has been replaced with the tyranny of economic consumption and fashionable whim. The successes of the West brought about the most incredible level of comfort, predictability, and public literacy the world has ever seen. But we may very well have sacrificed parenthood in the process. Some people may echo the line, "I am a spiritual being having a physical experience." A change in the variables brings another insight: "I am a biological being having an economic existence." We feel pressure to keep the wheels of innovation and social revolution greased. The problem considered and reconsidered remains: we may not know what we do when we give authority to the novelties of our emotions.

We don't know what the imagination has unleashed. We are not just telling our stories in different media now. We are participating in our stories and engaging the things that compel us in entirely new relationships. Anakin Skywalker, Luke Skywalker, and Princess Leia are all presented as ultimate individuals, shining examples of the power of the dark and light side of the Force in their galaxy. But each one of them, through the progress of the *Star Wars* episodes, murders and hurts others to fulfill the desires they serve. Anakin kills children and becomes a broken man obsessed with control. He ruthlessly destroys his allies and enemies with little distinction. Luke Skywalker blows up a space station the size of a small moon, killing everyone on it. Leia fires a blaster at her enemies and orders military commands. Her son murders his own father. This family gives and takes suffering that would make Agamemnon and Jephthah reconsider their own ambitions.

Nietzsche's madman, frantic about the death of a god in Europe in the late 1800s, said that no amount of water would wash away the blood from our hands. Now, in one of the most celebrated science fiction mythologies, the audience fully suspended disbelief as entire planets were destroyed. It was so easy for us to accept that individuals could be motivated to do such things. Spiritually, then, it is not just the blood of the gods on our hands, but the blood of every living thing on a planet that is on our hands. These are the stakes. The twentieth century faces us as direct proof of it.

In Luke's greatest test of identity, he chooses to not slay his own father. The idea of rescuing a father from the depths of the underworld is one of the oldest mythological stories of the West, and all the world. But that story, told again and again, has not stopped the rise and the fall of the civilizations that have passed along. These myths still resonate with us. We know the stakes are high. We know the hero can be a villain, depending on the perspective and the imagination. In the *Star Wars* saga, the birth of the siblings, Luke and Leia, coincides with the death of their mother and the mechanical reconstruction of their father. In terms of archetypes, it is worth asking ourselves what the vision of that family is telling us. In that universe, the father of tyrannical order, the fixed culture of past control, needs technology to keep him alive and in power. The mother of abundance and life dies while giving birth to her twins. The children are born, according to the third episode in the series, in a facility built on a barren asteroid, only to be transported to vastly different worlds and separated by all the distance in a galaxy.

Contrast the birth of twins Luke and Leia to the birth of brothers Cain and Abel. The dynamic relationship between Luke and Leia is wholly other in comparison to the competition between Cain and Abel. It may be so conceptually different that the story radically changes their figurative relationships with their father, their mother, and between themselves. This might be on a plane of perception we do not yet fully understand. We may not even have a proper name for it. But we can look to the faces before us. We can ask ourselves if we want blood on our hands, or the sweat and dirt of good work instead. How do we give this new aspect of our perception a moment of our time without diminishing the lessons learned from Cain and Abel?

The stakes are so high that some might think it worth sacrificing our world and our very nature as human beings in order to transcend, or destroy, our past. The people working to bring social, economic, and political destruction are certainly motivated enough to do it. But destruction of the past is like ignorance of the past. We multiply our risks and make ourselves fragile. Before we act on that pursuit, we need a new hope to find a new way to bring the family together, if for no other reason than to share a meal and start a conversation where all may be heard.

Jack Miles suggested in his book *God: A Biography* that the ultimate sign of success for a writer would be to have a story taken up religiously by an audience.[58] In Frye's terms, this would be kerygmatic—readers find in it a story to live by. We can't testify to what time will do to the *Star Wars* stories and its followers. But it is worth appreciating how popular this pop culture narrative has become, especially since it comes at a time of descent for so many other traditional belief systems in the West. People quite literally embody the characters and play out the events in the *Star Wars* universe, and other purely fictional narratives, just as they would take up religious rites of passage. What may have started as a novel thing to do on official government documents has become quite a serious category of identification for a minority of people. In the 2001 national census, 21,000 Canadians identified their religion as Jedi or Jedi Knight. It reached the most popular faith in the "Other Religions" category for census information in England.[59] Some people have responded to this with criticism or ridicule, waving it away as imaginary, meaningless, not *real*. In comparison, a few thousand people may have started the Christian communities in the first hundred years after the story of Jesus.[60] Christianity was granted status as a religion recognized by the state after followers were ignored, laughed at, and persecuted. Small communities bring big changes to the world.[61]

The imaginative expression of ideas puts aside the authority of what is, what should be, and even, what I want out of some other. Instead, it tries to express *what could* be. And in that potentiality, the artist and audience find something so inspirational and compelling they are together willing to explore where it might take them. Another writer of science fiction brought home the perennial beauty and persistent puzzle found in the relationship between artist, art, imagination and truth. In the words of Ursula K. LeGuin:

> In reading a novel, any novel, we have to know perfectly well that the whole thing is nonsense, and then, while reading, believe every word of it. Finally, when we're done with it, we may find that we're a bit different from what we were before we read it, that we have been changed a little, as if by having met a new face, crossed a street we never crossed before.
>
> The artist deals with what cannot be said in words. The artist whose medium is fiction does this in words. Words can be used thus paradoxically because they have, along with a semiotic usage, a symbolic or metaphoric usage. They also have a sound. A sentence or paragraph is like a chord or harmonic sequence in music: its meaning may be more clearly understood by the attentive ear, even though it is read in silence, than by the attentive intellect.
>
> All fiction is metaphor. Science fiction is metaphor. What sets it apart from older forms of fiction seems to be its use of new metaphors, drawn from certain great dominants of our contemporary life—science, all the sciences, and technology, and the relativistic and the historical outlook, among them.
>
> I'll make my report as if I told a story, for I was taught as a child on my homeworld that Truth is a matter of the imagination. The soundest fact may fail or prevail in the style of its telling: like that singular organic jewel of our seas, which grows brighter as one woman wears it and, worn by another, dulls and goes to dust. Facts are no more solid, coherent, round, and real than pearls are. But both are sensitive.[62]

Aduri

> The west shall shake the east awake. Walk while ye have the night for the morn, lightbreakfastbringer, morroweth whereon every past shall full fost sleep.
>
> —James Joyce[63]

Tanyss Munro was a teacher, principal, and district director of education in Canada. She advised the federal government and First Nations governments on school programs. When she met G. E. M. (Gem), a writer, artist, and fellow educator, they quickly became inseparable and took jobs teaching in an isolated First Nations reserve in northern Alberta.

Years later, Gem and Tanyss Munro were invited to Bangladesh to study the education system. They quickly realized a problem was growing in the country's city slums. People living in the slums couldn't afford to enrol their children in schools or keep them in school for any length of time. Many systemic problems tend to surround slum areas. Gem and Tanyss understood these children would likely remain illiterate throughout their lives. It would not be uncommon for girls to marry at the age of eleven or twelve and begin a life of domestic slavery. The expectation for any other kind of life was hardly thinkable for these children. How would anyone, let alone outsiders and people from the West, attempt to make a difference in a country of over 150 million people?

The Munros developed an idea that would lead them to work closely with mothers in the slums. The initiative was based less on intervention and more on establishing a solution for education that could grow from the mother's own motivations for their children. The ability to read and write could make a tremendous difference for work and life opportunities to families in these slums.

The Munros started an organization with no direct religious affiliations called the Amarok Society.[64] They went into a slum and found a group of mothers who wanted to learn how to read and write. Each mother promised to start a small, homegrown school of her own with at least five children in her neighbourhood. Mothers learned a lesson from an instructor, and then delivered it to their children and students in their own homes. The courses from Amarok Society included English, Bangla, and mathematics. By the slow, developmental steps of cumulative lessons, these mothers, children, and neighbourhoods gained the skills to build bridges out of their poverty.[65]

Gem Munro wrote a book to tell people of the work being done by the society.[66] The family returned to Canada to tour the country and promote the book in order to bolster support and funds for their organization. They spoke at events held in libraries and bookstores. One librarian gave a copy of the book to someone she knew who had an education centre. His name was Michael Maloney. He read Gem's book in about a day and immediately sought out how to contact the Munros. They met at a road stop between speaking engagements, where Maloney gave the Munros a new idea. He was a member of Rotary International, and an active member in his club's literacy committee. Each Rotary Club sets goals for community education programs and global literacy efforts. Maloney and the Munros were able to coordinate further speaking engagements for the Munros with a series of motivated audiences ready to help.

But Gem wanted to do more than explain what the Amarok Society did for mothers and children. He wanted to show Rotarians and others what the mothers involved in the Amarok Society were doing with the new opportunities that came with literacy. These mothers and their children now had an opportunity to move from a life of function to a life of purpose.

In his presentations, he talked about one mother by the name of Shamaya. Shamaya's father had given her to a man in marriage when she was eleven years old. The man was more than twice her age. She was expected to fulfill the role of wife. In that part of the world, this meant she would do all the cooking and cleaning to serve her husband, and to start bearing children. Shamaya happened to live in a slum in which the Amarok Society established a school. She agreed to teach children what she learned and began working through the lessons and classes in the organization.

Shamaya had a young daughter at the time by the name of Aduri. Aduri learned from her mother. But even at an age younger than eight years old, Aduri wasn't satisfied with the role of *student*. She wanted to be something more, and she identified with something more.

In Munro's words:

> It is beyond question that Shamaya's life has been immeasurably improved by moving from a life of function to a life of purpose, as a teacher of the children of her slum. It is possible we won't be able to rescue her from every unfortunate aspect of her life, however. What we can be very hopeful about though, is that her little daughter will have a very different experience than she had. This spirited little girl will be able to retain that spirit, escape the normal process of stamping out or tamping down whatever spark might be found in a little girl and she will be able to achieve an educated adulthood with that spirit intact.[67]

Aduri thought about this change and thought about her mother's role as a teacher in the community. Her mother would attend a lesson, and then afterwards teach Aduri and other children in the slum. Aduri watched and learned and then thought she could do the same thing.

> Every day Shamaya attends our school and then goes to her own home and conducts her own school. One of her students is, of course, little Aduri. Then Aduri, every day after she attends her mother's school, conducts her own little school, where she teaches five children of the ages of three and four. And she is very serious in this undertaking. She, like her mother, conducts a school for the same children at the same time for the same period of time.[68]

The ambitions of a child can be inspiring enough, but the Munros and the Amarok Society witnessed something come from this little girl's initiative that was even more remarkable:

> Aduri's grandfather observed her teaching these children. And one day he said to her, "Granddaughter, you are teaching these children to read and write and do arithmetic, and yet your own grandfather cannot read or write or do arithmetic. May I join your school?"
>
> And she said, "Yes, grandfather, you may."[69]

The grandfather then attended Aduri's school every day. He sat down with the other students in Aduri's class. He took part in the lessons and answered his teacher's questions. He received instruction on how to hold a pencil and form letters. Munro used this story to show how this man's mind had been changed.

> Let's consider for a moment, this man's journey. He has gone from finding it worthwhile to dispense with his daughter and to operate under the prevailing prejudice that girls and women are brainless baby machines, to welcoming education as delivered to him by his granddaughter, as delivered to her by his daughter. This is a long way to come.
>
> What we can expect is the little boy taught by Aduri won't have to take that same journey. He will grow up with the understanding that he is gaining his education from a girl who has gained it from a woman. He will grow up thinking that at least in our slums, girls and women equal education.
>
> Now, in terms of Aduri's grandfather, I (Gem Munro) am the first foreigner he's ever known. It's quite possible I'm the first foreigner he's ever seen, that's how non-cosmopolitan these circumstances are. And yet he says that he loves me. In fact, he says that he loves every North American who has contributed to the benefit of his family....
>
> We have a very serious problem in our world. Our failure to educate all of humanity stands as our greatest sin of omission. And the wages of that sin are terrible, including that we have made available to the terrorist, millions upon millions upon millions of people who have no developed capacities of reason by which to assess the ridiculous lies he will tell them, no independent moral sense by which to consider and judge the wicked deeds he's going to call upon them to carry out.
>
> It has been said that extremism is the great challenge of our age. Unfortunately, the governments of the developed world don't seem to have found a better answer to that challenge than to bomb Aduri's little school. That is the reality of modern warfare. But what else can we do? What else can we do in the face of admitted barbarism?[70]

Munro used this presentation to Rotary clubs to raise funds for the Amarok Society and thank Rotary members for their support. However, in his presentation he answers his question with something that could unite and inspire many people of the West. Despite the current crisis of identity in today's culture and the unintended consequences of the march of ambition, the West has contributed something remarkable to the development of the world, something worth fighting for. In a testament against the tests of entropy, the Munro family found a triumph in the most unlikely of places. But the way we face these tests, the way in which we fight, must change.

You all have highly developed capacities of reasoning. You have a world of information available to you. These two things combine to provide you with genuine wisdom. And to that wisdom, you add love and compassion, which we know are yours.

These are not your weaknesses against bald brutality. They are your strengths. And the extremist has no answer to them.

Of course, he's going to try to draw you out of the realm of your strength and into the arena of his. But why would you ever go? Why would you ever do anything he wants you to do? You should do exactly what he doesn't want you to do. And we know what that is by what he so desperately tries to prevent, everyday. It isn't war. He prospers in a state of warfare, he knows it. It isn't bombs. He welcomes bombs. He says, "We rejoice in death!"

If he rejoices in death, what can possibly frighten him? Well, there is something that strikes terror into the heart of the terrorist.

It's her.

An educated, reasoning mind, that has learned to love the world. Because there is absolutely nothing he can do with her or anyone she teaches. When we give her a reason to live, and she gives her students a reason to live, he has no opportunity to provide them with that opportunity to die.

If we are truly serious about creating and maintaining peace, we have got to stop rattling the sabres and start ringing the school bells. And we can't do any better than to place those school bells in the hands of the world's mothers.[71]

Munro often emphasizes in his talks that this story of Aduri and her grandfather is not unique. Men often stand or sit outside of the little schools and follow the lessons given by neighbourhood mothers. Older children pass on the lessons to younger siblings or children in other families. Almost everyone in these neighbourhoods seems to understand that education will transform their lives, families, and neighbourhoods. The role of communication in a community is almost as sacred as the role of love in a family.

The Munros have found a story to live by in the work they do in Bangladesh. Aduri has demonstrated how to take up the role and responsibility of the hero, bringing positive change and growth to her community. And her grandfather has demonstrated that he was willing to learn something from his granddaughter. The first foreigner he might have ever met changed the fortunes of his family in ways unimagined. This one humble man from a slum in Bangladesh has created for himself a moral identity that giants like Agamemnon and Jephthah never achieve in their stories. He was willing to be led by the wisdom of a little girl. In doing so, he found a love for the West. That love could change the families of the slum communities in Bangladesh for generations. The West may very well have shaken the East awake by putting an idea in the head of a little girl. And in turn, if we are courageous enough to look up and learn something from the story, it might mean a very different kind of salvation for us now.

When Malidoma Somé was a little boy in West Africa, his grandfather told him a story. His grandfather said that before the boy was even born, they had talked. The child was in his mother's womb. His grandfather asked the child in the womb what would be his purpose in life. According to his grandfather, the unborn child had answered:

Gold shall flow with silver, East shall shake hands with the West. To make an enemy a friend is to end the need for war, to vanquish the powers of destruction.[72]

Somé's grandfather was not likely aware of or even deliberately expanding on James Joyce's text when he used the symbolic directions of East and West. As well, he could not know that decades later a family from Canada would initiate an education program in the slums of Bangladesh. However, the story between grandfather and child might have planted a seed in the boy's mind, in terms of what could be his supreme way of being, the best use he could make of his life. The use of East and West may still appear poetic or vague, even after all these stories. But together, they could illustrate a relationship between any two individuals who meet, symbolically East and West. Aduri models our path away from disaster and resentment, a way to pass the tests of entropy together. We can make a difference here and now, and even redeem the past generations of our families, if we take a moment to see this child and hear her voice.

The Munros brought to Bangladesh a handful of ideas about education. Spiritually, that is metaphorically, those ideas could shake the world awake to a new attitude toward daughters. If we welcome this awakening with the proper attitudes of hosts and guests, then East and West may shake hands, vanquishing the powers of destruction.

REFLECTION

In 1958, a young boy from Egypt immigrated with his family to Canada. They settled in Toronto. In the 1970s, the boy started hanging out at a guitar store downtown. He played folk music at coffee houses for a while and then hitchhiked to Vancouver in search of fame and fortune. When he returned to Toronto, a public school invited him to put on a concert for the students. He wasn't sure about performing for children, but he agreed and prepared a number of songs. The kids loved him. They followed his lead and sang along with him. This one moment of novelty, a change in perspective, gave Raffi Cavoukian an incredible opportunity and a new personal identity. He became known as a global troubadour and one of the most popular children's singers in the English-speaking world.

In 2006, Raffi and his friend Dr. Sharma Olfman compiled an anthology, *Child Honouring: How to Turn This World Around*. The book includes what Raffi called a "covenant for child honouring" as a way to restore communities and ecosystems.

> One morning in late 1996, the phrase "Child Honouring" woke me up from a sound sleep. In that pivotal moment, I realized that all my years of singing and talking with young children, learning all I could about child development—and then of watching, with growing alarm, the disintegration of communities and the deterioration of our planet—had been a preparation of sorts, a way of showing me the link between the state of the world and the health of its children. I knew I had to speak out in a new way on behalf of the world's young. This sparked a dialogue with people in a wide range of disciplines.
>
> On New Year's Eve, 1998, on the University of Virginia campus, an important part of the Child Honouring vision emerged. I'd been visiting with Bill McDonough, then dean of architecture, who began his sustainable-design course each year with the question, "How do we love all the children?" Bill spoke of the importance of not imposing "remote tyranny" on children to come, of society's current activities not compromising their future lives. (This was the same message I'd heard 12-year-old Severn Cullis-Suzuki deliver in 1992 at the Earth Summit in Rio de Janeiro.) Later that night, I pulled a copy of the Declaration of Independence from a bookcase and began reading. In those pages, there was no mention of children. I wondered what a similar emancipatory proclamation about

them might say, and began writing what became "A Covenant for Honouring Children"—a declaration of duty to this and future generations.[73]

Raffi looked through a political document for inspiration with the form and content of his covenant. It is worth noting that he did not go to a sacred religious document. The Ten Commandments of the Judaeo-Christian tradition mention nothing about the rights of a child either. The only demand that comes close seems to be a demand on children to honour their mothers and fathers. Many people who have studied the development of civilization suggest that there is a common ground in the basic rules we have learned to live by. It has taken us more time and development to demand in writing that mothers and fathers and communities should honour children. This covenant can be considered a way of recognizing the child as divine, in the sense that a child has implications for our behaviour.

A Covenant for Honouring Children

We find these joys to be self-evident:
That all children are created whole, endowed with innate
intelligence, with dignity and wonder, worthy of respect.

The embodiment of life, liberty and happiness,
children are original blessings, here to learn their own song.
Every girl and boy is entitled to love, to dream, and to
belong to a loving "village." And to pursue a life of purpose.

We affirm our duty to nourish and nurture the young,
to honour their caring ideals as the heart of being human.
To recognize the early years as the foundation of life, and to
cherish the contribution of young children to human evolution.

We commit ourselves to peaceful ways and vow to keep
from harm or neglect these, our most vulnerable citizens.
As guardians of their prosperity we honour
the bountiful Earth whose diversity sustains us.
Thus we pledge our love for generations to come.[74]

Raffi is an advocate for children's rights. This covenant does not mean that children rule over us, as in have the power to dictate their interests over the good of a family or community. In Raffi's own words: "The best parenting is neither permissive nor punitive. It is authoritative. Sometimes the parent must say to the child: this is not your decision, it is mine. And that's how it's going to be."[75]

This same advice provides a model to adopt toward our own emotions and motivations. The child, like each archetypal character in our story, or each sequence of events or each social environment, has the potential for both good and evil. Rights do not simply offer protections, but articulate responsibilities. Honouring the child, as Raffi poetically expresses, is a call to bear responsibilities and commit ourselves to something other than the burning of Troy or the sacrifice of a daughter.

Part of this covenant, according to Raffi, means each child has a right to live free of commercial exploitation. This would mean decreasing children's exposure to instrumental language and commercial messages. In 1983, companies spent about $100 million on advertising directed toward children. In the last three decades, that number has increased to about $15 billion.[76] The change in media, business, and public attitude required in such a shift may appear insurmountable. Marketing to children generates profit. It generates jobs for the economy. It is not just a simple matter of correcting ambitions, unfortunately. Severe regulation could put families as well as companies and markets into chaos. But the stakes involved make it worth facing the challenge and finding better resolutions. By changing our attitudes toward children, and toward the observed other, maybe we can balance honour with ambition, responsibility with profit. The restoration of civilization and the transcendence of our own cycles of failure are pursuits worth fighting for.

Raffi has consistently refused offers for commercial endorsements. He has gone to great lengths to avoid marketing directly to children in his own projects. He turned down a movie proposal because the funding for the production would have come from methods against his covenant. His music company uses what is called a "triple-bottom-line" framework of accounting. Instead of just measuring a profit or loss, a triple-bottom-line company keeps social, ecological, and financial ledgers to expand the perspective of the company's impact. It is an attempt to manage and take up responsibilities that would otherwise be considered externalities.[77]

Imagine the strength of character needed to measure the things that seem outside or irrelevant to a precious and single-minded goal. Imagine the strength of vision needed to challenge the social architecture of the most intransigent institutions. Imagine the attention needed to avoid the use of instrumental language against children. Imagine the strength of will needed to accept and honour the gifts of children over the gifts of personal financial reward. This kind of commitment and attitude would suggest that everything we do matters, and that it is worth considering the unintended consequences of our actions. It is difficult enough for adults to parent themselves and limit personal screen time, maintain a home, and live as responsible individuals. But the test of entropy wasn't resolved with past generations and won't reach a conclusion with this one. It is an heirloom passed on with each decision we make.

The Biblical character of Abraham is known as a patriarch for Judaism, Christianity, and Islam. Abraham's relationship with his god undergoes many changes in the narratives of these religions. He argued with his god. He didn't believe the promises of his god. But when his god told Abraham he must kill his son, Abraham made the journey to the top of a hill and prepared a sacrificial altar. He laid his child on the stone, like an object instead of a living person, and raised his knife in preparation.

Some take this story as an exuberant display of faith and commitment to a god. Abraham proved himself worthy to his god. He was willing to sacrifice something so precious as his son.

And yet, according to the story, Abraham did not finish the action. A messenger—new information—stopped his hand. This messenger gave Abraham a moment to observe, not act, thus changing his perspective. This change of perspective turned out to be important, if our knowledge of Agamemnon and Jephthah helps us with this story. The destruction of a child in a family, by a quick sacrifice or the slow twisting of the child's development to ruin, ultimately means the potential destruction of the family and community as well. If it weren't for the change in perspective, Abraham's family and all the generations after would have collapsed in the dust under his feet.

Other interpretations of this story suggest the relationship between Abraham and his god can be understood as a clash of wills. Both characters are stubbornly committed to what they want. One pushes the other, as if they are playing a game of dares between opponents. God, as singular authority, commanded Abraham to sacrifice his son, and Abraham complied as a show of bravado. The tension of the story escalates on who would back down first.[78]

Abraham's god, his precious goal, the thing that compelled Abraham, what Abraham thought he must serve, is the one who dropped the game of dares and had a change of perspective. If this is the case, then the change of heart and change of mind is worth celebrating and worth worshipping.

Another useful perspective on the story comes from an earlier passage in the text, when Abraham was still named Abram. "And when Abram was ninety years old and nine, the Lord appeared to Abram, and said unto him, I am the Almighty God; walk before me, and be thou perfect."[79]

What is the significance of a god giving a command to "walk before me" instead of behind or beside? Abram must lead his own life and make his own decisions, even if bare before the omniscient presence always behind him. Even in this man's vulnerability and imperfection before his god, he has the responsibility to direct himself.

When directed to climb the hill and sacrifice his child, Abraham followed without question. But in following, giving up his own will, how could Abraham possibly walk before his god? He was not perfectly conscious of what his motivation was making him do in that moment. It seems more like he was following orders, as though full of fear and lacking the courage to take responsibility for his own actions. According to popular Biblical study, fear of the Lord is the beginning of wisdom. If a god is what compels action, then we must be very careful to not make fear the end. If we become loyal to fear then we make fear into a god, into something that compels our actions.

In religious language, the divine individual has a responsibility to make proper sacrifices and calculations before that individual's god. However, that responsibility doesn't manifest itself in behaviour that would mean using another individual as an object or piece of property, even when that observed other is one's own child. If the individual is considered sacred in the West, it means we carry a responsibility to see and name the individual in the observed other as divine as well. Otherwise, we may fail our own tests of entropy. God interrupted Abraham's behaviour with a messenger, a correction from a teacher to a student. Using a child as a scapegoat is no way to bring an individual closer to perfection or to pass these tests. This was a chance to begin again.

The character of Abraham presumed that he had some right or claim over the life of his child. Even something as intimately close to him as his own child was not seen or heard as divine. If each individual is to be considered divine, then the decision of the sacrifice rests upon the individual and the individual's god, or what that individual feels compelled to serve. In this story, Abraham felt he had justification to sacrifice an other to his god. But he never questioned if that justification was in fact worthy of his worship. It could be said Abraham only ever had the right to sacrifice two things—himself or the motivation he worshipped. He tested both by thinking he could sacrifice a child instead. Abraham's god tested him. Perhaps Abraham needed to differentiate between sacrificing his child to his ultimate concerns and presenting his child as an ultimate concern.

Like a relationship between call and response, the art of living our lives depends on how we communicate. The form of expression, the way we say something, can guide the other to know how to process the content of our message and the worth of our intentions. But this also allows us to reach new peaks in our own awareness. With communication comes consciousness and then choice.

To quote Shakespeare, "The play's the thing."[80] When preparing for a role, an actor asks, "What's my motivation?" If we are more conscious of the settings and stories we find ourselves in, we can identify the roles we are playing and evaluate if the motivations ruling us are worthy of our worship. Like a child who realizes when a game is no longer worth playing, we can have the courage to stop. We can have the presence of mind to find better rules through use of language, communication and agreement.

Munro suggested in his presentation that we are haunted by the question of what this world could be if we ever got around to opening all our gifts. Each child, word, breath, and gift give us an opportunity to consider what possesses us, and then reflect on what might be most worthy of our attention and our pursuit.

CODA

Standing on New Shores

The work to be done was no longer proto- or super-human; it was the labor specifically of man—control of the passions, exploration of the arts, elaboration of the economic and cultural institutions of the state. Now is required no incarnation of the Moon Bull, no Serpent Wisdom of the Eight Diagrams of Destiny, but a perfect human spirit alert to the needs and hopes of the heart.

—Joseph Campbell
The Hero with a Thousand Faces

Self-knowledge—in the total meaning of the word—is not a one-sided intellectual pastime but a journey through the four continents, where one is exposed to all the dangers of land, sea, air and fire. Any total act of recognition worthy of the name embraces the four—or 360!— aspects of existence. Nothing may be 'disregarded.' When Ignatius Loyalus recommended 'imagination through the five senses' to the meditant, and told him to imitate Christ 'by use of his senses,' what he had in mind was the fullest possible 'realization' of the object of contemplation. Quite apart from the moral or other effects of this kind of meditation, its chief effect is the training of consciousness, of the capacity for concentration, and of attention and clarity of thought. The corresponding forms of Yoga have similar effects. But in contrast to these traditional modes of realization, where the meditant projects himself into some prescribed form, [self-knowledge] is a projection into the empirical self as it actually is. It is not the 'self' we like to imagine ourselves to be after carefully removing all the blemishes, but the empirical ego just as it is, with everything that it does and everything that happens to it. Everybody would like to be quit of this odious adjunct, which is precisely why in the East the ego is explained as illusion and why in the West it is offered up in sacrifice to the Christ figure.

—Carl Jung
Mysterium Coniunctionis

> Resolution with your god
> was the depth and growth
> of your identity.

Pushing, Proving, and Improving

> In order to learn from tradition, one has to be able to push against it, and not be bowed by a surfeit of reverence. The point isn't to replicate the *conclusions* of tradition, but rather to enter into the same problems as the ancients and make them one's own. That is how a tradition remains alive.
>
> —Matthew Crawford[1]

In *The World Beyond Your Head*, Matthew Crawford explores what it takes to become an individual in an age where your attention, your identity, and your individuality are all commodities traded over the hyper-economy. Part of his book concentrates on the craft of making and restoring pipe organs. For hundreds of years, pipe organs filled cathedrals, churches, university halls, and (more recently) sports arenas with music. The people who have dedicated their careers to pipe organs feel their work will affect hundreds of years of music into the future. Their efforts may not challenge the radio and media sensations that flash and burn bright in the instant stardom of popular culture. The scales are measured differently, one might say. The point is not to "heroize" the present moment. But these dedicated crafters do not ignore new information for the sake of replicating past conclusions, either. Their point is to participate in a conversation, to contribute to something that's been going on for hundreds of years and may well continue into the future.[2]

Crawford observed these professionals as they used simple tools from long ago alongside complex electronic tools of today. In the 1950s and 1960s, many organs were updated or modified with replacement plastic components. Plastic was the wonder product of its day. But in the pipe organ business, leather and wood parts came back to replace many of the plastic ones that didn't withstand decades of wear. Older solutions, it turned out, worked. This doesn't mean the spirit of innovation died upon a few failed pieces of polymer. The crafters now explore carbon fibre materials, which show promise. It doesn't mean the old tradition of leather and wood was wrong, either. It means certain materials worked in that day, again in Karen Armstrong's use of the word. But in making these problems one's own, today's dedicated professional takes up the conversation of the craft more than the conclusions of the past.

Crawford's observations can be applied to our religious, political, and scientific beliefs. Often with traditional practices, we draw the covers up over ourselves and make our Procrustean beds as comfortable as possible. But in our desire for certainties, we mix up the variables, thinking the conclusions of the tradition are hard and absolute. The conclusions, however, were the response made from those in the past to problems faced at the time. Those problems didn't go away with simple and stultifying reverence to tradition. We still wrestle with the problems of regulating our emotions and managing our motivations. Whether we respect the work of the ancients, attempt to invent completely new paths, or explain away the problems with new-found vocabulary, we still find ourselves in the millennia-long conversation that is playing out in the human experiment of consciousness.

Religious traditions will collapse unless the leaders of spiritual practice push against the conclusions of their traditions. We can replace old conclusions that no longer work. We can start replacing the innovative but failed plastic additions that have become entrenched over decades, centuries, and millennia. The task now is to enter into the more difficult but consequently more rewarding challenges of facing the same problems and making them our own. We have newer tools to manage motivations and authorities. We have better measures for what works. We have ways of inviting new information into our homes as a diligent host would invite an honoured guest. The scientific revolution has helped us understand our love of inquiry. It is now our task to guide that love and curiosity to better peaks and vistas.

Jordan Peterson states:

> The image of the devil is the form that the idea of evil has taken, for better or worse, at least in the West. We have not yet developed an explicit model of evil that would allow us to forget, transcend or otherwise dispense with this mythological representation.... *Our ancestors were at least constantly concerned with the problem of evil* [emphasis mine]....The dogma of Original Sin forces every individual to regard himself as the (potential) immediate source of evil and to locate the terrible underworld of mythology and its denizens *in intrapsychic space*. It is no wonder that this idea had become unpopular: nonetheless, evil exists somewhere. It remains difficult not to see hypocrisy in the souls of those who wish to localize it somewhere else.[3]

The recognition of evil today, or even naming something as evil, can seem antiquated to the modern mind. And yet in our quick judgments, we immediately label people's motivations as wrong or right. Recognition can also stand for awareness, consciousness—being attentive to new information and ancient wisdom at the same time. That means we can still have this conversation and ask what our roles and responsibilities might be as motivated individuals in regulating our fears, our emotions, and our gods.

Followers of religious traditions today, instead of identifying with the conclusions, can instead participate in what Peterson described as our ancestors' constant concern with the problem of evil. Instead of rationalizing it away or localizing it in the other, religious practitioners can take up that conversation with the ancients. We might still listen to those old stories, but that doesn't mean we must wrap future generations in the anticipated, antiquated Procrustean bedsheets of supernatural explanations or totalizing ideologies. Beyond listening, we can participate in those stories. This is our time to envision and embody the different characters, to identify our own biases and motivations, and to act in a way that solves the problem of evil within ourselves. Decline the invitation of Procrustes and instead walk a little further with the past, present, and future in a conversation that consciously honours each and all. If we don't, then Agamemnon and Jephthah stand by our shoulders prepared to make their mistakes again. This time, it will be our sons and daughters they sacrifice.

What would it mean today to recognize and name the other, the observed, or novelty as something deserving of fear, reverence, or authority? Would such a spiritual symbol expand the sacred family and help us take up the problem of evil as our own? The scientific method gave birth to a new authority in our consciousness, differentiating between motivation, action, perspective, and observation. Instead of faith in our motivations, we can now have faith in the idea that the observed may be in some way divine, independent of how we look upon it. Agamemnon, for example, may have taken a moment to reflect on his motivations if his daughter Iphigenia had shone in his eye like a god worthy of his awe and allegiance. Jephthah may not have become a broken man if he had placed his daughter above his pride.

The Greek goddess Athena draws our attention to an archetypal observing, contemplative advocate. Sophia rejoiced, delighted, and played in the world as Wisdom. The Hindu story of Ramayana presents another perspective on loyalty with Sita. And even our contemporary mythologies ask us, "What is our relationship to the observed?" If we enter into these traditions, these ancient stories, or any story, and identify with the characters, we can still examine their choices and the consequences of those choices without making the same mistakes they did. Whether we read a biased historical account or a purely imaginative fiction, we are ultimately only on the shoulders of the text. We can bring a different set of perspectives, tools, and vocabularies to the situation. Beyond the horizon of the text and the ledger, there is another landscape, another inquiry in which to fall in love.

Whatever our ambitions and beliefs, the challenge now is to consider the unintended consequences. When we hesitate, even for just a moment, we make a place for the metaphorical, or spiritual, guest at the table. If we take the time to hesitate, we are not lost.[4] Humility was once considered a virtue worth nurturing. When the effects of our actions wash out, we want to know we have not simply handed our daughters over to men like Agamemnon and Jephthah. In the religions of the West, one passage has been used to summarize the spiritual pursuit: "What is required of thee but to do justly, and to love mercy, and to walk humbly."[5] If this summary holds, then reflection upon justice, mercy, and humility can bring a new framework of wisdom. If a god is temporarily understood to mean the force that compels your behaviour, just for the length of time it takes to read a book, this framework could be untethered to superstitious explanations, and instead point toward intentions. What's more, we can add something to this passage because of our new relationship to information and to the observed: But you are also invited to fall in love with the process of inquiry.[6]

One-Eyed Giants and Generational Debts

> Now I a fourfold vision see,
> And a fourfold vision is given to me:
> 'Tis fourfold in my supreme delight
> And threefold in soft Beulah's night
> And twofold always, may God us keep
> From single vision and Newton's sleep!
>
> —William Blake[7]

Acknowledging his own accomplishments, Isaac Newton said, "if we have seen farther it is by standing on the shoulders of giants."[8] Newton's supposed humility didn't seem to comfort Blake's worries about his singular vision of a clockwork universe. This sentiment of standing on the shoulders of giants has also been associated with Bernard of Chartres from the twelfth century.[9] Bernard was a scholar and teacher interested in reconciling the works of Plato and Aristotle. But Bernard lived in an environment of cathedral traditions and monastic schools. He may have been familiar with the icon of the *Vierge Ouvrante* in a way that we have lost today. He looked on his past and realized how much debt his knowledge carried from the ancients. Bernard was making a comment as much as a compliment. The word "debt" can hint at a conflict in meanings, such as the gratitude and bitterness that come from owing somebody something. Margaret Atwood, Canada's grandmother and our resident dragon, cautioned us that debt can be both leverage and burden.[10]

We owe a great debt to the giants in our past for what they found worked in their day. Unfortunately, we are also burdened with a great debt of unfulfilled responsibility. We can take this opportunity to join the conversation. If we adopt a broad understanding of what religious traditions attempt to accomplish, then we could say spiritual practice addresses two problems:

1. How do we manage fear or regulate our emotions?
   The fear of death, the fear of pain and suffering, and the fear of meaninglessness in the face of an infinite world we cannot fully comprehend or control—these emotions can utterly overwhelm an individual.

2. How do we address evil in ourselves and in the world?
   Each individual has the power to create and to destroy, to foster inspiration while encouraging mindfulness as well as initiate disorder and disrupt consciousness.

Many people fear the unpredictable and see it as a threat. We are creatures who anticipate and bargain with the future. And that desire for control and predictability can lead us to become one-eyed tyrants, similar to Agamemnon and Jephthah. We rashly sacrifice our daughters for the sake of our goals, ambitions, and our dominance over the world. In our pursuit to establish order, we invite chaos into our own homes. We attempt to leash entropy to our designs only to realize that entropy is not subject to us. As a result, we never open the unexpected gifts that could bring a much better world. But the soft, still voices around us and within us can help manage these motivations. Our task is to observe their calls, name them for what they are, and expand our identities with new knowledge.

Religious thinking, when tied to the mythological, also gives us a way to look at words and symbols that might at times conflict with the modern world. In religious thinking, a god can be both great and terrible. Mother Nature can be both abundantly nourishing and dangerously devouring. A hero of a story can also play the villain. The religious way of thinking uses symbols in ways that appear to cast both a light and a shadow. The religious way of thinking can help us recognize when something is in tune or off-key. This multi-fold meaning to actions, observations, intentions, and stories can be hard to understand from a modern perspective. But just as the modern world has shaken the traditional world awake, the two might be able to shake hands and find the relationship that transcends each other's limitations.

The modern world challenges religious traditions, but also offers new light for addressing and overcoming the two persistent problems of regulating emotions and limiting evil. Often the followers of a religion face a choice—to build their personal identities with the *call* to take up these problems or to build their personal identities from the *conclusions* already settled upon by the traditional sources. This choice illustrates how we choose to manage the debt, in both senses, from our past.

Agamemnon and Jephthah did not live in a world with the benefits of modern progress, rule-of-law governments, the mechanistic clockwork precision of physical sciences, the expanded vocabularies of today's languages, the resources of an industrial economy, or access to the entire library of world literature. Even so, much of the identity of the Western world stands on the cultural shoulders of giants like them. Unfortunately, no matter how tall and mighty they might have been, these giants of antiquity were partly blind. Seeing things with only one eye causes problems with depth perception. They could not see over the walls of their own limitations, think beyond the reach of their own ambitions, or understand the tides of information future generations would navigate. Like one-eyed monsters, fixated on one view, they lacked the ability of opening the other eye to get a better perspective. Their worship of a singular interest left them blind to the unobserved, the ignored, the not-valued gifts before them. In both stories, the gift turned out to be a daughter. Today, we have just as many or more defences against changing our minds. In the past, when gods revealed themselves and lifted individuals to some greater awareness, the characters would change their mind, resolved to a new course of action. Today, it is just as likely that spiritual revelations will only harden the hearts of those adhering to old conclusions, traditions, horizons, and ambitions.

Jephthah's daughter isn't named in his story. This book is intended to be a naming ceremony in order to recognize and see the divine daughters in our journeys. For the sake of the next journey, I encourage you to substitute the name of your own daughter or a child you know.

Past interpretations of the word "God" tend to individualize the character, setting, process, or revelation associated with it. God is one. God is all in one. This has led to questions. Is this God masculine or feminine? Inclusive or exclusive? Should we look upon our creator as Father or Mother? Perhaps the next shift in our consciousness is to ask if that word "God" could be understood as a family instead of an individual. A family contains a plurality on one level but acts as one on another level. A family in love with being a family can celebrate the parts and the whole. A family in love embraces the reduction, emergence, development, and transition of roles and relationships within it.

Standing on One Foot

> I hope you don't imagine that I am advocating or favouring any of these developments [in media and technology]. I regard the twentieth century with horror! But I don't see any alternative but careful study for survival.
>
> —Marshall McLuhan[11]

Where is Ariadne to provide the simple clue that will give us the courage to face our challenges? Ariadne fell in love with the hero Theseus. Ariadne spent her end of days on the shore of an island without her love. Theseus used her but then pursued his own motivations.

The Greek hero Perseus found a different relationship with his observed other. Athena gave him a polished silver shield and Hermes gave him a sword to cut off the Gorgon's head. Perseus used gifts from a goddess of wisdom and a god of communication to find a solution to his problems and master his fears. On the return journey, he saw the princess Andromeda chained to rocks as a sacrifice to a sea monster. He defeated the monster and saved Andromeda. Andromeda came from a royal family ruling another land. She was wholly other in the context of the West—not Greek and not Hebrew. Yet Perseus committed himself to her rescue and pledged himself to her as husband. Unlike Ariadne with Theseus, Andromeda joined her hero Perseus. According to legend, one of their children became the mythological patriarch of the Persians, a culture that could be thought of as wholly other in relation to the West. Perseus also found a potential solution to the problem of evil. With the Gorgon head, he wielded the power to turn anyone he observed into stone. In time, he gave wise Athena the Gorgon head, voluntarily relinquishing such power in order to live a noble life with his wife. His gift of the head and his gratitude went to the advocate of his adventure, Athena, and not to his own ambitions.

Imagine for a moment if some dashing hero descended upon Agamemnon and freed Iphigenia from her father's knife.[12] What would Jephthah have done if such a foreigner snatched his daughter away from her fate? To probe further, would either of these giants find the resolve to give up the Gorgon head and offer it as a gift to Athena or Sophia? Would they have been able to give it to their own daughters? Today's hyper-economy may be partly blind to the tragedies and tests of transitions. If we can look on the world's figurative sons and daughters as valued gifts and inheritors, the family might prove to be a workable model for the call and response involved in transitions of power.

The ancient Sphinx of Thebes asked a riddle: What stands on four legs in the morning, on two at noon but then three in evening? It is a story of how time changes our posture. Babies crawl on legs and arms. Adults stand on two legs. The elderly stoop with support of a cane or crutch. What would the Sphinx have said to Agamemnon before he sacrificed his daughter Iphigenia to his ambitions? Would it warn the bold leader that such sacrifices may leave him with no family support later in life? After all his glorious victories, his own wife killed him. And she was killed in turn by their other children. Instead of a crutch to help him later, Agamemnon received only a sharp blade and a pyre built on a ruined family.

The Talmud records an incident where a brazen gentile challenged Rabbi Hillel. The outsider would convert to Judaism if the rabbi recited the entire wisdom of the Torah while standing on one leg. Rabbi Hillel chose to accept the challenge with grace. Instead of making a grand, lengthy display of recall, this teacher summarized: Whatever is hateful to you, do not do that to anyone you come to know.[13] The idea of standing on one foot can be symbolic. The gentile wished to put the teacher in a precarious situation. The teacher found a way to lift the challenger onto his shoulders—like the act of a parent—so the gentile might see further, deeper.

What would Rabbi Hillel have said if he heard Jephthah boast before his battle that he would sacrifice the first thing to come out of his home to greet him? Maybe he would ask Jephthah to stand on one leg and think about the consequences of his pronouncement, the wisdom of such a rash prayer, the throwing away of such gifts.

The stories of Agamemnon and Jephthah show us what happens if you do not treat daughters with the divinity they deserve. However, we can see this golden-rule-of-thumb from a different perspective. A new rule might be:

Act toward others as you would have them act toward your daughter.

This of course influences our behaviour only if we can see divinity in our daughters—something that has the authority to compel our behaviour. We stand in two realms, with one foot in certainty, the things we know, and the other in uncertainty, the things we do not. The challenge is to keep a balance. Ignoring this invites the chance of a great fall, as the test of entropy demonstrates. If we are to stand on just one foot, in one realm or the other, then our foundations and balance are precarious. If we develop a family contract between observer and observed, we might find a better way to hold one another up. Sons and daughters move from sitting on our shoulders as children—so they can see further and better—to standing by our side. Later, we may need them to lead us with their strength.

But what if we make the wrong ambitious sacrifices? What if our goals are more important than our sons and daughters and the world they will live in? Will our children be there to follow us, and ultimately to guide us, as they take up the conversation with a craft or tradition? Perhaps they won't sit beside us in the cave to explain the fearsome shadows flickering on the wall. They won't come back home from their journeys into the abyss, within and without. Why would they, if there is nothing compelling them, nothing worthy of their return? They will build on their own. They will preserve only ashes rather than tend to the fire. They will forget all that has come before them because other ambitions took their place in the family. Children will take up their own journey while we are bound to be left behind.

The story of the rape of Lucretia is foundational to the West, and after millennia it still offers us wisdom. Historians date the story of Lucretia to around 510 BCE. Part history, part legend, it tells a story of the birth of a republic in ancient Rome. Her story touched the imaginations of artists, including Titian and Shakespeare.

In the time of Lucretia, Rome was ruled by the king Lucius Tarquinius Superbus. His son, Sextus Tarquinius, visited the home of Collatinus and his wife, Lucretia. The household served the noble son with grace and honour. During the visit, Sextus came to desire Lucretia. He slipped into her bedchamber one night and threatened her with a blade. If she did not sleep with him he would kill her and a servant, place the bodies together, and claim he found them in the throes of adultery.

Sextus left the next day. Lucretia explained the entire event to her husband and his friend Lucius Junius Brutus. According to writer Titus Livius, she asked the two of them for an oath of vengeance: "Give me your right hands, and your honour, that the adulterer shall not come off unpunished."[14] She then put a dagger in her heart.

The witnesses did more than punish the adulterer. The act of rape became a symbol of the reign of the leader and his entire family. They took Lucretia's body to the forum, a public place, so that more people would witness and identify with her. They won the favour of the public, gathered a force, and exiled the entire king's family. They revolutionized the form of government. From the outrage of the rape of a daughter of Rome, the people established a new republic and a new relationship with authoritative rule.

According to Lucretia's story, a family line of monarchical kings lost all power because of one act and one moment of desire. One moment of not seeing an other as an authority over at least her own body, changed the course of history. The unintended consequences grew to be so much more consequential, so much more real, than the mere satisfaction of exercising will over what was observed and desired. Despite the shame that was supposed to come from the act of the rape, the authority of kings collapsed. The audience, and the authority of the heroes who took up the oath with Lucretia, broke the monarchic rule.

One daughter of India, a medical student celebrating the end of exams, fell victim to a gang rape in 2012. The men involved were not in positions of governmental power, but again they felt as though they could act on their desires and resentments without consequence. They felt that shame would keep any victim quiet. Through the media and the story, the public identified with the woman, not the men. And they rose up for change.

David Hume suggested that one of the most curious paradoxes in history is how the few come to govern the many:

> Nothing appears more surprising to those who consider human affairs with a philosophical eye than the easiness with which the many are governed by the few; and the implicit submission, with which men resign their own sentiments and passions to those of their rulers. When we enquire by what means this wonder is effected, we shall find that, *as Force is always on the side of the governed,*

the governors have nothing to support them but opinion. It is therefore, on opinion only that government is founded [emphasis mine]; *and this maxim extends to the most despotic and most military governments, as well as to the most free and most popular.*[15]

Power collects as much as power corrupts. And absolute power tends to collect absolutely. But a conscious audience can rub up against the inertia of a tradition's assumptions and change the game. Institutional government is not the only thing founded "on opinion only." Any assumption of dominance or of human right can be consciously observed, tested, and measured to see if it works, if the governed take up that inquiry. The mythic lesson for today in all of this might be something we understand well but haven't articulated properly: when you rape a child, or sacrifice your daughter, refusing the voice of wisdom, you create an entire republic that will rise against you and lay your legacy to ruin.

The shining and distracting lights of new information call to us and ask us to respond. Economic ambitions have driven men and women into new roles, completely unfamiliar with old traditional cultures. The pressure to compete has turned each member of a family into an economic unit measured by income or investment. In the development of industrial processes and information technologies and scientific discoveries, we have become reliant on how we sell or persuade, how we manage opinion. As a result, we have found that we can no longer ignore the authority of the observed and the effects of the audience. We can no longer simply watch how our authorities face the tests of entropy. As McLuhan suggested, careful study may mean survival.

The call now in the contemporary world is to make smaller steps of faith rather than unnecessary leaps. As an example, Aduri watched her mother being educated, became educated herself, and then taught her grandfather. Small changes can make great improvements in the slums of Bangladesh and in the lives of the global family. The call of the present age is to be aware of the role of the other and the observed in our world. Even though the other is not necessarily primary or singular, and even if she does not rule in any absolute sense, she holds a position of authority in each experience, along with every other member of the family. She is the observed, and we do well to learn when to give her our attention. She can captivate us with novelty or she can guide us with wisdom.

For peak experiences of life and flourishing health in the world's humanity, we can take up today's challenge—recognize and differentiate our roles as both actors and observers. And in doing so, we can initiate a new conversation, pushing up against formidable problems while facing the observed, rather than bowing under the yoke of past conclusions.

Looking into the Maelstrom

A civilization in decline digs its own grave with a relentless consistency. It cannot be argued out of its self-destructive ways, for argument has a theoretical major premise, theoretical premises are asked to conform to matters of fact, and the

> facts in the situation produced by decline more and more are the absurdities that proceed from inattention, oversight, unreasonableness, and irresponsibility.
>
> —Bernard Lonergan[16]

Darren Aronofsky, a filmmaker, wanted to tell a story about Noah, his family, and the ark. Aronofsky's goal was not to tell the same old story, word for word, with a surfeit of reverence toward the Bible. Instead, he pushed up against the Biblical tradition of the story and entered into the problems the story addresses. In the movie, Noah is portrayed as a man determined to do what he thinks is his god's will. He thinks he knows the desires of his god so well he stops further inquiries—he decided to save the animal life on the world but to finish the chapter of human life. He acts against his family's wishes and by the end of the story they hardly recognize or trust him. When brought to the crucial moment of decision in the story, he feels asked to do something monstrous—kill two infants, his two granddaughters.

In that moment, mercy and love rule him instead of certainty and will. He stays his hand and kisses the infants. The decision breaks the character. He cannot tell if his failure to act in the moment of uncertainty meant betrayal to his god. His son's wife, however, suggests a new perspective for him. She tells him his god, what was guiding him to act throughout the story, ultimately gave Noah the choice of what should rule over him. God, in this sense, asked Noah to stand before all the supposed omniscient power of imagination and reality, and make the decision. What Noah in Aronofsky's story felt he must serve, ultimately, was not what he thought and felt was right—a goal of the mind. Instead, it was what he observed and identified as meaningful. As a result, he found a resolution and justice in the relationships that made up his family.

Although the movie earned seventeen award nominations, it shared the fate of many other productions in the oversaturated market of motion picture storytelling. It didn't earn massive popularity in the public consciousness. Still, it is a telling example precisely because its fate is so common. The audience moved on. Our unconscious worship of novelty takes our attention away from some ideas that truly matter, such as the health of our families and maybe even our survival.

Aronofsky's attempt to tell a story about evil, motivation, and choice shows us again that these problems never go away. Popular dismissal of, or disinterest in, religious themes just makes us more unaware and more susceptible to the problems. Such stories have the potential to draw us up to a peak experience of consciousness. That experience can help us face our families and our problems, making them our own. How do we prepare ourselves for the conversations ahead? Let's ask ourselves why each of our motivations has won authority. How can we recognize what should rule over us in one environment but not rule in another? What are the consequences, intended or unintended, of the assumption of authority? Let's sit together like a family at dinner and hear from each member in conversation.

Rituals, Celebrations, and Dances

> Oh, East is East, and West is West, and never the twain shall meet,
> Till Earth and Sky stand presently at God's great Judgment Seat;
> But there is neither East nor West, Border, nor Breed, nor Birth,
> When two strong men stand face to face, though they come from
> the ends of the earth!
>
> —Rudyard Kipling[17]

The suggestion from each chapter of this book is that an individual is the hero of his or her own story. The characters, settings, events, and style of expression all give clues as to what's important in making each story a tragedy or comedy. The following list of rituals all have a basic, repeated gesture. Look back and forth, then down and up. Look east and west, then look south and north. In this way, the mind prepares to look in four places for vital clues, to listen to four different sources for echoes.

Leonard Cohen's first collection of poems examined religious themes, young love, and family relationships. With his blessing and guidance, I hope the following rituals are read more as personal poems than prescriptive advice. They are reminders I use to draw my attention to the relationships between the known and the unknown, the observer and the observed. Suzanne takes you down, and she holds the mirror. It is time for us to look over our reflection. Let us compare mythologies, equations, and apologies.[18] The medicine wheel of our world, the spice box of earth, offers in every moment a chance for us to walk in dreams and work in hope.

The Ritual of Naming

Watch people. Watch yourself, especially. Look for those moments your emotions take possession of you, when you are at a loss for words, or when words come out of you as though something else is using you. Think about the actions you and others take in terms of the categories known, unknown, individual, and other. Name what you observe. Call and respond. Identify the figure and ground of your perspective. Name the motivations you recognize in yourself and others.

The Ritual of Constructing and Deconstructing the Architecture

An environment can possess you and have its way with you. It will direct your behaviour and turn you into a part of the setting of your story as much as prepare you to fulfill your character. Understand the costs and benefits in constructing and deconstructing pyramids. Evaluate the desire for homogeneity. Reflect on the behaviours, rewards, and punishments that come from the processes of panopticons. Turn your attention to both the audience and the stage when in a theatre. And go down to the crossroads of the marketplace to engage in the conversation.

The Ritual of Reading the Maps and Exploring the Territories

Fall in love with inquiry. Identify the path you follow. Recognize the domain of what is and the domain of what should be in your thinking. If teachers guide you out of a cave, into the light, and back down to the darkness, consider the motivations in their work and the development of your skills. If you find yourself on the threshold of a choice, understand that voluntarily travelling from the comfort zone of home and into the abyss of the unknown is the process of transforming your fragility into resilience. Work hard and boost your skill of pattern recognition. Spot corruption and the bondage it creates. Restore order in yourself and your family through shouldering responsibility. Be your hero and manage the villain inside.

The Ritual of Conscientious Expression

Make friends with both courage and embarrassment. Keep a cordial respect for, and distance from, confidence and shame. Whenever possible, declare your honest intentions. Bow in humility. Embrace in gratitude. Communication can be used to express what you want from the other, what you believe is real, what you believe should be and what you imagine could be. The practice of separating what is from what should be, descriptive language from prescriptive, could be enough to save a conversation, elevating an experience to a peak moment of consciousness.

SOMETHING OLD, SOMETHING NEW, SOMETHING BORROWED, SOMETHING BLUE

> Est aliquid prodisse tenus.[19]
> [It is something to have made a start.]

A wedding brings families together. Parents dance with children and families unite as one. The theme of the event, it is hoped, is celebration, not competition. In the *all-at-once* experience of the modern age, the figurative competition between the West and the East has changed into a dance, spurred by the sounds and lights and motivations of our cultures.

Perhaps inadvertently, perhaps inevitably, even the most heated dance can lead to romance. Instead of cultural appropriation, there is a chance for cultural collaboration. The danger and potential in a dance might inspire worry in the most open and traditional parents alike. The fourfold advice given to brides can transform in meaning when the stakes rise to the proportion of civilizations. I invited Agamemnon and Jephthah to join you through this journey. Neither Agamemnon nor Jephthah ever got to walk their own daughters down the aisle. They had already sacrificed their daughters to ambitions. Here at the end, let us raise a glass together and talk of things old, new, borrowed, and blue.

Something Old

Build a place for yourself where the known, anticipated, and ordered reigns in your life. Find conscious comfort in the healthy routines of your day and the skills you practise. Recognize when an environment plays upon your behaviour, and when you are letting your expectations rule over you. But know there is something beyond. There is no place like home, but there is nothing quite like the call to inquiry.

Something New

Take the initiative. Act on the power and skills you have prepared. Be the conscious change you want to see in the world. Use your words. Bargain with reality by telling your story. Bargain with reality by inviting it as a guest to your dinner. Prepare to share your best ideas. Bring incredible gifts to the table for trade.

Something Borrowed

Think of a moment when you corrected yourself or changed your mind. What have you adopted or followed from someone else? How do you demonstrate your conscious gratitude for what others have done for you? Who needs you to act as advocate or apostle for them? Become a fan of other people, changing their day with your support. Prepare to adapt when presented with something from the novel innovations or the performances of an other.

Something Blue

Blue is just one colour we have named in the ocean. We may not know what will come from the wine-dark sea. Spend a conscious moment in the presence of the unknown, in a place that tests your understanding and vocabulary, something that cannot be understood in the net of what you have already experienced. Ask better and better questions. Peer into the unknown with humility and answer its call.

§

We can be brides and bridegrooms, together. We can travel in and travel out, two directions at once. We can entertain two ideas, maybe even four ideas, giving none of them the authority of absolute belief unless the role, setting, sequence of events, and theme call to us. We can recognize objects and subjects, insiders and outsiders, and the barriers and bridges between them. We can be hosts and guests, with all the responsibilities these roles create. We can communicate with ourselves and with the other. We can bow to our own divinity, and bow to the divinity of the observed, and share a glass together.

Still, we can
fall in love,
We can write
songs about it,
And begin again,
with all blessings.

ACKNOWLEDGEMENTS

Mom and Dad—they never really seemed to know what to do with me, but they encouraged me to keep going. One time in 2008 or so, they watched a TVO panel and thought I'd be interested in a University of Toronto professor who wrote a book about meaning. Also, they voluntarily helped finance this book project. Who else would invest in such an enterprise?

Joel and Jeananne—for filling the shelves with books.

John D.—he introduced me to Bernard Lonergan. Also, he was the first to make it through one of the first drafts. He was ridiculously gentle with it.

Scott M.—illustrator, writer, collaborator. Friend from high school. I hope we keep finding or inventing odd projects to share.

Sneha P.—for the much-needed help with illustrations and images.

David G. S.—for directing me to Doug, and giving me a few more books to read.

Doug V.—a great editor who knows how to enforce his points with a novice, stumbling writer. Also, he directed me to Geri S-F.

Geri S.-F.—another great editor and kind chaperone through the formatting of the notes and sources.

Ann Louise B.—for help with the introduction and first chapter. I hope you get to read your full copy some day at the cottage.

Jackie P.—time and time again, she brought me back to "Why?" and "What does the reader do with this?"

Michael M.—for finding the projects that helped keep the lights on while I pursued this project.

The Munro family—for permission with the photo, for their work, and for telling the world about Aduri.

Rob G.—the musician I want to be, the friend who let me enjoy both Tool and Bread without much teasing.

Deepak M.—a good friend, a frustrating friend.

David M.—for reading the first line and just knowing it would be great without reading the rest.

Jenn S.—for conversations on god, theocratic dictatorship, physics, art, and entropy.

David D. S. and his family—for appearing at the right time, like a surprise chorus of support and collaboration and fun brainstorming.

Sylvia and Lindsay T.—fellow creators and writers on these journeys.

Millie Grumpaloo—our divine dawghter.

And my source of grace, the quiet wise one, Shannon. I love you.

RESOURCES, RETRIEVALS

DON'T PANIC

Adams, Douglas. *The Hitchhiker's Guide to the Galaxy*. New York: Random House, 1989.

Adams, Douglas. *The More Than Complete Hitchhiker's Guide*. New York: Random House, 1989.

Aeschylus. *The Oresteia*. Translated by Robert Fagles. New York: Penguin Books, 1977.

Alexander, Caroline. "A Wine-Like Sea." *Lapham's Quarterly*. https://www.laphamsquarterly.org/sea/winelike-sea.

American Masters—Dorothea Lange: Grab a Hunk of Lightning. Directed by Dyanna Taylor. Santa Fe: Raven Rouge, Katahdin Productions and Thirteen Productions, 2014. http://www.pbs.org/wnet/americanmasters/dorothea-lange-full-episode/3260

Armstrong, Karen. A *History of God: The 4,000-Year Quest of Judaism, Christianity and Islam*. New York:

Alfred A. Knopf, 1994.

Atwood, Margaret. *Payback*. Toronto: House of Anansi Press, 2008.

Atwood, Margaret. *Negotiating with the Dead*. Cambridge: Cambridge University Press, 2002.

Austin, James. *Philosophical Papers*. Edited by J.O. Urmson and G.J. Warnock. Oxford: Oxford University Press, 1970.

Bailey, Alison and Chris Cuomo. *The Feminist Philosophy Reader*. New York: McGraw-Hill, 2008.

Ballard, Nancer, Katerina Daley and Sage Hahn. *The Heroine Journeys Project*. https://heroine-journeys.com/.

Batters, Stephanie M. "Care of the Self and the Will to Freedom: Michel Foucault, Critique and Ethics." Paper 231. Senior Honors Projects, 2011. http://digitalcommons.uri.edu/srhonorsprog/231.

Beavers, Anthony, F. "Introducing Levinas to Undergraduate Philosophers." Colloquy Paper to the Undergraduate Philosophy Association at the University of Texas at Austin, 1990. http://faculty.evansville.edu/tb2/PDFs/UndergradPhil.pdf.

Berman, Marshall. *All That Is Solid Melts in to Air: The Experience of Modernity*. London: Verso, 2010.

Bliss, Michael. *Right Honourable Men*. Toronto: HarperCollins Publishers, 1995.

Bloom, Howard. "Reality is a Shared Illusion." http://pialogue.info/books/Bloom-Reality-is-a-Shared-Hallucination.pdf

Boehm, Christopher. *Hierarchy in the Forest: The Evolution of Egalitarian Behavior*. Cambridge (Massachusetts): Harvard University Press, 2001.

Bookchin, Murray. *Post-Scarcity Anarchism*. Montreal: Black Rose Books, 1986.

Brown, Rachel. "Mary in the Scriptures: The Unexpurgated Tradition." Milwaukee: Marquette University Press, 2014.

Brown, Rachel. *Mary and the Art of Prayer*. New York: Columbia University Press, 2017.

Burgess, Anthony. *A Clockwork Orange*. Harmondsworth, Middlesex: Penguin Press, 1972.

Also, *A Clockwork Orange*. Directed by Stanley Kubrick. New York: Polaris Productions Hawk Films, Warner Bros., 1971.

Byrne, Patrick. *Insight and Beyond*. Boston College, 2009-2010. https://bclonergan.org/insight/#insight-about.

Cain, Susan. *Quiet: The Power of Introverts in a World That Can't Stop Talking*. New York: Broadway Paperbacks, 2013.

Campbell, Joseph. *The Hero with a Thousand Faces*. Princeton: Princeton University Press, 1973.

Campbell, Joseph. *The Masks of God*. Harmondsworth: Penguin Press, 1976. Joseph Campbell Foundation. https://www.jcf.org/

Camus, Albert. *The Myth of Sisyphus and Other Essays*. New York: Knopf, 1955.

Carter, Codell and Barbara Carter. *Childbed Fever: A Scientific Biography of Ignaz Semmelweis*. Piscataway: Transaction Publishers, 2005.

Carter, Lin. *Tolkien: A Look Behind the Lord of the Rings*. New York: Ballantine Books, 1975.

Cavoukian, Raffi and Sharna Olfman. *Child Honoring: How to Turn This World Around*. Westport: Praeger Publishers, 2006.

CBC News. "Can an atheist be a United Church Minister?" March 25, 2016. http://www.cbc.ca/news/canada/gretta-vosper-united-church-minister-atheist-1.3506390

Chittister, Joan. *Welcome to the Wisdom of the World*. Grand Rapids: Wm. B. Eerdmans Publishing, 2007.

Clive, John. *The Philosophy of Nietzsche*. New York: Penguin Books, 1964.

Cohen, Leonard. *Let Us Compare Mythologies*. Toronto: McClelland & Stewart, 1966.

Cohen, Leonard. *The Spice-Box of Earth*. London: Random House. 1987.

Collins, Suzanne. *The Hunger Games*. New York: Scholastic, 2008.

Collins, Suzanne. *Catching Fire*. New York: Scholastic, 2009.

Collins, Suzanne. *Mockingjay*. New York: Scholastic, 2010.

Campbell, Joseph. "Mythic Reflections: Thoughts on myth, spirit and our time." Interviewed by Tom Collins. *In Context—A Quarterly of Humane Sustainable Culture*, Winter 1985/86. https://www.context.org/iclib/ic12/campbell/.

Cox, Harvey. *The Future of Faith*. New York: HarperOne, 2010.

Crafton, Lisa. "'A sick man's dream': Jephthah, Judges, and Blake's *Daughters of Albion*." *Romanticism on the Net*, *érudit*, Number 45, February 2007. https://www.erudit.org/fr/revues/ron/2007-n45-ron1728/015819ar/.

Crawford, Matthew B. *The World Beyond Your Head: On Becoming an Individual in an Age of Distraction*. Toronto: Penguin Pres, 2016.

Crysdale, Cynthia S. W., ed. *Lonergan and Feminism*. Toronto: University of Toronto Press, 1994.

Csikszentmihalyi, Mihaly. *The Evolving Self: A Psychology for the Third Millennium*. New York: HarperPerennial, 1994.

Csikszentmihalyi, Mihaly. *Flow: The Psychology of Optimal Experience*. New York: HarperPerennial, 1991.

Davies, Philip. "The Bible: Utopian, Dystopian, or Neither? Or Northrop Frye Meets Monty Python." *Relegere: Studies in Religion and Reception 2*, no.1, 2012.

Davies, Tony. *Humanism*. New York: Routledge, 1997.

Dawkins, Richard. *The God Delusion*. London: Bantam Books, 2006.

Day, David. *Tolkien's Ring*. London: HarperCollins Publishers, 1995.

de Botton, Alain. *Religion for Atheists*. Toronto: McClelland & Stewart, 2012.

de Waal, Frans B. M. "Primates—A Natural Heritage of Conflict Resolution." *Science*, Vol. 289, July 28, 2000.

de Waal, Frans B. M. "Morality and the Social Instincts: Continuity with the Other Primates." *The Tanner Lectures on Human Values*. Princeton University, November 19-20, 2003.

de Waal, Frans B. M. *The Age of Empathy: Nature's Lessons for a Kinder Society*. Toronto: Emblem, McClelland & Stewart, 2010.

Dennett, Daniel. *Darwin's Dangerous Idea*. Simon & Schuster, 1996.

Dennett, Daniel. *Breaking the Spell: Religion as a Natural Phenomenon.* London: Penguin Books, 2007.

Derrida, Jacques and Gayatri Spivak. *Of Grammatology.* Baltimore: Johns Hopkins University Press, 1980.

Derrida, Jacques and Allan Bass. *Writing and Difference.* University of Chicago Press, 1978.

Derrida, Jacques. *Speech and Phenomena, and Other Essays on Husserl's Theory of Signs.* Evanston: Northwestern University Press, 1973.

Diamond, Jared. *Guns, Germs and Steel: The Fates of Human Societies.* New York: W. W. Norton & Company, 1999.

Dodds, Eric R. *The Greeks and the Irrational.* Berkeley: University of California Press, 1973. http://ark.cdlib.org/ark:/13030/ft0x0n99vw/.

Doidge, Norman. *The Brain that Changes Itself.* New York: Viking Press, 2007.

Dostoevsky, Fyodor. *The Brothers Karamazov.* Translated by Andrew MacAndrew. New York: Bantam Books, 1983.

Dostoevsky, Fyodor. *The Brothers Karamazov.* Translated by Constance Garnett. New York: The Lowell Press, 1892.

Dowd, Michael. *Thank God for Evolution! How the Marriage of Science and Religion Will Transform Your Life and Our World.* New York: Plume, 2009.

Dowd, Michael. http://www.thankgodforevolution.com/.

Dunne, Tad. *Bernard Lonergan (1904—1984).* http://www.iep.utm.edu/lonergan/.

Eisler, Riane. *The Chalice and the Blade.* New York: HarperCollins Publishers, 1988.

Eliade, Mircea. *The Sacred and the Profane: The Nature of Religion.* New York: Harcourt, Brace & World, Inc., 1959.

Ellenberger, H.F. *The Discovery of the Unconscious: The History and Evolution of Dynamic Psychiatry.* New York: Basic Books, 2006.

Falck, Colin. *Myth, Truth and Literature: Towards a True Postmodernism.* Cambridge: Cambridge University Press, 1994.

Feynman, Richard. *Cargo Cult Science: Commencement Speech at California Institute of Technology,* 1974. http://calteches.library.caltech.edu/51/2/CargoCult.htm.

Fisher, Mark. *Capitalist Realism: Is There No Alternative?* Winchester: Zero Books, 2010.

Foucault, Michel. *Discipline and Punish: The Birth of the Prison.* London: Penguin Books, 1977.

Foucault, Michel. *The History of Sexuality.* Harmondsworth: Penguin, 1990.

Foucault, Michel. *The Order of Things*. New York: Vintage Books, Random House, 1994.

Foucault, Michel. *Fearless Speech*. Los Angeles: Semiotext(e), 2001.

Frankfurt, Harry. *On Bullshit*. Princeton: Princeton University Press, 2005.

Freud, Sigmund. *Totem and Taboo*. New York: Routledge, 2001.

Frye, Northrop. *Anatomy of Criticism: Four Essays*. Princeton: Princeton University Press, 1990.

Frye, Northrop. *The Great Code: The Bible and Literature*. New York: Harcourt Brace Jovanovich. 1982.

Frye, Northrop. *Words with Power Being a Second Study of "the Bible and Literature"*. Toronto: Viking, The Penguin Group, 1990.

Frye, Northrop and Bill Somerville. *The Bible and English Literature by Northrop Frye*. Toronto: University of Toronto, 1982. http://heritage.utoronto.ca/northropfryelectures.

Gibson, James. *The Ecological Approach to Visual Perception*. New York: Psychology Press, 1986.

Gillooly, Robert. *All About Adam & Eve*. Amherst: Prometheus Books, 1998.

Gladwell, Malcolm. *The Tipping Point*. New York: Little Brown, 2000.

Gladwell, Malcolm. *David and Goliath: Underdogs, Misfits and the Art of Battling Giants*. New York: Little, Brown and Company, 2013.

Gladwell, Malcolm. *Blink: The Power of Thinking without Thinking*. New York: Back Bay Books, 2013.

Gleick, James. *The Information: A History, A Theory, A Flood*. New York: Vintage Books, 2012.

Gleick, James. *Genius: The Life and Science of Richard Feynman*. New York: Vintage Books, 1993.

Goodenough, Ursula. *The Sacred Depths of Nature*. New York: Oxford University Press, 1998.

Grant, Michael. *Myths of the Greeks and Romans*. New York: Mentor, Penguin Books, 1986.

Haider, Shuja. "Postmodernism Did Not Take Place: On Jordan Peterson's 12 Rule for Life." *Viewpoint

Magazine*, January, 2018. https://www.viewpointmag.com/2018/01/23/postmodernism-not-take-place-jordan-petersons-12-rules-life/.

Haidt, Jonathan. *The Righteous Mind: Why Good People are Divided by Politics and Religion*. London: Penguin, 2013.

Hamilton, Edith. *Mythology: Timeless Tales of Gods and Heroes*. New York: Mentor, Signet Classic, Little, Brown and Company, 1969.

Hanh, Thich Nhat. *Touching Peace: Practicing the Art of Mindful Living*. Berkeley: Parallax Press, 2005.

Harpur, Tom. *The Pagan Christ: Recovering the Lost Light*. New York: Walker & Co., 2006.

Harris, Sam. *The End of Faith*. New York: W. W. Norton & Company, 2004.

Harris, Sam. *Letter to a Christian Nation*. New York: Knopf, 2006.

Harris, Sam. *The Moral Landscape: How Science Can Determine Human Values*. New York: Free Press, 2010.

Harris, Sam. *Waking Up: A Guide to Spirituality Without Religion*. New York: Simon and Schuster, 2014.

Harris, Sam. *Free Will*. New York: Free Press, 2012.

Harris, Sam and Maajid Nawaz. *Islam and the Future of Intolerance*. Cambridge: Harvard University Press, 2015.

Harrison, Ernest, John. *A Church Without God*. Toronto: McClelland & Stewart, 1967.

Hauser, Arnold. *The Social History of Art, Volume 1*. New York: Routledge and Taylor & Francis e-Library, 2005.

Hauser, Christine. "'Afghan Girl' in 1985 National Geographic Photo is Arrested in Pakistan." *The New York Times*, October 26, 2016. https://www.nytimes.com/2016/10/27/world/asia/afghan-woman-in-famed-national-geographic-photo-is-arrested-in-pakistan.html.

Hawley, John, Stratton. *Saints and Virtues*. Berkeley: University of California Press, 1987.

Hicks, Stephen. *Explaining Postmodernism*. Tempe: Scholargy, 2004.

Hirsi Ali, Ayaan. *Infidel*. New York: Atria Paperback, 2013.

Hirsi Ali, Ayaan. *Nomad*. Toronto: CNIB, 2011.

Hirsi Ali, Ayaan. *The Challenge of Dawa: Political Islam as Ideology and Movement and How to Counter It*. Stanford: Hoover Institution Press Stanford University, 2017.

Hitchens, Christopher. *God is Not Great*. Toronto: McClelland & Stewart, 2007.

Hoffman, Martin. *Empathy and Moral Development*. New York: Cambridge University Press, 200.

Homer. *The Iliad*. Translated by E. V. Rieu. London: Penguin Books, 1950.

Homer. *The Odyssey*. Translated by E. V. Rieu. London: Penguin Books, 1946.

Howard, Robert, Charles. "Horizontal Transcendence." https://www.poemhunter.com/poem/horizontal-transcendence/.

Ingram, Daniel. *Mastering the Core Teachings of the Buddha*. The Interdependent Universe, 2007.

International Anthony Burgess Foundation. https://www.anthonyburgess.org.

Iris. https://www.iris.xyz.

Joyce, James. *Finnegans Wake*. New York: Garland, 1978.

Joyce, James. *Finnegans Wake*. Contemporary Literature Press, 2014. http://editura.mttlc.ro/fwliniarized/FW%20LINEARIZED%20full%20text%20pp%203-628.pdf].

Kahneman, Daniel. *Thinking, Fast and Slow*. New York: Farrar, Straus and Giroux, 2013.

Kegan, Robert and Lahey Lisa L. "The Real Reason People Won't Change." *The Harvard Business Review*, 2001. https://hbr.org/2001/11/the-real-reason-people-wont-change.

Keshavarzian, Ramin and Abbasi Pyeaam. "Visions of the Daughters of Albion: The Influence of Mary Wollstonecraft's Life and Career on William Blake." *International Letters of Social and Humanistic Sciences*, Volume 40, 2014. https://www.scipress.com/ILSHS.40.48.pdf.

King, Stephen. *On Writing*. New York: Simon & Schuster Inc., 2000.

King, Thomas. *The Inconvenient Indian: A Curious Account of Native People in North America*. Toronto: Anchor Canada, Random House Canada, 2012.

King, Thomas. *The Truth About Stories*. Toronto: House of Anansi Press, 2003.

King, Thomas. *Green Grass, Running Water*. Boston: Houghton Mifflin, 1993.

Kingwell, Mark. *Unruly Voices*. Toronto: Biblioasis, 2012.

Kocher, Paul. *Master of Middle-Earth*. New York: Ballantine Books, 1988.

Korzybski, Alfred. *Science and Sanity, 5th Edition*. Brooklyn: Institute of General Semantics, 1994.

Kovacs, George, A. "Iphigenia at Aulis: Myth, Performance and Reception." PhD diss., University of Toronto, 2010.

Krooshof, Stijn. "Foucault, Christianity and the Care of the Self." Master's thesis, Radboud University, 2016.

Krygier, Martin. "The Rule of Law: Pasts, Presents, and a Possible Future." *Center for Study of Law & Society, and Kadish Center for Morality, Law & Public Affairs*. Berkeley: University of California Berkeley, 2016.

Lakoff, George and Johnsen, Mark. *Metaphors We Live By*. London: The University of Chicago Press, 1980.

Langer, Susanne K. *Philosophy in a New Key: A Study of Symbolism of Reason, Rite and Art*. Cambridge: New American Library, 1964.

Langer, Susanne K. *Feeling and Form: A Theory of Art*. New York: Charles Scribner's Sons, 1953.

Lapham's Quarterly. https://www.laphamsquarterly.org

Le Guin, Ursula K. "The Carrier Bag Theory of Fiction." In *The Ecocriticism Reader: Landmarks in Literary Ecology*, edited by Cheryll Glotfelty and Harold Fromm. Athens: University of Georgia Press, 1996.

Lessig, Lawrence. *Code version 2.0*. New York: Basic Books, The Perseus Books Group, 2006.

Levinas, Emmanuel. *Totality and Infinity: An Essay on Exteriority*. Norwell: Kluwer Academic Publishers, 1991.

Levinas, Emmanuel. *Difficult Freedom: Essays on Judaism*. Baltimore: Johns Hopkins University Press, 1990.

Levinas, Emmanuel. *Emmanuel Levinas Collected Philosophical Papers*. Dordrecht: Martinus Nijhoff Publishers, 1987.

Levitin, Daniel. *A Field Guide to Lies*. Toronto: Allen Lane Penguin Canada, 2016.

Light, Alan. *The Holy or the Broken*. New York: Simon & Schuster, 2012.

Lipton, Bruce H. *The Biology of Belief: Unleashing the Power of Consciousness, Matter & Miracles*. Carlsbad: Hay House, 2016.

Lombardo, Tom. "Science Fiction: The Evolutionary Mythology of the Future." In *Journal of Futures Studies*, December, 2015.

Lonergan, Bernard Joseph Francis. *Insight: A Study of Human Understanding*. London: Longmans, 1964.

Lonergan, Bernard Joseph Francis. *Method in Theology*. Toronto: University of Toronto Press, 2003.

Marsh, James. "Postmodernism: A Lonerganian Retrieval and Critique." *Postmodernism and Christian Philosophy*. Edited by Roman Ciapalo. Mishawaka: American Maritain Association, 1997.

Maslow, Abraham. *Motivation and Personality*. New York: Harper & Row Publishers, 1970.

Maslow, Abraham. *Toward a Psychology of Being*. New York: Van Nostrand Reinhold, 1968.

McCurry, Steve. "'Afghan Girl': Taking National Geographic's Most Famous Photo." In FORA. tv, 2010. https://youtu.be/BIgx-nkFL6c

McDonald, Ian. *Introduction to Spiral Dynamics*. Cheshire: Hot Snow Books, 2010.

McGilchrist, Iain. *The Master and His Emissary*. New Haven: Yale University Press, 2010.

McLuhan, Eric. "Marshall McLuhan's Theory of Communication: The Yegg." In *Global Media Journal—Canadian Edition*. Volume 1, Issue 1, 2008.

McLuhan, Marshall. *The Classical Trivium: The Place of Thomas Nashe in the Learning of His Time*. Edited by Gordon W. Terrence. Berkeley: Gingko Press, 2009.

McLuhan, Marshall, and W. Terrence Gordon. *Understanding Media: The Extensions of Man*. Corte Madera: Gingko Press, 2003.

McLuhan, Marshall, and Philip B. Meggs. *The Mechanical Bride: Folklore of Industrial Man*. London: Duckworth Overlook, 2011.

McLuhan, Marshall, Wilfred Watson, and W. Terrence Gordon. *From Cliché to Archetype*. Berkeley: Gingko Press, 2011.

McLuhan, Marshall, and Eric McLuhan. *Laws of Media: The New Science*. Toronto: University of Toronto Press, 1989.

McLuhan, Marshall, Quentin Fiore and Jerome Agel. *The Medium is the Massage: An Inventory of Effects*. Corte Madera: Gingko Press, 2005.

Merel, Peter (Interpolator). *The Dude De Ching: A Dudeist Interpretation of The Tao Te Ching*. Los Angeles: The Church of the Latter Day Dude, 2015.

Miles, Jack. *God: A Biography*. New York: Vintage Books, 1996.

Morford, Mark and Robert Lendardon. *Classical Mythology*. White Plains: Longman Publishers, 1971.

Morozov, Evgeny. *To Save Everything, Click Here: The Folly of Technological Solutionism*. New York: PublicAffairs, 2014.

Munro, G.E.M. *South Asian Adventures with the Active Poor*. Hagensborg: Tangent Books, 2010.

Murdock, Maureen. *The Heroine's Journey: Woman's Quest for Wholeness*. Boulder: Shambhala, 1990.

Neumann, Erich. *The Origins and History of Consciousness*. New York: Harper Torchbook Harper & Brothers, 1962.

Neumann, Erich. *The Great Mother: An Analysis of the Archetype*. Princeton: Princeton University Press, 1972.

Newberg, Andrew and Mark, R. Waldman. *How God Changes Your Brain*. New York: Random House, 2010.

Newman, Cathy. "A Life Revealed." *National Geographic*, April, 2002. https://www.nationalgeographic.com/magazine/2002/04/afghan-girl-revealed/.

Nietzsche, Friedrich. *The Birth of Tragedy: An Attempt at Self-Criticism*. Translated by Ian Johnston. Public Domain, 2003. http://www.russoeconomics.altervista.org/Nietzsche.pdf.

Nietzsche, Friedrich. *Beyond Good and Evil: Prelude to a Philosophy of the Future*. Translated by R.J. Hollingdale. Mineola: Dover Publications, 1997.

Nietzsche, Friedrich. *Thus Spoke Zarathustra: A Book for All and None*. Edited by Adrian Del Caro. Cambridge: Cambridge University Press, 2006.

Nietzsche, Friedrich. *The Gay Science*. Translated by Walter Kaufmann. Toronto: Random House, 1974.

Noah. Directed by Darren Aronofsky. New York: Regency Enterprises, Protozoa Pictures, Paramount Pictures, 2014.

Orwell, George. *The Road to Wigan Pier*. London: Victor Gollancz, 1937.

Orwell, George. *1984*. New York: Penguin Books, 1956.

Paglia, Camille. *Sexual Personae: Art and Decadence from Nefertiti to Emily Dickinson*. New Haven: Yale University Press, 1990.

Paglia, Camille. *Glittering Images: A Journey Through Art from Egypt to Star Wars*. New York: Vintage, 2013.

Paglia, Camille. *Vamps & Tramps: New Essays*. New York: Vintage Books, 2004.

Paglia, Camille. "Junk Bonds and Corporate Raiders: Academe in the Hour of the Wolf." 1994. https://www.bu.edu/arion/files/2017/09/Arion-Camille-Paglia-Junkbonds-Corporate-Raiders.pdf

Paglia, Camille. "The Magic of Images: Word and Picture in a Media Age." *Arion* 11.3 Winter, 2004.

Paglia, Camille. "Erich Neumann: Theorist of the Great Mother." *Arion* 13.3 Winter, 2006.

Papadopoulos, Renos, ed. *The Handbook of Jungian Psychology*. New York: Routledge, 2006.

Papal Encyclicals. http://www.papalencyclicals.net

Parrinder, Geoffrey. *Religion in Africa*. Middlesex: Penguin Books Ltd., 1969.

Pennebaker, James W. *The Secret Lives of Pronouns: What Our Words Say About Us*. London: Bloomsbury Press, 2013.

Pennebaker, James W. http://www.secretlifeofpronouns.com/videos.php

Peperzak, Adrienne. *To the Other: An Introduction to the Philosophy of Emmanuel Levinas*. West Lafayette: Purdue University Press, 1993.

Perrin, R. T. *From Cambridge to Communication: McLuhan Beyond McLuhanism*. Masters Thesis: Simon Fraser University. 2000.

Peter, Burkhard. "Gassner's exorcism—not Mesmer's magnetism—is the real predecessor of modern hypnosis." *International Journal of Clinical and Experimental Hypnosis*, 53(1), 2005.

Peterson, Jordan, B. *Maps of Meaning: The Architecture of Belief*. New York: Routledge, 1999.

Peterson, Jordan, B. *12 Rules for Life: An Antidote to Chaos*. New York: Penguin Random House, 2018.

Peterson, Jordan, B. "Three Forms of Meaning and the Management of Complexity." *The Psychology of Meaning*. Edited by K. Markham, T. Proulx and M. Linberg. Washington: American Psychological Association, 2013.

Peterson, Jordan B. "Peacemaking Among Higher-Order Primates" *The Psychology of Resolving Global Conflicts: From War to Peace: Volume III, Interventions*. Edited by C.E. Stout and M. Fitzduff. Westport: Praeger, 2005.

Peterson, Jordan, B. and Maja Djikic. "You Can Neither Remember No Forget What You Don't Understand." *Religion & Public Life*, 33, 2003.

Peterson, Jordan B. *Jordan Peterson Videos*. https://www.youtube.com/user/JordanPetersonVideos/videos

Petrovic, Lena. "Remembering and Dismembering: Derrida's Reading of Levi-Strauss." *Facta Universitatis Series: Linguistics and Literature Vol. 3, No 1*, 2004.

Plato. *The Republic*. Translated by Desmond Lee. Toronto: Penguin Books, 1987.

Plato. *The Republic*. Translated by G.M.A. Grube. Indianapolis: Hackettt Publishing Company, 1992.

Plutarch. *The Rise and Fall of Athens: Nine Greek Lives*. Translated by Ian Scott-Kilvert. Toronto: Penguin Books, 1960.

Pinchbeck, Daniel. *Breaking Open the Head*. New York: Broadway Books, 2003.

Pirsig, Robert M. *Zen and the Art of Motorcycle Maintenance*. London: Vintage Books, 2014.

Pius IX. "Ineffabilis Deus The Immaculate Conception" (1854). http://www.papalencyclicals.net/pius09/p9ineff.htm

Pius XII. *Munificentissimus Deus Defining the Dogma of the Assumption*, November 1, 1950. http://w2.vatican.va/content/pius-xii/en/apost_constitutions/documents/hf_p-xii_apc_19501101_munificentissimus-deus.html

Pogue, Carolyn. *After the Beginning*. Kelowna: CopperHouse, Wood Lake Publishing, 2006.

Powe, B. W. *Marshall McLuhan and Northrop Frye: Apocalypse and Alchemy*. Toronto: University of Toronto Press, 2014.

Premdas, Ralph. "Ethnicity and Identity in the Caribbean: Decentering a Myth." *The Kellogg Institute for International Studies*, 1996.

Pulp Fiction. Directed by Quentin Tarantino. Story by Quentin Tarantino and Roger Avary. Los Angeles: A Band Apart and Jersey Films, 1994.

Rabinow, Paul, ed. *The Foucault Reader*. New York: Pantheon Books, 1984.

Rabkin, Eric, ed. *Fantastic Worlds: Myths, Tales and Stories*. Toronto: Oxford University Press, 1979.

Rabstejnek, Carl. *History and Evolution of the Unconscious Before and After Sigmund Freud*. 2011. www.HOUD.info

Ramsey, Paul. *Nine Modern Moralists*. Englewood Cliffs: Prentice-Hall, 1962.

Rand, Ayn. *The Fountainhead 25th Anniversary Edition with Special Introduction by the Author.* Indianapolis: Bobbs-Merril, 1968.

Rand, Ayn. *Atlas Shrugged.* New York: Signet, Penguin Books, 1996.

Rand, Ayn. *The Virtue of Selfishness.* New York: Signet Books, The Penguin Group, 1964.

Rifkin, Jeremy. *The Empathic Civilization: The Race to Global Consciousness in a World in Crisis.* New York: Penguin Books, 2016.

Rogers, Carl. *On Becoming a Person: A Therapists View of Psychotherapy.* Boston: Houghton Mifflin, 1961.

Rogers, Liam. "Sabrina and the River Severn." Beltane, 1999. https://www.whitedragon.org.uk/articles/sabrina.htm

Ross, Floyd and Tynette Hills. *The Great Religions.* Greenwich: Fawcett Publications, 1961.

Rowling, J. K. *Harry Potter and the Philosopher's Stone.* New York: Scholastic, 1997.

Rowling, J. K. *Harry Potter and the Chamber of Secrets.* New York: Scholastic, 1997.

Rowling, J. K. *Harry Potter and the Prisoner of Azkaban.* New York: Scholastic, 1997.

Rowling, J. K. *Harry Potter and the Goblet of Fire.* New York: Scholastic, 1997.

Rowling, J. K. *Harry Potter and the Order of the Phoenix.* New York: Scholastic, 1997.

Rowling, J. K. *Harry Potter and the Half-Blood Prince.* New York: Scholastic, 1997.

Rowling, J. K. *Harry Potter and the Deathly Hallows.* New York: Scholastic, 1997.

Rushkoff, Douglas. *Program or Be Programmed: Ten Commands for the Digital Age.* New York, O/R Books, 2010.

Rudd, Jeff. "Falling Apple Story (Anecdote)." Edited by Laura Schmidt.1999. http://www.sfu.ca/phys/demos/demoindex/mechanics/mech1l/falling_apple.html

Sandars, N.K., trans. *The Epic of Gilgamesh.* London: Penguin Books, 1972.

Sanguin, Bruce. *Darwin, Divinity, and the Dance of the Cosmos: An Ecological Christianity.* Kelowna: CopperHouse, 2007.

Saracino, Michele. *On Being Human: A Conversation with Lonergan and Levinas.* Milwaukee: Marquette University Press, 2003.

Schermer, Michael. *The Believing Brain: From Ghosts and Gods to Politics and Conspiracies— How We Construct Beliefs and Reinforce them as Truths.* New York: Times Books Henry Holt and Company, 2011.

Schucman, Helen (penned), *A Course in Miracles.* New York: Viking, The Foundation for Inner Peace, 1976.

Schwartz, Jeffrey. *You Are Not Your Brain*. New York: Avery, 2011.

Scott, James. *Seeing as a State: How Certain Schemes to Improve the Human Condition Have Failed.* New Haven: Yale University Press, 1998.

Seaton, Jeffery Allen. "Who's Minding the Story? The United Church of Canada Meets A Secular Age." Thesis, Duke University Divinity School, 2016.

Shippey, Tom. *J.R.R. Tolkien: Author of the Century*. London: HarperCollins Publishers, 2001.

Shriners International Organization. http://www.shrinersinternational.org

Sloterdijk, Peter. *Derrida, an Egyptian: On the Problem of the Jewish Pyramid*. Cambridge: Polity, 2009.

Smith, Jonathan, Z. *Imagining Religions: From Babylon to Jonestown*. Chicago: University of Chicago Press, 1982.

Sokal, Alan and Jean Bricmont. *Fashionable Nonsense: Postmodern Intellectuals' Abuse of Science*. New York: Picador, Pan Books, 1998.

Somé, Malidoma Patrice. *Ritual: Power, Healing and Community*. Arkana: Swan Raven & Company, Penguin Compass, 1997.

Spiegelmann, J. Marvin. "C. G. Jung's Answer to Job: A Half Century Later." *Journal of Jungian Theory and Practice*, Vol. 8 No. 1, 2006.

Spitz, René A. "The first year of life: a psychoanalytic study of normal and deviant development of object relations." New York: International Universities Press, 1965.

Spong, John, Shelby. *The Sins of Scripture*. New York: HarperCollins Publishers, 2005.

Spretnak, Charlene. "Anatomy of a Backlash: Concerning the Work of Marija Gimbutas." *Journal of Archaeomythology* 7, 2011.

Star Trek: The Motion Picture. Directed by Robert Wise. Story by Alan Dean Foster and Gene Roddenberry. Hollywood: Paramount Pictures, 1978.

Star Trek: The Original Series. Created by Gene Rodenberry. Hollywood: Desilu Productions and Paramount Television, CBS Television Distribution, 1966-69.

Star Wars: A New Hope. Directed by George Lucas. San Francisco: Lucasfilm Ltd., Twentieth Century Fox, 1977.

Star Wars: The Empire Strikes Back. Directed by Irvin Kershner. Story by George Lucas. San Francisco: Lucasfilm Ltd., Twentieth Century Fox, 1980.

Star Wars: Return of the Jedi. Directed by Richard Marquand. Story by George Lucas. San Francisco: Lucasfilm Ltd., Twentieth Century Fox, 1983.

Star Wars: The Phantom Menace. Directed by George Lucas. San Francisco: Lucasfilm Ltd., Twentieth Century Fox, 1999.

Star Wars: The Attack of the Clones. Directed by George Lucas. San Francisco: Lucasfilm Ltd., Twentieth Century Fox, 2002.

Star Wars: Revenge of the Sith. Directed by George Lucas. San Francisco: Lucasfilm Ltd., Twentieth Century Fox, 2002.

Stark, Rodney. "Reconstructing the Rise of Christianity: The Role of Women." *Sociology of Religion*, 56:3, 1995.

Statistics Canada. http://www.statcan.gc.ca

Stromer, Richard. "The Good and the Terrible: Exploring the Two Faces of the Great Mother." http://soulmyths.com/

Swayze, Beulah, ed. *Magic of Myth & Legend*. Toronto: Ryerson Press, 1961.

Szasz, Thomas. *The Myth of Mental Illness: Foundations of a Theory of Personal Conduct*. New York: HarperPerennial, 2010.

Taleb, Nassim. *The Black Swan: The Impact of the Highly Improbable*. New York: Random House, 2007.

Taleb, Nassim. *The Bed of Procrustes*. New York: Random House, 2010.

Taleb, Nassim. *Antifragile: Things That Gain From Disorder*. London: Allen Lane, 2012.

The Globe and Mail. https://www.theglobeandmail.com

The Matrix. Directed by Larry & Andy Wachowski (Now Lana & Lilly). Sydney: Roadshow Entertainment, Warner Brothers, 1999.

The Matrix Reloaded. Directed by Larry & Andy Wachowski (Now Lana & Lilly). Sydney: Roadshow Entertainment, Warner Brothers, 2003.

The Matrix Revolutions. Directed by Larry & Andy Wachowski (Now Lana & Lilly). Sydney: Roadshow Entertainment, Warner Brothers, 2003.

Thorsby, Mark. "Phenomenology." https://www.youtube.com/user/PhilosophicalTechne/playlists

Tillich, Paul. *The Courage to Be*. New Haven, CT: Yale University Press, 2014.

Tolkien, J. R. R. *The Lord of the Rings*. London: Unwin, 1974.

Tolkien, J. R. R. *The Hobbit, or There and Back Again*. London: HarperCollins, 1997.

Tolkien, J. R. R. *On Fairy Stories*. Oxford: Oxford University Press. 1947.

Tzu, Lao. *Tao Te Ching*. Translated by Ursula K. Le Guin. Boston: Shambhala, 2011.

Udwin, Leslee. "India's Daughter." Mumbai: Assassin Films, Tathagat Films. 2015.

United Church of Canada. "A Song of Faith" http://www.united-church.ca/community-faith/welcome-united-church-canada/song-faith

United Church Observer. http://www.ucobserver.org

Vosper, Gretta. *With or Without God: Why the Way We Live is More Important than What We Believe.* Toronto, Ontario, Canada: Harper Perennial, 2014.

Vosper, Gretta. http://www.grettavosper.ca/

Wade, Nicholas. *The Faith Instinct.* New York: The Penguin Press, 2009.

Warrick, Patricia, Martin Greenberg and Joseph Olander, eds. *Science Fiction: Contemporary Mythology.* New York: Harper & Row Publishers Inc., 1978.

Watson, John B. "Psychology as the Behaviorist Views It." *Psychological Review*, 20, 158-177. http://psychclassics.yorku.ca/Watson/views.htm

Weber, Max. "Science as a Vocation." In *From Max Weber: Essays in Sociology.* Translated by H.H. Gerth. Edited by C. Wright Mills. New York: Oxford University Press, 1946.

Wiener, Norbert. *God and Golem, Inc.* Cambridge: Massachusetts Institute of Technology, 1990.

Wiener, Norbert. *The Human Use of Human Beings: Cybernetics and Society.* New York: Da Capo Press, 1954.

Wilbur, Ken. "Psychologia Perennis: The Spectrum of Consciousness." A revision and expansion of ideas in the magazine *Human Dimensions, Summer*, 1974.

Wilkinson, Richard, and Kate Pickett. *The Spirit Level: Why More Equal Societies Almost Always Do Better.* London: Allen Lane, 2009.

Willey, Basil. *The Seventeenth Century Background.* New York: Doubleday Anchor Books, 1953.

White, Lynn. "The historical roots of our ecologic crisis [with discussion of St Francis; reprint, 1967]." In *Ecology and Religion in History.* New York: Harper and Row, 1974. http://www.siena.edu/ellard/historical_roots_of_ou r_ecologic.htm

Whitehead, A. N. *Symbolism: Its Meaning and Effect.* New York: Fordham University Press, 1985.

Whitehead, A.N. *An Introduction to Mathematics.* London: Williams & Norgate, 1911.

Wright, Ronald. *A Brief History of Progress.* Toronto: House of Anansi Press, 2004.

Young, William P. *The Shack.* Los Angeles: Windblown Media, 2007.

Yousafzai, Malala and Christina Lamb. *I Am Malala.* Thorndike, 2013.

Wikipedia, The Free Encyclopedia. https://en.wikipedia.org

ENDNOTES, EXTENSIONS

INTRODUCTION

1. Aeschylus, *The Oresteia*, trans. Robert Fagles (New York: Penguin Books, 1977).

2. Judges 11–12.

3. Caroline Alexander, "A Wine-Like Sea," in Lapham's Quarterly, https://www.laphamsquarterly.org/sea/winelike-sea.

4. Leslee Udwin, *India's Daughter*, Assassin Films, Tathagat Films, 2015.

5. H. F. Ellenberger, *The Discovery of the Unconscious: The History and Evolution of Dynamic Psychiatry* (New York: Basic Books 2006), chap. 2. For this section, see also: Burkhard Peter, "Gassner's Exorcism—Not Mesmer's Magnetism—Is The Real Predecessor of Modern Hypnosis," *International Journal of Clinical and Experimental Hypnosis* 53, no. 1 (2005), 5–8; Carl Rabstejnek, *History and Evolution of the Unconscious Before and After Sigmund Freud* (2011), 6–9, https://www.HOUD.info.

6. Genesis 1–4.

7. Jeff Rudd, "Falling Apple Story (Anecdote)." Edited by Laura Schmidt. 1999, http://www.sfu.ca/phys/demos/demoindex/mechanics/mech11/falling_apple.html. See also: Robert Klara, "The story behind the Apple logo's evolution," 2011, http://www.adweek.com/creativity/story-behind-apple-logos-evolution-11672/.

8. Jane Bosveld, "Isaac Newton, World's Most Famous Alchemist" 2010, http://discovermagazine.com/2010/jul-aug/05-isaac-newton-worlds-most-famous-alchemist.

9. Pantone Matching System, https://www.pantone.com/the-pantone-matching-system.

10. Erich Neumann, "Art and Time," as quoted in Camille Paglia, "Erich Neumann: Theorist of the Great Mother," in *Arion*, Spring 2006, 14, https://www.bu.edu/arion/files/2010/03/Paglia-Great-Mother1.pdf.

11. Quentin Tarantino and Lawrence Bender, *Pulp Fiction* (A Band Apart and Jersey Films, 1994).

12. Mark Fisher, *Capitalist Realism: Is There No Alternative?* (Winchester: Zero Books, 2010), 13.

13. CBC News, "Can an atheist be a United Church minister?" March 25, 2016, http://www.cbc.ca/news/canada/gretta-vosper-united-church-minister-atheist-1.3506390.

14. United Church of Canada, *A Song of Faith* Preamble, http://www.united-church.ca/community-faith/welcome-united-church-canada/song-faith.

15. United Church of Canada, *A Song of Faith*, page 2.

16. Susanne K. Langer, Philosophy in a New Key: A Study of Symbolism of Reason, Rite and Art (Cambridge: New American Library, 1964), 19.

17. Northrop Frye used this as an illustration of "superstition." This can also be understood as "tradition." For further context: Northrop Frye and Bill Somerville, *The Bible and English Literature by Northrop Frye* University of Toronto, 1982, Lecture 18, http://heritage.utoronto.ca/content/bible-and-english-literature-northrop-frye-full-lecture-18. See also: chap. 1, note 17.

18. Camille Paglia, Sexual Personae: Art and Decadence from Nefertiti to Emily Dickinson (New Haven: Yale University Press 2001), 8.

19. William Butler Yeats, "The Second Coming," https://www.poets.org/poetsorg/poem/second-coming. See also: Chinua Achebe, *Things Fall Apart* (New York: Anchor Books, 1994), https://archive.org/details/thingsfallapart-00ache_ldx.

20. Jeremy Rifkin, The Empathic Civilization: The Race to Global Consciousness in a World in Crisis (New York: Penguin Books, 2016), 2.

21. Ibid., 26.

22. Ibid., 40–42.

23. Joseph Campbell, *The Hero with a Thousand Faces* (Princeton: Princeton University Press), 23.

ONE

1. John Kenney, "Shriners Hospital Opening In Montreal" in *Montreal Gazette*, August 20, 2015, http://montrealgazette.com/gallery/gallery-shriners-hospital-opening-in-montreal. See also: Tim Sargeant, "Montreal Shriners Hospital opens its doors October 5," *Global News*, August 20, 2015, https://globalnews.ca/news/2175727/montreal-shriners-hospital-opens-its-doors/.

2. Kalina LaFramboise, "Haitian girl set to return home after life-changing treatment at Montreal Shriners," CBC News, December 30, 2015, http://www.cbc.ca/news/canada/montreal/waina-dorcelus-montreal-haiti-surgery-shriners-1.3384389.

3. See Shriners International, http://www.shrinersinternational.org/Shriners/History/Beginnings.

4. For further examination see Gretta Vosper, *With or without God: Why the Way We Live is More Important than What We Believe* (Toronto: Harper Perennial, 2014). See also: http://www.grettavosper.ca/.

5. Gretta Vosper, "A Letter to Gary Paterson Regarding Paris," http://www.grettavosper.ca/letter-gary-paterson-regarding-paris/.

6. Mike Milne, "United Church committee finds atheist minister 'not suitable'" September 2016, http://www.ucobserver.org/faith/2016/09/atheist_minister_unsuitable/.

7. Colin Perkel, "United Church postpones hearing for atheist minister indefinitely," November 14, 2017, https://www.thestar.com/news/gta/2017/11/14/united-church-indefinitely-postpones-hearing-for-atheist-minister.html.

8. Margaret Wente, "The collapse of the liberal church," July 28, 2012, https://www.theglobeandmail.com/globe-debate/the-collapse-of-the-liberal-church/article4443228/. See also: Mike Milne, "Survey: Predicting the future," July 2010, http://www.ucobserver.org/faith/2010/07/survey3_july2010/; Ken Gallinger, "Interview with Kevin Flatt," October 2013, http://www.ucobserver.org/interviews/2013/10/interview_kevin_flatt/. "In November of 2018, the UCC and Vosper came to an agreement. Vosper remains an ordained minister in the church. https://www.ucobserver.org/faith/2018/11/gretta_vosper_decision/"

9. Mireille Vézina and Susan Crompton, "Volunteering in Canada," http://www.statcan.gc.ca/pub/11-008-x/2012001/article/11638-eng.htm.

10. Joseph Campbell, "On Becoming an Adult," https://youtu.be/aGx4IlppSgU; https://www.jcf.org/.

11. Wendy Piersell, as quoted in Rick Whittington, "Why You Can't Ignore Content Marketing to Improve Brand Awareness," *Iris*, May 11, 2016, https://www.iris.xyz/digital-marketing/why-you-cant-ignore-content-marketing-improve-brand-awareness.

12. Michael Dowd, "God is Reality Personified, Not a Person," in *The Evolutionary Evangelist*, http://www.thankgodforevolution.com/node/2010.

13. Northrop Frye, "Third Book," *Notebooks*, 69, as quoted in B. W. Powe, *Marshall McLuhan and Northrop Frye: Apocalypse and Alchemy* (Toronto: University of Toronto Press, 2014), 70–71.

14. Jordan B Peterson, *Maps of Meaning: The Architecture of Belief* (New York: Routledge, 1999), 20.

15. Joseph Campbell in interview with Tom Collins, "Mythic Reflections: Thoughts on myth, spirit and our time," in *In Context—A Quarterly of Humane Sustainable Culture* (Winter 1985/86), 52. https://www.context.org/iclib/ic12/campbell/.

16. Karen Armstrong, *A History of God: The 4,000-Year Quest of Judaism, Christianity and Islam* (New York: Alfred A. Knopf, 1994), xxi.

17. Northrop Frye used this as an illustration of "religion" as separate from superstition. This is the role of revelation, apocalypse, and transcendence in religious practice, according to Frye. This can also be understood as "adaptation" or "adoption" in a more social sense of the words. For further context: Northrop Frye and Bill Somerville, *The Bible and English Literature by Northrop Frye*. University of Toronto, 1982, Lecture 18, http://heritage.utoronto.ca/content/bible-and-english-literature-northrop-frye-full-lecture-18. See also Introduction: Note 17.

18. Christopher Boehm, *Hierarchy in the Forest: The Evolution of Egalitarian Behavior* (Cambridge: Harvard University Press, 2001), 227–28.

19. Sigmund Freud in conversation with Marie Bonaparte, as quoted in Ernest Jones, *Sigmund Freud: Life and Work* (Hogarth Press, 1953) vol. 2, part 3, chap.16, 421.

20. Jordan Peterson, *Maps of Meaning*, 124–48. Throughout this section, I am relying on Peterson's explanation as a guiding source for this archetype.

21. Rachel Fulton Brown, *Mary and the Art of Prayer* (New York: Columbia University Press, 2017), 68–69.

22. Rachel Fulton Brown, *Mary in the Scriptures: The Unexpurgated Tradition* (Milwaukee: Marquette University Press, 2014), 33.

23. John Paul I, "Angelus," September 10, 1978, https://w2.vatican.va/content/john-paul-i/en/angelus/documents/hf_jp-i_ang_10091978.html. See also: http://www.lastampa.it/2013/06/10/vaticaninsider/eng/the-vatican/the-francisjohn-paul-i-connection-gods-love-is-like-a-mothers-love-z45KrCnBpwCR1RvekjOxFP/pagina.html.

24. Pius IX, "Ineffabilis Deus The Immaculate Conception" (1854), http://www.papalencyclicals.net/pius09/p9ineff.htm; Pius XII, *Munificentissimus Deus Defining The Dogma of the Assumption*, November 1, 1950, http://w2.vatican.va/content/pius-xii/en/apost_constitutions/documents/hf_p-xii_apc_19501101_munificentissimus-deus.html.

25. Erich Neumann, *The Great Mother: An Analysis of the Archetype* (Princeton: Princeton University Press, 1972), xlii.

26. Lillian Smith, as quoted in Ursula K. Le Guin, "The Carrier Bag Theory of Fiction," in Cheryll Glotfelty and Harold Fromm, eds., *The Ecocriticism Reader: Landmarks in Literary Ecology* (Athens: University of Georgia Press, 1996), 151. See also: Lillian Smith lecture on autobiography, Audio Collection, Special and Area Studies Collections, George A. Smathers Libraries, University of Florida, Gainesville, Florida.

27. "Arvid Carlsson" in *Encyclopedia Britannica*, https://www.britannica.com/biography/Arvid-Carlsson. See also: Vikram Yeragani, Manuel Tancer, Pratap Chokka, and Glen Baker., "Arvid Carlsson, and the story of dopamine," *Indian Psychiatry*, January-March 52, no. 1, 2010, 87–88, https://www.ncbi.nlm.nih.gov/pmc/articles/PMC2824994/.

28. Jordan Peterson. *Maps of Meaning*, 153–74. Throughout this section, I am relying on Peterson's explanation as a guiding source for this archetype.

29. Jonathan Bowden, "The Strange Case of Anthony Burgess' A Clockwork Orange," in *Counter Currents Publishing*, https://www.counter-currents.com/2011/03/the-strange-case-of-anthony-burgess-a-clockwork-orange/. See also: Roger Lockhurst, "An Introduction to A Clockwork Orange" in *British Library Discovering Literature: 20th Century*, Dec 2016, https://www.bl.uk/20th-century-literature/articles/an-introduction-to-a-clockwork-orange; Wind Goodfriend, "Classical Conditioning in A Clockwork Orange" in *Psychology Today*, May 2012, https://www.psychologytoday.com/blog/psychologist-the-movies/201205/classical-conditioning-in-clockwork-orange; https://www.anthonyburgess.org/about-anthony-burgess/burgess-a-brief-life/.

30. John B. Watson, "Psychology as the Behaviorist Views It" originally in *Psychological Review*, 20, 1913, 158-177. http://psychclassics.yorku.ca/Watson/views.htm

31. Frans de Waal, *The Age of Empathy: Nature's Lessons for a Kinder Society* (Toronto: Emblem, McClelland & Stewart, 2010), 12. Frans de Waal tells the story of Little Albert with a white rabbit. Others tell the story with a white rat. When it is your turn to tell the story, what animal will you choose? See also: "John B. Watson" in *Encyclopedia Britannica*, https://www.britannica.com/biography/John-B-Watson; T. DeAngelis, "'Little Albert' regains his identity" in *Monitor on Psychology*, January 2010 (American Psychological Association), http://www.apa.org/monitor/2010/01/little-albert.aspx; B. Harris, "Whatever Happened to Little Albert?" in *American Psychologist* vol. 34, no. 2 (1979), 151–60, http://psycnet.apa.org/record/1979-25006-001.

32. Ogden Lindsley, as recounted by Gary Wilkes, "Evidence-Based Knowledge: The Fool's Gold standard of behavior analysis," May 2015, https://clickandtreat.com/wordpress/?p=1465.

33. R. David Cole, "Choh Hao Li" in *Biographical Memoirs: V.70* 1996 (The National Academies Press), 221–39. See also: "A History of UCSF: People—Choh Hao Li (1913–1987)" (University of California San Francisco), http://history.library.ucsf.edu/li.html. Choh Hao Li also wrote articles for Scientific American—October 1950 and July 1963.

34. Harold Schmeck Jr., "Synthetic Growth Hormone Cleared" in the *New York Times*, October 19, 1985, http://www.nytimes.com/1985/10/19/us/synthetic-growth-hormone-cleared.html. See also: Mallory Warner, "The big story behind synthetic human growth hormone" in *O Say Can You See? Stories from the National Museum of American History*, http://americanhistory.si.edu/blog/2012/10/human-growth-hormone.html.

35. Alistair Corbett, Graeme Henderson, Alexander McKnight, and Stewart Paterson, "75 years of opioid research: the exciting but vain quest for the Holy Grail" in *British Journal of Pharmacology*, January 2006, 147(Suppl 1): S153–S162, https://www.ncbi.nlm.nih.gov/pmc/articles/PMC1760732/.

36. Peterson. *Maps of Meaning*, 145–53. Throughout this section, I am relying on Peterson's explanation as a guiding source for this archetype.

37. Colin Stokes, "How Movies Teach Manhood" as presented to *TEDxBeaconStreet*, https://www.ted.com/talks/colin_stokes_how_movies_teach_manhood.

38. Susan Pass, *A Biographic Comparison Tracing the Origin of Their Ideas of Jean Piaget and Lev Vygotsky* (a paper prepared for the Annual Meeting of the American Educational Research Association, 2003), 8, https://files.eric.ed.gov/fulltext/ED478987.pdf. See also: Richard Kohler, *Jean Piaget* (New York: Bloomsbury Academic Publishing, 2014), 26–30; "Jean Piaget" in *Encyclopedia Britannica*, https://www.britannica.com/biography/Jean-Piaget.

39. Jordan Peterson, *Maps of Meaning*, 288

40. Jordan Peterson, *Maps of Meaning*, 288.

41. Lea Minerman, "The mind's mirror" in *Monitor on Psychology* vol 36 (October 2005), 48, http://www.apa.org/monitor/oct05/mirror.aspx. See also: J. M. Kilner and R. N. Lemon, "What We Know Currently about Mirror Neurons" in *Current Biology* vol. 23, no. 23, R1057–R1062, https://www.ncbi.nlm.nih.gov/pmc/articles/PMC3898692/.

42. Christopher Boehm, *Hierarchy in the Forest*, 164.

43. Jordan Peterson., "Dragons, Divine Parents, Heroes and adversaries: A complete cosmology of being" (Jordan B Peterson, Jun 2014), 42:00, https://youtu.be/nqONu6wDYaE.

44. Jordan Peterson, *Maps of Meaning*, 188–97. Peterson does not specifically address anomaly or novelty as an archetypal character differentiated from his three Great and Terrible characters. Throughout this section, I am exploring the characterization of the idea of novelty. I use as a start Peterson's ideas from "The Appearance of Anomaly: Challenge to the Shared Map" in Chapter 3.

45. A retelling from a retelling: Joseph Campbell and Bill Moyers, *Joseph Campbell and the Power of Myth Episode 2* (PBS, June 1988), http://billmoyers.com/content/ep-2-joseph-campbell-and-the-power-of-myth-the-message-of-the-myth/. See also: Joseph Campbell and Bill Moyers, *The Power of Myth* (New York: Doubleday, 1988).

46. Pope Francis, "Laudato Si' on Care For Our Common Home." *Encyclical Letter, 1*, http://w2.vatican.va/content/francesco/en/encyclicals/documents/papa francesco_20150524_enciclica-laudato-si.html.

47. Carl Rogers, *On Becoming a Person: A Therapist's View of Psychotherapy* (Boston: Houghton Mifflin Company, 1961), chap. 1 through 12. See also: Carl Rogers, "Empathic: An Unappreciated Way of Being" in *The Counseling Psychologist* vol. 5, no. 2–10 (1975).

48. Abraham Maslow, *Toward a Psychology of Being* (New York: Van Nostrand Reinhold, 1968), 5.

49. Carl Rogers, *On Becoming a Person*, 24.

50. Jeremy Rifkin, *The Empathic Civilization*, 12.

51. Ibid., 26.

52. Homer, *The Odyssey*, trans. E. V. Rieu (London: Penguin Books, 1946), 230.

53. Daniel Kahneman, *Thinking Fast and Slow* (New York: Farrar, Straus and Giroux, 2013), chap. 1–9. In comparison, see also Iain McGilchrist, *The Master and His Emissary* (New Haven: Yale University Press, 2012).

54. Marshall McLuhan, Quentin Fiore, and Jerome Agel. *The Medium is the Massage: An Inventory of Effects* (Corte Madera: Gingko Press Inc., 2005), 68–69.

55. Riane Eisler, *The Chalice and the Blade: Our History, Our Future.* (New York: HarperCollins, 1995), chap. 6–9.

56. Christopher Boehm, *Hierarchy in the Forest*, chap. 3 through 8. The idea of "hierarchy" and Boehm's "reverse dominance hierarchy" are further explored in verse 2—The Pyramid.

57. Camille Paglia, "Erich Neumann: Theorist of the Great Mother," 9.

58. Charlene Spretnak., "Anatomy of a Backlash: Concerning the Word of Marija Gimbutas" in *Journal of Archaeomythology* vol.7 (2011), 10-20.

59. Ibid., 23.

60. Riane Eisler, *The Chalice and the Blade*, 54–56, 78–81.

61. Ibid., 78. See also: Aeschylus, "The Eumenides" in *The Oresteia*, lines 820–33.

62. Northrop Frye, *The Great Code: The Bible and Literature* (New York: Harcourt Brace Jovanovich. 1982), 94.

63. Ibid., 120.

64. Leo Tolstoy, *Anna Karenina* (New York: Penguin Classics, 2004), 1.

65. Marshall McLuhan, Quentin Fiore, and Jerome Agel, *The Medium is the Massage*, 63.

66. Leslee Udwin., "India's Daughter," Assassin Films, Tathagat Films, 2015. Throughout this section, I am relying on Udwin's exploration as a guiding source.

67. Ibid.

68. Michael Dowd, *Thank God for Evolution!*, 103.

69. "Leslee Udwin, "Making India's Daughter" at *Because I am a Girl*, Plan International, 2015, https://plan-uk.org/blogs/leslee-udwin-making-indias-daughter. See also: Sonia Faleiro and Leslee Udwin, "In Conversation: Interview with Leslee Udwin" in *Granta* 130: India, April 2015, https://granta.com/interview-leslee-udwin/.

70. The Economic Times Bureau, "Ban wasn't needed. For truth to be known, filth has to come out, says Nirbhaya's father Badrinath Singh" in *The Economic Times*, March 5, 2015, https://economictimes.indiatimes.com/news/politics-and-nation/ban-wasnt-needed-for-truth-to-be-known-filth-has-to-come-out-says-nirbhayas-father-badrinath-singh/articleshow/46462402.cms.

71. Jeremy Rifkin, *The Empathic Civilization*, 443.

72. Mike Gabriel and Eric Goldberg, *Pocahontas* (Walt Disney Pictures, 1995). The actual name of the historical girl might have been Matoaka and not the nickname Pocahontas—an interesting aside considering this book is about a naming ceremony. Whatever historical inaccuracies or storytelling embellishments there are to bring up, the movie was a new beginning in pop culture. The character Pocahontas was the first Native American Disney Princess and the first marginalized woman, to use a phrase, to be a lead in a Disney film. See also: Thomas King, *The Inconvenient Indian: A Curious Account of Native People in North America* (Toronto: Anchor Canada, Random House Canada, 2012), 8–9; Tom Brook, "The controversy behind Disney's groundbreaking new princess," BBC, November 28, 2016, http://www.bbc.com/culture/story/20161128-the-controversy-behind-disneys-groundbreaking-new-princess.

73. B. W. Powe, *Marshall McLuhan and Northrop Frye: Apocalypse and Alchemy* (Toronto: University of Toronto Press, 2014), 173. A Canadian call and response

74. Rabbi Moshe Reiss, "Jephthah's Daughter: Jewish Perspectives," http://www.moshereiss.org/articles/16_jephthah.htm. See also: Tamar Kadari, "Jepththah's Daughter: Midrash and Aggadah" in *Jewish Women's Archive*, https://jwa.org/encyclopedia/article/jephthahs-daughter-midrash-and-aggadah.

75. "A Clockwork Orange Net Notes," *The Guardian*, March 16, 2000, https://www.theguardian.com/news/2000/mar/16/netnotes. See also: Christian Bugge, "The Clockwork Controversy," http://www.visual-memory.co.uk/amk/doc/0012.html.

76. Jeffrey Schwartz, *You Are Not Your Brain* (New York: Avery, 2011) See also: Norman Doidge, *The Brain That Changes Itself* (New York: Viking Press, 2007).

77. Samir Selmanovic, *It's Really All About God: How Islam, Atheism, and Judaism Made Me a Better Christian* (Hoboken: Jossy-Bass, 2011), chap. 3.

78. "Constitution of the Republic of Ecuador," Article 71, 47, http://constitutionnet.org/sites/default/files/ecuador_constitution_english_1.pdf.

TWO

1. Marshall McLuhan, as quoted by B. W. Powe, *Marshall McLuhan and Northrop Frye: Apocalypse and Alchemy* (Toronto: University of Toronto Press, 2014) 190. Quote from John Ayre, *Northrop Frye A Biography* (Toronto: Random House Canada, 1989).

2. Sam Harris, *Waking Up: A Guide to Spirituality Without Religion* (New York: Simon and Schuster, 2014), chap. 2.

3. Northrop Frye, "Third Book" *Notebooks*, 69, as quoted in B. W. Powe. *Marshall McLuhan and Northrop Frye: Apocalypse and Alchemy* (Toronto: University of Toronto Press, 2014), 70–71. See also chap. 1, n. 13.

4. Susanne K. Langer, *Feeling and Form: A Theory of Art* (New York: Charles Scribner's Sons, 1953), 92–103.

5. Matthew Crawford, *The World Beyond Your Head: On Becoming an Individual in an Age of Distraction* (Toronto: Penguin, 2016), 182.

6. Northrop Frye, *Words with Power Being a Second Study of The Bible and Literature* (Toronto: Viking, The Penguin Group, 1990), 139.

7. Ibid., 42.

8. Paul Tillich, *Systematic Theology Volume I* (Chicago: University of Chicago Press, 1973), 44.

9. Marshall McLuhan, *Mademoiselle: the magazine for the smart young woman* vol. 64 (1966), 114.

10. Marshall McLuhan, crediting A. N. Whitehead, *The Medium is the Massage*, as a subheading. To further play with sources, see also J.M. Culkin, "A schoolman's guide to Marshall McLuhan" (The Saturday Review, March 1967), 51-53, 70-72.

11. Marshall Berman, *All That Is Solid Melts into Air* (London: Verso, 2010), preface to the Preface.

12. Malidoma Patrice Somé, *Ritual: Power, Healing and Community* (Arkana: Swan Raven & Company, Penguin Compass,1997), 66.

13. Christopher Boehm, *Hierarchy in the Forest*, 20–29.

14. Ibid., 66–88.

15. Ibid., 183, 198, 253.

16. Gary Olson, "Jacques Derrida on Rhetoric and Composition: A Conversation" in *Journal of Advanced Composition* vol 10, no. 1, http://www.jaconlinejournal.com/archives/vol10.1/olson-derrida.pdf.

17. Ayn Rand, *Atlas Shrugged* (New York: Signet, Random House, 1957), 680.

18. Ibid., 989.

19. Nassim Taleb, Antifragile: *Things That Gain From Disorder* (London: Allen Lane, 2012), Preface.

20. A. N. Whitehead, *Symbolism: Its Meaning and Effect* (New York: Fordham University Press, 1985), 88.

21. Jeremy Rifkin, *The Empathc Civilization*, 430.

22. Genesis 11:1–9.

23. I wanted to add this part on Sisyphus because of Albert Camus. In the process of editing, I removed direct mention of Camus. Maybe I will come back to his sympathies for Sisyphus; Albert Camus, *The Myth of Sisyphus and Other Essays* (New York, Knopf, 1955), chap. 3.

24. Genesis 4.

25. Ibid., 26–34.

26. Thirugnanam, *Devi Mahamyam English Transliteration*, 2010.

27. Malidoma Patrice Somé, *Ritual*, 65.

28. A. N. Whitehead, *An Introduction to Mathematics* (London: Williams & Norgate, 1911), 61.

29. Richard Dawkins, *The Greatest Show on Earth: The Evidence for Evolution* (New York: Free Press, 2009), chap. 12. See also: Jag Bhalla, "Richard Dawkins' Tree Metaphor: Why Free Markets Are So Inefficient" at Big Think, 2016, http://bigthink.com/errors-we-live-by/how-free-competition-can-create-dumb-costs.

30. Michel Foucault, *Discipline and Punish: The Birth of the Prison* (London: Penguin Books, 1977), 228.

31. Matthew Crawford, *The World Beyond Your Head*, 40–41.

32. "Step Two" of the 12-Step Program, https://www.aa.org/assets/en_US/en_step2.pdf.

33. James Christopher, "Sobriety Without Superstition" in *Free Inquiry*, 1985. See also: White, W. (2012), "The history of Secular Organizations for Sobriety—Save Our Selves: An interview with James Christopher," http://www.williamwhitepapers.com/pr/James%20Christopher%20Interview%202012.pdf; http://www.sossobriety.org/

34. Paul Rabinow, ed., *The Foucault Reader* (Toronto: Random House, 1984) ,11. See also: Bob Robinson, "Michel Foucault: Ethics" in *Internet Encyclopedia of Philosophy*, https://www.iep.utm.edu/fouc-eth/.

35. Karl Marx, "Critique of the Gotha Program" in Marx/Engels Selected Works, Volume Three (Moscow: Progress Publishers, 1970), 13–30, https://www.marxists.org/archive/marx/works/download/Marx_Critque_of_the_Gotha_Programme.pdf.

36. Malidoma Patrice Somé, *Ritual*, 87.

37. Ibid., 25. Compare with A. N. Whitehead's commentary, chap. 2, n. 20.

38. Emmanuel Levinas, "The Name of a Dog, or Natural Rights" in *Difficult Freedom: Essays on Judaism* (Baltimore: Johns Hopkins University Press, 1990), 151–53.

39. Emmanuel Levinas, "Philosophy and the Idea of Infinity" in *Emmanuel Levinas Collected Philosophical Papers* (Dordrecht: Martinus Nijhoff Publishers, 1987), 48. Levinas was commenting on Plato's Republic, Book X.

40. Bernard Lonergan, *Insight: A Study of Human Understanding* (London: Longmans, 1964), 243.

41. Bernard Lonergan, *Method in Theology* (Toronto: University of Toronto Press, 2003), 53. See also:

Tad Dunne, "Bernard Lonergan (1904–1984)" at *Internet Encyclopedia of Philosophy*, http://www.iep.utm.edu/lonergan/.

42. Exodus 11: 7, mentioned in Emmanuel Levinas, "The Name of a Dog, or Natural Rights" in *Difficult Freedom*, 152.

43. Emmanuel Levinas, *Totality and Infinity: An Essay on Exteriority* (Norwell: Kluwer Academic Publishers, 1991), 110–15.

44. Ibid., 276, 306. See also: Adrienne Peperzak, *To the Other: An Introduction to the Philosophy of Emmanuel Levinas* (West Lafayette: Purdue University Press, 1993), 198, 207–08.

45. Marshall McLuhan, *The Gutenberg Galaxy* (Toronto: University of Toronto Press, 2002), 36.

46. Jeremy Rifkin, *The Empathic Civilization*, 555, 564–66.

47. Christopher Boehm, *Hierarchy in the Forest*, 198, 253. See also chap. 2, n. 13.

48. René Spitz, "Psychogenic Disease in Infancy," 1952, https://archive.org/details/PsychogenicD.

49. Georgette Mulheir, "Institutions not only separate children from families, but also their communities" at *Lumos*, https://www.wearelumos.org/news-and-media/2015/01/01/institutions-not-only-separate- children-families-also-their-communities/.

50. Emmanuel Levinas, *Totality and Infinity*, 214, 244.

51. Northrop Frye, *Anatomy of Criticism* (Princeton: Princeton University Press, 1990), 167–74.

52. Malidoma Patrice Somé, *Ritual*, 96, back cover.

53. Ibid., 75.

54. Lumière Brothers, "L'Arrivée d'un Train en Gare de La Ciotat," 1895, https://archive.org/details/youtube--e1u7Fgoocc.

55. Friedrich Nietzsche, *The Gay Science* (Toronto: Random House, 1974), 181.

56. David Brancaccio and Katie Long, "How independent businesses kept New Orleans afloat" in *West Virginia Public Broadcasting*, August 10, 2015, http://wvpublic.org/post/how-independent-businesses-kept-new-orleans-afloat#stream/0; http://www.nolaba.org/news-2/how-independent-businesses-kept-new-orleans-afloat/.

57. Roberta Brandes Gratz, *We're Still Here Ya Bastards: How the People of New Orleans Rebuilt Their City* (New York: Nation Books, Hachette Book Group, 2015).

58. David Brancaccio and Katie Long, "How independent businesses kept New Orleans afloat," http://wvpublic.org/post/how-independent-businesses-kept-new-orleans-afloat#stream/0.

59. Jordan Levine (Producer), "Dr. Jordan B Peterson full-length 2015 interview" at *Transliminal*, November 2015, https://youtu.be/07Ys4tQPRis.

60. Michael Bradford, "Louisiana moves to upgrade building code in wake of Katrina" at *Business Insurance*, November 27, 2005, http://www.businessinsurance.com/article/20051127/ISSUE01/100017957/louisiana-moves-to-upgrade-building-code-in-wake-of-katrina. See also: "Statewide Code to Guide Rebuilding in Louisiana" at *Insurance Journal*, December 4, 2005, https://www.insurancejournal.com/magazines/mag-features/2005/12/04/151023.htm; "Louisiana's Statewide Building Code on Chopping Block" (Baton Rouge: America Press) at *Construction Equipment Guide*, May 25, 2007, https://www.constructionequipmentguide.com/louisianas-statewide-building-code-on-chopping-block/8701.

61. Camille Paglia, *Vamps and Tramps: New Essays* (New York: Vintage Books, 2004), xiii.

62. James Gleick, *The Information: A History, A Theory, A Flood* (New York: Vintage Books, 2012), chap. 1, 1.

63. Job 1–21.

64. Kevin Draine, "India's Wandering Lions" on PBS, April 13, 2016, http://www.pbs.org/wnet/nature/indias-wandering-lions-full-episode/14114/

65. Matthew Crawford, *The World Beyond Your Head*, 153–55.

66. Nassim Taleb's 2018 book has the title, *Skin in the Game: The Hidden Asymmetries in Daily Life*. Taleb has used the phrase elsewhere: Nassim Taleb, *Antifragile: Things That Gain from Disorder*, 5. He considers the absence of skin in the game is the greatest generator of crises in the world. Agamemnon and Jephthah were willing to contribute their daughter's skins, failing their tests of entropy and jeopardizing their families.

67. Rudro Chakrabarti, "This Mom Just Did The Most Amazing Thing For Her Kids. Childhood Made." January 19, 2018, https://www.tickld.com/wow/2168270/tckldthis-mom-just-did-the-most-amazing-things-for-her-kids-childhood-made/. See also: Caroline Picard, "How to Tell Your Kids About Santa Without Breaking Their Hearts" in *Good Housekeeping*, December 8, 2016, http://www.goodhousekeeping.com/life/parenting/news/a41821/how-to-tell-kids-about-santa/.

68. Malidoma Patrice Somé, *Ritual*, 24–25.

69. Friedrich Nietzsche, *Thus Spoke Zarathustra: A Book for All and None* (Cambridge, Cambridge University Press, 2006), 5.

70. Carl Jung, *The Portable Jung* (New York: Viking Press, Penguin Books, 1977), 161, 373. See also: Carl Jung, "Answer to Job" in *The Portable Jung* (New York: The Viking Press, Penguin Books, 1977), 595, 624.

71. Erich Neumann, *The Great Mother: An Analysis of the Archetype*, xlii.

72. Pia Skogemann points out one example in "The Psychological Aspects of the Kore," *Carl Jung, Archetypes and the Collective Unconscious* (Princeton: Princeton University Press, 1969), 182. See also: Pia Skogemann, "The Daughter Archetype" at Pia Skogemann, https://www.piaskogemann.dk/artikler/the-daughter-archetype.aspx; Carl Jung, "Psychological Aspects of the Mother Archetype" in *Archetypes and the Collective Unconscious* (Princeton:Princeton University Press, 1969), 75–111, especially The "Nothing-But" Daughter," 97. In the next sections and chapters I

am going to follow Northrop Frye's work with the Biblical child-daughter in order to develop the context for the distinction. In simple names, *Sophia* is not *Mary*. That said, I am drawn to this particular mention of Perseus: "What Perseus has to do with the Gorgon's head would never occur to anyone who did not know the myth. So it is with the individual images: they need a context, and the context is not only a myth but an individual anamnesis."—"The Psychological Aspects of the Kore" in *Archetypes and the Collective Unconscious*, 189. The same cannot be said about Theseus and the string from Ariadne. Maybe this is why these two heroes appear in the Introduction.

73. Ziauddin Yousafzai, "My Daughter Malala," March 2015, https://www.ted.com/talks/ziauddin_yousafzai_my_daughter_malala.

74. Ibid.

75. Malala Yousafzai, *I Am Malala* (Thorndike, 2013), chap. 1, chap. 10.

76. Ziauddin Yousafzai, "My Daughter Malala."

77. Amulya Chandra Sen, "Ashoka Emperor of India" in *Encyclopedia Britannica*, https://www.britannica.com/biography/Ashoka. See also: Cristian Violatti, "Ashoka" in *Ancient History Encyclopedia*, September 2013, https://www.ancient.eu/Ashoka/; Radhakumud Mookerji, Asoka (Gaekwad Lectures) (London: MacMillan and Co., Ltd., 1928), https://archive.org/details/asokagaekwadlectradh.

78. *The Epic of Gilgamesh*, trans. N. K. Sandars (London: Penguin Books, 1972), Introduction.

79. Ralph T. H. Griffith, *The Ramayana of Valmiki* (London: Trubner & Co., 2008).

80. Huston Smith, *The Religions of Man* (New York: Mentor Books, Harper & Row, Publishers, 1963), 250.

81. Kings 1:21.

82. As an example and link: http://www.mindfulness-kingston-upon-thames.org/ten-bulls.

83. Northrop Frye and Bill Somerville, *The Bible and English Literature by Northrop Frye*. University of Toronto, 1982. Lecture 18, http://heritage.utoronto.ca/content/bible-and-english-literature-northrop-frye-full-lecture-18. See also: Northrop Frye, *The Great Code*, 125; William Butler Yeats. "Among School Children," https://www.poetryfoundation.org/poems/43293/among-school-children.

THREE

1. Ovid, "The Story of Narcissus" in Book III of *Metamorphoses*, trans. Samuel Garth and John Dryden, 402—510, http://classics.mit.edu/Ovid/metam.mb.txt.

2. Marshall McLuhan, *Understanding Media* (Cambridge: Massachusetts Institute of Technology Press, 1964), 41.

3. Aeschylus, *The Oresteia*, trans. Robert Fagles (New York: Penguin Books, 1977), 110–11.

4. Jeremy Rifkin, *The Empathic Civilization*, 183.

5. Ibid., 555.

6. "Plato's Stepchildren," November 22, 1968 at *Memory Alpha*, http://memory-alpha.wikia.com/wiki/Plato%27s_Stepchildren_(episode).

7. "Nyota Uhura" at *Memory Alpha*, http://memory-alpha.wikia.com/wiki/Nyota_Uhura.

8. Bernard Lonergan, *Method in Theology*, 53. Paraphrase, extending the invitations into questions.

9. Jordan Peterson, *Maps of Meaning*, 197.

10. Camille Paglia, "Junk Bonds and Corporate Raiders: Academe in the Hour of the Wolf" in *Arion*, Spring 1991, 197.

11. Jordan Peterson, "2016/10/03: Part 1: Fear and the Law" at Jordan B Peterson Videos, https://youtu.be/fvPgjg201w0.

12. Jordan Peterson, *Maps of Meaning*, 7.

13. Ibid., 13.

14. Muriel Rukeyser, "The Speed of Darkness," https://www.poetryfoundation.org/poems/56287/the-speed-of-darkness.

15. Jordan Peterson, *Maps of Meaning*, Figure 1, 24.

16. Ibid., Figure 5, 46 and Figure 6, 47.

17. Ibid., 24, 28.

18. Genesis 18.

19. Ibid., 19:8.

20. For further discussion on sexuality, power, and motivation, in the context of our relationships with a god, see also Jack Miles. *God: A Biography* (New York: Vintage Books, 1996), 63–75.

21. Douglas Adams, *The Hitchhiker's Guide to the Galaxy* (New York: Random House, 1989), 1.

22. Desmond Lee, "Translator's Introduction" in Plato, *The Republic* (Toronto: Penguin Books, 1987), 13–16.

23. Plato, *The Republic* (Toronto: Penguin Books, 1987), 316–25.

24. George Orwell, *1984* (New York: Penguin Books, 1956). See also: Richard Brautigan, "All Watched Over By Machines of Loving Grace" at https://allpoetry.com/All-Watched-Over-By-Machines-Of-Loving-Grace; https://www.poetryfoundation.org/harriet/2011/06/richard-brautigan-poem-inspires-bbc-documentary-series.

25. "The Dalai Lama walks into a pizza shop," https://youtu.be/xlIrI80og8c.

26. Otto Rank, *The Myth of the Birth of the Hero* (New York: The Journal of Nervous and Mental Disease Publishing Company, 1914); Lord Raglan, *A Study in Tradition, Myth and Drama* (London: Watts & Co, 1936).

27. Joseph Campbell, *The Hero with a Thousand Faces* (Princeton: Princeton University Press, 1973), 3. For further discussion on the similarities and differences between Carl Jung and Joseph Campbell (and Mircea Eliade and Northrop Frye) see also Glen Gill, "Northrop Frye and the Phenomenology of Myth," thesis paper at McMaster University, April 2003. 18, 93–130, https://macsphere.mcmaster.ca/bitstream/11375/6152/1/fulltext.pdf.

28. Nassim Taleb, The Bed of Procrustes: Philosophical and Practical Aphorisms (New York: Random House, 2010).

29. Joseph Campbell, *The Hero with a Thousand Faces*, 25.

30. J. R. R. Tolkien, *The Lord of the Rings* (London: Unwin, 1974).

31. Northrop Frye, *The Great Code*, 169. See also: Northrop Frye and Bill Somerville, *The Bible and English Literature by Northrop Frye* University of Toronto, 1982. Lecture 2, http://heritage.utoronto.ca/content/bible-and-english-literature-northrop-frye-full-lecture-2.

32. Northrop Frye and Bill Somerville. The Bible and English Literature by Northrop Frye, Lecture 2. See also: Shakespeare, A Midsummer Nights Dream, Act 5, Scene 1.

33. Revelation 11:8.

34. Patrick Byrne, *Insight and Beyond*. Boston College and bclonergan.org, Class 12, https://bclonergan.org/insight/. See also: Tad Dunne, "Bernard Lonergan Part 6: Categories" at *Internet Encyclopedia of Philosophy*, http://www.iep.utm.edu/lonergan/.

35. I asked a friend what he thought of the 2013 *Star Trek Into Darkness*. His response was both flippant and pregnant: "There's no Trek in it." Will Wheaton commented on this too: https://wilwheaton.tumblr.com/post/50514989060/jenniferdeguzman-he-said-star-trek-is-too; https://wilwheaton.tumblr.com/post/50587610082/a-lot-of-people-have-pointed-out-to-me-that-if. The 2013 movie did make almost half a billion dollars at the box office, which would suggest some audience members identified with the story. See also: Miriam Kramer, "Why We Still Love 'Star Trek,' Final Frontiers and All," at *Space.com Entertainment*, May 2013, https://www.space.com/21162-star-trek-fan-love-endures.html. For all of *Star Trek's* love of progress, some have found the franchise does not go boldly enough: https://www.wired.com/2013/05/star-trek-lgbt-gay-characters/.

36. Northrop Frye and Bill Somerville, *The Bible and English Literature by Northrop Frye*, Lecture 18.

37. Proverbs 8:30–33.

38. Northrop Frye and Bill Somerville, *The Bible and English Literature by Northrop Frye*, Lecture 18.

39. Jeremy Rifkin, *The Empathic Civilization*, 213.

40. Bernard Lonergan, *Insight: A Study of Human Understanding* (London: Longmans, 1964), 228.

41. Ibid., 267.

42. Plato, *The Republic* (Toronto: Penguin Books, 1987), 319.

43. Although outside the original intentions of my project, and not in my current competence, this could be a place to involve theories that map out other developmental levels of consciousness. See also: Clare Graves, Don Beck and Ken Wilber, "Spiral Dynamics Integral," http://www.spiraldynamics.net/; Lawrence Kohlberg, "Stages of Moral Development," https://www.britannica.com/biography/Lawrence-Kohlberg; Robert Kegan and Lisa Lahey on topics such as Minds at Work, Immunity to Change, Stages of Mind, An Everyone Culture: Becoming a Deliberately Developmental Organization, http://mindsatwork.com/.

44. Jordan Peterson, *Maps of Meaning*, 173.

45. Ignaz Semmelweis, *The Etiology, Concept and Prophylaxis of Childbed Fever*, trans. Codell Carter (University of Wisconsin Press, 1983), 67–69, 120–158. See also: Geneva: World Health Organization, *WHO Guidelines on Hand Hygiene in Health Care: First Global Patient Safety Challenge Clean Care Is Safer Care*, 2009, https://www.ncbi.nlm.nih.gov/books/NBK144018/; Howard Markel "In 1850, Ignaz Semmelweis saves lives with three words: wash your hands," (*PBS News Hour*, May 15, 2015).

46. Lewis Carroll. "Jabberwocky," https://www.poetryfoundation.org/poems/42916/jabberwocky.

47. Codell Carter and Barbara Carter, *Childbed Fever: A Scientific Biography of Ignaz Semmelweis* (Piscataway: Transaction Publishers, 2005), 76–78.

48. Michael Shermer. *The Believing Brain: From Ghosts and Gods to Politics and Conspiracies—How We Construct Beliefs and Reinforce Them as Truths.* (New York: Times Books Henry Holt and Company, 2011), 149.

49. Ibid., 148.

50. Speaking of Great and Terrible archetypes, it may be possible to accuse Louis Pasteur's work today as a stereotyping of germs and bacteria, thinking they only caused disease in healthy hosts. Antoine Béchamp, a critic of Pasteur, offered a different interpretation and used the word "microzymes" in developing what came to be known as host theory. Perhaps germs and bacteria can be marginalized as much as social aggregations. So it goes.

51. Ayaan Hirsi Ali, *Infidel* (New York: Atria Paperback, 2013), 28.

52. Ibid., 30.

53. Ibid., 90.

54. Jordan Peterson, *Maps of Meaning*, 21.

55. Martin Hoffman, *Empathy and Moral Development: Implications for Caring and Justice* (New York: Cambridge University Press, 2000), 10–20. For a response to induction discipline, and the role of love in parenting, see also Michael Slote, *A Sentimentalist Theory of the Mind* (Oxford: Oxford University Press, 2014), chap. 5, 120–28.

56. Martin Hoffman and H. D. Saltzstein, "Parent discipline and the child's moral development" in *Journal of Personality and Social Psychology*, vol.5, no. 1 (1967), 45–57. See also: Renee B. Patrick, *Adolescents' Perceptions of Parental Discipline Techniques: Induction and the Moral Self*, thesis for Graduate Program in Psychology, Ohio State University 2009, Abstract, 12–13, 27–28; Julia Krevans and John Gibbs, "Parents' Use of Induction Discipline: Relations to Children's Empathy and Prosocial Behavior" in *Child Development*, 1996, 67, 3263–277.

FOUR

1. B. W. Powe, *Marshall McLuhan and Northrop Frye: Apocalypse and Alchemy*, 12.

2. Attributed to Fred Menger, chemistry professor. "If you torture data sufficiently, it will confess to almost anything." Apparently, he also joked that when he started his career, "fire had yet to be domesticated." Here's another good one, from William Watt: "Do not put your faith in what statistics say until you have carefully considered what they do not say." See also: Mahendra Tiwari and Ramje Dixit, *Data Mining Principles, Process Model and Applications* (eBooks2go Inc, 2017).

3. John Kenneth Galbraith, *Economics, Peace and Laughter* (New York: New American Library, 1971), 50. See also: "Do not be alarmed by simplification. Complexity is often a device for claiming sophistication, or for evading simple truths"—*The Age of Uncertainty* on BBC Television, 1977.

4. T. S. Eliot, "The Love Song of J. Alfred Prufrock" at https://www.poetryfoundation.org/poetrymagazine/poems/44212/the-love-song-of-j-alfred-prufrock.

5. B. W. Powe, *Marshall McLuhan and Northrop Frye: Apocalypse and Alchemy*, 62.

6. Hewitt Bernard, brother to Agnes Bernard, first objected when Macdonald asked him about marrying Agnes. Macdonald promised to change his ways. He may have genuinely meant to change. He may have tried. It is possible Agnes extended his life by helping him manage his drinking and holding him to daily routines, http://www.biographi.ca/en/bio/macdonald_john_alexander_12E.html; http://www.biographi.ca/en/bio/bernard_susan_agnes_14E.html.

7. Emmanuel Levinas, *Totality and Infinity*, 21.

8. Marshall McLuhan., The Classical Trivium: The Place of Thomas Nashe in the Learning of His Time (Berkeley: Gingko Press, 2009), 8.

9. Augustine, *Confessions*, trans. Albert Outler. Book 6, chap. 3, https://www.ling.upenn.edu/courses/hum100/augustinconf.pdf.

10. Max Roser and Esteban Ortiz-Ospina, "Literacy" (2018) at OurWorldInData.org., https://ourworldindata.org/literacy.

11. Marshall McLuhan, "The Medium is the Message" in *Understanding Media: The Extensions of Man* (Cambridge: Massachusetts Institute of Technology Press, 1964), 14. Speaking of failed tests of entropy, see Humpty Dumpty and the Wall in Marshall McLuhan, "Wheel, Bicycle and Airplane" in *Understanding Media: The Extensions of Man*, 205. Or, perhaps the better riddle would be: What if today's chicken is just the yegg's way of making another yegg? — "Many of the conundrums of modern media and culture are understood most effectively through research that transcends the constraints imposed by seeking to make the case for or against the truth of a particular theory. Begin with theory, you begin with the answer; begin with observation, you begin with questions."—Eric McLuhan,

"Marshall McLuhan's Theory of Communication: The Yegg" in *Global Media Journal—Canadian Edition* vol. 1, Issue 1 (2008), 25–43.

12. Northrop Frye and Bill Somerville, *The Bible and English Literature by Northrop Frye*, Lecture 1.

13. Ibid.

14. Northrop Frye, *The Great Code*, chap. 1, 13–30.

15. David Hume, *A Treatise of Human Nature* (1739), Book III, Part 1, Section 1. For a more detailed introduction and examination of Hume's point, and if we should do much about it, or if you just feel like quibbling over the distinction, see also: Charles Pigden, "Hume on Is and Ought" in *Philosophy Now*, Issue 83, March/April 2011; Charles Pigden, ed., *Hume on 'Is' and 'Ought'* (Palgrave Macmillan, 2010).

16. John Austin, "How to Do Things With Words," *William James Lectures at Harvard University 1955* (Oxford: Oxford University Press, 1962), 4–6.

17. Harry Frankfurt, "On Bullshit" essay on *California State University Dominguez Hills*, http://www5.csudh.edu/ccauthen/576f12/frankfurt__harry_-_on_bullshit.pdf. See also: Harry Frankfurt, *On Bullshit* (Princeton: Princeton University Press, 2005), 13; "On Bullshit Part 1" at Princeton University Press, https://www.youtube.com/watch?v=W1RO93OS0Sk.

18. Marshall McLuhan, "Cokes and Cheesecake" in *The Mechanical Bride: Folklore of Industrial Man* (London: Duckworth Overlook, 2011), 118.

19. Camille Paglia, "City in Motion" in *Glittering Images* (New York: Vintage, 2013), 201–06 (ebook).

20. Edouard Manet, *A Bar at the Folie-Bergère*. See also: *A Bar at the Folie-Bergère* at *Art and Architecture*, http://www.artandarchitecture.org.uk/fourpaintings/manet/picture/suzon.html; *A Bar at the Folies-Bergere* (1881-2) at *Art Encyclopedia*, http://www.visual-arts-cork.com/paintings-analysis/bar-at-the-folies-bergere.htm.

21. Robert Hare's work is mentioned in: Jordan Peterson, "2017 Maps of Meaning 3: Marionettes and Individuals (part 2)" at Jordan B Peterson, January 30, 2017, 44:00—49:00, https://www.youtube.com/watch?v=Us979jCjHu8. See also: Martha Stout, *The Sociopath Next Door* (Broadway Books, Random House, 2003), 12, 136. Robert Hare is quoted as saying he believes our society is moving in the direction of permitting and valuing some of the traits listed in his Psychopath Checklist —impulsivity, irresponsibility, and lack of remorse. All the more reason to voluntarily seek a better sense of regulation on our fears and motivations. See also: Robert Hare, *Psychopathy: Theory and Research* (Hoboken: John Wiley & Sons, 1970); Robert Hare, *Without Conscience* (New York: The Guilford Press, 1999); http://hare.org/welcome/.

22. Francis Bacon, *The New Organon*. Book I, cxxix. See also: *Dorothea Lange: Photographer of the People*, http://www.dorothea-lange.org/text.home.htm.

23. Dyanna Taylor, "American Masters – Dorothea Lange: Grab a Hunk of Lightning" on PBS, 2014, http://www.pbs.org/wnet/americanmasters/dorothea-lange-full-episode/3260.

24. Jörg M. Colberg, "Looking at Dorothea Lange's Migrant Mother" at *Conscientious Photography Magazine*, May 20, 2013, https://cphmag.com/migrant-mother/.

25. Roy Stryker, as quoted in Robert Harriman and John Louis Lacaites, *No Caption Needed: Iconic Photographs, Public Culture, and Liberal Democracy* (Chicago: University of Chicago Press, 2007), 55.

26. Dorothy Lange, "Migrant Mother" in *Farm Security Administration Collection*, Library of Congress, http://www.loc.gov/rr/print/list/128_migm.html. See also: Francis Luis Mora, "Morning News" in *Wikimedia Commons*, https://commons.wikimedia.org/wiki/File:Morning_News_by_Francis_Luis_Mora,_San_Diego_Museum_of_Art.JPG.

27. John Nici, *Famous Works of Art—And How They Got That Way* (Rowman & Littlefield Publishers, 2015), 213.

28. Richard Feynman, "Cargo Cult Science" at California Technical Institute Commencement, 1974, *Caltech Magazine* (Formerly *Engineering & Science*) vol. 37, no. 7, http://calteches.library.caltech.edu/51/2/CargoCult.htm.

29. Ibid.

30. Marshall McLuhan., "Freedom – American Style" in *The Mechanical Bride*, 117–18.

31. Richard Feynman, "Cargo Cult Science."

32. Ibid.

33. Homer, *The Odyssey*, Book IV, 73–78.

34. Kings 1:19.

35. Ayn Rand, *The Fountainhead 25th Anniversary Edition with Special Introduction by the Author* (Indianapolis: Bobbs-Merril Co., 1968), Introduction.

36. Ibid.

37. Fyodor Dostoevsky, *The Brothers Karamazov*, trans. Constance Garnett (New York: The Lowell Press, 1892), 665 (762 ebook). For a discussion on translations, or different versions of the quote, see also Andrei Volkov, "Dostoevsky Did Say It" at *The Secular Web*, https://infidels.org/library/modern/andrei_volkov/dostoevsky.html.

38. Ayn Rand, *Atlas Shrugged* (New York: Signet, Penguin Books, 1996), 153.

39. Ken Levine (Writer), Scott Sinclair (Artist), Paul Hellquist (Designer), and Christopher Kline (Programmer), *Bioshock* (2K Games, 2007).

40. Ayn Rand believed it was trade, in part, that liberated society in the nineteenth century. Ayn Rand, *Capitalism: The Unknown Ideal* (New York: Signet Books, 1986). "During the nineteenth century, it was free trade that liberated the world, undercutting and wrecking the remnants of feudalism and the statist tyranny of absolute monarchies."

"Capitalism was the only system in history where wealth was not acquired by looting, but by production, not by force, but by trade, the only system that stood for man's right to his own mind, to his work, to his life, to his happiness, to himself."

"The concept of individual rights is so new in human history that most men have not grasped it fully to this day. In accordance with the two theories of ethics, the mystical or the social, some men assert that rights are a gift of God– others, that rights are a gift of society. But, in fact, the source of rights is man's nature."

"The economic value of a man's work is determined, on a free market, by a single principle: by the voluntary consent of those who are willing to trade him their work or products in return. This is the moral meaning of the law of supply and demand."

41. Ayn Rand, *Atlas Shrugged*, 699–758. In Chapter 2, "The Utopia of Greed" in Part 3, *A is A* of *Atlas Shrugged*, she comes close to making two young boys characters in the story. They are seen, respected, idealized, but not heard. Rand does use childhood memories to reveal elements of her characters. But children are not presented as characters involved in or moving the plot. As another telling example of relationships between adults absent of children, her characters do not experience pregnancy.

42. Fyodor Dostoevsky, *The Brothers Karamazov*, trans. Constance Garnett (New York: The Lowell Press, 1892), 265 (302–3 ebook).

43. Marshall McLuhan, "Love Goddess Assembly Line" in *The Mechanical Bride*, 93–94.

44. Ibid., 96.

45. Cathy Newman, "A Life Revealed" in *National Geographic*, April 2002, https://www.nationalgeographic.com/magazine/2002/04/afghan-girl-revealed/. See also: The original story in Debra Denker, "Along Afghanistan's

War-torn Frontier" in *National Geographic*, June 1985, http://ngm.nationalgeographic.com/2002/04/afghan-girl/original-story-text; Steve McCurry, "'Afghan Girl': Taking National Geographic's Most Famous Photo", FORA.tv, 2010, https://youtu.be/BIgx-nkFL6c; Steve McCurry website, http://stevemccurry.com/.

46. Cathy Newman., "A Life Revealed" in *National Geographic,* April 2002. See also: In a 2017 update to the story, Sharbat Gula was given a home and property in Afghanistan: Nina Strochlic, "Famed 'Afghan Girl' Finally Gets a Home" in *National Geographic*, December 2017, https://news.nationalgeographic.com/2017/12/afghan-girl-home-afghanistan/.

47. "Photographer of the Year: Steve McCurry" in *American Photo*, XIII, July–August 2002, 43–45.

48. Camille Paglia, "Red River" in *Glittering Images*, 375 (ebook).

49. Ibid., 376 (ebook).

50. George Lucas, as quoted by Camille Paglia, "Red River" in *Glittering Images*, 382 (ebook).

51. Camille Paglia, "Red River" in *Glittering Images*, 387 (ebook).

52. Ibid., 388 (ebook).

53. George Lucas, *Star Wars: A New Hope*. Lucasfilm Ltd.: 20th Century Fox, 1977. Photo from promotional material.

54. Camille Paglia, *Vamps and Tramps: New Essays* (New York: Vintage Books, 2004) Introduction.

55. Carrie Fisher, as quoted by Bethan Holt, "Carrie Fisher's complicated relationship with her iconic Princess Leia gold bikini" in Lifestyle Fashion *The Telegraph*, December 28, 2016, https://www.telegraph.co.uk/fashion/people/carrie-fisher-iconic-princess-leia-gold-bikini-costume/. See also: "Slave Leia Costume" at Wookieepedia: The Star Wars Wiki, http://starwars.wikia.com/wiki/Slave_Leia_costume.

56. Camille Paglia, *Vamps and Tramps: New Essays*, Introduction.

57. Marshall McLuhan, "Heading for Failure" in *The Mechanical Bride*, 40.

58. Jack Miles, *God: A Biography* (New York: Vintage Books, 1996), Keynote.

59. The official number declined in Canada with the 2011 census. The Canadian Press. "Canada's Jedi Knights not as much of a religious force" in CBC News, May 8, 2013, http://www.cbc.ca/news/canada/canada-s-jedi-knights-not-as-much-of-a-religious-force-1.1321650. See also: Lorrayne Anthony, Canadian Press. "Jedis have some fun with Statistics Canada" in *The Globe and Mail*, May 14, 2003, https://www.theglobeandmail.com/news/national/jedis-have-some-fun-with-statistics-canada/article1015194/; Henry Taylor, "'Jedi' religion most popular alternative faith" in *The Telegraph*, December 11, 2012, https://www.telegraph.co.uk/news/religion/9737886/Jedi-religion-most-popular-alternative-faith.html; Tim Donnelly. "Thousands of people have converted to the Jedi faith" in *Living*, *The New York Post*, December 14, 2015.

60. Rodney Stark, The Rise of Christianity: A Sociologist Reconsiders History (Princeton: Princeton University Press, 1996), 4–13. See also: Rodney Stark, "Reconstructing the Rise of Christianity: The Role of Women" in *Sociology of Religion* vol. 56, no. 3 (1995), 229–44; Luke Muehlhauser, "The Explosion of Early Christianity, Explained" at *Common Sense Atheism*, February 28, 2009.

61. Nassim Taleb, "The Most Intolerant Wins: The Dictatorship of the Small Minority," a chapter from *Skin in the Game*, on Medium, August 14, 2016, https://medium.com/incerto/the-most-intolerant-wins-the-dictatorship-of-the-small-minority-3f1f83ce4e15.

62. Ursula K. LeGuin, *The Left Hand of Darkness* (New York: Ace Books, 1976), Introduction and page 1.

63. James Joyce, *Finnegans Wake* (Contemporary Literature Press), 794, http://editura.mttlc.ro/fwliniarized/FW%20LINEARIZED%20full%20text%20pp%203-628.pdf.

64. For information on the Munros and the Amarok Society: http://amaroksociety.org/.

65. Bridges out of Poverty is the name of another independent program. It is part of the Aha! Process Inc. with Ruby Payne, https://www.ahaprocess.com/.

66. G.E.M. Munro. *South Asian Adventures with the Active Poor.* (Hagensborg: Tangent Books Inc., 2010).

67. G.E.M. Munro. "On the Work of the Amarok Society" in a video presentation for Rotary Shares, February 2017.

68. Ibid.

69. Ibid.

70. Ibid.

71. Ibid.

72. Malidoma Patrice Somé, *Ritual: Power, Healing and Community* (Arkana: Swan Raven & Company, Penguin Compass,1997), 36.

73. Raffi Cavoukian and Sharna Olfman, *Child Honouring: How to Turn This World Around* (Westport: Praeger Publishers, 2006), xx–xxii.

74. Ibid.

75. Mary Hynes and Raffi Cavoukian, "Raffi on why we need to honour children" on *Tapestry*, CBC Radio, August 21, 2016, http://www.cbc.ca/radio/tapestry/children-and-spirituality-part-2-1.3412058/raffi-on-why-we-need-to-honour-children-1.3413868. See also: Raffi Cavoukian and Sharna Olfman, "Good Parenting Takes More Than Good Intentions" in *Child Honouring*, 24–27.

76. Susan Linn, "Honoring Children in Dishonorable Times: Reclaiming Childhood from Commercialized Media Culture" in *Child Honouring*, 201.

77. "Raffi Cavoukian Receives 2006 Fred Rogers Integrity Award" at Campaign for a Commercial-Free Childhood, October 18, 2006, http://www.commercialfreechildhood.org/blog/raffi-cavoukian-receives-2006-fred-rogers-integrity-award. See also: Benjamin Wagner, "Bedtime, Raffi, And Integrity" at *Mister Rogers and Me*, September 8, 2006, http://www.misterrogersandme.com/2006/09/08/bedtime-raffi-and-integrity/.

78. Jack Miles, *God: A Biography*, 67–69.

79. Genesis 17:1.

80. Shakespeare, *Hamlet*, Act 2, Scene 2.

CODA

1. Matthew Crawford, *The World Beyond Your Head*, 244.

2. Ibid., 209–46.

3. Jordan Peterson, *Maps of Meaning*, 248.

4. Joseph Campbell, *The Hero with a Thousand Faces*, 64.

5. Micah 6:8.

6. Paraphrase from Bernard Lonergan, *Method in Theology*, 104–05.

7. William Blake, "Letter to Thomas Butts," November 22, 1802, http://www.bartleby.com/235/146.html. Northrop Frye used this letter as inspiration for one of his books: *The Double Vision, Language and Meaning in Religion*,

(Toronto: University of Toronto Press, 1991). See also: William Blake, "Visions of the Daughters of Albion," 1793. https://www.bartleby.com/235/256.html

8. Isaac Newton, "Letter to Robert Hooke," February 15, 1676, http://www.newtonproject.ox.ac.uk/view/texts/normalized/OTHE00101.

9. John of Salisbury quoted Bernard of Chartres in his *Metalogicon*, 1159, Christophe Grellard and Frederique Lachaud, *A Companion to John of Salisbury* (Boston: Brill, 2015), 49, 177–78, 211, https://archive.org/details/ACompanionToJohnOfSalisbury.

10. Margaret Atwood, *Payback* (Toronto: House of Anansi Press Inc, 2008). See also: http://www.cbc.ca/radio/ideas/the-2008-cbc-massey-lectures-payback-debt-and-the-shadow-side-of-wealth-1.2946880; Margaret Atwood, *Negotiating with the Dead: A Writer on Writing* (Cambridge: Cambride University Press, 2002).

11. Marshall McLuhan, "1967 Fordham University Tapes #2" at Fordham University, 40:00, https://mcluhangalaxy.wordpress.com/2011/09/16/audio-recordings-of-mcluhan-carpenter-at-fordham-1967/. See also: https://youtu.be/Tx2ed93_Lpc.

12. Some writers tried to save Iphigenia. See Euripides, *Iphigenia in Tauris*; Euripides, *Iphigenia in Aulis*; Ovid, *Metamorphoses*, 12. A number of more recent iterations and stories exist as well.

13. Rabbi Hillel, Talmud, Shabbath 31a.

14. Titus Livius, *The History of Rome*, trans. D. Spillan (Bungay: John Childs and Son, 1868), Book 1, chap. 1, http://www.gutenberg.org/files/19725/19725-h/19725-h.htm. Thomas King mentions a North American story that fits with parts of the Lucretia pattern. In 1858, a group of miners in what is now British Columbia raped a Nlaka'pamux woman. The event brought about the Fraser Canyon War and the Snyder Treaties. Thomas King, *The Inconvenient Indian: A Curious Account of Native People in North America* (Toronto: Anchor Canada, Random House Canada, 2012), 26–27.

15. David Hume, "Of the First Principles of Human Government" in *Essays By David Hume*, https://www.gutenberg.org/files/36120/36120-h/36120-h.htm.

16. Bernard Lonergan, *Method in Theology*, 55.

17. Rudyard Kipling, "The Ballad of East and West," http://www.kiplingsociety.co.uk/poems_eastwest.htm.

18. Leonard Cohen, *Let Us Compare Mythologies* (Montreal: Contact Press, 1956); Leonard Cohen. *The Spice-Box of Earth* (Toronto: McClelland & Stewart, 1961).

19. Giordano Bruno, as quoted by Northrop Frye, *The Great Code*, xxiii. "It may still be something to have made a statement, if only to stimulate the writing of better books [and telling better stories]."

CPSIA information can be obtained
at www.ICGtesting.com
Printed in the USA
LVHW040204200419
614901LV00001B/1/P